T0295610

Rethinking Career Studies

Careers are studied across many disciplines – particularly from the social sciences – but there is little conversation between them. Many scholars are studying the same thing in different ways, too often missing opportunities to learn from one another and draw on each other's ideas and findings to enrich their own. Gunz and Mayrhofer bridge these scholarly discourses as they explore the meaning of 'career' and answer the question: What is it that career scholars do when they study careers? The framework that emerges from this answer – the Social Chronology Framework (SCF) – vitally facilitates valuable conversations between scholars in different intellectual traditions. Building on the SCF framework, this comprehensive introduction to career studies encourages students, researchers and practitioners to identify commonalities between the topics that they are studying and those examined in other fields, such as organization studies, drawing together interdisciplinary insights into career outcomes and their influencing factors.

HUGH GUNZ has a PhD in Chemistry and in Organizational Behavior, and is Professor of Organizational Behavior at the University of Toronto. He is the author of the book *Careers and Corporate Cultures* (1989), and the co-editor of the *Handbook of Career Studies* (2007). He serves or has served on the editorial boards of a number of journals, including *Journal of Professions and Organization, Academy of Management Journal*, and the *Journal of Managerial Psychology, and Emergence*, and is a former chair of the Careers Division of the Academy of Management.

WOLFGANG MAYRHOFER is Full Professor and Head of the Interdisciplinary Institute of Management and Organizational Behavior, Vienna University of Economics and Business, Austria. He has (co-)authored/(co-)edited 31 books and (co-)authored more than 210 peer-reviewed articles and book chapters. He serves as editorial or advisory board member of several international journals and research centers and regularly consults with organizations in the for-profit and non-profit world. He has received national and international awards for outstanding research and service to the academic community.

Rethinking Career Studies

Facilitating Conversation across Boundaries
with the Social Chronology Framework

Hugh Gunz

University of Toronto

Wolfgang Mayrhofer

Vienna University of Economics and Business (WU Vienna)

CAMBRIDGE
UNIVERSITY PRESS

University Printing House, Cambridge CB2 8BS, United Kingdom

One Liberty Plaza, 20th Floor, New York, NY 10006, USA

477 Williamstown Road, Port Melbourne, VIC 3207, Australia

314–321, 3rd Floor, Plot 3, Splendor Forum, Jasola District Centre, New Delhi – 110025, India

79 Anson Road, #06–04/06, Singapore 079906

Cambridge University Press is part of the University of Cambridge.

It furthers the University's mission by disseminating knowledge in the pursuit of education, learning, and research at the highest international levels of excellence.

www.cambridge.org
Information on this title: www.cambridge.org/9781107057470
DOI: 10.1017/9781107414952

© Hugh Gunz and Wolfgang Mayrhofer, 2018

First published 2018

Printed in the United Kingdom by Clays, St Ives plc

A catalogue record for this publication is available from the British Library.

ISBN 978-1-107-05747-0 Hardback

Contents

List of Figures   *page* vii
List of Tables   ix
Preface and Acknowledgments   xi

Part I   Point of Departure   1

1   Establishing the Need for the Social Chronology Framework   3
    What Is Career? Is There a Field of Career Studies?   6
    Conversation within and between Career Discourses and Its Obstacles 13
    Finding a Common Language: The Supportive Role of Perspectives   14
    Outline of the Book   17
    Summation   20

2   Exploring Career as a Concept   21
    Views of Career   21
    Core Ideas in Career Definitions   25
    Career Actors   29
    Summation   37

Part II   The Social Chronology Framework (SCF)   39

3   The Three Perspectives and Their View of Career   41
    Perspectives: Creating Reality and Meaning   41
    Spatial Perspective   47
    Ontic Perspective   53
    Temporal Perspective   57
    Interplay between Perspectives   62
    A Theoretically Grounded Definition of Career   63
    Summation   73

4   A Heuristic Model of Career   74
    Career Transitions   75
    Modeling Career Transitions: The Basic Building Block   78
    Assembling the Blocks: The Elaborated SCF Model   85
    Summation   91

5   Exploring the Architectonics of the SCF   92
    Theory in the Social Sciences   92
    Frameworks and Models   96
    The SCF as a Framework   98
    Activities When Applying the SCF   100
    Summation   107

Part III   Putting the SCF to Work   109

6   Facilitating Conversations within Career Studies   111
    The Importance of Conversation   112
    Conversations between Career Fields   122
    Identity-Related Conversations: A Narrative of the OMC Field's History   130
    Summation   145

7   Stimulating Cumulative Research within Career Studies   147
    Mapping and Reviewing Constructs and Their Relationships   149
    Looking for Missing Connections   156
    Moving beyond the Current Bounds   160
    Summation   168

8   Bringing Ideas In from Organization Studies   169
    Coevolutionary Theory, Complementarity Theory, and Mentorship 170
    Neo-institutionalism and Career Success   183
    What Career Studies Can Learn   193
    Summation   201

9   Contributing to Organization Studies   202
    Reframing Individual Studies   203
    Reframing Fields   208
    Summation   235

Part IV   Conclusion   237

10 Taking the SCF Forward   239
    Main Messages of the Book   239
    Some Further Directions   244
    Coda: Defamiliarization, Imagination, and Conceptual Combination   255

References   257
Index   296

Figures

1.1 Fields, proto-fields, and nascent commonalities of interest   *page* 13
4.1 Career transition – basic building block   79
4.2 SCF heuristic model chained over time   86
4.3 Elaborated SCF heuristic model (partial view)   90
5.1 The stages of the SCF and its applications   99
5.2 Reconstructing contextual perspectives on career in terms
of the SCF   104
6.1 Ideal types of career research   122
6.2 Development of the OMC field   144
7.1 Betz and Hackett's model of career-related self-efficacy   151
7.2 Reconstructing Betz and Hackett's model within the SCF   152
7.3 Reconstructing the Seibert *et al.* (2001) model within the SCF   153
7.4 Reconstructing Seibert *et al.* (2001) to show a lagged effect on
objective career success   155
7.5 Career success and social capital (Seibert *et al.*, 2001):
supplementary hypothesis   158
7.6 Reconstructing CEO succession and non-appointed managers
(Boyer and Ortiz-Molina, 2008)   159
7.7 Refinement of the reconstruction of Betz and Hackett's model   161
7.8 Further extension of Seibert *et al.* (2001) model   165
7.9 Extended model of reconstructing CEO succession and non-
appointed managers (Boyer and Ortiz-Molina, 2008)   166
9.1 Recasting Shen and Cannella's (2002) model in terms of the
SCF – view 1   205
9.2 Recasting Shen and Cannella's (2002) model in terms of the
SCF – view 2   207
9.3 Major events and offices in the political life of Nelson Mandela   214
9.4 de Klerk, Mandela, and Mbeki – major events and offices in
their political lives   218
9.5 Interconnections between the PSF's principal actors (based on
Hinings *et al.*, 2015a: 19)   224

9.6   Model of the career of the focal professional, chained over time   226
9.7   Elaborated model of focal professional's career, showing
      propositions   231
10.1 Conversations between fields, proto-fields, and nascent
      commonalities of interest   240

Tables

2.1 Potential "units" to which careers are attributed   *page* 33
3.1 Elements of the SCF   46
6.1 Life-course theory paradigmatic principles (from Elder,
     Johnson, and Crosnoe, 2003: 11–13) and the SCF   127
8.1 Institutional pillars and carriers (Scott, 1995: 52)   191
9.1 Interplay between discourses and career as a research focus   203

Preface and Acknowledgments

This book addresses some deceptively simple questions: what is career, what do those of us who study career actually do, and why do we find it so hard to talk to each other about our work? Books about careers take many forms, from academic monographs through edited collections of academic writing to a vast array of books intended to be helpful to people who actually have careers. This one falls into the first camp: it targets anyone who is interested in research on careers. That is a much wider audience than it at first appears. One of our themes, and it is not an original one, is that career puts in an appearance almost anywhere you look. There are certainly scholars whose primary interest is career (or an obvious synonym for it), but they are in some ways a minority. Social scientists and scholars of the humanities, of almost any imaginable kind, may at one time or another find themselves reflecting on what happens as people pass through life. Our aim here is not quite as broad as this: we are addressing anyone who does research on career, whether or not it is their primary interest, with a specific focus on colleagues working in the broad field of organization studies. At the moment few of us in these disparate areas of enquiry talk to each other about our mutual if varying interest in career; what we hope to do in this book is suggest an approach to stimulating this kind of conversation.

Because we are addressing what, for us at least, are fairly basic questions about career scholarship, there are places in this book, especially in Part II, where we get caught up in the weeds about basic issues. What we are trying to do is be as precise as we can about the ideas we are working with. We are pretty sure that this will interest some readers and irritate others. Some of the latter won't understand why we have to analyze every syllable and punctuation mark, so to speak, and some will regard our efforts as perhaps not bad for beginners but really needing an awful lot more work to be credible. We are signaling ahead on this point because our expectation is that different parts of this book will appeal to different readers and that by no means all of it will interest everyone. This means that anyone who has the endurance to read it all might find certain ideas coming back at them more times than they might wish. We apologize in advance for this. But there are some points that we do not want the reader to miss, in particular that we think of the Social Chronology Framework (SCF) as a facilitator of conversation, *not* as a straightjacket for all thinking about career; that the studies we discuss are excellent pieces of scholarship on which it has been our pleasure to try to build; and that the SCF is by no means the only possible way of generating the ideas we claim for it.

It is very hard to be sure where an idea comes from. We – the authors – have been collaborating for a good many years on a number of projects, typically to do with conferences of one kind and another. Over that time we discovered a shared interest in a deceptively simple question: what on earth is career research all about? One of us (Hugh Gunz) had just finished coediting, with Maury Peiperl, a handbook that purported to define the field and where it might be heading. But at the end of that lengthy process he found himself as uncertain as ever about just what comprises the field of career studies (assuming that there is one). The other (Wolfgang Mayrhofer) was getting increasingly startled about what he had got himself into after setting up a longitudinal study on business school graduates' careers and the discussions about what a career "is" that were raging when doing this in an interdisciplinary team.

One of the ideas that emerged from the handbook, to which proper reference will be made when we get down to business in Chapter 1, was of career studies not being so much a field as a perspective on social enquiry. Whether that really was the origin of the idea for this book is hard to be sure because conversations ramble in many directions and ideas pop up out of them unexpectedly and randomly. We certainly had plenty of conversations like that. But the key point to be made here is that neither of us individually is the originator of the notion of the Social Chronology Framework: it has been a genuinely collaborative effort. Of course, this means that we carry equal blame, too.

The plan originally was for a journal article, which kept us going for longer than we prefer to remember. Gradually the structure of the argument took shape, and the clearer the shape became, the longer the article grew. We did submit it to a couple of journals (as well as present the ideas to a variety of meetings), and the reaction was constructive but pointed. There is too much here, they said, for a single article. One editor said quite bluntly that it looked to them as if we had the outline of a book manuscript, which was good to hear because by then Cambridge University Press had accepted our proposal for a monograph.

If it is hard in retrospect to identify where the idea for this book comes from, it is easy to identify friends and colleagues who have supported us along the way with their thoughtful and constructive criticisms and suggestions. Among them are John Arnold, Michael Arthur, Silvia Bagdadli, Joel Baum, Matthew Bidwell, Laurie Cohen, Audrey Collin, Gina Dokko, Nicky Dries, Jo Duberley, Daniel Feldman, Jeffrey Greenhaus, David Guest, Peter Heslin, Kerr Inkson, Candace Jones, Maria Kraimer, Kathy Kram, Mila Lazarova, Barbara

Lawrence, Mary Dean Lee, Michael Meyer, Renate Meyer, Celia Moore, Nigel Nicholson, Thomas Schneidhofer, Johannes Steyrer, Stefan Titscher, Pam Tolbert, and Yoav Vardi as well as numerous other colleagues who have suffered our numerous presentations. Whether any of this wonderfully distinguished group of colleagues will recognize their advice in this book only time will tell, but we are deeply grateful for their contributions. We learned a lot from you: thank you. If we have failed to learn adequately, please accept our apologies. But the process has, for us, been enormous fun and incredibly stimulating.

We also thank Renate Gellner-Bächer and Gisela Ullrich-Rosner who dealt with a number of editing issues. As well we are most grateful to Valerie Appleby, James Gregory, and David Moore of Cambridge University Press and Paula Parish, formerly of Cambridge (who commissioned this book), whose enthusiastic support of the project from the initial submission of the book proposal to getting the first copies to our desks has been greatly appreciated.

The fun and stimulation accompanying writing the manuscript happened during a great many writing sessions, almost all of which took place at the home of one or the other of us. That required great tolerance on the part of our wives, Elizabeth Badley and Andrea Mayrhofer, both successful professionals in their own areas of expertise, who we are sure were convinced that all this endless talk was never going to go anywhere. We thank them for their unfailing hospitality and support and for not throwing us out of their respective homes as the SCF rolled over everything else in seemingly endless repetition. Finally, we are grateful to the distillers of numerous fine whiskeys and bourbons, whose support for morale at the end of a long day's writing was always appreciated.

Part I

Point of Departure

1 Establishing the Need for the Social Chronology Framework

Most people who study careers have had an experience such as the following when explaining to an acquaintance what they do. The conversation is usually brief:

> "What do you study?"
> "Careers."
> "Oh."

But some time later it might be that the person in question finds themselves needing career advice, and it is now that an interesting ambiguity in the word "career" may become apparent. Of the great many people who study careers, only a small proportion do so in a way that qualifies them any more than a layperson to provide advice of this kind. Little does one's credibility more damage than to be forced to reply: "Sorry, I don't do *that* kind of career research."

Mirroring that variety of interest is the widely encountered observation in the opening remarks of scholarly books about career, remarks that typically comment on, even lament, the many meanings that the term has attracted, how many disciplines show an interest in it, and how little conversation there is between these many discourses (e.g. Gunz and Peiperl, 2007a; Hall, 2002; Collin and Young, 2000, 1986). We have no intention of departing from this venerable tradition; indeed, we address it in the next paragraphs. But this book is an attempt to do something about it. Rather than merely celebrate the extraordinary richness of career as these other books do, we accept that as given and ask the question: Can we find a way of viewing career that subsumes much, if not all, of this richness into a new and overarching framework? If so, can this framework be used to help us and our colleagues in what we call here the field of organizational and managerial career (OMC) studies – which is very much the focus of this book and which we define with greater care later in this chapter – to find new ways of doing their research? Can it help OMC researchers see hitherto missed connections between their work and that of colleagues who do not see themselves as OMC scholars but whose insights have high relevance for the study of OMC careers? And, perhaps most ambitiously of all,

3

might such a perspective help these other colleagues – those working in a career field outside OMC studies or with the construct of career but not necessarily seeing themselves as scholars of career – to find new and productive ways of framing their work?

Our starting point is to address two questions: What do we mean by the term "career," and what do career researchers (i.e., researchers who study careers, as opposed to those who make a career out of doing research) do? This needs some explanation. "Career" is, after all, a word in common if not daily use, so where is the ambiguity?

As we discuss in Chapter 2, the term "career," in Hall's (2002: 8) memorable phrase, "suffers from surplus meaning":

If "career" were used in a free-association test, it would undoubtedly elicit an impressive range of meanings and feelings. Career conjures visions of political gamesmanship, the "organization man," the Wall Street jungle, and government civil servants, slowly but steadily working their way upward, grade by grade. (ibid.: 8)

For many people careers are things that only successful people or people in specific, usually highly regarded professions have; for others, everyone has them. They can be the list of positions that appear in one's CV or résumé, the subjective experience of moving through those positions, a particular kind of occupation, or just getting ahead in life. Depending on how a career is defined it can be one's working life, one's life in a particular occupation, or life from birth to death. Careers can be studied from as many angles as there are academic disciplines and subdisciplines with an interest in them, and there are a lot of disciplines and subdisciplines that do have this interest. In addition to people describing themselves as career researchers the list can include (but is not limited to) sociologists, demographers, labor economists, organizational theorists, developmental psychologists, educational and vocational psychologists, economists, historians, anthropologists, political scientists, and geographers. Even the current (2017) Chair of the US Federal Reserve, Janet Yellen, can get drawn into talking about careers, albeit without using the term, when assuming that "a tight labour market might draw in potential workers who would otherwise sit on the sidelines and encourage job-to-job transitions that could also lead to more efficient – and, hence, more productive – job matches" (Schneider and Herbst-Bayliss, 2016).

Each perspective brings with it its own unique view of career, ranging from a focus on the individual and their path through life to what this tells us about the nature of the society in which the individual lives:

... a study of careers – of the moving perspective in which persons orient themselves with reference to the social order, and of the typical sequences and concatenations of office – may be expected to reveal the nature and 'working constitution' of a society.

Institutions are but the forms in which the collective behaviour and collective action of people go on. In the course of a career the person finds his place within these forms, carries on his active life with reference to other people, and interprets the meaning of the one life he has to live. (Hughes, 1937: 413)

We explore these distinctions and differences in greater depth later in this book. For now, let us simply accept that "career" is a term used in many different senses and that it is of interest to an extraordinarily broad range of scholarly disciplines.

Therein lies both the great strength and the great weakness of career as a concept. On the one hand it matters a great deal in a practical sense to lay-people, i.e. people who have careers, namely everyone, and people who find themselves worrying about other people's careers, for example parents worrying about their offspring, as well as to a very broad range of researchers. On the other, not only is it used in many different senses – it is almost as if it is a term that everyone understands but that everyone understands differently – but different disciplines have different interests in it. And precisely because they come from such different directions there is, typically, surprisingly little inter-action between them: scholars studying career in field A very rarely read the work of scholars studying career in field B, and vice versa. If there is little or no conversation between different discourses, it is hard for each to learn from the other (Arthur, 2008).

Hence the starting point for this book: exploring the meanings of career and of career research. Flowing from this proximal aim is our distal one: to find a way of facilitating conversation about career between different disciplinary discourses. Our approach is to propose a framework for viewing career and career research that transcends narrow disciplinary boundaries and that provides a way of viewing career that can be recognized by anyone interested in career. Our assumption is that if you and I find that what we are studying can be described in the same terms and thus enables us to share a language, it will help us to establish a meaningful conversation. Language-sharing is not the whole story, of course: there is a lot more to developing understanding than just sharing words and concepts. But unless you and I both speak the same language we cannot even begin to develop any kind of mutual understanding. Such a conversation would allow the field of career studies, if there is such a thing, to profit from insights generated elsewhere and, hopefully, vice versa. This is what we hope will be the outcome of this book, the product of both proximal and distal aims.

We call this shared language the Social Chronology Framework (SCF), for reasons that we explain later in this chapter. Before doing so we address a number of fundamental questions about what career is and what we might mean when we refer to the "field" of career studies.

What Is Career? Is There a Field of Career Studies?

We address the first question – what is career? – in greater depth in Chapter 2, including many of the distinctions that have been made between different senses in which the term "career" is used, but we need at this stage at least to establish the broad outlines of how we use the term in order to orient the reader to the material that follows.

As has been pointed out elsewhere (e.g. Gunz and Peiperl, 2007b), the English word "career" derives from the late Latin *carraria*, meaning a carriage-road or road, which was reflected in its sixteenth- and seventeenth-century usage in English. Over time its English meaning has evolved to: "A person's course or progress through life (or a distinct portion of life)" (OED, 2017), although it often has overtones that give it a richer set of meanings. The German *Duden*, the most authoritative reference for German language issues, refers in its online version to career as the successful advancement in one's occupation. In addition, the *Oxford English Dictionary* (OED), in the entry on career, goes on to add "*esp.* when publicly conspicuous, or abounding in remarkable incidents: similarly with reference to a nation, a political party, etc." (emphasis in the original). This supplementary observation makes two interesting points. First, it seems to be saying that careers are things that interesting people have and, by implication, that ordinary people do not. Second, that it is not just people who have careers; one of the citations from the entry in question refers to "the career of France, Prussia, etc." We shall return to the second point later in this chapter and in Chapter 2; for now, let us reflect on the idea that career might be about status.

There is no question that, for many, a career is more than just what happens to everyone as they proceed through life. We refer to someone as being "career-minded" if they show signs of being driven by more than just the need to work at something they find rewarding, either financially or in other ways. The expression is typically intended to indicate that the person in question has ambitions to become something that they are not at present; that they are showing signs of wanting to get ahead. It can be used disparagingly, as Mark Anthony speaks of Caesar in Shakespeare's *Julius Caesar*:

> The noble Brutus
> Hath told you Caesar was ambitious.
> If it were so, it was a grievous fault,
> And grievously hath Caesar answer'd it.   (Act 3, Scene 2)

or admiringly, as one might of a young person with ambitions to rise above their humble origins. It all depends on the observer's opinion of the person's ambition.

However, career does not have to imply only a sense of getting ahead or of ambition. It can be used in conjunction with a profession or an occupation so that someone may talk of their career for instance as an accountant, an executive, a painter, a writer, an architect, or a politician. Each of these examples refers to an occupation in which it is possible to conceive of the individual as progressing over time to become a more senior and successful accountant, a more renowned painter, and so on. So when a profession or an organization produces publicity material describing careers in their profession or organization, the clear implication, accurate or otherwise, is that more is being talked about than simply a job: the profession or organization is offering some kind of future. This implication derives from the way that the word "career" is less likely to be used in everyday usage in connection with lower-status occupations. Indeed if someone were to refer to "their career as a dishwasher" it is likely that they would be heard to be doing so somewhat wryly or sarcastically (e.g. Anonymous, 2016; Isom, 2006).

There is a branch of the literature, which we shall call in this book the study of organizational and managerial careers (OMC) and with which the book is most closely concerned, that extends the use of the term "career" to any working life. It has its origins in the work of scholars interested in organizational careers, most commonly traced to the MIT school led by Edgar Schein, Donald Super's work at Harvard, and the group organized by George Milkovich at Cornell (Gunz and Peiperl, 2007b). Many of these scholars, particularly the MIT group, in turn owe an intellectual debt to the Chicago school of sociology led by Everett Hughes (although not all members of the "school" regarded it as such; see Becker, 1999). We shall return in Chapter 6 to the question of just how the focus of this succession of groups and schools, and of OMC research generally, has changed over time, for example, in terms of the role that organizations play in these careers (Arthur and Rousseau, 1996a). Suffice it for now to say that some scholars, particularly the Chicago school (Barley, 1989), see a career as lasting the career actor's lifetime, while most, especially more recently, think of it as covering the actor's *working* life. We return to this debate in Chapter 3, but in brief the position we take in this book matches that of the Chicago school: we see a career as that which happens to a career actor over their life to date and a working career as a subset of that broader span.

Such an account with its North American focus seriously oversimplifies the origins of the study of careers. Moore *et al.* (2007) identify three contributory streams in the literature. The first they call the sociological tributary, which is the one to which we refer in the previous paragraph, although they go back further in history to Durkheim and Weber. The second they label vocational, which can be traced back at least to Plato's *Republic* and is to do with finding a fit between the career actor and the range of occupations on offer. The third they call the developmental, tracing its origins to the writings of Freud and Jung and encompassing work on the development of the individual over the course of their life. It comes as no surprise, then, that career can have such a breadth of meaning, and not just the breadth that we have outlined thus far. Career can be approached from so many angles the effect can be dizzying and, more seriously, divisive. A sociologist may be interested in the way that advantage is passed on between generations or the patterns of intergenerational mobility within countries; an OMC researcher may want to understand more about the pattern of careers within and between organizations or occupations, what the precursors might be for career success, or how different career actors define success in their terms; and a vocational researcher may be interested in new ways of providing counseling to young people struggling to make their way in a world dominated by global economic forces. At first sight there does not seem to be a lot in common between these directions of inquiry.

Many discourses, then, converge on the topic of career; we have only touched on the list of possibilities here. This raises the question, in turn, of whether career studies generally can be thought of as a field and, if so, what might belong in that field. We shall address this question at three levels of analysis: (1) research in the field of OMC studies; (2) career research carried out across a range of other fields outside OMC studies, such as vocational or life-course research; and (3) research that involves the construct of career, even when carried out by scholars who do not see themselves as career researchers since they contribute to other fields such as human resource management (HRM), strategic management, or demography.

OMC Studies

First, what do we mean by a field? One definition is offered by Whitley:

Scientific fields can, I suggest, be best understood as particular kinds of work organization which produce intellectual novelty by working on intellectual artifacts to solve intellectual problems. They are institutionally committed to constructing intellectual innovations – only "new" knowledge is considered publishable – and yet restrict the extent of such innovations by making reputations, and hence rewards, dependent upon the use made of them for others' research ... Research in reputational work organizations is conducted with a view to convincing fellow specialists of the importance and correctness of the results and thus enhancing one's reputation in the field. (Whitley, 1984: 776–777)

A number of candidates offer themselves for consideration as fields of career research. We shall focus most closely here on OMC studies because that is the field that we inhabit and that forms the major focus of this book. But there are others, for example, vocational psychology and life-course studies, both of which we return to in the next section.

OMC studies has at least some aspects of Whitley's description of a field. There is no doubt that there is a loosely coordinated community of scholars who see themselves as being involved in the same project as their colleagues. OMC researchers are certainly united in their fascination with career and see fellow OMC researchers as allies, people to be joined with, for example, in groupings like the Careers Division of the Academy of Management or the long-standing succession of working groups on careers at the European Group for Organizational Studies. Indeed, in a landmark publication, the 1989 *Handbook of Career Theory*, the editors made a strong claim for career studies as a field:

In a word (or two), career theory has 'gone legitimate.' We (people who study careers) have become established. We have become a *field*. (Arthur, Hall, and Lawrence, 1989c: xv; emphasis in the original)

Whether there really is a body of career theory, "the body of all generalizable attempts to explain career phenomena" (Arthur, Hall, and Lawrence, 1989a: 9), that could be described as legitimate does not matter for present purposes. What does matter is that there is an identifiable group of scholars who see themselves as sharing an interest in career and who undoubtedly think of themselves as belonging to a common field. But it is a very loosely defined, partitioned field. One has only to attend a meeting of any such group to discover the breadth of topics in which the researchers are interested and the lack of overlap between them, reflecting all that we have described previously. One view (Gunz and Peiperl, 2007b) is that OMC studies is an example of what Whitley (1984) calls a fragmented adhocracy:

The fragmented adhocracy is characterized by a low degree of interdependency between researchers, which implies a rather "loose" or flat research organization. Since the researchers are facing very few restrictions in this type of organizational configuration regarding the choice of theoretical framework and the choice of research method, the degree of technical and strategic task uncertainty is very high. This implies a relatively fragmented knowledge structure and the existence of much disagreement about the relative importance of different problems to be solved by the field. As a result, the problem solving activity within the field takes place in a rather arbitrary and ad hoc manner, with limited attempts to integrate new solutions with the existing structure of knowledge. Management studies and contemporary American sociology are mentioned by Whitley (1984a) as examples of this type of reputational organizational form. (Knudsen, 2003: 278)

There is no question that OMC studies fits this description. OMC researchers feel few restrictions on the theoretical frameworks or research methods they can choose to make use of. As we have seen, the knowledge structure is extremely fragmented, and arguably it is fair to say that there is no real agreement on the relative importance of problems to be solved. It is not clear whether there have been attempts to integrate new solutions with the existing structure of knowledge; the main attempts at integration have been to produce books or articles that have provided an overview of the field (e.g. Gunz and Peiperl, 2007a; Sullivan, 1999; Arthur, Hall, and Lawrence, 1989b; Collin and Young, 1986; Van Maanen, 1977b; Hall, 1976; Glaser, 1968), but they have not tried to provide a theoretical integration of the field. So we shall refer in this book to OMC studies as a field, with the proviso that it has the characteristics of a fragmented adhocracy, with all that that implies for the coordination and collaboration, or lack thereof, that happen within it.

Career Research Carried Out across a Range of Fields outside OMC Studies

OMC scholars are interested in careers within and between organizations, but there are others for whom career, or an obvious synonym of it, is the central object of their research yet who do not, by and large, either publish in the same journals as or cite OMC literature. Nor do OMC researchers pay much attention to the work of these other scholars. Perhaps the gulf that has been most commented on is the one between OMC and vocational career research (Collin and Patton, 2009). On the face of it each field has a lot in common. We previously introduced OMC; the vocational is "the study of vocational behaviour and development (Crites, 1969). It is particularly concerned with career choice and work adjustment, career decision making, the influence of context upon choice, and effective interventions to facilitate the above (Fouad, 2007)" (Collin, 2009: 11).

So, in brief, the vocational field focuses on the way that individuals make choices about the careers studied in the field of OMC and how they can be helped to make those choices. As Collin (2009) points out, many scholars, for many years, have deplored the lack of contact between the two fields and called for a more multidisciplinary approach. But it is evident from the length of time these calls have been coming – Collin traces them back at least to 1977 – that this contact is not easy to establish or, if established, to maintain.

The OMC–vocational career research divide is just one example of the way that career studies generally consists of many relatively independent areas of scholarship. Peiperl and Gunz (2007) suggest that at least part of the explanation comes from the great many researchers working in a great many subdivisions of career studies, publishing in a great many different journals, so that it is not easy to keep track of what is going on. But there is more to it than that. Conducting conversations across disciplinary boundaries is not easy. At the most straightforward level, languages or sociolects (varieties of language associated with particular social groups) differ so that people may find themselves using different words for the same phenomenon and the same word for different ones. The term "career" is perhaps the best example of this: as we have seen, almost everyone has their own view of what precisely it means. And, of course, each discipline comes with its own education and training, intellectual foundation and epistemologies, preferred methodologies, founders, iconic figures, and publications.

If this is a fair description of the careers "field," and many writers have suggested that it is (e.g. Collin, 2009; Gunz and Peiperl, 2007b; Schein, 2007), then can it be called a field at all? Is there really an overarching field of career studies that unites, for example, vocational psychology and OMC studies?

To return to Whitley's view of what constitutes a field, the term "work organization" implies some sense of consciousness of a collectivity, however loosely defined. But it is far from clear that everyone who sees themselves as having career as a central research interest also sees themselves as part of the same intellectual community. To take two examples: We have just seen how the vocational and OMC communities barely talk to each other; we shall refer in Chapter 6 to the extensive life-course literature, which also appears to have a relationship of mutual oblivion with OMC studies. So while career research generally has some aspects of Whitley's view of a field, it is hard to argue that it really meets all of the criteria. There are clearly communities within the general category of researchers interested in career, such as OMC studies, vocational psychology, and life-course scholarship, that are closer to his definition, and we shall refer to them here as fields, albeit fields with varying degrees of integration. But it is hard to see the term "field" applying to the broader area of research that includes all of these fields.

If we cannot regard career researchers generally as forming a field, at least for now, is there another term that might do? Whitley (2016) suggests that it could be called a proto- or embryonic field *if* common elements between the constituent parts could be identified and the circumstances imagined that might cause them to come together to "constitute a distinct intellectual enterprise" (ibid.). Is it possible to find commonality beyond the not very helpful statement that they all study careers even if they do not necessarily use that term? That, as we shall shortly show, is one of the tasks we set ourselves in formulating the SCF.

Research Involving Career Carried Out by Noncareer Researchers

There are a great many researchers who certainly would not describe themselves as career specialists but who nevertheless have an interest in career. In the not-too-distant field of strategic management, for example, many scholars have introduced the career construct to their work without explicitly referencing the OMC literature (e.g. Sorensen, 1999; Boeker, 1997; Haveman and

Cohen, 1994). The same is true for many other fields, for example, HRM (e.g. Mayrhofer, Meyer, Iellatchitch, and Schiffinger, 2004; Ferris and Rowland, 1990) or health sciences (Boadi-Kusi *et al.*, 2015; Gigliotti and Makhoul, 2015).

At times it can seem that there is practically no area of the social sciences and humanities that does not, at one point or another, introduce the concept of career. Arthur, Hall, and Lawrence (1989a), for example, list psychology, economics, sociology, demography, and organization studies but also anthropology, political science, history, and geography, and others have extended the list (Chapter 2). A great many scholars are interested in what happens to people, how their backgrounds might affect the way they do things, and what all this might mean for the social forms of which they are part. Yet, as with the strategic management examples just cited, it is not at all common for writers outside the field but nevertheless working with career concepts to refer to work within the career literature in general or, for organization researchers in particular, the OMC field. Nor is it common for those within the OMC field to reference the work of those outside it, even when the field is closely related, as it is, for example, in the case of strategic management.

We are describing here something that, at best, could be described as a nascent commonality of interest without it even approaching being a proto-field. There is certainly a commonality of interest to the extent that the concept of career appears in this work. The commonality is nascent in the sense that any recognition of the commonality has yet to emerge beyond the suggestions of perceptive writers such as Arthur, Hall, and Lawrence (1989a).

To sum up where we have got to (Figure 1.1): We start with the observation that career is a multifaceted concept that is used in many different senses in a broad range of literatures that overlap to varying degrees. From there we go on to examine the question of whether, in view of this complexity, career studies can be thought of as forming a field. We show that there do seem to be a number of fields of study that meet this description, including the one with which this book is most closely involved, namely OMC studies. However, OMC studies in particular is an amalgam of many different approaches and can be described as a fragmented adhocracy. Despite that, there certainly exists a community of scholars who see themselves to be involved in a common task that is the study of careers within and between organizations. In the same way, other communities of scholars examine, for example, vocational psychology or the life course.

Although linked by a common interest in career, these fields of study do not together form a meta-field: there is no real indication that those working in the fields are particularly aware of or influenced by those working in the others. We call the collection of fields with a focus on career a proto-field, indicating that if it is possible to detect commonality between them – other

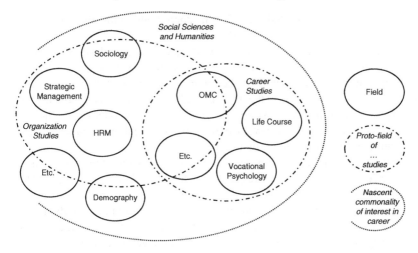

Figure 1.1 Fields, proto-fields, and nascent commonalities of interest

than the observation that they all work with career even though they may not call it that – researchers in the fields, if they see that commonality as valid, may be moved to develop a community of interest that could eventually be recognized as a field of study.

Finally, we turn to the large number of disciplines in which career puts in an appearance, ranging from other disciplines within organizational studies to the social sciences and humanities, not that there is any real recognition of this among the researchers and writers involved. While far from being a field, one still can describe it as having a nascent commonality of interest in career.

Where does this mapping of the territory get us? It indicates the extraordinary breadth of interest in career, which in turn points to the potential benefits from scholars being able to talk to and learn from each other across this breadth of interest. We turn to this next.

Conversation within and between Career Discourses and Its Obstacles

It is not hard to see why it might be a good thing for the many different discourses in which career appears to be able to connect with each other: to be able to conduct conversations across the boundaries surrounding them (Arthur, 2008). In Chapter 6 we address the question of the benefits that could accrue from such conversation; in brief, there is much to be gained in terms of mutual learning from making these connections. Yet as we saw previously these conversations have proven hard to initiate, and hard to maintain even if initiated, as Collin documents with the vocational psychology–OMC gulf (Collin, 2009).

Our book is an attempt to find a way of framing the work of those taking different approaches to the study of career and publishing in different and non-overlapping literatures, such that a commonality is exposed that goes beyond the not very helpful statement that they all study career. If that commonality can be expressed in terms that make sense to the different communities, our hope is that it can form the basis of increased dialogue between these communities, or discourses as we shall refer to them often in this book.

One aim of this book, then, is to find a way of facilitating conversation between discourses within the fragmented field of OMC studies, between fields within the proto-field of career studies, and between fields that are not career studies but in which career puts in an appearance. This is not unambitious. We try to provide a common language that links research in the field. It is a high-level language in the sense that it deals at a high level of abstraction, but we shall show how this can, nevertheless, focus attention on the commonalities between research conducted in different corners of the field of OMC studies.

It is very important that we underline what this does *not* imply. We offer the SCF as a framework, as the name implies, but as neither a theory nor a straightjacket. It is not intended as a *theory* but as a *support for building career theory*. Likewise, it is not a unifying theory of career, within which all "legitimate" career research should be located. For one thing, as we explain in Chapter 5, it is highly unlikely that a grand unifying theory of career, of the kind sought by theoretical physicists to explain the nature of matter, could ever be formulated (although in Chapter 10 we speculate on what such a theory might look like if it were to be developed). For another, as Van Maanen (1995) argues, what he calls *paradigmatic consensus* – which would have to underpin any acceptance of a grand unifying theory of career – would have a deadening effect on the creativity of research in the field. Again, we return to this point in Chapter 5. We do argue, however, that the SCF constitutes a joint frame of reference that can be flexibly used for various purposes but, above all, provides a common language. We turn to this next.

Finding a Common Language: The Supportive Role of Perspectives

So how does one go about finding a common language to be shared by anyone interested in studying career? Obviously the approach has to be discipline independent; otherwise it could not claim to be genuinely transdisciplinary. In language that can be understood by anyone with an interest in career it needs to describe what career is and what career research involves; it must lead to a flexible, discipline-independent definition of career that can be translated into the working definitions used by the many different fields studying career and be adaptable to their concrete research questions and various theoretical viewpoints; and it should point the way to theories of career that can be used to build models that can develop career scholarship.

That is a tall order. Our starting point is the suggestion by Gunz and Peiperl that career studies "may not be a field at all, but a *perspective on social enquiry*. Its central concept is *the effect on people of the passage of time*" (Gunz and Peiperl, 2007b: 4; emphasis in the original). This suggestion attracted us because it moves the conversation beyond that of constructs, which are inevitably tied to a particular disciplinary approach. Nor does it say anything about fields of any kind, other than to locate career studies somewhere in the social, which can encompass both the social sciences and the humanities. It simply says that studying careers is about adopting a particular way of looking at social phenomena. By analogy, one might define the physical sciences as a perspective on the physical world based on observation, inference, and deduction rather than dogma. Clearly a philosopher of science would take issue with the triteness of that way of putting it, but most physical scientists would certainly recognize it, both in terms of their everyday work in the laboratory and also as an explanation for why they reject the alternative explanations of, for example, creationists.

So perspective is at the core of this book: our argument is that anyone studying career is adopting a particular set of perspectives on social phenomena. The perspectives relate to three domains, those of space, being, and time. In brief, the argument runs as follows.

At the core of the concept of career is the career actor, namely the entity that has a career. Pretty much anyone would assume that the entity in question is an individual person, and indeed the literature to which we have been referring so far takes that as a basic, unquestioned assumption. But the term has also been used in connection with collectivities – the OED citation quoted earlier refers to "the career of France, Prussia, etc." – and, as we shall suggest in Chapter 2, it can be used in connection with any entity that persists over time.

This is no mere playing with words. People certainly have careers, and the careers of individuals are basic to this book. But a career is not lived in the absence of context. People live in a broader social space – at its most general: their society – consisting of various social entities and governed by various rules. As their careers progress, two things inevitably happen: their position within their society changes, and the social entities they relate to change as well. Examples of the former include the way that over time their family circumstances change, they become students, they belong to groups of many kinds, they may join and leave work organizations or occupational groups such as professions (or both), their national residency and citizenship may change, as they get older they may enter a phase of retirement that involves a shuffling of organizational and social connections, and so on.

All this also affects their position in their social space, within which the social entities that form the social space are not static. Consider the career of a young British woman who in the mid-2010s goes to university aiming for a career that will take her to Europe to practice her profession as an architect. On June 23, 2016, the Brexit vote means that her career plans crumble: at least for the next few years until the situation is clarified it is evident that her dream will become much more difficult to realize. Britain, in choosing to leave the EU, has taken a further step in its career as a nation, and this will profoundly affect the careers of millions of individuals, both British and EU citizens. Furthermore, the reasons for the British voting as they did have a great deal to do with the way that many of them feel that their careers have been affected by Britain's membership of the EU. What we are describing here is a coevolutionary process, in which the careers of individuals – in the example, British and EU citizens – and the country in which they live coevolve, the one affecting the other in a cyclic process. That is why it is not just playing with words to assert that social entities, as well as people, can have careers.

Beyond putting the actor who has the career at the core of the concept of career, examining career involves three things: the characteristics of a career actor, the positions the actor occupies in their social and geographical space, and the time over which the career happens – and, in addition, how these things interrelate. That, in a nutshell, is the Social Chronology Framework. It says that studying career involves the simultaneous application of three perspectives, to do with being, space, and time. We call the perspectives ontic (a word that derives from Heidegger's existential philosophy and simply means "of or relating to entities and the facts about them"; OED, 2017), spatial, and temporal. It implies that career denotes first and foremost an actor's *social chronology*: a chronology that traces the "path" of a unit – a career actor – through a given social (and, of course, also geographical) space over a given time.

This is the view of career that we shall be working with in this book. It is, of course, a very abstract way of conceptualizing career, but if we are to find a way of viewing career that makes sense to anyone studying it from any discipline we might care to think of in the social sciences or humanities, it needs to be. How might it be translated into more familiar terms? Let us provide an example.

The career of expatriates is a traditional topic in the literature (e.g. Harvey and Moeller, 2009; Brewster, 1991; Tung, 1988; Miller, 1975; Heenan, 1970). Major topics in this discourse include personal characteristics that help expatriates to be successful in their assignment (e.g. Caligiuri, 2000), adapting to the new environment in the host country (e.g. Haslberger, Brewster, and Hippler, 2014) including how long it takes to adapt on various dimensions (e.g. Hippler, Brewster, and Haslberger, 2015), and the role of HRM policies and practices in the expatriation cycle of selecting, training, assigning, and repatriating expatriates (e.g. Peterson, Sargent, Napier, and Shim, 1996). These areas of research clearly reflect the three perspectives. The spatial perspective is interested in how different aspects of the social space such as other actors, e.g. the HRM department, rules of the field like expatriation policies, or observable practices such as compensation schemes influence careers. From an ontic perspective the personal characteristics of the career actor, in this case the expatriate, and their consequences for careers are at the center of interest. The temporal perspective is primarily focused on the role of time in careers, for example, when the actor makes a career transition such as a move abroad.

This outlines, very briefly, the basis of the SCF. In this book we explore each of the concepts we introduce in this chapter and ask the question: Where does this get us? Our aim is to show how the SCF provides a guide to developing career theory, providing a fresh way of viewing career research, asking new questions within the field of OMC studies, and showing how the conversations it enables between the career discourse and other discourses such as organizational studies can lead to novel questions and new approaches to old ones. In the next section, we outline the steps we take to get there in a little more detail.

Outline of the Book

Part I of this book concludes with Chapter 2, which examines career as a concept. It begins by reviewing many different meanings of the term "career," focusing on those drawn from the OMC literature that, as noted previously, is the main point of reference for this book. We show that these various approaches to defining career share three common themes already introduced: a focus on context, a career actor and their characteristics, and the time over which the career takes place. These themes lead us to the three perspectives – spatial, ontic, and temporal – that form the basis for the SCF. Next, we consider the entity that has the career, explaining why we adopt the concept specifically of actor as opposed to other ways of conceptualizing the individual. But it is not just individuals who have careers; we go on to discuss the notion of collective actors and why they are important to the SCF. The chapter ends on a semi-whimsical note, pointing out that the concept of career has even been used in the context of inanimate objects, an idea that is not as bizarre as it first appears.

Part II gets into the theoretical foundations of the SCF. In Chapter 3 we tackle two issues: the perspectives on which the SCF is based and how this view of career leads to a theoretically grounded definition of career. We start by exploring the epistemology of perspective: How do we understand perspective to create reality and meaning? Observation, we argue following Luhmann (2000) and Spencer-Brown (1972), is based on drawing distinctions and making indications, i.e. choosing which of the states that arise from drawing a distinction one wishes to focus on. It is rather like defining figure and ground (distinction) and choosing which – figure or ground – is which (indication). Perspectives are specific modes of observation that apply a particular "guiding difference" to make sense of what is being observed. Each of the three SCF perspectives – spatial, ontic, and temporal – depends on a particular guiding difference and an operation associated with that guiding difference to make a particular core construct manifest. Next, we explore the three SCF perspectives in greater depth, explaining their meaning and application to the study of career and showing that there are circumstances under which there is interplay between them. This enables us, as a final step in this chapter, to develop a theoretically grounded definition of career, which forms the foundation for what follows: career is a pattern of a career actor's positions and condition within a bounded social and geographic space over their life to date.

In Chapter 4 we continue the unfolding of the SCF by developing a heuristic model of career. The definition of career presented in Chapter 3 refers to a pattern of positions and condition, and for there to be a pattern there needs to be a series of transitions from one position within the actor's geographical and social space to another. To be sure, if there are no transitions there is still a pattern that says something about the actor and the respective social space. Transitions, therefore, are fundamental to career. We show how the SCF suggests a heuristic model for career transitions, that is, a model that provides a framework for applying more specific theories to more specific instances of career transitions. But this model, which we call the basic building block, can be elaborated on in several ways to provide a more complex and richer set of heuristics. The basic building block can be chained over time as a series of transitions, the actors involved may be collectivities as well as individuals, and the careers of the actors – collective and individual – within the focal actor's social space may coevolve with the career of the focal actor. This provides a rich set of ideas for developing career theory.

We conclude Part II with Chapter 5, which considers what we call the architectonics of the SCF. Although this book is fundamentally a theoretical work the SCF is not a theory of career in itself. We explain what we mean by theory, distinguishing it from models and frameworks as well as the process of theorizing, from which it becomes apparent why the SCF is a framework, not a theory. Having cleared this epistemological ground we are then able to describe the steps involved in using the SCF to develop theory and identify interesting questions in, perhaps, established fields of inquiry. There are three: (1) selecting an interesting area to study: (2) reconstructing it in the language of the SCF, which is where the heuristic model of Chapter 4 can help; and (3) equivalizing, i.e. finding areas of inquiry elsewhere in either the field(s) of career studies or social research more generally in which it is possible to identify (again, using the language of the SCF) analogous problems being studied, understanding the nature of the connection, and importing these ideas to help reframe the original problem.

We call Part III of the book "Putting the SCF to Work." To do this we look both within the field of OMC studies and outside it. In Chapters 6 and 7 we focus on research within what we call here the proto-field of career studies; in Chapters 8 and 9 we look outside. In Chapter 6 we begin by showing how the SCF can facilitate conversations within career studies, in particular OMC studies. We return to the observations we make in the present chapter about the fragmentation of the field and consider its consequences as well as the benefits of conversation as a way forward. Ideal types in a Weberian sense are widely used in social research as a way of clarifying concepts, and we show how the SCF suggests three ideal types of career research that differ in the extent to which they focus on one, two, or three SCF perspectives. We suggest ways in which these ideal types can facilitate conversation across different areas of interest within career studies, partly by establishing common ground between different viewpoints and partly by emphasizing understanding, even-handedness, and social ties between the discourses. We then use the ideal type framework to reconstruct the history of OMC studies, showing how it has followed a curious narrowing of focus over time, perhaps reflecting a gradual change in the institutional context within which OMC studies are conducted.

In Chapter 7 we examine ways in which the SCF might stimulate cumulative research within career studies. Using a number of well-received studies within the field, we show how by following the steps outlined in Chapter 5, based on the heuristic model from Chapter 4, one can come up with new ideas for research. The process might be as simple as mapping the study on to the SCF heuristic model and reviewing constructs used in the research; sometimes the mapping process reveals hitherto unstudied connections that lead in interesting directions; or it could involve using the heuristic model to move beyond the original framing of the problem, introducing new constructs and variables for study.

It is important that we note here – and we shall repeat the point later to avoid any possible misunderstanding – that none of the research ideas that emerge in Chapter 7 and also in the following two chapters absolutely requires the SCF. It is entirely possible that they could have been arrived at by other means. What we *do* claim is that the process we introduce in Chapter 5 is a surprisingly useful one and that the framework of thinking provided by the SCF has the potential to get the researcher somewhere interesting faster and in a more systematic way than might otherwise have been the case. That, after all, is what a heuristic is for.

In Chapters 8 and 9 we connect OMC studies to scholarship outside the proto-field of career studies, specifically within the broader field of organiza-tional studies. In Chapter 8 we work through two examples of OMC topics – mentorship and career success – to show how the SCF facilitates bringing ideas *in* from organizational studies to suggest new approaches to these well-studied topics. In Chapter 9 we move in the opposite direction, showing how the framework can be used to suggest new ways of framing areas of study *outside* the OMC field. We look first at some individual studies and then two more general fields of study (organizational succession and professional service firms), seeking to demonstrate how the SCF suggests novel approaches to each.

Part IV consists of one chapter, our concluding one. In Chapter 10 we review the book and consider what, to us, are three of the most significant issues that emerge from it. The first is to do with the social part of social chronology, the second the chronology part, and the third some thoughts about where we might go from here in developing career theory.

Summation

Fundamentally, this book offers a novel way of viewing career, a way that, we suggest, has the potential to facilitate conversation between the many scholarly discourses that have an interest in career. We imply at the beginning of this chapter that our intended primary audience is our fellow OMC scholars, but we hope that our ideas will be of broader interest. Indeed it would not be an unreasonable test of the SCF's utility, given the way we introduce it here, to see whether it does indeed appeal to others working with the construct of career but who do not see themselves as scholars of career, let alone organizational and managerial careers.

Enough of introductory remarks. In the next chapter we tackle the first of our questions: What is career?

2   Exploring Career as a Concept

In this chapter we lay the conceptual groundwork for what follows in the book. If "career" does not quite mean all things to all people, it certainly covers a lot of territory, and our first task is to map that territory. Looking at the different views of career taken in various disciplines and that are evident in established career definitions, we show how three common threads run through these views. However it is addressed, career is something to do with (1) a career actor, (2) the physical and in particular social space within which their career unfolds, and (3) the time during which this happens. These form the basis for the three-perspective (ontic, spatial, and temporal) view that underpins the SCF as its basic element.

Finally, before developing these perspectives further in Chapter 3 we address what, on the surface, seems a nonissue but which is actually fundamental to the concept of career: What do we mean when we use the term "career actor"? In both the career literature and everyday life it seems pretty unambiguous; a career actor is someone who has a career. However, at least two questions emerge from this. First, who or what exactly is this "someone" having a career? And second, does this "someone" necessarily have to be an individual or can collectivities such as groups or organizations also have a career? Regarding the first question, we argue that the concept of actor – rather than individual, human being, subject, or person – best captures what is meant. In terms of the second question, the sociological literature makes it clear that actors do not have to be individuals; they can be entities of varying levels of social complexity. Building on that, we propose that not only individual but also collective actors have careers in their own right. In later chapters, we use this simple extension for developing a multi-level and coevolutionary model of career transition. We end this chapter on a semi-whimsical note: Can the concept of career actor be extended to include inanimate objects? First, however, we turn our attention to the basic question: What is career?

Views of Career

Career is one of those words that everyone relates to in one way or other, but just as with what constitutes good art, there is not a great deal of consensus about what it means. Using a word or concept does not ensure mutual agreement in everyday life:

"And only one for birthday presents, you know. There's glory for you!"
    "I don't know what you mean by 'glory,'" Alice said.
    Humpty Dumpty smiled contemptuously. "Of course you don't – till I tell you. I meant 'there's a nice knock-down argument for you!'"
    "But 'glory' doesn't mean 'a nice knock-down argument,'" Alice objected.
    "When I use a word," Humpty Dumpty said, in rather a scornful tone, "it means just what I choose it to mean – neither more nor less."
    "The question is," said Alice, "whether you can make words mean so many different things."
    "The question is," said Humpty Dumpty, "which is to be master – that's all."
(*Through the Looking Glass*, Lewis Carroll)

The situation in the scientific fields dealing with career is hardly any different. Career studies is a field of great complexity and richness, and we need to explore both in order to identify the common threads that hold it together and form the basis for the SCF's perspectives. Testifying to this complexity and richness is the evident difficulty scholars have had in agreeing on what belongs "inside" the field of career studies. A number of handbooks and collections of scholarly writing on careers have been published over the past forty years, the period during which the field of careers from an organizational and management perspective (OMC studies) has developed. Yet there is surprisingly little overlap in topic coverage between them (Peiperl and Gunz, 2007). There are probably two reasons for this. First, careers feature in a remarkably wide range of disciplines within organization studies and the broader social sciences (Arthur *et al.*, 1989a); indeed it is hard to find a field in which careers do not put in an appearance. This provides an extraordinarily broad choice of topics for any compendium of writing on career. Given that every collection has to be selective, it is perhaps no surprise that no two collections overlap greatly. Second, the term "career" is used many different senses. We shall consider these two reasons in turn.

First, the ubiquity of careers in the social sciences is remarkable. To begin with, there are those scholars who see themselves to be working in the field of organizational and managerial careers (OMC). The kind of topics they might examine include anything from the following list, itself highly selective: boundaryless careers; career choice; career counseling; career development; career management; career motivations; career patterns; career phases/stages; career planning; career success; careers across cultures; careers of particular categories of people such as women, minorities, ethnic groups, or members of a particular occupation or profession; contextual issues in careers; developmental theories; global careers; late career; life stages; mentoring and developmental networks;

personality and career outcomes; psychological contracts and career; the role of external agencies in career management; and work/family career issues.

Next, there are many in the social science literature who may not see themselves as career scholars but who explicitly work with career phenomena. Gunz and Peiperl (2007b: 3) give eight examples:

- Sociologists interested in intergenerational mobility and societal life changes, the structure and behavior of business elites specifically, and the social origins and demography of managers in general
- Organizational demographers studying the factors underlying promotion rates and mobility
- Labor economists investigating the structure of inter- and intra-firm labor markets
- Organizational theorists working on the structure of careers within and between organizations
- Developmental psychologists investigating the life stages through which people pass
- Educational and vocational psychologists involved in training and counseling
- Social psychologists and sociologists with an interest in patterns of work experience and the interaction among the many roles that people experience, sequentially and in parallel
- Sociologists and social psychologists with an interest in comparative studies of careers in different societies and in the impact of new organizational forms on careers in developed societies
- Strategic management and finance scholars studying the impact of managerial background on the strategic behavior of companies and their experience with capital markets

As we saw in Chapter 1, Arthur, Hall, and Lawrence (1989a) extend this list of disciplines in which careers are studied to include psychology, economics, sociology, demography, organization studies, anthropology, political science, history, and geography. If the concept of career is of such apparent ubiquity, are we sure that everyone is talking about the same thing? This turns out not to have a simple answer, providing the second reason for the lack of agreement between career scholars about what should be included in a compendium of writing on careers. Career as the object of career scholarship is a surprisingly ill-defined construct with multiple meanings (Young and Collin, 2000: 1):

Perhaps the primary issue in the study of career is, what do we mean by career? Is it different from occupation or job? When we speak of career, are we concerned with the lifelong behavioral processes and the influences upon them that lead to individual work values, choice-making style, work salience, preferences and interests, continuity and discontinuity of a career pattern, work salience, role integration, self and career identity, pre- and postwork involvement, and related phenomena? On the other hand, are we principally concerned with the subset of individual career development, which might be defined in organizational terms as the stages that one undergoes in different work settings from induction to consolidation to retirement? Do we really mean that we are concerned with who enters particular occupations and why, the individual differences in interests and abilities found in particular groupings, and the overlap in these character-istics across occupational grouping, or are we really concerned with job satisfaction and work adjustment? The answers to the above questions are neither right nor wrong . . . In broad terms, this question is, "What are the boundaries in which research can be legitimately conceived to express the study of career?" (Herr, 1990: 3–4)

Hall (2002: 8) refers to career as "suffer[ing] from surplus meaning" since, he suggests, drawing on a combination of common conceptions and scholarly definitions, it is used in four distinct senses. The first implies advancement: "vertical mobility – moving upward in an organization's hierarchy . . . [or] in the overall status hierarchy of the world of work" (ibid.: 8–9). The second looks at career as profession. In this view "certain occupations represent careers, whereas others do not" (ibid.: 9) because the former – for example, law, medicine, management, and teaching – have within them different levels of status, the passage through which form a career. The third and fourth senses focus on lifelong sequences of jobs and role-related experiences, respectively. A sequence of jobs is a more neutral term than the first sense because it does not imply advancement: it is simply a description of the jobs that someone has held over their working life. The sequence of role-related experiences, on the other hand, is concerned with the subjective experience of the career actor as they move through life.

It is by no means uncommon, as Hall (2002) notes, for career to be thought of as something that professional or managerial people have but ordinary people do not because it is so often associated with the idea of getting ahead (as in references to someone being "career-minded"). Indeed this sense in which professionalism, career, and progress go together is found in English and German language dictionary definitions of "career":

a field for or pursuit of consecutive progressive achievement especially in public, professional, or business life . . . a profession for which one trains and which is under-taken as a permanent calling. (Merriam-Webster, 2016)

A person's course or progress through life (or a distinct portion of life), esp. when publicly conspicuous, or abounding in remarkable incidents: similarly with reference to a nation, a political party, etc. . . . In modern language (after French carrière) frequently used for: A course of professional life or employment, which affords opportunity for progress or advancement in the world. Frequently attrib. (orig. U.S.), esp. . . . designat-ing one who works permanently in the diplomatic service or other profession, opp. one who enters it at a high level from elsewhere. (OED, 2017)

successful advancement in one's profession. (Duden Online 2016; translation by WM)

This sense of getting ahead or success in life seems inevitably linked with career; Hall (2002: 9; emphasis in the original) refers to *"directionality* ('up is good, low is bad') [as] a pervasive theme in our thinking about careers." By contrast, however, Hughes and his fellow members of the Chicago school of sociologists, who as we note in Chapter 1 are seen by many as the progenitors of OMC studies, mean career to cover life in a very general sense (Barley, 1989). For them, it refers to everything that happens to a person over their lifetime, both work-related and unrelated to work, and they by no means confine themselves to high-status professions. Examples of the "occupations" that they studied include hobos (Anderson, 1923), taxi hall dancers (Cressey, 1932), professional thieves (Sutherland, 1937), and jack rollers (Shaw, 1930). In the OMC literature, on the other hand, career tends to be understood to mean *work* career. Popularly, the term is widely used to denote a fragment of a career, as when it is said that people can look forward to several careers during their working lifetime or when it is said that someone's career is "over," meaning that, for example, their career as a professional footballer is over because of age or a serious injury or someone's career as a banker is over because of their conviction for fraud. In neither case is their life necessarily over, meaning that in Hughes's terms they have just completed one phase of the career that their life comprises.

In this book, we put ourselves firmly in the camp of those for whom career has a broad and encompassing meaning. Rather than restricting it to one particular area of life, e.g. work, we see careers as cutting across different areas of life, linking and separating them at the same time, and requiring a comprehensive approach when dealt with both academically and practically. This, of course, does not prevent the concept of career being applied to different areas of life, so that we can talk of work, sports, or drug careers, to name a few.

So how is career defined by those working in the OMC field, and what common themes can be extracted from these definitions?

Core Ideas in Career Definitions

The OMC literature, as opposed to the wider set of discourses discussed in the previous section, typically makes a broad distinction between two kinds of career. On the one hand, careers can be seen as patterns of roles or offices, examined over an extended period of time. This has been called the objective (Hughes, 1958: 63), external (Schein, 1980: 357), or orderly (Wilensky, 1961: 522) career. It is nicely summarized in London and Stumpf's (1982: 4) "sequence of work-related positions occupied throughout a person's life." It is also probably the most frequent sense used by scholars who do not see themselves working in the careers field but who nevertheless use the career construct in their research (e.g. Sorensen, 1999; Boeker, 1997; Haveman and Cohen, 1994).

On the other hand, careers can be seen both as objective patterns of roles or offices and as the subjective experience of the individual (Van Maanen, 1977a: 1), again examined over an extended period of time. Here, the objective career is combined with a subjective element (Schein, 1980: 357; Van Maanen, 1977b: 1): "*Subjectively*, a career is the moving perspective in which the person sees his life as a whole and interprets the meaning of his various attributes, actions, and the things which happen to him" (Hughes, 1958: 63; emphasis added).

More recently such definitions have tended to be more concise; emphases have been added in the following quotes to identify a term that arguably includes a subjective component, for example:

the *individually perceived* sequence of attitudes and behaviors associated with work-related *experiences* and activities over the span of the person's life. (Hall, 2002: 12)

the evolving sequence of a person's work *experiences* over time. (Arthur *et al.*, 1989b: 8)

the sequence of employment-related positions, roles, activities *and experiences* encountered by a person. (Arnold, 1997: 16)

the pattern of work-related *experiences* that span the course of a person's life. (Greenhaus, Callanan, and Godschalk, 2010: 10)

These typical approaches to defining career have been elaborated on in at least five different ways, which we examine next.

1. Career as Retrospective Sense-Making This approach is concerned with understanding what careers mean to people. Hughes's subjective definition has a meaning-related component to it that Young and Collin (2000: 1) in effect rephrase: "Many in our complex and highly differentiated society use [career] to attribute coherence, continuity, and social meaning to their lives." Similarly, Nicholson and West (1989: 181) use sense-making to distinguish between work history ("sequences of job experiences") and career ("the sense people make of them"), or, in a more complex analysis:

Organizations are not pyramids, they are scattered encampments on a wide terrain of hills and valleys, and careers are not ladders, but stories about journeys and routes through and between these encampments. Some of these paths and stories are well trodden and well known, others are improvised and haphazard. Many have unclear beginnings and no obvious endings: they just peter out. Careers, as stories of these journeys, often get better with the telling. Logic, consistency and meaning are reassuringly accessible when one analyses the past, but become strangely elusive when one dispassionately appraises the present. Careers can be viewed as fictions about the past to help us feel good about the future. They are talismans, offering protection against the proximity of gaping uncertainties. They provide cognitive structures on to which our social identities can be anchored. (Nicholson and West, 1988: 94)

This theme of retrospective sense-making is echoed by many other writers (e.g. Patton, 2008: 147; Savickas, 2005; Parker, Arthur, and Inkson, 2004; Cohen and Mallon, 2001; Young and Valach, 1996; Herr, 1990: 4).

2. Career as a Means of Linking Different Levels of Social Complexity A frequently quoted statement about career is Hughes's (1958: 67) famous "moving perspective in which persons orient themselves with reference to the social order." The concept expressed here, of career "falling at the intersection between the individual and society" (Schein, 1980: 357), is not, as Schein remarks, unique to career; he points out that it is shared by role. But nevertheless it has been noted as a central property of career (Young and Collin, 2000; Gunz, 1989b; Grandjean, 1981; Mills, 1959).

3. Career as a Path through Space and Time Yet other writers build on the commonly used idea of career path (Gowler and Legge, 1989; Nicholson and West, 1989; Schein, 1977) by looking on careers as movement through space-time or across a complex landscape (Nicholson and De Waal-Andrews, 2005). This approach focuses on the space through which the career path finds its way. It can be geographical or social, in particular occupational or organizational, such that the "movement is contextualized, anchored in a specific space" (Collin, 2006: 62–63).

4. Career as Self-Construction In a sociological view, the concept of career can be regarded as an organizing and regulative principle in modern society. "Career links present, past and future through a series of stages, steps or progressions. Careers offer a vehicle for the self to 'become' ... Career can offer one of the most obvious sites for realizing the project of self" (Grey, 1994: 481–482). The self is construed as a self-governing entity where each actor, in work as much as outside, is engaged in a project to shape their life as an autonomous individual driven by motives of self-fulfillment (cf. Giddens, 1991: 75; Rose, 1989: 115; Sennett, 1980: 84ff.).

5. Career as Product Rather than Process Career can sometimes be referred to as a product of a life's work as typified in a résumé or CV rather than a process. The focus may be something relatively specific, as in Bird's (1996) definition of careers as repositories of knowledge, "accumulations of information and knowledge embodied in skills, expertise, and relationship networks that are acquired through an evolving sequence of work experiences over time" (ibid.: 150).

Looking at this complexity, we see three themes common to each approach to career. Each involves attention to the *context* in which the career happens, a *career actor* who "has" the career, and the *time* over which the career takes place (cf. Collin's "time, social space, and the individual" [2007: 560]). Next, we examine these in a little more detail.

First, neither objective nor subjective careers can be considered in the absence of some kind of context, be it the geographic space or, arguably most important, either the social order (for dimensions of space see, e.g. Boschma, 2005) referred to by Hughes (1958: 67) or the social space of Bourdieu (1989). Sometimes metaphorically referred to as the landscape through which the career actor travels (Inkson and Elkin, 2008), this space is the social and physical world that they move through over the course of their life. The phrase "sequence of work-related experiences" or its equivalent that appears in all of the preceding definitions of career can only be made sense of in terms of social space, given that these experiences are inevitably tied to position. Position might be mapped in terms of, for example, formal position within a hierarchy, relationships with other members of a community of practice (Barley, 1996), location within a social or kinship network, socioeconomic status, geographic location, or political affiliation. Subjectively, when career actors measure their success by reference to others (Heslin, 2003) they almost invariably measure their relationship to those others by reference to how they both fit into the social order as, for example, colleagues, fellow alumni and former teachers (Higgins, Dobrow, and Chandler, 2008), or family members.

Second, it is axiomatic that career requires a career actor. Any examination of an objective or subjective career involves an examination of some aspect of that actor: their status, income, sense of well-being or career satisfaction, age, and so on.

Third, time is implicit in any account of career. Each definition we cited previously uses terms like sequence, moving perspective, patterns of experiences spanning a life, continuity, movement (through space), or life's work, each of which implies the passage of time.

Two of these three themes, concerning career actor and time, are familiar to existential philosophy (Heidegger, 1962) in the sense that they evoke being and time. The third concerns space, in particular geographical or social space. In the absence of this necessary additional dimension the actor would be seen as an acontextual entity, improbably not interacting with any social structures or systems over the course of their life. These three themes, then, referring to being, time, and space, provide a useful basis for understanding the nature of career scholarship. They suggest that the study of career involves the examination of what happens to career actors as they move through a given geographical and social space over time, and implicitly, they also suggest that what happens to social spaces as career actors pass through them matters too (Jones and Dunn, 2007). Drawing on the idea that career studies "may not be a field at all, but a *perspective on social enquiry*" (Gunz and Peiperl, 2007b: 4; emphasis in the original), we suggest that career studies involves the simultaneous application of three perspectives to social phenomena, focusing on (1) the – primarily social – space(s) surrounding the career actor, (2) the career actor, and (3) the time over which the career happens.

This view of career studies makes it clear why careers are such pervasive phenomena in the social sciences, particularly when, as we shall argue later, it is acknowledged that career actors need not be individuals but can be collectivities – organizations, institutions, nations – as well (e.g. Coleman, 1974; Parsons and Shils, 1962 [Original 1951]). There are a great many ways in which these three perspectives can be combined theoretically and empirically and a pretty much unlimited number of contexts to which they can be applied, which is what we see across a wide range of literature in the social sciences and humanities.

In this book we shall call these three perspectives spatial, ontic (Feenberg, 2000; meaning "of or relating to entities and the facts about them"; OED, 2017), and temporal. Each depends on the others, providing complexity for each other (Luhmann, 1995: 213). In the next chapter we develop them in greater detail, but before doing so we need to address the entity that is central to career: the career actor.

Career Actors

The notion that careers are linked to someone (or perhaps something, as we will briefly discuss at the end of this section) is implicit and largely undisputed in any discussion about careers, be it in a more academic fashion outlining major characteristics of careers as we did previously or in an everyday conversation with our neighbors about the latest happenings in our work life. Yet it is not entirely clear who this someone is: an individual, a human being, a subject, a person, or an actor? While we use these terms more or less interchangeably in daily matters, a more thorough look reveals that choosing one or the other is not a trivial matter since they each come with a substantial theoretical and historical heritage of meaning.

In this section we will first clarify the various potential options and consequences when conceptualizing the reference point of careers at the individual level and why we opt for actors as the point of reference of the SCF at the individual level. Building on this, we go on to elaborate on the concept of actor and argue that career actors can be entities both at the individual level and at higher levels of social complexity, e.g. a group, an organization, or a nation state. In a closing remark, we briefly touch on the issue of whether inanimate objects such as paintings, guitars, or songs can have a career, too.

The Concept of Actors

When conceptually deciding about the entity that "has" or "makes" a career, a number of different options are available, which we listed previously: individual, human being, subject, person, or actor. They differ in terms of usefulness for our endeavor of uncovering the basic characteristics of careers based on a notion of career that emphasizes its embeddedness in a broader social space. We shall go through these options in turn.

A first candidate is the individual. However, while this concept emphasizes the individual unit and singles it out from larger groupings, it lacks a focus on humans. Consequently, it also covers a number of entities that mainstream career research does not have at its focus: organisms such as dolphins and bees and even slime molds, parts of organisms such as placentas, or groups made up of organisms such as aggregates of bacteria or giraffe populations (Wilson and Barker, 2014). It is hard to see how this term would be a good candidate for career studies.

The next most obvious, but at the same time impractical and misleading, candidate is the empirically observable human being *in toto*. When talking about human beings the implicit assumption is that the discussion covers everything that can be linked to them. This ranges from, for example, human beings' cell and chromosome structure and hormone levels to the makeup of the skeleton and hair color or the composition of the brain and what goes on in there. As others have convincingly argued, it is highly impractical to include the human being in all of its facets in serious social analysis (e.g. Luhmann, 1991). It increases the complexity and number of analytical angles to the point that it is virtually impossible to bring the various facets of human beings together theoretically and relate them to each other as well as to the factors that influence – and are influenced by – their careers. It is also analytically not helpful since it tends to blur a major aspect of analyzing careers: Who "has" a career? If we take the whole human being as the central entity, would such different elements as gonads, teeth, nails, brain, or tongue have a career? While all of them undoubtedly belong to human beings at least under normal circumstances, would it be necessary or even possible to take these angles into account when analyzing careers? Very unlikely.

Subject is also a possibility. It can be thought of as a "being (or power) that thinks, knows, or perceives ... the person or self considered as a conscious agent" (OED, 2017). The concept of subject plays an important role in some traditions such as transcendental theory in the wake of Kant, German neo-humanist thinking by, e.g. Lessing, Herder, or von Humboldt (Luhmann, 2002:

39), or critical theory of the Frankfurt School with major figures such as Horkheimer, Marcuse, and others (Geuss, 1981). The subject has the ability to critically reflect social norms, ideologies, and so forth and is not socially determined but can govern its own action. While this concept clearly is a potential candidate, it also comes with a lot of baggage in terms of theoretical and ideological underpinnings arising from its use in the kinds of schools of thought to which we have just referred. In addition, the concept of subject clearly gives precedence to the subject and its self-directing potential over the influence of the broader social context.

As a consequence of these difficulties, person is another possibility. Person comprises those aspects of human beings that take part in societal communication, to which communications, actions, and decisions are attributed, and that link, set apart and protect them from what happens at the societal level. Referring to person is helpful for regulating social interaction, by pointing toward persons' embeddedness in their closer and broader social surroundings. As a classical Latin lexicon puts it: "... persona est conditio, status, munus, quod quisque inter homines et in vita civili gerit"[1] (Forcellini and Facciolati, 1828 [Original 1771]: 150). In addition, the concept of person allows the reduction of the potentially limitless variety of individual behaviors to those aspects that are relevant and discussable in a concrete setting. An example concerns the sets of behaviors an athlete has to show on the field and has the right to keep private within their own apartment. Similarly, touching the private parts of an otherwise distantly known man during a medical examination in the morning and during an extramarital affair in the evening can be done by the same human being or subject but is being done by two different persons (albeit that the former – the medical professional – risks censure from their profession in behaving as the latter does). In this sense, person as a concept is a better candidate than individual, human being, or subject for serving as the point of reference for careers. Yet it lacks a crucial aspect of modern society emerging, at the latest, in the twentieth century, namely the increased actorhood that is possible – and expected – in contemporary Western social settings. This leads to the concept of actor.

The concept of actor is embedded in a broader and changing understanding of the relationship between nature, society, and human beings. Realist theoretical thinking points out that actorhood is nearly inevitably the result of processes of rationalization of society and nature. If individual action is no longer largely predetermined by social requirements, spiritual and natural laws, or traditions, actors have options and have to choose between options. An institutionalist view emphasizes the importance of cultural construction, in

---

[1] "Person" signifies the position, the task, and the duties that everybody has within the community and in social life (translation based on the interpretation kindly provided by C. Lang).

particular for acting on behalf of itself due to the authority and capacity that come from, respectively, "Man" as actor and the wider cultural system (Meyer and Jepperson, 2000):

We argue that in the modern system, this capacity comes from the wider cultural system, and can best be seen as the cultural devolution of originally spiritual agency. "Man" as actor – individuals, organizations, states – carries almost the entire responsibility for the now-sacralized human project, with gods, other spiritual forces, ancestors, or an animated nature drained of agency ... The constructed capacity for responsible agency is the core of modern actorhood. (ibid.: 104 ff.)

From this, two major characteristics of actors emerge:

First ... the natural human entity with valid and lawful functions and interests ... the human individual or group that can be represented as behaving in terms of natural (scientifically expressible) laws. Second, devolving from rationalized spiritual authority ... the legitimated agent and carrier of authority, responsibility, and capacity to act in history. The integration of these two elements in a single imagined natural-and-spiritual entity is what moderns mean by the term "actor." (ibid.: 106)

This view of actor allows for both variation and commonalities. "Despite the obvious substantive differences among individuals, groups, and states, the cultural reduction of all to the agent-actor identity produces great commonalities. . . . Agentic actors at any level are to form clear boundaries and purposes, effectively integrated sovereignty, coherent control systems, and rational technologies" (Meyer and Jepperson, 2000: 112). Among other things, this leads Meyer and Jepperson to reasonably assert not only that "increased individualism emerges as a concomitant of increasing modernity, but also that human beings enact highly standardized individualism" (ibid.: 111).

To be sure, such a view of actorhood and the requirements "to form clear boundaries and purposes, effectively integrated sovereignty, coherent control systems, and rational technologies" (Meyer and Jepperson, 2000: 111) does not assume authenticity of any kind. On the contrary, the widely acknowledged discrepancy between preferred and actual behavior is still prevalent and a traditional theme in much of organization- and individual-related research. Examples include concepts such as espoused theories versus theories-in-use (Argyris and Schön, 1978), decoupling of structural elements and actual activities (Meyer and Rowan, 1977), logics of action (Karpik, 1978), or planned versus emergent strategies (Mintzberg and Waters, 1985). What Perrow succinctly put more than half a century ago – "[t]he type of goals most relevant to understanding organizational behavior are not the official goals, but those that are embedded in major operating policies and the daily decisions of the personnel" (Perrow, 1961: 854) – is not only still true, but *mutatis mutandis* also applies to modern actors. They "wear masks, too, now carrying the devolved authority of a high god. The modern mask is actorhood

Table 2.1 *Potential "units" to which careers are attributed*

	Characteristics	Career-related issues	Adequacy
Individual	Focus on individual unit; covers various sorts of beings	Missing focus on humans	Low
Human being	All-inclusive and holistic; includes all physical and psychic levels	Too complex and all-encompassing	Low
Subject	Self-directed action; able to distance themselves from societal pressures	Overemphasis of actorhood; theoretical and ideological ballast	Medium
Person	Embeddedness in social surroundings; emphasis on concrete settings	Relative lack of actorhood	Medium
Actor	Competent; responsible agency; bound by cultural and institutional context	Balances actorhood and contextual influences	High

itself, and in wearing it modern participants acquire their agentic authority for themselves, each other, and the moral (and natural) universe" (Meyer and Jepperson, 2000: 116f.).

Such a view of actorhood and actor fits the SCF. While it suggests a competent actor (see also Boltanski and Thévenot, 2006 [Original 1991]), it also is a far cry from seemingly boundaryless, autonomous individuals steering their career with aplomb, largely unfazed by what goes on around them. Instead, intricate, dynamic relationships exist between actor and their environments.

Table 2.1 gives an overview about the various candidates for entities having a career. From now on we shall use the term "actor" in this context.

Collective Actors

It is largely undisputed that not only individual actors but also different forms of collectives can be viewed as actors in their own right. Certainly by the time of Coleman (1974) the idea that not only individuals but also collectives, i.e. corporate actors, have rights that give them substantial freedom to act but that also make them hard to control by natural persons has established a foothold in organizational analysis. Indeed, corporations have been regarded in law, in one way or another, as persons since at least 1444 (Schane, 1986–1987). Of course, there are a number of variations of this thought. Krücken and Meier choose the term "organizational actor" to denote "the image of an integrated, goal-oriented entity that is deliberately choosing its own actions and that can thus be held responsible for what it does" (Krücken and Meier, 2006: 1). Laumann and Marsden point out that not only formally organized entities such as corporations but other types of collectivities also qualify as actors. They focus on collective decision-making systems and define collective actors as the set of members who (1) share an outcome preference in some matter of common concern and (2) are in an effective communication network with one another. A collective actor thus constitutes the maximal opportunity structure for coalition formation on a given issue (Laumann and Marsden, 1979: 717).

From this it follows that a comprehensive analysis of careers has to take into account the possibility of both individual and collective career actors. Both can have careers of their own, and as we shall see in Chapter 4, they mutually provide context for each other's careers. While at the individual level this is more or less accepted wisdom, the role of collective career actors requires some more explanation.

First, collective actors can have their own careers. Clarke (1991: 134), for example, assumes careers of social worlds by remarking that "[f]or Strauss and his colleagues, a natural history, career, or trajectory approach is useful in analyzing social worlds of all kinds in their various stages of becoming, maintaining, expanding, or deteriorating." The development of rock bands is described as these bands' careers (Waksman, 2001: 253; 269). Historians trace the history of countries through the centuries, showing how their social, demographic, economic, and legal compositions change along with those of the countries that they interact with, merge with, separate from, conquer, and so on, as with, for example, the case of Afghanistan and its career from a war economy to a drug economy (Maaß, 2010). Organizations have careers involving moving from one position in their respective space to another, often traceable to some form of "birth" – for example, entrepreneurs working on product ideas in their bedroom or garage or from humble beginnings (e.g. Tata Steel in India, Apple or Hewlett-Packard in the USA), a merger of several smaller corporations (e.g. GlaxoSmithKline, Penguin Random House, PricewaterhouseCoopers), being spun off from larger corporations (e.g. wireless tower operator Telesites spinning off from Mexican giant America Móvil), or a larger corporation being split up (e.g. Alibaba splitting up Taobao, a big commerce site in China, into three sites and entities). In no particular order they grow, change their structure, stagnate, decline, and ultimately "die" (e.g. former "big five" accounting firm Arthur Andersen), lose their independence by merging with another corporation (e.g. Chrysler's merger with Fiat), or disappear into another organization that absorbs the remnants of their operations (e.g. former UK chemical giant ICI). It would, of course, be misleading to over-reify organizations as career actors. The change processes to which we have just alluded mean that it can be hard to be sure, at times, whether we are talking about the same entity over time. This can be seen most strikingly in the histories of European countries that have emerged, been swallowed by neighbors, reemerged as independent jurisdictions only to be swallowed by another neighbor or invader from another continent, and so on or whose boundaries have constantly been in flux as a result of disputes with neighbors. However, the same questions can be raised about the identity of a twenty-year-old immigrant to the USA without any financial means who turned into one of the richest people of his time by the time of his death at age eighty-five, an abstract description of the case of John Jacob Astor, born in Germany in 1763. Overall, it is hard to see any substantial differences between individual and collective career actors that would make it seem far-fetched to look at the latter through a career lens.

Second, while all actors potentially provide context for other career actors (Chapter 4), this role is more evident in the case of collective actors. For example, the organization in which an individual career actor makes their career has its own career but also comprises a key part of that individual's social space for as long as they are a member of the organization. Take the example of a business school such as WU Vienna, academic home to one of the authors (WM). Around the beginning of the millennium, the university's leadership decided that for its positive long-term development, participation in the emerging field of European business schools competing for students, faculty, and reputation was essential (cf. the account by Kutner, 2014, of Northeastern University's gaming of university rankings). Consequently, WU invested heavily in various areas in order to be accredited by internationally recognized agencies such as EQUIS, AMBA, or AACSB and to climb up in various rankings such as the *Financial Times* ranking. Fifteen years and various career steps later, WU has established itself as a visible player in the European landscape of business schools as indicated by its triple accreditation and its respectable position in the *FT* ranking. These career steps have not left the careers of (some of) its members unaffected. On the contrary, by making a career in the field of (European) universities, WU also provided a favorable developmental context for its individual members and supporting their own career steps. While initially coming from WU was no plus, having WU in one's vita is now, at least at the European level, considered an advantage.

Inanimate "Actors"

Our last category of career actor sounds whimsical, but it is not meant to be. We include it for completeness even though we shall not be addressing it further in this book. What does it mean to say that an inanimate object can have a career? Or, rather, why should the "career" of an inanimate object be of any interest?

Objects, according to G. H. Mead, are socially constructed:

First, the nature of an object is constituted by the meaning it has for the person or persons for whom it is an object. Second, this meaning is not intrinsic to the object but arises from how the person is initially prepared to act toward it. Readiness to use a chair as something in which to sit gives it the meaning of a chair; to one with no experience with the use of chairs the object would appear with a different meaning, such as a strange weapon. It follows that objects vary in their meaning. A tree is not the same object to a lumberman, a botanist, or a poet ... Third, objects – all objects – are social products in that they are formed and transformed by the defining process that takes place in social interaction. The meaning of the objects – chairs, trees, stars, prostitutes, saints, communism, public education, or whatnot – is formed from the ways in which others refer to such objects or act toward them. Fourth, people are prepared or set to act toward objects on the basis of the meaning of the objects for them. In a genuine sense the organization of a human being consists of his objects, that is, his tendencies to act on the basis of their meanings. (Blumer, 1966: 539)

So although an object over time may do little other than get older, it may attract many different meanings from the people who use it or interact with it. The 1998 movie *The Red Violin* traces the story of a violin from its making by the fictional violin maker Bussotti through three centuries of varied ownership. The violin plays a part in the lives of each of its owners, in settings ranging from an Austrian orphanage to Cultural Revolutionary China. It has moved through a complex social space over an extended period of time, and the core concept of the movie is the way that the violin's meaning to its various owners has changed from owner to owner and, during each period of ownership, to that owner. Following Mead, it could be said that its nature – its condition – has changed as its meaning to its owner changed, making it somewhat less than fanciful to talk about it having a career within the terms of the SCF.

There is also some debate about career-like qualities of objects of the kind found on display in various surroundings such as private homes and exhibitions (e.g. Wintle, 2008). Pearce (1995) points out that "[o]bjects are not inert or passive; they help us to give shape to our identities and purpose to our lives. We engage with them in a complex interactive or behavioural dance in the course of which the weight of significance which they carry affects what we think and feel and how we act. This both contributes to the stability of social structures and to that of our own lives, and adds its mite to the accumulation of mental shifts which we call social change" (18f.). Emphasizing the relationship between objects and narratives, Stewart (1993) outlines the dynamic quality of objects and their relationship to the social space within which they emerge, showing how they are both contextualized and decontextualized and are essential for various kinds of meaning generations.

In a similar vein but going beyond material objects, career is also used to denote the development and progress of fields of studies and of concepts

(Barber, 1995). Examples of the former include "The Career of Causal Analysis in American Sociology" (Bernert, 1983) or "Sanskritization: The Career of an Anthropological Theory" (Charsley, 1998); the latter is illustrated by "Nigger: The Strange Career of a Troublesome Word" (Kennedy, 2008) or "The Strange Career of Cold War Rationality" (Erickson *et al.*, 2013).

As noted previously, we do not pursue this idea in this book. We include it in order to make the point that the concept of career is extraordinarily broad with many angles to which the mainstream careers literature typically does not pay attention.

Summation

In this chapter we begin the process of establishing the theoretical concepts on which the rest of the book depends. While the term "career" may not quite mean all things to all people, it does pack a great deal of, to use again Hall's (2002: 8) memorable phrase, "surplus meaning." We show how most views of career focus on the entity that has the career and their moves through geographical and social space over time. The three corresponding perspectives that emerge from this view of career are, respectively, the ontic, spatial, and temporal, which underpin the Social Chronology Framework. We go on to examine how to conceptualize the entity that has the career. We propose that the term "actor" is indeed the most appropriate and show the breadth with which it can appropriately be used in the context of career, covering both individuals and collectivities.

In Part II of this book we use the starting points presented in this chapter to develop the SCF. We do this in three steps. After outlining the three perspectives and their view on career we present a heuristic model of careers based on the assumption that career transitions are at the heart of much of career studies. At the end of Part II we explore the architectonics of the SCF, explaining why it is a framework guiding theory building rather than a theory itself. However, we start it with an in-depth exploration of the three perspectives.

Part II

The Social Chronology Framework (SCF)

3 The Three Perspectives and Their View of Career

In Chapter 2 we draw on the idea that career studies "may not be a field at all, but a *perspective on social enquiry*" (Gunz and Peiperl, 2007a: 4; emphasis in the original) to lead to our suggestion that studying careers involves the application of three distinct perspectives: spatial, ontic, and temporal. In this chapter we enlarge on them and show how they lead to a definition of career that offers the possibility of unifying the disparate definitions of career we encountered in the previous chapter. But first we need to explain how "perspective" fits in: Where does the concept come from, and how do we use it in this book?

Perspectives: Creating Reality and Meaning

We take as our point of departure the assertion that observation is at the core of any analysis and explain our concept of observation based on the view put forward by Spencer-Brown (1972). Drawing on social systems theory in the wake of Luhmann (1995), we then argue that perspectives consist of three major characteristics – guiding differences ("*Leitdifferenzen*"), operations, and core constructs – and their specific interplay.

Observation

In line with Luhmann's (e.g. 2000) reading of Spencer-Brown (1972), we view observation as the core element of any kind of analysis (for the following, see also Seidl, 2005). In its most basic sense, observation goes beyond optical perception and "refers to any operation from communication to thoughts and even to operations of machines; even the observer himself is an observation" (Seidl, 2005: 47). So the focus is not on the outcome of an observation but on the process of observing, on how it is possible to observe. Each observation requires two basic elements: distinction and indication.

Drawing a *distinction* is the basis of any observation. Observing everything at the same time is impossible – observers have to choose a distinction and determine their focus in order to observe something within a given space. This rests on Bateson's (2000 [Original 1972]: 459) epistemological view that difference is the basic building block for producing information:

There are many differences ... Of this infinitude, we select a very limited number which become information. In fact, what we mean by information – the elementary unit of information – is a difference which makes a difference.

In this sense, information is the combination of differences. Guiding differences guide the process of producing information, which for the social or psychic system applying them emerges as meaning. So, for example, let us assume that a police officer's guiding difference when observing a crowd of people is: "potentially a public safety risk/not potentially a safety risk." A good officer is trained to watch crowd members for potentially threatening behavior and separate the crowd mentally into those showing the behavior and who therefore need closer surveillance and those who are not. A bad (or badly trained) officer might use an invalid difference, for example, the ethnicity of crowd members.

Making sense always requires placing restrictions on the manifold possibilities that might be; these possibilities require selection. Zerubavel (1995: 1098) argues that

[a]fter all, any notion of orderliness presupposes at least some element of structure, which inevitably presupposes some boundaries ... Without at least some mental horizons that would help scholars curb their curiosity, organize their intellectual attention in a more "focused" manner, and essentially separate the relevant from the irrelevant, for example, it would be absolutely impossible to establish any coherent scholarly agenda at all.

Making a distinction transforms the initial space of potential observations into two spaces. The observer then has to make an *indication*, i.e. choose which of the states they want to focus on. By focusing on one space – the "inside" – this becomes the so-called marked space; the outside turns into the unmarked space. Using different terminology we might call the marked space the figure and the unmarked space the ground. Take the example (see Spencer-Brown, 1972: 69 ff.) of a plane space, e.g. an otherwise empty sheet of paper. If we want to observe the whole sheet, we draw a distinction using the four edges and mark the whole sheet as the "inside." What is beyond the sheet is of no interest to us; it is the unmarked space. When reading a newspaper, for example, we focus on what is inside the borders of the sheets of paper; anything outside them is irrelevant. In case we want to observe specific parts of the paper, we have to make a different kind of distinction and indication. For example, someone might have drawn a circle around a particular article to draw our attention to it; they are encouraging us to define what is inside the circle as marked space, and we ignore the unmarked space, i.e. everything outside it. Alternatively, we might define the marked space as everything printed in the paper's standard font. Anything not is likely to be an advertisement, which we ignore (or try to).

The processes of distinction and indication are crucial because they determine what we see and what is left in the dark. Observers – e.g. an individual or a social system like an organization – have to decide what they are interested in. Normally, they can choose among a great variety of distinctions and indications. Their choice depends on a myriad of factors such as drives, personal interests, organizational culture, political pressure, economic logic, or societal norms, to name just a few. Scientific disciplines such as psychology, biology, sociology, organizational science, or economics inform us extensively about determinants of individual and collective action. Once these decisions are made, they have consequences: you only can see what you choose to see.

Let us illustrate this by using two examples. There are many ways of viewing public buildings: beauty, cost, materials, durability, color, and so on. Officials responsible for marketing a city might tend toward using a distinction that relates to prestige and makes the city unrivaled throughout the world, giving it an edge over other tourist destinations. They might refine this high/low prestige distinction by focusing on a more specific and easily quantified one: "tall/short" in relation to the height of buildings. The officials might indicate that they are interested in "tall." In this sense, Dubaians will focus on how much taller Dubai's Burj Khalifa is than Toronto's CN Tower, and consequently, inhabitants of Toronto are no longer able to boast of living in the city with the tallest free-standing structure in the world (to the chagrin of one of the authors, HG).

Another example comes from the area of careers. Imagine a business school graduate weighing her options after graduating. When analyzing various job offers, she uses different kinds of distinctions for her observations. The job offers resemble the sheet of paper in the previous example. They constitute the existing "unstructured empty space," here, of course, filled with data about the offers. Using the distinction "net income beyond the threshold of … " she differentiates the otherwise "unstructured" job offers into two groups: those that meet the threshold criterion and those that do not. Strictly speaking, the graduate collapses two observations into one. First, she decides to use net income as distinction and not, for example, potential hierarchical advancement, ethical standards, personal development, or geographical location. Second, within the focus on net income, she indicates that she is interested in only those offers that meet the criterion of a given net income. During her musings about which offer to take up, the graduate most likely switches constantly between different kinds of observations using different kinds of distinctions such as the ones mentioned previously, i.e. advancement, personal develop-ment, and so on.

Returning to the conceptual level, the distinction together with the marked/ unmarked spaces are called the *form* of the distinction. This emphasizes that

[t]he form of something is not sufficiently described by the defined – the marked state – but the unmarked state is a constitutive part of it. The marked side cannot exist without its unmarked side. . . . A distinction, thus, has a double function: like any boundary it both distinguishes and unites its two sides. (Seidl, 2005: 47)

Strictly speaking, it is not possible to focus on the marked and the unmarked space at the same time. Likewise, as with the famous saying "fish can't see water," once you are "inside," the distinction itself becomes invisible. Only from the outside – looking down at the fishbowl – or, more formally, only through a second-order observation where you observe how an observer observes can the distinction itself be observed. In this case, the marked space, the distinction, and the unmarked space of the first observer (the fish) constitute the "inside," which is the marked space of the second observation (made by the observer of the fishbowl).

Against the backdrop of this conceptualization of observation, we will next develop our view of what perspectives mean and how perspectives create both meaning and reality.

Perspectives

As an organizing framework, the SCF is, in the language used earlier, a second-order observation, i.e. it concerns itself with observing how career research up to now has observed the underlying phenomena associated with career. Within the SCF, perspectives are specific modes of observation. As we shall shortly see, they apply a guiding difference to unstructured career-relevant data "out there" by means of an operation connected with the perspective and relate it to a core construct for that perspective. In so doing, this observation provides meaning and, at the same time, creates new reality. We deal with these issues in turn, briefly introducing the basic ideas behind this approach and then, in the following sections, providing a more detailed explanation for each perspective.

Our starting point is the notion of distinction or of difference that we outlined in the previous section. In order to produce information to make sense of unstructured data "out there," one has to apply a meaningful difference. Guiding differences are the basis for selecting since they force the system to indicate what is of interest and what is not, the latter always being the much larger part (in the way that the smaller region is more likely to be assigned to "figure" than "ground"; Vecera, Flevaris, and Filapek, 2004).

When your boss chooses to observe tangible output instead of emotional fulfillment or another topic from a nearly endless list of potential candidates, she makes a choice indicating her priorities. A nation focusing on economic welfare or supposed safety from terrorism and not on integrating refugees from poorer or dangerous countries abroad does the same.

We can now move from perspectives in general to the three SCF perspectives in particular: spatial, ontic, and temporal. First, we sketch out the approach we shall be taking when we examine them in detail later. The SCF argues that the perspectives with their respective guiding differences are essential in order to look at careers. The spatial perspective, using "in/out" as its guiding difference, places career actors in a social and geographical space that is bounded in the sense that it is internally differentiated and externally enclosed vis-à-vis the overall environment. By applying an "Ego/Alter" differentiation, the ontic perspective relates career actors to each other. Finally, the temporal dimension, using "precedes/follows" as its guiding difference, acknowledges that careers take time to unfold.

Guiding differences require operations that lead to constructs. By operations we mean the process by which the guiding difference is applied. Each of the guiding differences in the SCF draws on such operations, each of them is specific and generates a construct and statements about it with which we make sense of the world. "Constructs are the means by which science orders observations" (Jenner, Smith, and Burdick, 1983: 1) because they reduce the potentially indefinite number of observations and help us to explain reality:

Without this faith, no science could ever have any motivation. To deny this faith is to affirm the primary chaos of nature and the consequent futility of scientific effort. The constructs in terms of which natural phenomena are comprehended are man-made inventions. To discover a scientific law is merely to discover that a man-made scheme serves to unify, and thereby to simplify, comprehension of a certain class of natural phenomena. (Thurstone, 1947: 51)

The spatial dimension's *operation* is mapping. It locates elements such as positions, individual and collective career actors, or rules into different segments of the social space. This leads to boundaries as the *core construct* that internally structure and externally limit the social and geographical space in question, thus influencing career actors' careers. The ontic perspective uses comparing as its *operation*. Comparing relates career actors, located in the bounded space, to each other. Comparing leads to evaluating the condition of career actors – its *core construct* – in terms of an almost infinite number of possible criteria, for example, income, social status, fulfillment, leaving a legacy, and so on. Finally, the temporal dimension has sequencing as its *operation*. By putting career transitions and their elements (i.e. conditions of

Table 3.1 *Elements of the SCF*

Domain	Perspective	Guiding difference	Operation	Core construct
Space	Spatial	In/Out	Mapping	Boundary
Being	Ontic	Ego/Alter	Comparing	Condition
Time	Temporal	Precedes/Follows	Sequencing	Chronology

career actors, characteristics of social space, and its relationships) into a temporal order along dimensions of time, this kind of observation leads to its *core construct*, chronologies of various kinds.

Overall, this results in the elements of the SCF tied to the three domains of space, being, and time shown in Table 3.1.

We argue earlier in the chapter that applying the SCF's perspectives creates both meaning and reality. Regarding the former, the interplay of guiding differences, operations, constructs, and the choices linked with them transforms data into meaning. At the same time, this is also a process of creating reality. Mapping, comparing, and sequencing create a new reality that offers a starting point for future processes creating meaning. Take, for example, the case in which an HR manager maps the careers of expatriates working in her company along the lines of cultural proximity of the host countries the expatriates went to. She then compares the conditions of these expatriates in terms of their next career transition after they came back to the home country, e.g. promotion, equal position, demotion, or leaving the organization altogether. This means that she develops unique condition/chronology assumptions about each expatriate, for example: persons have been moved to different countries for different periods of time, they have gained a variety of experiences and skills depending on the length of their stay, their next career move is systematically linked to both host country and length of stay abroad, and so on. In this way, she not only allocates meaning to what she observes, but she also creates a new reality on which she bases her future decisions. This includes, for example, organizational guidelines on how long expatriates should stay in certain countries, policy decisions about supporting certain types of expatriation more than others, or insight into what is most promising for individuals whom the HR department wants to put on a fast track. Beyond that, it also provides a new reality for the rest of the organization, e.g. future expatriates who need to decide whether to take up an offer of going abroad.

Now that we have sketched out the approach we shall be taking, we can examine the three perspectives of the SCF and their respective guiding differences, operations, and constructs in more detail.

Spatial Perspective

Context in Organizational Research

Talking about context in organizational research seems to be a no-brainer. Embedding individuals and organizations in their broader context is a classic issue in the scientific discourse on individuals and organizations. An early example is the basic behavioral formula of Lewin (1936: 12) claiming that behavior results from the interplay between person and environment, which in recent years has become prominent as the AMO (abilities, motivation, opportunities) approach in human resource management (HRM; Boxall and Purcell, 2003). It appears in perspectives such as the open systems view of organizations (Scott, 2004; Katz and Kahn, 1978), contingency approaches to the study of organizations (Lawrence and Lorsch, 1967), or institutional viewpoints of different kinds (e.g. Tolbert and Zucker, 1996; DiMaggio and Powell, 1983; Meyer and Rowan, 1977), all of which give evidence of the central part context plays in organization research. Of course, how context is conceptualized and what is meant by it differ greatly in different theoretical approaches. It seems safe to say, though, that beyond the material context of soil and natural resources the social context plays a crucial role for understanding organizations and individuals. Again, foci differ greatly. Some approaches emphasize national culture (e.g. Hofstede, 1980); others point toward various kinds of actors in the socioeconomic context (e.g. Maurice and Sorge, 2000) or different forms of capitalism (e.g. Hall and Soskice, 2001).

The picture starts to change slightly once we move from general organizational research to more specific areas related to career studies. For example, in HRM an extensive debate exists on the universalist versus the contextualist view of HRM (see e.g. Brewster and Mayrhofer, 2011). Despite a firm place for context in the original models of HRM (Beer, Spector, Lawrence, Quinn Mills, and Walton, 1984; Fombrun, Tichy, and DeVanna, 1984) as well as strategic (e.g. Jackson and Schuler, 1999) and international HRM (e.g. Dowling, Festing, and Engle, 2013; Sparrow, 2009), the universalist view emphasizes the shared and invariant characteristics of organizations and individuals. Consequently, research efforts in this tradition are looking for HRM best practices that support overall organizational performance. In contrast, the contextualist view focuses on the contextual specifics that organizations and individuals face when making choices. Research in this tradition underlines the importance of taking into account crucial elements in social contexts in order to understand how HRM works. In a similar vein, in organizational behavior research there is a constant stream of reminders that context matters (e.g. Johns, 2001, 2006; Rousseau and Fried, 2001; Rousseau and House, 1994). Hardly surprisingly, the understanding of context differs greatly, ranging from situational or intra-psychic micro-factors (e.g. Joshi and Roh, 2009) to well-known macro-factors such as culture (Bandura, 2002).

When looking specifically at career studies, it becomes evident that contextual factors do play a minor role in theoretical and empirical research, in particular when going beyond micro-factors such as group or organizational context. Of course, there is no basic disagreement that both individual and contextual factors – sometimes captured by the buzzwords of agency versus structure or micro versus macro – are essential to understanding careers. Careers inevitably are careers in context (Collin, 1997; Young and Collin, 1992; Schein, 1984). They are located at the "intersection of societal history and individual biography" (Grandjean, 1981: 1057) and link micro- and macro-frames of reference (Barley, 1989; Gunz, 1989a). Consequently, the two parts of the picture – individuals on the one hand, context on the other – have received considerable attention. However, despite calls for a stronger integration of contextual issues in career studies (Mayrhofer, Meyer, and Steyrer, 2007a), a focus on the individual and, at best, the organizational context clearly dominates. In recent years, though, we observe a revived interest in context-based career studies. Examples include the new interest in boundaries (e.g. Rodrigues, Guest, and Budjanovcanin, 2016; Inkson, Gunz, Ganesh, and Roper, 2012), the integration of institutional contexts in career analysis (Kaulisch and Enders, 2005), and the growing field of comparative career studies, looking into the importance of national and institutional factors for career phenomena such as career success or career transitions (Briscoe, Hall, and Mayrhofer, 2012b).

Elements of the Perspective

The spatial perspective's focus is on the social and geographical space within which careers happen. Its *operation* is mapping, i.e. defining a map of the career-relevant characteristics of the career actor's social and geographical space. In a topographical sense this means locating career actors and their careers in a defined space internally structured by boundaries constraining and enabling careers. We might describe this location in terms of the firm the career actor works for or is under contract to; where they are in the firm's hierarchy and in its horizontal division of labor; how a self-employed person fits into the economy and which professional group or community of practice they identify with; if unemployed, whether the actor is in a pool of those seeking work or whether they are in a special category (e.g. of those suffering from long-term disability) that means that paid work is either impossible or only possible under very constrained circumstances; whether they locate themselves in the voluntary sector, the retired sector; and so on. Mapping also includes the social order and its components relevant for the career actors, including the norms and rules governing access to and movement within various career fields (Iellatchitch, Mayrhofer, and Meyer, 2003). Therefore, the spatial perspective also covers issues such as the location of career actors in social hierarchies, formal and informal access regulations governing how to get into positions, or career logics (Gunz, 1989a) underlying career patterns. These social facts about the career actor have in common that they define the actor's location in relation to a social order and also to those *Alters* who might play a role in determining the future of their career.

The examples of defining location in the previous paragraph have both subjective and objective aspects to them, both of which, as we see in Chapter 2, are central to career as it is conceived of in the literature. Division of labor is an objective concept, typically expressed in terms of documents such as job descriptions. However, it has a subjective element to it given that it depends on the actor's individual response to a specific arrangement of division of labor, involving such constructs as career goals, individual need for growth, or personal convictions about a just way of dividing labor between different members of society. Similarly, defining oneself as part of a given community of practice or deciding how one divides one's energy among paid work, voluntary work, and family life depends on a subjective interpretation of the meaning to the actor of these three domains.

How the social space is mapped and what its elements are depend on the specific research question being asked and the underlying theoretical foundation in use. For example, in the Parsonian tradition one would argue that the social space relevant to career studies consists of social objects such as other individuals, physical objects such as things that do not interact with or respond to the actor, and cultural objects such as norms and beliefs that are not internalized by the actor but treated as situational objects (Parsons, 1991 [Original 1951]). By contrast, in a Bourdieuan sense one would conceptualize the social space as a field with a patterned set of practices and as a playground or battlefield in which actors, endowed with a specific field-relevant capital, try to advance their position (Bourdieu, 1986).

Mapping requires drawing boundaries, the *core construct* of the spatial perspective. A geographical map is characterized by its use of boundaries: physical boundaries depicting coastlines, rivers, lakes, deserts, mountainous areas and political boundaries depicting countries, provinces, cities and so on. Boundaries separate, but they also connect because they imply the existence of a reality on the other side of the boundary that Lewis (1973: 84 ff.) describes as "possible worlds." In the Batesonian sense (Bateson, 2000 [Original 1972]: 459) they are differences that make a difference and, hence, provide information and lead to meaning as they structure social space. Boundaries have been well recognized in the careers literature to shape careers in fundamental ways (Inkson *et al.*, 2012). They constrain careers by restricting the kinds of changes people can make in their working lives (Vardi, 1980), enable them by structuring status passages (Glaser and Strauss, 1971), and punctuate them by providing the markers that help structure people's careers into episodes (Roth, 1963) and develop *rites de passage* (van Gennep, 1960 [Original 1909]). It has often been argued that boundaries come before and define structure (e.g. Nicholson and De Waal-Andrews, 2005; Heracleous, 2004; Hernes, 2004; Lamont and Molnar, 2002; Abbott, 1995).

Overall, boundaries constitute a very useful construct for conceptualizing the way in which social and geographical space shapes career, and vice versa. They help to make sense of the transitions (Nicholson, 1984), both subjective and objective, that career actors make in crossing these boundaries. Applying the *guiding difference* "in/out" leads to boundaries and, as a consequence, to a bounded social space in a twofold sense. On the one hand, it creates a defined social space that is distinguished from the rest of the world and denotes the arenas within which careers take place, for example, certain professions or specific countries. This reduces complexity by creating an "internal milieu" with more order than outside, favoring the emergence of specific relations between elements within the boundary (Willke, 1987: 259). For example, the existence of occupation-specific boundaries forms medical interns, during their medical education, into a specific group as they face similar tests, are uncertain about similar aspects of their future, and so on. In brief, boundaries differentiate a specific space from others that are not necessary for the analysis. On the other hand, drawing a boundary and differentiating between in and out establish internal structure by demarcating the social space internally. So the space occupied by medical interns is structured by internal boundaries separating interns of different specialties and in terms of seniority, the latter with varying expectations placed on them in terms of knowledge and performance and, perhaps, minor managerial responsibilities such as scheduling the work shifts of other interns.

Movement within and out of the bounded social space involves boundary crossing (Luhmann, 1984: 52). Boundaries can be thought of as that which is crossed (or not crossed) when making (or not making) a career transition. To the person making transitions, they feel like boundaries. A pre-adult feels excluded from adulthood until they have crossed the boundary separating the two conditions. Students feels "outside" a company or profession they plan to join until they have gone successfully through the admission process, crossing the boundary separating the organization from the outside world. Gunz *et al.* (2007a) argue that these boundaries begin as subjective feelings about the possibility of making the transition: the less possible it seems to be, the less permeable it seems to be to the focal person. They argue that this permeability is actually the result of a negotiation between the focal person and the gatekeepers controlling access to whatever is the other side of the boundary and that the greater the consensus there is about the rules for crossing the boundary the more it takes on an appearance of objectivity. The boundary examples we have already used (adulthood rituals, boundaries controlling access to organizational or professional membership) are typically objectified in this way because the rules are well understood by everyone involved. To be sure, Inkson *et al.* (2012) point out there may be hidden aspects too to objectified boundaries, for example, in the way that organizations or professions may quietly exclude people of particular religions or ethnicities.

Conceptually, this calls attention to the differentiation between elements and relations. While elements have to be either "in" or "out" and can only be at one side of the boundary or the other at a given time, relations can cut across boundaries. For example, two academics may be on different sides of career boundaries, as North American academics often are when some faculty have crossed the boundary of tenure and others have not. Yet their personal and professional networks cut right across the tenure-related boundary. This does not rule out situations where elements seemingly are on neither one side nor the other. Two major constellations emerge. First, sometimes a boundary crossing can take considerable time. During this time an in-between or liminal state can occur in which an element is on neither the one side nor the other (see, for example, van Gennep's [1960] preliminary *rites de separation* and the third, postliminal *rites d'aggregation*; Glaser and Strauss's [1971] temporality dimension of status passages; or Mayrhofer's [1996] intermediary steps in international job transitions). Second, elements can zigzag between different sides of a boundary at great speed. While in essence these are multiple boundary crossings, they look like an in-between state. For example, rapid, often daily changes in the social structure of a group – who is coalescing with whom, who is "in" and "out" – can indicate such changes.

The concept of position in the social space is inextricably linked with a focus on boundaries and boundary-crossing. Positions are locations within the social fabric endowed with rights and obligations, emerging at the intersection of social relationships. They derive their existence and meaning from their relationships to other positions. Positions are the result of social differentiation, of "who does what" and "how valuable this is in relationship to other positions." In principle, positions are not linked with any specific person but are non-personal, i.e. they exist independent of potential incumbents. Positions can take on widely varying forms. In their most institutionalized variant, positions appear in the form of office. Office is "a standardized group of duties and privileges" (Hughes, 1937: 404), often formally regulated. Examples of offices abound and range from head of state to secretary to the dean of studies. Most positions, however, are less well defined than office, with duties and rights rarely legally fixed. In their weakest form, they appear in a specific aggregate state of "positional solidification/ hardening" with an awareness of vacancy if the position is not or no longer filled (Popitz, 1967: 10). Examples of these more fuzzy forms of positions include informal leadership positions in groups, the scapegoat position in an organization, or bloggers in the public societal discourse. Note that positions are not necessarily permanent or long term. They also can exist as "potential empty space" that is filled under specific circumstances, e.g. the position of "host" when guests come to a private home. In organizations, positions are absolutely crucial: "Persons without positions cannot function as executives, they mean nothing but potentiality. Conversely, positions vacant are as defunct as dead nerve centers" (Barnard, 1971 [Original 1938]: 218).

Two further concepts related to that of position are role and status (see the classic discussion in Linton, 1936). An extensive debate that in recent years has somewhat died down discusses these concepts and their relationship to position. As usual, no unanimous view exists. Yet it seems safe to say that roles are tightly linked with the bundle of expectations existing in the social space vis-à-vis individuals filling positions. "Roles have been viewed as the boundary between individuals and the organization, consisting of expecta-tions of the individual and the organization" (Dougherty and Pritchard, 1985: 141). They lead to "standardized patterns of behavior required of all persons playing a part in a given functional relationship, regardless of personal wishes or interpersonal obligations irrelevant to the functional relationship" (Katz and Kahn, 1966: 37). Status, on the other hand, has a more evaluative component. It is the result of a social evaluation of elements of a position or the position itself. For example, in many countries rankings exist that evaluate the societal appreciation of different professions, with firefighters and nurses often being on top of these lists and insurance brokers and politicians at the bottom (GFK Verein, 2016).

To sum up, by locating career actors within a social or geographical space we establish their position. Within an organizational or professional space this might be expressed in terms of hierarchical level or professional specialization; within a geographical space, national location; within a political space, party affiliation; or within a kinship space, position in a given family. Spaces and positions may be occupied sequentially, as, for example, when someone moves from university to their first employing organization, or contemporaneously: typically, people simultaneously occupy positions at work, in their families, and in all probability in many other roles they fill in life – for example, in voluntary, social, or religious groups they belong to or at their gym or sports club. Even this is an oversimplification: their work lives can comprise filling more than one position. They may be under contract to more than one company; within any one organization they may fill more than one position – for example, their primary position, membership of official or semiofficial groups such as supervisory boards or unions, and even, as Ashforth *et al.* (2000) point out, the distinct roles of subordinate and supervisor. Although these positions are all occupied during the same period they are seldom occupied at exactly the same time; we make micro-transitions (Ashforth *et al.*, 2000) between them so that, at any one moment, we probably occupy only one position. The rarity with which this does *not* happen is evidenced by the awkwardness created if we find ourselves genuinely occupying two positions at once – for example, if one's angry spouse appears at one's office while something particularly difficult is happening there.

Three additional aspects of the bounded social space are of particular importance here. First, various types of individual or collective actors (Coleman, 1990) are part of the social space. The possibilities include individuals such as peers and supervisors; collectivities including organizations offering career opportunities, facilitating career opportunities (Cappelli and Hamori, 2007; Fernandez-Mateo, 2007), or constituting major players in the field such as trade unions; or even nation states undergoing roller-coaster experiences as debtors. Second, the social space is governed by power relations (Emerson, 1962). The power distribution in the field influences the behavior of the career actors and their interactions. For example, the relative power of labor unions and management can make a substantial difference in the way career transitions such as firing can be carried out. Third, power relations are formed by and express themselves through rules in the social space (Bourdieu, 1989), which in turn express themselves as various types of boundaries. Examples include cultural boundaries controlling social access to a group or organization; legal boundaries such as rules regulating access to a profession; or boundaries of meaning (Luhmann, 1995: 194 ff.) that constitute collective identities and point toward possibilities and limits of crossing over from "us" to "them," as in the case of an academic faculty member becoming an administrator.

Ontic Perspective

Being and Condition

The term "ontic" or "ontical" (the terms seem interchangeable, so we have arbitrarily chosen the briefer one, which also has the advantage of not being as easily confused with "ontological") derives, as we note in Chapter 1, from Heidegger's work on *Being and Time* (Heidegger, 1962). "Ontological inquiry is concerned primarily with *Being*; ontical inquiry is concerned primarily with *entities* and the facts about them" (ibid.: 31, translators' note; emphasis in the original). For example:

Ontical refers to the traditional approach of the sciences, including psychology, of categorizing, labeling, and objectifying that which is studied. It is the explaining of "things" and their generalized ways of being. Ontology is the study of the meaning of human experience. In the case of multiculturalism, ontological study represents a focus on understanding, not explaining, the individual's unique, subjective experience as a member of a cultural group. (Karcher and Nakkula, 1997: 211)

We describe perspectives as modes of observation, so our primary concern here in understanding the ontic perspective is: What do we observe when using this perspective? The ontic perspective focuses on the entity called the career actor and the facts about it and asks the question: How can we describe the actor in a way that is useful from the theoretical perspective that we have chosen for the purpose we have in mind? For example, if we are interested in the effect that general mental ability might have on occupational prestige and income (proxies for extrinsic career success, from the study by Judge, Klinger, and Simon, 2010), then we need to describe the actor's general mental ability, occupational prestige, and income, along, perhaps, with a short list of other mediating and control variables. That still leaves a vast number of other measures that will not be considered.

The ontic perspective operates within the domain of being, a term that in Heideggerian philosophy is somewhat elusive. Heidegger's main opus on it, *Being and Time* (Heidegger, 1962), does not include a concise definition; indeed the book is an exploration of its meaning:

Thus to work out the question of Being adequately, we must make an entity – the inquirer – transparent in his own Being. The very asking of this question is an entity's mode of *Being*; and as such it gets its essential character from what is inquired about – namely, Being. (Heidegger, 1962: 27; emphasis in the original)

This is not easy stuff to engage with, and we shall not get diverted into a discussion about Heidegger's concept of Being. Suffice it to say that what we have in mind here is a focus on the existence of the entity that is the career actor. As we note in Chapter 2, the actor is essential for careers, in the sense that one cannot talk about career without a clear sense of who the career actors are in any given context. Are they, as we also discuss in Chapter 2, an individual or a collectivity? What value is attached to them by the society they are found in? Where are they in their life-course? If they are individuals, are they involved in work, and if so, what kind? If they are not involved in work, what kind of status do they have: Are they, for example, unemployed, retired, on long-term disability? What do we know about their ethnicity, social class, socioeconomic classification, personality, gender, physical characteristics, wealth, education? And so on; the possible questions are almost endless. So to make sense of careers, one of the things we have to do is collect facts about the respective entities that are career actors. This is what Heidegger's (1962: 31) translators refer to as ontic inquiry.

Elements of the Perspective

The *core construct* we use to describe the results of this inquiry is the career actor's condition, namely what we see of a career actor from the ontic perspective at any given moment in time. In the example we have just used, the actor's condition is described in terms of general mental ability, occupational prestige, and income. We use "condition" instead of the more familiar term "state" because the latter tends to be used in a rather more restrictive sense, typically in connection with someone's psychological or mental condition.

Condition, defined in this way, is a very open construct; it encompasses everything that we can say about a career actor. For it to be useful in concrete analyses, it needs to be more specific, and that, as we argue in Chapter 5, is the difference between a framework (as we use the term here) and a model or theory. The framework (SCF) says that the ontic perspective provides a view of a career actor's condition; the specific model or theory that one adopts for the purpose of any given study defines which aspects of condition one is interested in and what they might be related to and leads to more precise, theoretically founded constructs and variables.

To return to the study cited previously of the relationship between general mental ability and extrinsic career success (Judge *et al.*, 2010), the model developed for that study includes a range of ontic constructs: core self-evaluations and a group labeled by the authors "human capital" (educational attainment, training, and job complexity), with age, gender, race, and socioeconomic status as control variables. The study involves a relatively complex view of condition involving all of these constructs. But it does not, nor could it, cover everything. For example, it does not include occupation itself; the authors use a standard index to code occupational prestige and another to code job complexity. Nor, in its view of race, does it include anything beyond whether the respondent was white; all other races are coded as "other." Educational attainment does not include information on the level achieved (e.g. secondary school, undergraduate degree, or graduate degree) because the data source only reported "highest grade or year of regular school," which is coded as the number of years spent in education. And so on.

None of these constraints to the complexity with which condition is viewed in this paper are meant in any sense to be criticisms, of course. They are the inevitable consequence of several factors: (1) the data that are available in the large longitudinal data source that is used; (2) the theoretical model that the authors are testing, which defines the variables to be included; and (3) straightforward practicality: there is only so much that can be included in any given study. Our point is simply that condition is a general concept that, in any given study, gets used in a specific way.

Examining aspects of condition implies measuring, essentially, a process of comparison that is the *operation* of the ontic perspective. For example, to say that someone is 200 centimeters tall implies a comparison to the standard meter: their height is twice its length. The standard meter in turn has been defined over the years by comparison with a variety of things: the distance from the equator to the North Pole, the length of a pendulum that has a half-period of one second, the length of a platinum bar stored in Paris (or, subsequently, the distance between two lines marked on a platinum-iridium bar), the wavelength of a particular emission line of krypton-86, and the distance light travels in a particular fraction of a second. As an ultimate blow to imperialism, in 1959 the imperial inch was redefined by comparing it to the standard meter, as exactly 0.0254 meters.

Of course, for most of the time nobody gives these comparisons a moment's thought, even when they measure length with a tape measure that involves comparing the length of the object with the distance between markings on the tape measure. For most practical purposes, length just "is" – until, that is, we discover that the tape measure we have been using has a damaged hook and all of our length measurements have a systematic error. But the issue becomes more critical when, for example, we start making psychometric measurements. The numbers that emerge from a psychometric instrument such as one measuring personality or cognitive capacity carry no useful information until they are compared with the results from applying the same instrument to a defined population. For example, to say that someone has a neuroticism score of 7 on a 10-point scale is not helpful in itself. For all we know, the instrument is such that almost anyone is likely to end up with a score of 7. It only begins to make sense when we start making comparisons with other people's scores. Even then one has to be very careful in defining the populations they are drawn from, ensuring that the instrument is measuring the same thing for each part of the population, and so on.

From the ontic perspective, the *guiding difference* that is needed to make comparisons is between a focal actor (Ego) and other actors or standards with whom or which we wish to compare them (Alter). The social networking literature has recently made extensive use of the Ego/Alter distinction. Here, however, we use it in its more original sense widely employed in the social sciences (e.g. Parsons, 1960; Bogardus, 1924) to refer simply to the distinction between a focal actor and the actors with whom or which the focal actor interacts. We use it in an even more general sense because the comparisons that are made may well be with people with whom Ego never directly interacts, as, for example, when someone's general mental ability is being measured. Our point is simply that when someone's condition is being assessed, because this involves measurement, which is a process of comparison, it must involve a comparison between the focal career actor and some other actor or set of actors.

To sum up, then, the ontic perspective provides a picture of the career actor's condition. This picture is the result of a process of comparison between the career actor (Ego) and any number of other actors (Alters). The precise nature of the comparisons – what is measured – depends on the theoretical foundation and purpose of the study being conducted. We may be interested in a very restricted range of facets of the actor's condition, for example, if we are carrying out a simple study to see how language ability affects success in job-finding within a defined labor market. But things can get very complicated by the time we have added in all the variables our theory requires of us, including appropriate control variables.

Temporal Perspective

Time in Social Research

Time is central to social research, although its role is often only implicitly acknowledged. Accounts from various disciplines include, for example, a sociology of time (e.g. Bluedorn, 2002; Bergmann, 1992), a social psychology of time (e.g. McGrath, 1988), an anthropology of time (Gell, 1992; Hall, 1989), or a geography of time (Levine, 1997). Great thinkers relevant for organizational theory such as Durkheim, Evans-Pritchard, Geertz, Husserl, Lévi-Strauss, or Piaget have dealt with the problem of time in their own ways. In management research, too, there are substantial contributions about the importance of time for theory building and empirical research (e.g. Shipp and Fried, 2014a, 2014b; Sonnentag, 2012; Whipp, Adam, and Sabelis, 2002; Mitchell and James, 2001; Ofori-Dankwa and Julian, 2001). Some contributions have focused on the importance of different conceptualizations of time. For example, Ancona, Okhuysen, and Perlow (2001) distinguish between different types of time such as clock time, cyclical time, predictable/unpredictable event time, and life cycle time as well as socially constructed time where different social groups have their own view of time. In addition, they point toward the importance of various mapping activities to time and how actors relate to time through their respective temporal perception and temporal personality. Mosakowski and Earley (2000) analyze research classifying time and point toward five major dimensions: the real versus epiphenomenal nature of time; its subjective or objective experience; the novel versus cyclical versus punctuated flow of time; the discrete versus continuous versus epochal structure of time; and the referent anchor lying in the past, present, or future.

At the empirical level, while studies explicitly focusing on the role of time in the work context do not abound, they are not rare either. Examples range from single studies about the temporal structure of technical contracting (Evans, Kunda, and Barley, 2004) or the integration of individual work patterns with the broader social and temporal contexts (Perlow, 1999) to analyses at the team level examining the role of shared temporal cognitions for meeting deadlines (Gevers, Rutte, and Van Eerde, 2006).

Time is also fundamental to career: without a time dimension, one cannot talk about career because career is about a passage through life or part thereof. It is integral to Arthur et al.'s (1989a: 8) adopted definition of career [which] is the evolving sequence of a person's work experiences *over time*. A central theme in this definition is that of work and all that work can mean for the ways in which we see and experience other people, organizations, and society. However, *equally central to this definition is the theme of time*, along which the career provides a 'moving perspective' (Hughes, 1958, p. 67) on the unfolding interaction between a person and society. (emphasis added)

Acknowledging the great variety of different approaches toward time in career research, Gunz and Peiperl state that "whichever way one looks at it, career and the passage of time are inextricably entangled" (Gunz and Peiperl, 2007b: 4).

Elements of the Perspective

The temporal perspective of the SCF focuses on time. Both the spatial and the ontic perspective require time to record (a) transitions across the spatial construct of boundaries and (b) changes in the ontic construct of condition. At their simplest, changes in condition involve things like getting older or becoming knowledgeable and skilled as the result of education, training, and experience. These changes can be ordered in a sequence over time, leading to observations about the changeability of some aspects versus the relative unchangeability of others. Expertise and social capital, for example, are much more changeable than personality traits, which, although not unchangeable, are "stable patterns in each individual and distinguish him or her from other individuals" (Specht, Egloff, and Schmukle, 2011: 862; see also Roberts and DelVecchio, 2000), and it can be of great interest to see how different career processes affect these two variables. In a more fundamental sense,

the structural contexts of action are themselves temporal as well as relational fields – multiple, overlapping *ways of ordering time* toward which social actors can assume different simultaneous agentic orientations. Since social actors are embedded within many such temporalities at once, they can be said to be oriented toward the past, the future, and the present at any given moment, although they may be primarily oriented toward one or another of these within any one emergent situation. (Emirbayer and Mische, 1998: 963–964; emphasis in the original)

Tracking transitions across boundaries is central to career research, too. For example, when analyzing the effects of mentoring on the advancement of women within private sector organizations from a classic organizational design view, which dissects organizations into different divisions and hierarchical levels, tracking women's movements across various divisions and hierarchical levels of the organization results in a sequential list of job transitions, e.g. a move from deputy head of global services to head of retail technical services. Boundaries and boundary-crossing are inextricably linked (Luhmann, 1984: 52). As we note previously, every boundary implies the existence of a reality on the other side of the boundary, of what has been called "possible worlds" (Lewis 1973: 84, cited in Miller, 1987b: 198). At any given time a career actor may be on one side of a transitional boundary or the other or be in the process of crossing it. Again as noted earlier, the crossing process always takes time; one of Glaser and Strauss's (1971) dimensions of status passage is the time taken to make the passage, for example, as a new recruit moves from probationer to full organizational member. It can also be reversible, for example, as people change back and forth from being "in" and "out" members of a group or as they move back and forth between office and home (Ashforth *et al.*, 2000; Glaser and Strauss, 1971).

Studying careers from a temporal perspective, then, is a process of tracking changes in condition and transitions across boundaries by putting them in sequence. The *operation* is sequencing, which leads to information about the temporal aspect of careers. The required *guiding difference* is precedes/follows, and the *core construct* that emerges from this is a chronology. As outlined earlier in our description of the foundations of the SCF (Table 3.1), we need the core elements of a perspective – guiding difference, operation, core construct – in order to observe and create meaning as well as new reality. Applying the distinction "precede/follows" to career phenomena directs our attention and the focus of analysis to the time dimension underlying careers. Through sequencing, we can order the units of analysis along different dimensions of time. As a result, we are able to create chronologies, i.e. a sequential arrangement of our units of analysis along the time dimensions chosen. In its simplest form this operation could involve arranging them in the order of occurrence as one regularly does, for example, in CVs.

A closer look reveals, however, that using these three elements is not quite as straightforward as one might be tempted to assume. We exemplify this by highlighting the difficulties arising from different concepts of time, from the implicit assumption of being able to infer causality, and from different time concepts that individuals and socials systems have.

When constructing a chronology of, say, life events through sequencing, we have two basic options. On the one hand, we can order these events as being in the past, present, or future. As McTaggart (1908: 458) puts it:

Positions in time, as time appears to us prima facie, are distinguished in two ways. Each position is Earlier than some, and Later than some, of the other positions. And each position is either Past, Present, or Future. The distinctions of the former class are permanent, while those of the latter are not. If M is ever earlier than N, it is always earlier. But an event, which is now present, was future and will be past.

McTaggart calls the distinction between earlier and later (resembling our guiding difference of "precedes/follows") the B series of time, which also relates to the duration of events and their frequency. He calls the distinctions between past, present, and future the A series (Zerubavel, 1981). This points toward an inevitable fluidity since present becomes past, future becomes present, and so on. McTaggart goes as far as concluding that our perception of time is an illusion (McTaggart, 1908). For us, this points toward the dynamic and diverse view one gets as soon as one starts seriously analyzing careers from a temporal perspective.

Looking at career phenomena through the "precedes/follows" distinction using sequencing and chronologies is relevant for two additional reasons. First, it introduces the possibility of inferring causality. Second, it helps career actors and their observers impose some kind of meaning on their past. The two are closely intertwined, as we discuss now, but the distinction is not trivial.

Sequencing leads not only to a sequential structure but also to decisions about durations of events (i.e. how long they last), their temporal location (i.e. when they take place), and their rate of recurrence (i.e. how often they occur) (Zerubavel, 1981). As Jaques (1982) points out, sequencing does not by itself imply causality. He introduces two dimensions, which he labels the axes of succession and intention. Using the axis of succession simply involves assembling events in a sequence. This first dimension, the axis of succession, runs from earlier to later. Although it appears to be directional, it is, in fact, not. Only retrospectively is it possible to say that one thing, e.g. joining company X, has preceded another thing, e.g. becoming chairwoman of professional association Y. However, it makes no sense to say that the former is moving toward the latter, which at the time did not even exist. Hence, sequencing on this dimension retrospectively creates a temporal sequence as events are ordered according to their relative position on the axis of succession. It constitutes "a statement of a reconstruction of what has already succeeded what, and cannot be a statement of what *will* at some time in the future succeed what" (Jaques, 1982: 99; emphasis in the original). Novelist Ann Patchett (2016: 159) picks up this point nicely in her book *Commonwealth*:

If Beverly or Bert were to tell the story now, they would say they divorced after Cal died. And of course that was true, they had, but in this instance the word "after" would be misleading. It linked together the death and the divorce as if they were cause and effect, as if Beverly and Bert were one of those couples who, upon a child's death, are led down such separate paths of grief that they can no longer find their way back to one another. This was not the case.

Jaques's second dimension, the axis of intention, however, introduces an examination of causality, acknowledging that doing something has conse-quences for what happens next. Whether or not this causality reaches the strict requirements of path dependence, in which "singular historical events . . . may, under certain conditions, transform themselves into self-reinforcing dynamics, and . . . possibly end up in a . . . lock-in" (Sydow, Schreyogg, and Koch, 2009: 690), can only be determined empirically. Although path dependence has been studied in many branches of the social (and nonsocial) sciences (see, e.g. Magnusson and Ottosson, 2009; Garud and Karnoe, 2001; Garrouste and Ioannides, 2000), curiously the term has had little currency in the careers literature (rare exceptions include DiPrete and Eirich, 2006; Chan, 1999; Brüderl, Diekmann, and Preisendorfer, 1991; Forbes, 1987; Rosenbaum, 1984).

Attributing meaning and causality works both prospectively and retrospectively. Prospective sense-making is about predicting future events or about intentions to make these future events happen. It is, in a sense, "a probability statement at time ti_n of the likelihood of occurrence of an event at some time later than ti_n," (Jaques, 1982: 99). It contains teleological behavior that is goal directed and purposeful. Retrospectively, attributing meaning and causality has often been referred to as retrospective sense-making (Young and Collin, 2000: 1; Weick, 1995b: 25 ff.; Nicholson and West, 1989). We cannot go back and unmake the past, but we can construct a narrative that reinterprets our past, perhaps, following typical attribution tendencies, framing unsuccessful outcomes as being caused by events that were out of our control and successful outcomes as being the result of our initiative. As events unfold, these interpretations can change. Note that retrospective sense-making is analytically distinct from the process of living the career. As Kierkegaard (1960: 111) wryly observes:

It is quite true what Philosophy says: that Life must be understood backwards. But that makes one forget the other saying: that it must be lived – forwards. The more one ponders this, the more it comes to mean that life in the temporal existence never becomes quite intelligible, precisely because at no moment can I find complete quiet to take the backward-looking position. (Part 5, Section 4, No. 136)

Note also that sequencing on both of Jaques's dimensions of time does not imply some kind of objective scientific method or truth. Career actors or their observers also can create chains of causality and meaning through personal stereotyping ("accountants lack the imagination to move into marketing"), superstitious beliefs ("Friday 13th was a bad day to be appointed to my new job"), or cultural folklore ("long-term career planning is difficult for Southern Europeans").

Some have argued that individuals and social systems hold different concepts of time (Boniwell, 2009; Luhmann, 2000: Chapter 5), leading to different universes of time. Indeed even our concept of the time of day is socially constructed, with standardization initially the result of the growth of railroads in the nineteenth century (Zerubavel, 1982). If members of these universes communicate with each other, the same concept – say, urgency – can have varying meanings in, for example, a fire department and a library. A call for urgent action to the fire department causes an immediate reaction with the fire truck being set into motion within minutes; performance standards for response times may be specified in seconds (e.g. Haden, 2012). By contrast, a call for urgent action for borrowing a book from a library usually takes days, if not weeks, to have any effect. The question of how the necessary temporal alignment between different actors happens is bound up with the concept of *entrainment*, which is about "the adjustment of the pace or cycle of an activity to match or synchronize with that of another activity" (Ancona and Chong, 1996: 253).

Interplay between Perspectives

Despite the apparent clarity of the distinctions between spatial, ontic, and temporal perspectives, there are times when it can be hard to know which perspective we are dealing with. Any taxonomy is bound to have areas of fuzziness because the world is never as tidy as theoreticians would like it to be:

> If construct and "reality" exactly correspond, you are in the morass of the particular. You are talking about this thing at this time in such a way that explicit comparison with anything else becomes virtually impossible. (Becker, 1940: 51)

Sometimes the fuzziness comes about because we use one perspective to categorize career actors from another perspective. It is common, for example, to group people by the apparently temporal constructs of age (e.g. young, middle-aged, old) or career stage (early career, mid-career, late career) when our real interest is in some ontic correlate of age or career stage such as skill level, experience, social capital, or cognitive abilities. Or we may group them by the apparently temporal constructs of birth cohort such as baby boomer or Generation X, Y, or Z when our interest is in, for example, ontic constructs such as their employment experience or life chances. To give some more specific examples:

- *Confusing Ontic and Temporal:* These perspectives become confused when, for example, we describe someone as being in early or late career or even sometimes by specifying their age. If the reason for doing so is because we are aiming to locate a career actor on a timeline so that we can try to establish how other aspects of the condition of someone in early career – for example, their education – affects another aspect of their condition in late career – for example, objective career success – then we are using "early career" in a temporal sense because we are using it to set up a sequence of events. But it may be that the intention is to describe some other aspect of the career actor, such as their level of skill or work experience: someone in early career is likely to be lower in these than someone in late career. Here, temporal language is being used to describe an aspect of the actor's condition.
- *Confusing Ontic and Spatial:* It is common to use spatial language to define some aspect of a career actor's condition, for example, by describing some-one as an "experienced CEO." The use of the CEO job title implies their

position in the hierarchy of a firm, which is spatial language. However, it may be that our interest is not in their position but instead in the knowledge, expertise, and skills that the position of CEO requires of its incumbents, so the spatial label is being used in an ontic sense. Specialization implies a particular set of activities that require or develop a particular expertise and skill set. But, typically, it also implies a position within some kind of social structure. Sometimes the link is strong: the title "CEO" pretty much inevitably implies that the holder is to be found at the top of an organizational hierarchy. Sometimes it is less so: an orthopedic surgeon may be found within a department of orthopedic surgery or may be a private practitioner. Once again, it is necessary to get behind the language to examine the purpose for which it is being used.

The inevitable entanglement between different perspectives is nicely summed up in Ortega y Gasset's (1914: 43) famous dictum: "Yo soy yo y mi circunstancia" ("I am me and my circumstances"). The position we adopt here to analytically set apart this entanglement is one of focus. When the focus is on the career actor, we are adopting an ontic perspective; when it is on the actor's context, we are adopting a spatial perspective.

A Theoretically Grounded Definition of Career

Now that we have described the three perspectives of the SCF, we can return to the puzzle we outline in Chapter 2: Why are there so many different ways of defining the deceptively straightforward concept of career? In the final section of this chapter, we show how the SCF leads to a definition that, we shall argue, draws together many of the approaches found both in the literature and in everyday life. Tempting though it may be, we shall steer away from the overly ambitious claim that it is an encompassing definition. Our aim is not to produce a definition for its own sake. Rather, it is to offer our view of what career is to give us an anchor for the rest of this book.

Classically, a definition does two things. It (a) relates the term – the *definiendum* (that which is being defined) – to a *superordinate concept* (*genus proximum*) and (b) finds a characteristic (*definiens*) or several characteristics (*definientia*) that differentiate(s) the *definiendum* from other terms that also are part of the superordinate concept. Based on an Aristotelian view, this is sometimes referred to as definitions requiring a *genus proximum* and *differentia specifica* (Locke, cited in Buldt, 2008). For example, a dog (*definiendum*) is an organism (*superordinate concept, genus proximum*) that houses fleas and barks (*definientia, differentia specifica*) (attributed to Kurt Tucholsky[1]). This whimsical definition

[1] 1890–1935, famous German-Jewish journalist, satirist, and writer and one of the most important journalists of the German Weimar Republic opposing the rising Nazi regime.

is useful if one can be certain that any living thing that either does not house fleas or does not bark or both is not a dog. Housing fleas may not be the most useful distinguishing feature between organisms, but barking certainly excludes, for example, cats.

So if the *definiendum* here is "career," what might be the (a) superordinate concept and (b) *definientia* that differentiate "career" from everything else that fits within the superordinate concept? We tackle this question by reframing it: What might the superordinate concept be for what is "seen" when you apply the three SCF perspectives?

So what is "seen"? We listed three core constructs that emerge from the perspectives: boundary, condition, and chronology, the point being that a construct is what we use in order to make sense of the world. Applying the three perspectives jointly means that we see something – a career – that we describe in terms of boundaries, condition, and chronology. Is there a less abstract way of putting this?

Thus far we have left out the career actor. Adding that in, we find ourselves saying that the perspectives reveal an actor whose position is defined in terms of the boundaries delineating and structuring a space and whose condition is defined by comparing its various facets with appropriate comparators (Alters) elsewhere. These observations of position and condition are not made just once but are repeated over a given period of time in order to produce a chronology. So what we are seeing is a sequence, or perhaps a pattern, of positions and conditions over a given period of time, all of this taking place within a given social and geographic space. For example:

- Person A is a plant manager at a large manufacturing location (position) and is new to the job with little experience of labor relations (condition). When a labor dispute breaks out at the location, his position means that he is seen to be representing the company in the eyes of the workers, but his inexperience means that he makes some comments to those workers that exacerbate the situation and extend the strike. Subsequently, he is sent back to the technical support job he came from.
- Person B is a senior researcher in a pharmaceuticals company lab (position) who has more experience of other therapeutic areas than her colleagues on the team (condition). Her experience allows her to spot a potential new use for the drug that is being worked on, and her position means that she is able to persuade the team to investigate this opportunity, leading the project in a new direction that turns out eventually to be highly profitable for the company. She ends up as VP of Research.
- Person C is a senior consultant for an international consulting firm (position) who has had many years of HR consulting for large companies in a particular group of countries (condition). Her position in the firm means that she is selected for a contract involving a company in Country X even though she

does not know it well. As a result of her inexperience with that country, she uses a compensation model that has worked well elsewhere but is quite inappropriate to the cultural context of Country X. The system fails, the consulting firm is no longer able to get business in Country X, and Person C eventually leaves for a firm that focuses on countries with which she does have experience.

In each of these examples a combination of position and condition influences the actor to respond in a particular way to circumstances and influences the responses of the actors with whom the focal actor interacts. This in turn has consequences for the organization in which the actor works (part of their social space) but also for their future position and condition. In the first example, the consequences are a return to a previous position and, presumably, a blow to self-esteem and income; in the second, they are the position of VP of Research and, presumably, enhanced self-esteem and income; and so on. So a career becomes a pattern or sequence of the positions occupied by and condition of the actor.

If so, sequences or patterns take center stage, and for careers (the *definiendum*), sequence or pattern is therefore the superordinate concept (*genus proximum*). What differentiates a career-related sequence or pattern from other kinds of sequence or pattern is that the former are sequences or patterns of position and condition of a career actor within a certain social and geographic space over a given time (the *definientia*, their *differentia specifica*).

If that is what a career is and having dealt with career actor, position, condition, space, and time in this chapter and the previous one, we need to settle two questions before we offer it as a definition. First, is sequence or pattern the more appropriate term? Second, while "certain social and geographic space" clearly refers to the space occupied by the actor over time, what do we mean by "given time," i.e. what is the appropriate period of time for defining a career?

Sequence or Pattern?

On the face of it, "sequence" seems the more likely candidate. It has a broad range of meanings, from "the following of one thing after another in succession" to "[a] continuous or connected series (of things)" (OED, 2017), but the central idea is ordinal: it is about things falling in some kind of order. They can, for example, be over time (e.g. one musical note following another), coexisting but experienced in a particular order (e.g. a sequence of rooms through which one passes), coexisting but assembled in a particular order (e.g. bases in a DNA molecule), coexisting but with different origins in time (e.g. geological strata or tree growth rings), and so on. As we have seen, careers are all about one thing following another, and indeed we use the term "sequencing" as our label for the operation of the temporal perspective.

But for our present purpose, can "sequence" cover all the possible combinations of position and condition? Clearly it cannot. Perhaps most obviously, researchers are often interested in several aspects of a career actor's condition that may not fall in any kind of sequence: at any given point of time, they are being examined cross-sectionally. The study of Judge *et al.* (2010) that we cited previously, for example, included core self-evaluations, educational attainment, training, job complexity, and the control variables age, gender, race, and socioeconomic status.

Furthermore, an actor can occupy several positions simultaneously, both work and nonwork. For example, they can have more than one part-time job; they may occupy several distinct roles in an organization; and of course nonwork life for most people involves a great many, often conflicting, roles, all of which have to be balanced simultaneously with work life. These roles can vary in their degree of segmentation or integration (Ashforth *et al.*, 2000), which refers to the extent to which they are experienced separately. Integrated roles, as occupied, for example, by someone who works at home and at the same time is responsible for child care, are evidently not occupied in sequence, except to the extent that anyone in this kind of situation is regularly switching attention between one set of responsibilities and the other. Even in the highly segmented extreme, such as when members of one role set may be completely unaware that the role incumbent occupies the other role (as can happen when someone works in a stigmatized occupation such as assassin or prostitute; Ashforth and Kreiner, 1999), on anything other than the micro-scale on which Ashforth *et al.* (2000) focus the actor for all practical purposes is occupying multiple roles simultaneously.

Sequence, then, although a central concept in the temporal perspective for which sequencing is the operation, is inadequate for a broader definition of career. For this, we need to turn to the term "pattern," which can also be used in many senses. It can mean something that forms a design that can be used on future occasions and can carry with it a sense of repeatability, in the way that a fabric or wallpaper pattern repeats. Pattern recognition is based on this view: a pattern that can be recognized is one that fits a particular cluster of similar objects (Freidman and Kandel, 1999: 3). It can also mean a chance arrangement, as in "the pattern of rainfall over the past year" (The Free Dictionary, 2016) or "the pattern of events" (Merriam-Webster, 2016). This sense is often encountered in chaos theory (Smith, 1998). The term also appears in Mintzberg's (1978: 934) well-known definition of strategy as "a pattern in a stream of decisions."

Perhaps the most concise way of looking at the distinction between pattern and sequence is to note that whereas there is an element of objectivity to a sequence – its core idea is ordinal – a pattern is something that is inferred by an observer. So one can find a pattern in a sequence by making some kind of sense of the sequence (even if the sense is simply that there is no logic to the sequence). For example, we may deduce a *pattern* representing a form of objective career success in a *sequence* of jobs in which each succeeding job is better paid than the previous one. Indeed techniques of sequence analysis such as optimal matching (Gubler, Biemann, and Herzog, 2017; Koch, Forgues, and Monties, 2016; Wu, 2000) are designed to look for patterns in large sets of data sequences.

Because the use of the term "pattern" does not necessarily imply any regularity or logic in the arrangement of the elements that make it up, in the case of career it can simply imply the arrangement, over time, of recognizably different aspects of a career actor's position and condition without the necessity for assuming that there is any governing logic to them. However, a complete lack of logic would be surprising. To put our point another way, if there were no such underlying regularity or logic in careers, then there would be very little for career researchers to do. Arguably, a central task of this area of scholarship is to discern what it is that connects the dots of careers: to uncover their regularities and the reasons for them to occur. Let us briefly examine two examples of where the regularities or logics can come from to help make this point.

First, any ontic or spatial variable is bound to demonstrate a high degree of autocorrelation given that, for example, the occupation someone has this year is likely to be a strong predictor of their occupation next year, as is their hierarchical level, compensation, or network of contacts. That is not to say that these relationships always hold – people lose their jobs, after all – but that for most people, for most of the time, they probably do. Whether this reaches the level of path dependency, which as noted previously implies that earlier events lock the entity into a pattern that is hard, if not impossible, to get out of (Sydow *et al.*, 2009), is less predictable, however, although it is certainly a strong possibility with careers (Rosenbaum, 1979b). Furthermore, the boundaries that constrain, enable, and punctuate careers (Gunz *et al.*, 2007a) contribute to their regularity or logic (e.g. Gunz, 1989a; Vardi, 1980).

Second, patterns have no ontological quality; they are not simply "there" but require somebody to put together the various facts into what they see as a pattern. More precisely, career patterns can, when regularity or logic is inferred, be an expression of retrospective sense-making (Young and Collin, 2000; Nicholson and West, 1989) or narratives, which also implies that individuals look back on their careers and impose a pattern on previous experiences that expresses a logic that "explains" what has happened over the course of their careers. This notion of pattern is implicit in the well-used metaphor of career path (Inkson, Dries, and Arnold, 2015), which certainly implies a form of pattern to which a logic applies. The career actor is not the only person who can construct this narrative; it could equally well be done by an observer such as a biographer. Depending on what forms of condition are being included in the sense-making, the interpretations could be subjective – for example, as the career actor constructs a story about how they have developed and matured – or objective – for example, if the story attempts to show how, regardless of the actual forces at work at the time, a series of disparate positions inevitably led to the position the career actor currently occupies.

So, to sum up, although the operation for the temporal perspective is sequencing, that is, arranging an actor's changing condition and position in geographical and social space over time, the richness apparent in the resultant sequence of condition and position is more helpfully conceptualized as a pattern, which allows for subjective interpretation and retrospective sense-making rather than just a sequence.

Over What Time Does a Career Last?

Thus far we have left the question open of what the time span is for a career. Does it mean "over a lifetime" or "over the actor's lifetime to date," as is implied by the Chicago school's work (Barley, 1989)? Or does it mean "over a part of the actor's lifetime, perhaps relating to the period during which they are practicing a particular occupation or occupying a particular role"? There is a great deal of difference between a definition of career that means what has happened during one's lifespan (to date) and one that means what has happened while, for example, one was a junior accountant, a product officer, or a CEO of a specific company. Do these latter examples describe careers or partial careers? This ambiguity reflects an equivalent ambiguity in the way in which the word is used in everyday life. It is as common for people to refer to their career as a whole as it is for them to refer to their career as, for example, a student, parent, engineer, athlete, or employee of a particular company, for example, "my Safaricom career" indicating one's time at East Africa's largest mobile telecommunications provider.

For Hughes, the career involves the career actor's entire life:

the moving perspective in which the person sees his life as a whole. (Hughes, 1958: 63)

as it does for Van Maanen and Schein:

a series of separate but related experiences and adventures through which a person passes during a lifetime. (Van Maanen and Schein, 1977: 31)

and a number of writers in the vocational tradition:

A career is one's life. (Norris, Hatch, Engelkes, and Winborn, 1979: 7, cited in Cochran, 1990: 71)

life is career unfolding and, conjointly, career is life empowered. (Tiedeman and Miller-Tiedeman, 1985: 223)

It is also, for Hughes, something that everyone has, regardless of whether they work in a formal organization.

For example, Hughes and his students were just as willing to talk about the careers of marijuana users (Becker 1953a) as they were about the careers of doctors (Hall 1948) and executives (Dalton 1951). One suspects, then, that Wilensky (1960: 554) had Chicago sociologists firmly in mind when he wrote:
Just as the concept of "profession" loses its precision when we speak of the "professionalization" of auto-workers in Detroit, so the concept of "career" loses utility when we speak of the "career of a ditch-digger." In dealing with the organization of work, it is better to take a more restricted view of career. (Barley, 1989: 45)

Perhaps in response to Wilensky's critique, the other definitions we cited in Chapter 2 refer to career as that which spans the actor's working life, either explicitly or implicitly:

the individually perceived sequence of attitudes and behaviors associated with work-related experiences and activities over the span of the person's life. (Hall, 2002: 12)

the pattern of work-related experiences that span the course of a person's life. (Greenhaus *et al.*, 2010: 10)

the evolving sequence of a person's work experiences over time. (Arthur *et al.*, 1989b: 8)

the sequence of employment-related positions, roles, activities and experiences encountered by a person. (Arnold, 1997: 16)

There is clearly, then, a preference in the OMC literature to depart from the colloquial use of the term "career" in its partial sense to refer to career if not as a whole-life phenomenon, then at least as a whole-working-life phenomenon. This makes sense because the implications of allowing a formal definition of career to apply to a partial career are intriguing given that this means that a career actor can have several careers simultaneously. Once the label "career" is attached to that part of the actor's life that is associated with a particular role, then any study of how, for example, one simultaneously held role affects another – as in the case of work-life research – becomes an *inter*-career, not an *intra*-career issue, which is not, we suspect, how most researchers in the field would see it. Inter-career issues seem best reserved for inter-actor rather than intra-actor phenomena, and indeed we examine this in more detail in Chapter 4.

For this reason it seems to us that it is better to reserve the term "career" for whole-life issues. What is colloquially called one's career as "x" – for example, one's working career or one's career as an accountant or a volunteer firefighter – then becomes a partial career. In addition to avoiding the multiple-career problem to which we refer previously, it also avoids the kind of confusion that results from the choice of different time periods. Are, for example, career counseling interventions directed at schoolchildren long before they start work dealing with careers? Are they work-related enough to count? What about the "careers" of the retired (excluding those who continue to work in paid employment)? What about people who care for their families but who do not engage with the labor market or who spend their lives in, for example, religious communities whose only dealings with the normal world of work are to serve it without recompense? Are they working, and if not, do they have careers?

It seems to us unnecessary to get involved in debates like these when it is possible, as Hughes encourages us, to regard a career as something that happens over one's entire life, or at least one's life to date (to quote Steven Wright, a comedian from the USA: "I intend to live forever – so far, so good"). As we see later, it is always possible to make a general definition selective, but not so easy to make a specific definition more general.

Defining Career

The upshot of these considerations means that we can define career as follows:

A pattern of a career actor's positions and condition within a bounded social and geographic space over their life to date.

This definition is not only rooted in the theoretical and conceptual considerations outlined in this chapter but also entirely consistent, with one obvious exception, with the well-established definitions cited previously. The exception concerns the time over which a career is believed to happen, and as we noted, it is clear from the examples we cite from the OMC literature that the writers see career as synonymous with working career. We return to this in a moment, but first we should explain our claim of consistency.

The use of the term "pattern" captures Hughes's interpretative approach and Hall's (2002) "individually perceived sequence" because, as we note earlier, a pattern is put together by someone. Our definition leaves it entirely open for the career actor to create the pattern themselves by means of the sense-making process described by, for example, Young and Collin (2000: 1) and Nicholson and West (1989).

The other cited definitions describe sequences or patterns in:
- work (or employment-related) experiences
- employment-related positions
- employment-related roles
- employment-related activities
- attitudes and behaviors associated with work-related experiences and activities

all of which can be accounted for in terms of position or condition.

The remaining issue concerns the question we addressed previously: Is a career a whole-life affair as Hughes asserts and with whom we concur, or should it be restricted to a work career as the other definitions we cite would have it?

In fact, the difference is less stark than it first appears. We made it clear when we described condition that although it describes everything one could know about a career actor, in practice one will always be selective, choosing one or a few facets. Similarly, only certain facets of position – for example, business function, professional affiliation, or hierarchical status – will be selected for attention. By the same token there is no reason not to be selective when it comes to defining space. Indeed the definition includes the phrase "[w]ithin a bounded social and geographic space" in order to reflect the need to ensure that statements about careers are related to specific "bounded social worlds" (Barley, 1989: 46). It is necessary in order to give "position" meaning. For example the position "CEO" only means something if its context is included: Does it refer to the CEO of Exxon or a small start-up with two employees?

So, if one's interest is in the working lives of the actors under the scholarly microscope, it makes sense to restrict examining the space they occupy to that linked with their working lives. It would be entirely consistent with the work-life literature for this to include their nonwork – for example, family – space as well because what happens there may well influence what happens at work, and vice versa. And if this is the focus, then it would make sense to restrict the "lifetime" to a working lifetime, thus converting our definition into one that would be recognizable to anyone working in the field of organizational and managerial careers, namely that of a work career, which could be defined as follows:

A pattern of a career actor's positions and condition within a work-related bounded social and geographic space over their working life to date.

For the purposes of this book we shall remain with the general: we shall regard a career as something that happens over an entire life and a working career as that part of a career connected with work. In this view, a working career is a special case of a career, in the same way as is a school career, a career as an invalid, or one's career as a retired person.

Our definition offers four advances over previous attempts. First, it emphasizes the key role of *pattern*, which, although not requiring it, directs the researcher's attention to the underlying logic and "gestalt-like" quality as the superordinate concept to career. Previous definitions vary in the extent to which they identify this aspect of career, which is curious given its centrality. Career scholarship has as one of its central themes the identification and understanding of the logic underlying the experiences, conditions, or whatever the chosen idea is from which the actor's career is built. To deny the nonrandom nature of career patterns is to leave the scholar with a puzzle: If life is completely random, is there much that can be said about it? To be sure, this position does not deny that random events, luck, and so forth can play a role in careers, but they typically have consequences, such as a chance encounter leading to an unexpected job offer that in turn leads to a previously unanticipated sequence of positions in a new organization. Pattern emerges from chance.

Second, the use of *condition* as one of the *definientia* broadens the scope of the phenomena to be studied. Previous definitions use terms such as experiences, roles, activities, positions, offices, moving perspective, things that happen to the actor, attitudes, and behaviors; indeed there is little overlap between the lists with the possible exception of experiences. It seems to us to be better to use deliberately a portmanteau word such as condition, which explicitly directs attention to the idea that *everything* about a career actor at any given moment may be relevant to their career.

Third, it directs attention to the broader *social and geographic space* – in itself bounded – within which careers are enacted over time, not limiting it to work or employment. That is not to say that work careers cannot be studied: as we have shown, by specifying the bounded social space as that applying to work, the definition is transformed into one that explicitly deals with work careers. But this kind of constraint should be imposed with care because the distinction between work and nonwork is fuzzy at best, as the extensive literature on work-family issues (Greenhaus and Foley, 2007) attests. What makes an experience work-related? How much of what happens in a person's so-called nonwork life is genuinely of no relevance to work, and how might this cross-influencing vary between individuals? If, however, we define a social space as enclosing the full set of roles occupied by an individual over the course of their career, we encourage ourselves to construct theories that connect certain roles and behaviors and fail to connect others and to design studies that explore the roles and behaviors that we are interested in. To take another example, one of the fundamental critiques that boundaryless career scholars (Arthur and Rousseau, 1996b) make of the organizational career literature is that it is bounded by the organization or, in SCF terms, that the social space under investigation is the organization only. In so doing, they argue, students of organizational careers miss seeing major changes that have been happening to the world of work (albeit that some researchers have argued that the evidence that these changes have happened is not strong: see Inkson *et al.*, 2012: 329; Rodrigues and Guest, 2010; there is, however, some ambiguity here because Arthur and Rousseau's point was that mobility by the mid-1990s was *already* high enough for them to take a fresh look at the structure of careers). By broadening the examined social space well beyond the organization, boundaryless career theorists argue, it is possible to make sense of these hitherto overlooked "new" careers.

Finally, the definition explicitly admits the possibility that *career actors* need be not just individuals but also collectives. This point becomes crucial later, as we show when we argue that the SCF provides a framework for connecting scholarship in previously not very well connected areas.

Summation

This is a chapter in which we delve deeply into the concepts on which the SCF is based. The spatial, ontic, and temporal perspectives and their interplay provide a comprehensive view of careers. Furthermore, they lead us to our definition of career as a pattern of a career actor's positions and condition within a bounded social and geographic space over their life to date. Beyond this broad conception, the perspectives and our definition of career also allow a more constrained use, for example, by applying it only to work careers, a major focus in this book.

This groundwork brings us in a position to be able to outline the SCF further by developing a heuristic model of career. To this we turn next.

4   A Heuristic Model of Career

The three perspectives outlined in the previous chapter provide the basis for a heuristic model of career processes, which constitutes the second element of the SCF. By "heuristic" we mean a guide to action – we shall argue here that it is a well-tried one – that shows a series of relationships between broad constructs. Both constructs and their relationships in the model constitute seasoned rules of thumb for the matter at hand and are grounded in different kinds of theoretical and empirical work. Yet the heuristic does not provide specific explanations or predictions about how and why these relationships work. Instead, it invites the user to introduce appropriate areas of theory to further elaborate on the constructs and explain the relationships in which they are interested, based on the research question under consideration and its theoretical background. An example drawn from a more everyday realm of life may help explain what we mean.

A heuristic, in the way we use the term here, might be to say that one's ability to move around depends *inter alia* on the nature of one's connection with the ground; if it is tenuous, such as happens when walking down an icy path, getting around can be a challenge. Two broad constructs – connection with the ground and ability to move around – are linked in a causal manner. While arguably that is a seasoned rule of thumb, it also sounds like a trivial observation until we reflect on the point that neither "connection with the ground" nor "moving around" is by any means a trivial construct. For example, the effectiveness of pretty much all automotive design depends on a remarkably small area of contact between tire and road. In order to make useful predictions about the way that this small area of contact works, we need further elaborations, i.e. we must specify what we mean by connection with the ground and how this connection works. Consequently, we must look for and understand quite a bit about the theory that explains how well a tire clings to the road surface. We have to know about the sources of tire friction, for example, what causes rubber to adhere to other surfaces and how it deforms to adapt to irregularities in the road surface and tears if subjected to sufficient stress. We need insight into how this friction varies with tire composition, pressure, and temperature and road conditions such as its composition and smoothness, its temperature, how dry it is, whether it has patches of ice, oil, gravel, and so on. We also have to master the mechanics of keeping wheels in contact with the ground, which involves a deep understanding of suspension design and following principles such as minimizing unsprung weight. All of this is relevant to the first of the heuristic's two broad constructs: understanding the connection with the ground. Similarly, the second construct – moving around – has to be properly understood: What does it mean in practice? What range of speeds, compression and shear forces, and so on, need to be accommodated?

So the simple heuristic – one's ability to move around depends *inter alia* on the nature of one's connection with the ground – when applied to automotive design leads to a large number of very searching questions drawing on a broad range of theory and practice. The heuristic does not solve these problems; it directs the designer's attention to the nature of the overall problem that has to be solved. Similarly, the SCF heuristic model, a set of propositions that emerge from thinking about the kinds of construct that derive from each of the three perspectives (spatial, ontic, and temporal) directs the researcher's attention to the problems that need solving with respect to understanding careers and how they are interrelated. It does not provide the theory that is needed; it shows what *kind* of theory is needed. In that sense the heuristic model is about *guiding inquiry* rather than *giving answers*, and its use is an example of what Lave and March (1975: 2) call "guiding speculation" about a particular research question.

We shall put the model together in two stages. First we develop what we call the basic building block, which takes as its unit of analysis a core element of careers, namely the transition between positions. This comprises eight propositions drawn from a variety of sources, including the field of organization studies. Second, we show how the basic building block can be elaborated on in a variety of ways to reflect the complexities and richness of careers.

Career Transitions

The definition of career that emerges from the SCF is, as we note in Chapter 3, a pattern of a career actor's positions and condition within a bounded social and geographic space over their life to date. The use of "pattern . . . over their life to date" implies two things: changes in position and condition and when these changes happened. Moving through a bounded social and geographical space implies mapping the series of positions between which the actor moved as well as the condition of the actor over the course of this time. If these are put together, they give a view over time of the actor's career.

So if we were interested in a straightforward objective work career, we might record first the changes in aspects of the career actor's condition that are most appropriate to such a view – for example, the actor's job title, salary, or level of expertise – and then the changes in position in terms of, for instance, level, function, or division in whichever organizations they worked, salary, span of control, or number of subordinates. Alternatively, if they are not the employee of an organization, we might trace their position in terms of its contractual relationships with other economic actors if the focal actor works on short-term contracts or their relationships with clients, customers, suppliers, or regulators if the actor is self-employed. If we were interested in someone's subjective career, the aspects of their condition that we might follow include changes in career satisfaction, life satisfaction, or various aspects of their psychological state including happiness or stress level. If we were interested in work career, the boundaries of the social space would enclose only the work organizations that the actor was involved with over the course of their work career. If we wanted to go beyond the work career to something closer to Hughes's (1937) concept of career as that which covers most of the person's life span, the boundaries would be drawn differently, encompassing other areas of social space.

Change in condition and position and when these changes happen, then, are at the heart of how a career is characterized, and we shall call them here career transitions. Such transitions have been variously called status passages (Glaser and Strauss, 1971), role transitions (Currie, Finn, and Martin, 2010; Allen and Van de Vliert, 1984), career transitions (Louis, 1980a, 1980b), work role transitions (Ashforth and Saks, 1995; Nicholson, 1984), macro work role transitions (Ibarra and Barbulescu, 2010), micro role transitions (Ashforth et al., 2000), or just plain transitions (Ibarra and Barbulescu, 2010; Louis, 1980a, 1980b).

We prefer the term "career transition" for present purposes because, although most writing in the area of career scholarship tends to focus on the work career, and our focus in this book largely echoes this, as we note in Chapter 3 we need to ensure that the SCF is not necessarily seen as being limited to the work career. Our use of the term "career transition" is meant to imply that it is a transition *within* rather than *between* partial careers because our definition of career, in common with most other definitions (Chapter 2), is of something that covers either a working lifetime or a lifetime. We do not talk, as is common in everyday parlance, of switching careers or starting new careers but of transitions that take place within a career and that may have greater or lesser consequences for that career.

Our concept of a career transition is close to that of Louis (1980a: 330):

we will define *career transition* as the period during which an individual is either changing roles (taking on a different objective role) or changing orientation to a role already held (altering a subjective state). (emphasis in the original)

The handling of the term "role" is somewhat ambiguous in that paper. It sounds as if roles are equivalent to positions that the career actor moves between;

however, role is defined earlier as "the task and other behaviors *associated with* a position in an organization or social system" (ibid.: 330; emphasis added). That said, Louis's definition usefully draws attention to transition as a period of time during which the change happens, a point echoed by Ibarra and Barbulescu (2010: 137), who "use the term to refer to a process that may begin long before an actual role change and that often extends significantly beyond it."

There are a variety of taxonomies of transitions. Ibarra and Barbulescu (2010: 136), for example, classify them on the basis of magnitude or radicalness; the extent to which they are institutionalized, novel or idiosyncratic; and their desirability (in the sense that a demotion is typically not). Glaser and Strauss (1971) have an even more complex scheme, differentiating between reversibility, temporality, shape, desirability, circumstantiality, and multiple status passages as major dimensions. For our purposes the most useful distinction is to do with *the rate of change in a career actor's condition*. There are times during a career when very little is happening in the way of change: the career actor is at a stable point, perhaps having recently gotten past the learning phase of their current role and settled into it. There are other times when the rate of change is very great, as might happen when an actor is in the process of changing jobs and countries. So change of position is most likely to be associated with a high rate of change of condition, and it is this kind of period that we associate with career transitions.

A career transition, then, involves changing (a) some aspect of a career actor's condition and (b) their position in their social and/or geographical space by crossing at least one boundary. It also involves (c) a period of time over which these changes happen. At least one of these changes has to be significant enough to be interesting to the career actor or an observer; it needs to involve a difference that makes a difference (Bateson, 2000 [Original 1972]).

Different kinds of transition are significant and interesting to different research traditions. Scholars of intergenerational mobility may examine the typically widely spaced transitions that mark mobility between socioeconomic or occupational groups (Western and Wright, 1994); those studying work–nonwork issues may look at the daily back-and-forth transitions between different spheres of life (Ashforth *et al.*, 2000); vocational psychologists (e.g. Herr, 2013; Holland, 1959) are particularly interested in the transition from education to work; and those who study internal labor markets (e.g. Bidwell and Mollick, 2015; Bidwell, 2011; Sonnenfeld, Peiperl, and Kotter, 1988; Rosenbaum, 1984) concentrate on transitions between roles within organizations. Next, we develop our model of career transitions, starting with what we label for reasons that will soon become evident the basic building block.

Modeling Career Transitions: The Basic Building Block

The heuristic model takes as its unit of analysis a career transition undertaken by a focal career actor. The ontic perspective directs our attention toward the way in which the actor's condition changes during the transition. The spatial perspective focuses on the social and geographical space, the boundaries that define this space and across which the transition takes place, and the positions between which the actor moves. The temporal perspective points to the chronology of the events. For the purposes of this model the three constructs linked with each perspective – (1) condition, (2) boundaries and positions, and (3) chronology – are not defined with any greater specificity. As we explain previously, the model is intended to be a general heuristic for the development of more specific models designed to investigate specific research questions. These specific models require theories selected to make particular predictions about the selection of specific ontic, spatial, and temporal variables of interest and how they are connected in that research context.

We start by considering a single transition, for simplicity starting at time t_1 and ending at time t_2 and influenced by characteristics of the social space in which the transition takes place and of the boundary that is crossed. This simplification is not meant to imply that the social and geographical space acts on the transition at one single moment in time, nor that it is precisely halfway between t_1 and t_2. Building on the basic assumption that career actors' condition at any given time influences their condition at a later time, the model adds eight propositions linking the three major elements of the model between t_1 and t_2 (Figure 4.1). The figure shows three arrows of time in order to reflect our discussion on the different views that the temporal perspective can take (Chapter 3).

The assumed link between condition at two different points in time (arrow 1) plays an important role in models of managerial action (e.g. Broschak, 2004). It appears axiomatic, but it needs to be spelled out, because of both its centrality to the SCF and its peculiarities.

The effect can be relatively straightforward. It may involve the same aspect of condition or the influence of one aspect of condition on another aspect at a later time. An example is occupation, which is partially predicted by occupation at an earlier time but also by skill acquisition (Shaw, 1987). So from an ontic perspective the condition of an actor at a later time is affected by their condition at an earlier time. Some aspects of condition will remain pretty much unchanged – for example, personality – while others – for example, compensation – are likely to be affected by the move. The longer the period of time over which the transition takes place, the greater the possibility that post-transition condition will be significantly different from pre-transition condition. Suppose, for example, the

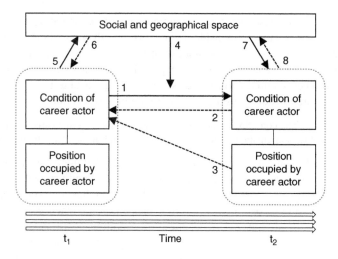

Figure 4.1   Career transition – basic building block

transition involves the change between late-stage medical traineeship in a specialty to becoming fully qualified in that specialty. This normally involves some form of exam, which requires considerable study. The fully qualified specialist is likely to be much better informed about their specialty after they have gone through the study and exam period than they were before. A further layer of complexity comes from the way that different aspects of the actor's condition may interact to affect the connection between condition at t_1 and at t_2. A flexible personality may make an actor more likely to adapt, while risk aversion may have the opposite effect, for example. We summarize these considerations in Proposition 1. Detail of this nature is not captured in the heuristic model but would be in a more in-depth model that is developed for a particular study that draws on specific theory for its predictions.

Proposition 1: A career actor's condition at the end of a career transition is affected by their condition before it.

In addition to the basic effect of condition in the direction of the time arrows there is also an anticipatory effect going "against" the flow of time (arrows 2 and 3 in Figure 4.1): someone's anticipation of their future position or condition may affect their current condition. Possible selves – people's ideas about what they might become – incentivize behavior (Ibarra, 1999; Markus and Nurius, 1986: 954). Successful recruitment requires, among other things, the building of realistic expectations of both the organization and the individual before establishing a work relationship (Wanous, 1980). Anticipatory socialization

(Merton, 1957b) describes the behaviors of people anticipating their future condition, for instance, life inside the organization they are about to join. So, for example, business students adopt what they think are the mannerisms and behaviors of the businesspeople they hope to become, and worries about one's ability to meet required performance standards might lead to tense feelings or additional preparation. This leads to the following proposition.

Proposition 2: The condition of a career actor at the beginning of a career transition is affected by their anticipation of their condition at the end of the career transition.

Following the same logic that led to Proposition 2 – that there have been many approaches to understanding the reasons people have for adjusting their current condition to future circumstances – we can also expect them to be influenced by anticipated future positions. This often happens, e.g. when current career aspirations of individuals – an element of condition – are shaped by their view of the number and availability of future positions. For example, when doctoral students scan the market for available positions at universities in different layers of the university system, they adjust their career aspirations accordingly, perhaps deciding, if there are few academic positions on offer, to abandon thoughts of an academic career and opting instead for working in the private sector or public administration. From this follows the next proposition.

Proposition 3: The condition of career actors before making a career transition is affected by their anticipation of their position following the transition.

Next, we examine a group of relationships that address the role of various elements of social and geographical space in the career transition. First, characteristics of the social and geographical space within which the transition takes place moderate the way in which condition and position change during the transition. For example, boundary permeability (Schein, 1971) affects the probability of the transition taking place at all: the less permeable the boundary, by definition the harder it is to cross it. Promotion through hierarchies is affected by the structure of the process that governs selection: tournament-style labor markets (Rosenbaum, 1984) are very different from those, such as one identified by Forbes (1987), in which early failure does not disqualify and the labor market is "more analogous to a horse race than to a tournament: position out of the gate had relatively little effect in comparison to position entering the home stretch" (ibid.: 122). Furthermore, because the social space is, among other things, a social network to which the career actor is connected, the nature of the ties is likely to be important. Castilla (2005), for example, found that when someone in a network left an organization, the people they referred to as network contacts were more likely to leave, too. In a similar vein, geographical issues such as climate, height above sea level, or availability of mountains or lakes for recreation can influence the career transition to the extent that they can affect the desirability of the new position in the eyes of the career actor.

In addition, the relationship between professional skills at the beginning and the end of a career transition within an organization will, among other things, be moderated by the level of organizational activities supporting skill transfer and lifelong learning. Similarly, whether coaches newly entering a professional sport will benefit from having been professional athletes before will depend on, among other things, the professional norms in the respective sport, public opinion about their performance as active athletes, and the spin the media give to such a transition.

In sum, the social and geographical space is bound to affect the change in condition marked by the transition.

Proposition 4: The change in career actors' condition and position is moderated by the characteristics of the social and geographical space in which the transition takes place.

We have treated social and geographical space thus far as something apart from the career actor, but of course in the case of social space it is not. Social environments are enacted by their inhabitants (Weick, 1979), so the social space of a career actor is, in part, enacted by that actor (Giddens, 1981: 171). It follows that the career actor's social space is affected by the career actor's condition at t_1. For example, suppose someone is offered an expatriate assignment that her superiors want her to accept. The less enthusiastic she is, the more her superiors are likely to try to convince her and the greater the incentives that might be offered. Indeed this reluctance might be feigned in order to produce just such an increase in incentives. It is probably no exaggeration to say that a great part of organizational life is about trying to shape one's social space to one's advantage, to the extent that it is one of the staples of literary fiction (as, for example, in the tongue-in-cheek book, converted into a very successful musical and film, *How to Succeed in Business without Really Trying;* Mead, 2011).

Similarly, position is not only the creation of the social space in which it is embedded. Its existence, modification, or creation also affects the social space within which it is embedded. For example, the creation by a company's senior management of a privacy compliance office sends a signal to the rest of the firm and the organizational environment that compliance with privacy legislation is now a matter of official concern. The location of the compliance position within the firm's hierarchy indicates how serious this concern is. If the compliance office reports to the CEO, the chances are that people will interpret the signal as a strong one and start taking privacy compliance seriously. If, on the other hand, it reports to a manager in a part of the firm that holds little power, as can be the case for the HR function, people are likely to interpret the signal as calling for perfunctory observance of the rules only. There is also an element of inertia to the creation and modification of positions (Sydow *et al.*, 2009) arising from processes such as imprinting (Johnson, 2007; Higgins, 2005; Stinchcombe, 1965) that means that the impact of this creation or modification can be long-lasting.

All of this can be important for career transitions, affecting, for example, whether such a transition is valued by the individual and the social environment as a promotion. Overall, this suggests the following link.

Proposition 5: The condition and position of career actors at the beginning of a career transition affect the characteristics of the social space relevant to the career transition.

In addition to social space being affected by condition and position in the early phase of career (t_1), there can be anticipatory effects working in the reverse direction. The career actor's condition will be affected by their view of the social space they are about to encounter or are already encountering. Social identity theory (Tajfel and Turner, 1986) predicts that boundary permeability should affect the way people identify with their in-group (Jackson, Sullivan, Harnish, and Hodge, 1996). When boundaries are permeable, people identify themselves more "as individuals (who may be associated with one group or another). A structure in which different status groups have impermeable boundaries does not offer the opportunity to change one's group affiliation ... Under these circumstances, people are more likely to identify primarily in terms of their social group" (Ellemers, 1993: 32), leading to different mobility strategies. Boundaries have signaling properties: people anticipate what their experience will be crossing them and prepare themselves for it. Additionally, role theory (Katz and Kahn, 1978) describes the way a role set projects its expectations onto a focal person, who adopts role behavior strongly affected by these expectations. So, for example, individuals in their probationary years will try hard to meet the expectations of their more established colleagues in order to maximize their chances of making it into permanent membership.

This leads to a proposed link between social space and condition at the beginning of the career transition:

Proposition 6: The condition of a career actor at the beginning of a career transition will reflect their anticipation of the characteristics of the social space in which the career transition will take place.

In addition to the moderating effect of the social space (Proposition 3), the space will potentially also directly affect the career actor's condition and position at the end of the transition (t_2). Effects of social structure on both action and its outcome are a cornerstone of sociological thinking. Mead (1934) introduces the figure of the generalized other, an abstract yet shared approach of a collective expressing what to expect from individual action; Durkheim (1951 [Original 1897]: 229) argues that the social space is a core determinant of individual action; Coleman

(1990: 27 ff.) points to the importance of mutual exchange between actors and their social micro-structure. For example, consider the situation of a CEO who is recruited by a family company (as Lee Iacocca was by Ford; this example closely follows the situation described in Iacocca and Novak, 1986). As soon as she arrives in the position, it becomes evident that, despite the way that the situation was described during the recruitment process, she has far less discretion for action than she was expecting because the family controlling the firm holds all the important cards. She loses face with her subordinates because her initiatives are blocked, affecting her personal power; her stress levels go up; and her organizational commitment goes down, in all probability leading to an early exit from the firm.

To be sure, social space can simultaneously have a direct and a moderating effect. For example, collective knowledge about the toughness of an exam will directly affect a candidate's degree of satisfaction after passing or failing the exam, an expression of the condition of a career actor at t_2. But the available collective knowledge about the toughness of the exam also moderates the relationship between pre-exam anxiety (condition at t_1) and post-exam relief (condition at t_2).

What happens in the social space might also affect positions at the end of career transitions, given that positions in social structures are to a very great extent the creation of social processes within that structure – Barnard (1971 [Original 1938]: 219) calls the definition of organization positions the "scheme of organization." In an organization, positions are typically created by someone other than the future occupant of those positions – for example, senior executives in leadership positions designing their organizations or HR specialists charged with specifying jobs within a given hierarchy. But it may also be the case that other developments in the social space will result in pressure within the social space to redesign positions. For example, the introduction of human resource management as a profession replacing personnel management (Armstrong, 2000; Legge, 1995; Guest, 1990) or the adoption of ideas connected with corporate social responsibility (Matten and Moon, 2008) led to the creation of new or redesigned existing organizational positions. A critical feature of social space, power relations (Emerson, 1962), clearly has a role to play here. The probability of changes happening to positions varies with the power of the actors within the social space advocating for such change.

For the resulting effects we suggest the following.

Proposition 7: Characteristics of the social space in which the transition takes place affect the condition and position of a career actor at the end of their career transition.

Finally, there are anticipatory effects from both condition and position of the career actor at the end of the career transition in relation to the social space. Individual or collective actors in the social space of the focal career actor anticipate possible conditions of the focal career actor and effects of the position at the end of their career transition and act accordingly in order to influence the career transition. Take the example of the supervisor of an expatriate who might anticipate that the expatriate will be overwhelmed when trying to adapt to a new work assignment abroad in a so-called hardship posting. This might lead the supervisor to offer additional emotional support during the transition. This not only eases the change between condition at the beginning of the transition (e.g. excitement, anxiety) and at the end (e.g. exhaustion) (moderating effect, arrow 4) but also directly affects the organizational commitment of the expatriate through signaling "we care." Or, from a spatial viewpoint related to position, actors in the social space such as heads of state might anticipate (arrow 8) the effects of a newly established position such as Secretary General at the UN. In that light they could try to influence the role transition of specific persons aiming at becoming Secretary General (moderating effect of social space, arrow 4) and/or influence the concrete responsibilities linked with that position (direct effect, arrow 7). Such anticipations can backfire, too. Consider the situation in which the superiors of a promising young person are thinking about how to persuade their protégé to accept a difficult assignment. Working on the assumption that the young person is ambitious and looking for opportunities to challenge themselves, they may present the assignment as a "stretch" (O'Mahony and Bechky, 2006). But when they do so, they discover to their dismay that their protégé is engaged to be married and, as a result, is adjusting their view of work-life balance. The last thing the youngster wants at the moment is a "stretch" assignment.

Against this backdrop, we formulate the following.

Proposition 8: Individual and collective actors in the social space are directly affected by anticipated characteristics of position and condition at the end of the career transition.

Taken together, these propositions form the basic building block of the SCF's heuristic model. As a heuristic, it comprises the central components, constructs and relationships alike, of career transitions that are at the core of careers. To be sure, the basic building block not only covers full transitions but also allows for the analysis of choice between various career transitions or refusing a transition. When focal career actors are at the early stage of a potential transition, they often have the choice between several options in the future, i.e. different future condition–position configurations. Indeed *any* transition is implicitly the outcome of a choice: Should I make this move or stay where I am? And any successful job-seeker is likely to be familiar with the problem of deciding which offer to accept and which to decline. In the logic of the basic building block, they might face an array of future conditions at times $t_2 \ldots {}_n$ and corresponding future positions. In the light of their own preferences expressed in terms of conditional elements, influences from the social space, and various anticipated effects from various future condition–position configurations $t_{2 \ldots n}$ they make their decision on which option to choose.

That completes our development of the basic building block, which models a single career transition. Next, we show how blocks can be assembled in different ways in order to elaborate on the basic model and allow us to examine larger segments of careers.

Assembling the Blocks: The Elaborated SCF Model

In this section we describe three approaches to elaborating on the basic building block, each of which, we shall show in subsequent chapters, is of fundamental theoretical interest. First, we extend the model "horizontally" through time by chaining basic building blocks into a sequence; second, we return to our point (Chapter 2) that career actors can be entities of a higher order of social complexity than individuals; and third, we extend the basic model "vertically," exploring the dynamics of the interactions between social space and focal career actor.

First Elaboration: Chaining through Time

The first elaboration involves extending the basic model backward and forward through time by chaining several basic building blocks to allow an exploration of a greater segment of the focal actor's career consisting of multiple periods, stages, episodes, and so forth. The post-transition condition and position for one career transition becomes the pre-transition condition and position for the next transition, and so on. This simply reflects the nature of life as noted concisely by Shakespeare – what's past is prologue (*The Tempest*, Act 2, Scene 1) – and reflects the perspective of Mc Taggart's (1908) so-called A series of time (Chapter 3). A particular influence on pre-transition condition is what came before that. For example, when someone's specific career aspirations lead to a job change, i.e. the crossing of a number of boundaries, perhaps organization or professional, leading to a resulting change in the available social network, it is likely that their new social network will influence the next starting condition – e.g. their career aspirations – for a new career transition. Each link in the chain models a career transition and represents its own building block. The chain shows how the career actor's condition changes over time as they move through a bounded social space modeled as a specified set of boundaries, characterized by the appropriate boundary variables. In this way the extended model can be used to illustrate a situation in which a career actor moves through a number of recognizable stages or episodes, perhaps hierarchical levels or developmental stages (Sullivan and Crocitto, 2007). Figure 4.2 shows this schematically.

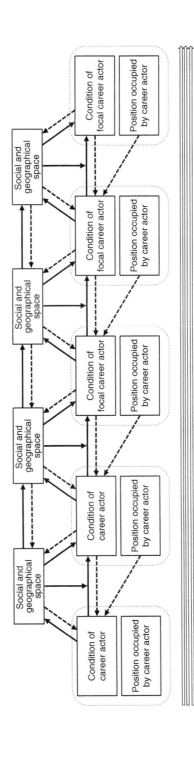

Figure 4.2 SCF heuristic model chained over time

We observe during our account of the basic building block that circumstances might well dictate that we are interested in different aspects of condition before and after the transition. In the same way, when the blocks are chained it might well be the case that the boundaries and aspects of condition that are of interest may vary from stage to stage. For example, in early stages of a set of career transitions – i.e. in early career – issues such as income or prestige tend to be more important than in late career; the opposite is true for intrinsic motives for work such as enjoyment and achievement (Kooij, De Lange, Jansen, Kanfer, and Dikkers, 2011).

Furthermore, the effects that need to be modeled may span more than one transition. Suppose, for example, we are interested in the way in which career actors strategize their route to a position that is organizationally some way from where they are at present; for simplicity, let us assume that the position they hope to be in is at t_3. This would involve, at t_1, looking ahead to the hoped-for position at t_3 and guessing at the position that the actor needs to be in and what their condition needs to be at t_2 in order to be considered for the desired position at t_3. So in a study of this nature one might be interested in the personality characteristics of the actor that distinguishes them from others who do not think about their careers as strategically, the critical aspects of condition that are needed at t_2 in order to enhance suitability for the t_3 position, and the characteristics of the social space during the t_1–t_3 period that the actor must deal with in order to make this series of transitions. More generally, variables in each period can build on each other, such that there is potential for feed-forward in the model as condition at t_n affects boundary variables at t_{n+1} and condition at t_{n+2}.

Second Elaboration: Collective Career Actors

The second elaboration relaxes the assumption that career actors must be individuals. In our development of the heuristic model thus far, our understanding of career actor was limited to this being an individual person. Yet, as we note in Chapter 2, there are other types of actors, for example, a dyad or a collective actor of higher social complexity such as a group or an organization (Coleman, 1990; Parsons and Shils, 1962 [Original 1951]).

The careers of collective social actors constitute an important part of the context for the career of the focal individual career actor, for example, the organization that employs the focal actor or a professional body if the actor is a professional such as a physician or lawyer. For simplicity, we shall continue to work here with the focal career actor as an individual, but we shall allow the career actors in the social space to take on different forms. Regardless of their form, they are important elements of the social space and, as we shall see, have to be taken into account when building a model looking at the focal career actor.

Yet it is important that we underline that, conceptually, career actors comprise individual as well collective actors: the model could equally well be drawn with a collectivity as focal career actor. So the SCF in principle also addresses careers of nonindividual career actors.

Third Elaboration: Coevolution with Elements of the Social Space

Our third elaboration introduces dynamic and relational aspects into the career actor's social space. The social space comprises the elements discussed previously and in Chapter 3 – for example, power relations, rules, individuals, organizations, and national cultures – giving the model a multilevel quality. Actors and segments of the social space may be related to different universes of time. The upshot is that the individuals and collectivities in the social space also have their own careers. All of these career actors, Ego as the focal actor and Alters as the other relevant career actors, constitute context for each other, and none is in principle independent of the others, which creates a highly dynamic situation of mutual dependence that, over time, may generate coevolutionary processes. Here coevolution is not just between person and environment as Nicholson (2007) describes it. Nor is it restricted to the kind of coevolution described in the "collective" or "shared" career literature (Svejenova, Vives, and Alvarez, 2010), which focuses on groupings that take career decisions collectively, intentionally pursuing career opportunities jointly. An example of collective careers is that of spouses who jointly plan their careers so that they coevolve in ways that have the potential to complicate or simplify the lives of both partners.

Instead, coevolution in the SCF model is about the way that the careers of any career actors within the focal actor's social space, individual or collective, may interact with that of the focal actor. Perhaps the most obvious example of the influence of an individual actor in the social space, to which we return in Chapter 8, concerns the mentoring relationship. Not only does the protégé benefit from this relationship, but so, potentially, does the mentor if the protégé's career succeeds. In Chapter 2 we discuss an example of the influence of a collective actor, the career move of a university from a nonaccredited to accredited institution, on the careers of individual faculty by giving them more credibility when trying to extend their social network and improve their position in the field. In turn, the more that they do this, the more prestige accrues to the university, which benefits reputationally from having scholarly stars as members of its faculty.

Obviously, the temporal dimension plays a role in these processes, in particular with regard to some kind of temporal alignment between the moves and developmental paths of the coevolving career actors. Arguably, the concept of entrainment is better than those of either strict synchronization or loose time connection for capturing the essence of the alignment. Originally developed as a concept in biology, entrainment in the realm of organization studies encompasses "the adjustment of the pace or cycle of an activity to match or synchronize with that of another activity" (Ancona and Chong, 1996: 253). Potentially cutting across various levels of social complexity, entrainment

> often occurs in a nested hierarchy. For example, an individual is nested in a department, which is nested in an organization, which is nested in a national culture. To further complicate matters, the individuals and collectivities may be part of several nested hierarchies that may, at times, exert conflicting entrainment demands on the individual, department, and so on. (Bluedorn and Jaussi, 2007: 213)

Entrained coevolutionary developments are not free of power relations, of course. The construct of social *zeitgebers* (Ehlers, Frank, and Kupfer, 1988; Grandin, Alloy, and Abramson, 2006), denoting the signal itself as well as the signaler and understood as a tangible synchronizer, a pace agent for marking the joint rhythm, is not only essential for entrainment processes but also linked to the power dimension. When mentors call, protégés usually come – and if they don't, this clearly has effects for the coevolutionary path and the power relationship between them.

Coevolution as envisaged by the SCF, then, can involve intentional relationships of the kind described in the collective or shared career literature but also unintentional relationships in the sense that they are the unintended, or perhaps unplanned, consequences of actors, individual and collective, occupying the same social space over time.

Elaborated Model

Combining these three elaborations results in a multiperiod, multilevel, and coevolutionary heuristic model within the SCF. It becomes impractical to draw a full schematic of the model because of the large number of possible constructs and interconnections between the focal actor and the various elements of the social space. The general idea can, however, be schematically outlined as a set of chains of basic building blocks across different levels of social complexity, each coevolving with the others with which they interact. Their precise specifications are flexible based on the respective aim and theoretical basis of the study in question. We depict this schematically in Figure 4.3.

Actor A (at the bottom of the figure) is the focal actor whose social space (the middle row) is populated by a number of other actors. We focus on one of them, Actor B, whose condition and positions are shown over the same time period at the top of the figure. For clarity, the broken-line wedge-shaped box shows the basic building block for Actor B at the beginning of the time series. Let us assume that B is A's mentor. As the figure makes clear, A is part of B's social space in just

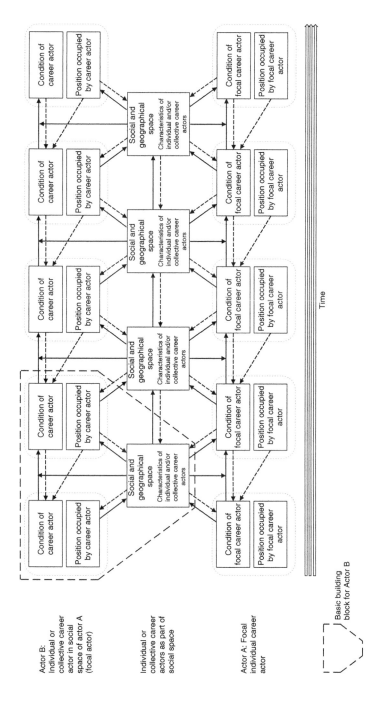

Actor B:
Individual or
collective career
actor in social
space of actor A
(focal actor)

Individual or
collective career
actors as part of
social space

Actor A: Focal
individual career
actor

Basic building
block for Actor B

Time

Figure 4.3 Elaborated SCF heuristic model (partial view)

the same way that B is part of A's. So we have a model showing the coevolution of the careers of A and B.

Of course, this is a highly schematic depiction in which chains of events dovetail nicely, alternating regularly between actors at different levels of social complexity. In real life, we are unlikely to encounter this regularity or simplicity. In addition, there could well be other combinations of individual and collective career actors that are of interest. To add together the two examples we use in the previous section and reframe them as shown in Figure 4.3, Actor A is the protégé, B the mentor, and C the university both work for. We now have a very complex model showing the coevolution of all three. Suppose, for example, Francis Crick and his protégé James Watson had been working in a small UK university instead of Cambridge's Cavendish Laboratory when they elucidated the structure of the DNA molecule (which is of course unlikely given the importance of their Cambridge colleagues' largely unacknowledged contribution to the work). It is easy to imagine that their university would have benefited greatly from the exposure that the discovery brought its illustrious researchers, who in turn would have benefited from the university's efforts to retain them, and so forth.

These examples illustrate the flexibility of the SCF. Its modular setup allows for "horizontal," "vertical," and relational enlargements as the situation requires.

Summation

This chapter has operated at a fairly high level of abstraction. To repeat the point that we made at its outset, the model we develop is heuristic: it is a guide to action, and the action involved is the development of more precisely formulated theories of career processes. In order to do this, it is necessary first to select an aspect of career for more detailed modeling and then draw on the heuristic model to select appropriate theories from the literature that might explain the relationships in question. One specifies what kind of conditions, positions, and elements of the social space one is interested in and then selects particular arrows – propositions – in the heuristic model and finds appropriate theory to explain why they might have the effect predicted, in the way that we chose various illustrative examples to show how each arrow might work.

In the remainder of the book we expand on these ideas by showing how they can be used to develop career research in a number of novel directions. But first we need to pause to reflect on the epistemological nature of the enterprise in which we are engaged. In short, if the SCF is not a theory, what is it? And how can this "it" be used? That is the task for the next chapter.

5   Exploring the Architectonics of the SCF

In this chapter, we pause to consider what lies at the heart of our venture. Theory is central to what this book is about. Yet, paradoxically, we are not presuming to offer a theory of careers. This needs some explaining, so this chapter is for anyone concerned about the nature of the theoretical claim we are making.

In brief, our argument is as follows. The SCF is not a theory of careers but a framework that delineates and maps the field of career studies and suggests an approach to theorizing (Weick, 1995b) about careers. It comprises a number of layers that we explore in the previous three chapters: the perspectives, the constructs that emerge from the perspectives, the concept of career implied by the constructs, and the heuristic models that can be devised from this view of career.

If that is a summary of the argument of the earlier chapters of this book, then we need to fill in some detail. We have been using terms such as framework, theorizing, model, and theory, yet if one thing stands out from the pretty extensive literature on these terms, it is that they are used in many different ways by different writers. So in the interests of intellectual precision – or, at least, in the hope that we might move in that direction – we take a moment in this chapter to review briefly some of the literatures on theory, model, and framework in order to give a sense of the variety of views that can be encountered and to provide context for the ways in which we use the terms in this book. That, in turn, allows us to sum up what lies within the SCF and its purpose, which provides a bridge between the conceptual considerations of Part II and the more concrete examples of the use of the SCF that we turn to in Part III. In addition, in the final section of the chapter, we also outline four interrelated activities that put the SCF to work when using insight generated outside career studies.

Theory in the Social Sciences

Within the field of organizational studies, the questions of what a theory is and is not and what makes a good theory have been extensively debated. These questions clearly generate considerable passion among organizational scholars, perhaps because social scientists – and humanists for that matter (see Haack, 1997, for an example of a critique on this point) – are affected to varying extents by what has been called science or physics envy (Lipton, 2003), the feeling that "real" science is being done elsewhere. Yet

[i]f there is one thing that philosophers of science, who go out and study the natural sciences, can teach us, it is that the practices of the natural sciences are not as we imagine them (Cartwright 1983). No one actually knows what it means for a discipline to be scientific, and any set of rules we could write down would be found to be violated routinely in fields regarded as indisputably scientific. There is no such thing as the Scientific Method, and most philosophers have given up the search for a single set of practices that defines one field as scientific and another as not (Laudan 1983; Caldwell 1988). Many of the features of a discipline that we think of as scientific come from nineteenth-century classical ... physics, which holds little relevance for modern physics and even less for the modern social sciences (Giere 1984). (Clarke and Primo, 2012: Section 1.3.1, para 1)

Clarke and Primo, writing about political science, go on to remark that "[t]he only people who still care about the scientific status of political science are political scientists motivated by a largely unnecessary academic inferiority complex" (ibid.: para 3). *Mutatis mutandis*, arguably the same is true in the organizational sciences.

Yet – or perhaps as a result – the passion surrounding the question of what constitutes "real" theory is real enough and ubiquitous within the social sciences. One cannot get a paper published in a good organizational journal unless it purports to develop or test theory. As one such journal's website puts it: "The mission of the *Academy of Management Journal* is to publish empirical research that tests, extends, or builds management theory and contributes to management practice" (*Academy of Management Journal*, 2016). By contrast, the web page that provides information for authors who wish to submit papers to *Nature*, one of the two arguably internationally leading general science journals, does not mention the word "theory" at all (*Nature*, 2016). The other such journal, *Science*, does mention the word on its equivalent page, where it sets out the rules for authorship. To be listed as an author, one must meet one or more of four criteria, the first of which is "[f]ormulation of theory and prediction" (*Science*, 2016); however, there is no mention of a requirement that *submissions* deal with theory. So what is "theory" in the eyes of organizational scholars, and why are we choosing not to develop one for careers and opt for a framework instead?

The word "theory" is derived from the Latin *theoria*, in turn derived from the Greek θεωρία, meaning "action of viewing, contemplation, sight, spectacle" (OED, 2017). By the late sixteenth century it had taken on a more purposive sense: "The conceptual basis of a subject or area of study ... [c]ontrasted with *practice*" (emphasis in the original) or "[a] conception of something to be done, or of the method of doing it; a systematic statement of rules or principles to be followed" (ibid.). By the seventeenth century it was being used in a sense that would be understood by the editors of present-day academic journals: "An explanation of a phenomenon arrived at through examination and contemplation of the relevant facts; a statement of one or more laws or principles which are generally held as describing an essential property of something" (ibid.).

Much of the debate on theory in organization studies is framed in terms of what makes for a good "theory" section in an empirical paper (DiMaggio, 1995; Sutton and Staw, 1995; Weick, 1995b; Whetten, 1989) or a good theoretical contribution to a review journal (Rindova, 2009; Kilduff, 2006). There seems fairly general agreement that theory is not lists of references, data, lists of variables or constructs, diagrams, or predictions/hypotheses (Sutton and Staw, 1995). Put more simply, theory is not description:

> Description, the "features or qualities of individual things, acts, or events" (Werkmeister, 1959, p. 484) must be distinguished from theory. As Hempel (1965) pointed out, the vocabulary of science has two basic functions: (a) to adequately describe the objects and events being investigated and (b) to establish theories by which events and objects can be explained and predicted. While descriptions may be the source material of theories, they are not themselves theoretical statements. In the organization and management literature, the two are often confused. Specifically, three modes of description must be distinguished from theory: categorization of raw data, typologies, and metaphors. (Bacharach, 1989: 496–497)

Theory, most writers agree, connects constructs or variables in order to explain and predict:

> Building on the works of previous students of theory construction (e.g. Dubin, 1969; Nagel, 1961; Cohen, 1980), researchers can define a theory as a statement of relationships between units observed or approximated in the empirical world. *Approximated* units means *constructs*, which by their very nature cannot be observed directly (e.g. centralization, satisfaction, or culture). *Observed* units mean *variables*, which are operationalized empirically by measurement. The primary goal of a theory is to answer the questions of *how, when,* and *why,* unlike the goal of description, which is to answer the question of *what.* In more detailed terms, a theory may be viewed as a system of constructs and variables in which the constructs are related to each other by propositions and the variables are related to each other by hypotheses. The whole system is bounded by the theorist's assumptions. (Bacharach, 1989: 498; emphasis in the original)

So a theory of careers has to identify something about the how, when, and why of careers. What might that be? Is there any possibility that we can find the career equivalent of the "theory of everything" that physicists seek as an explanation of the nature of the universe by uniting gravitational, electromagnetic, weak nuclear, and strong nuclear forces under one theoretical roof? Theory such as the standard model in physics provides the basis for predictions about the particles that will be found when theory-specified experiments are conducted – for example, the experiments using CERN's Large Hadron Collider that produced evidence of the hitherto elusive Higgs boson. Carroll (2012) describes the process concisely as follows: "Today, particle theorists scribble equations on blackboards, which ultimately become specific models, which are tested by experimentalists who gather data from exquisitely precise machines" (Chapter 1, para 4). What might the career equivalent look like?

In this book, we define career as a pattern of a career actor's positions and condition within a bounded social and geographic space over their life to date. This seems to be encouraging us to develop a theory that explains the pattern in position and condition, knowing something about the career actor, the time under consideration, and the bounded geographical and social space within which all this happens. As soon as we put it like this, it becomes obvious why developing such a general theory is, at best, an extremely ambitious undertaking or, at worst, impossible. Position is something that can be defined in myriad different ways depending on the purpose at hand. Condition is everything that can be said about a career actor: Which aspects of condition are we interested in? Indeed, is the career actor an individual or some kind of collectivity? What do we mean by pattern? How do we consider time and social space, let alone the nature of the boundaries that enclose and partition the space? And so on.

It is no surprise, then, that a search for the term "theory of career" in Google Scholar demonstrates that it is used in association with specific aspects of careers, not career as a whole. Prominent examples include the social cognitive theory of career and academic interest, choice, and performance (Lent, Brown, and Hackett, 1994); a social capital theory of career success (Seibert, Kraimer, and Liden, 2001); a social learning theory of career selection (Krumboltz, Mitchell, and Jones, 1976); a theory of career mobility (Sicherman and Galor, 1990); a theory of career motivation (London, 1983); a learning theory of career counseling (Krumboltz, 1996); and a theory of career development (Super, 1992). It is certainly true that the first handbook that drew the field of career studies together was titled a *Handbook of Career Theory* (Arthur *et al.*, 1989b). However, that volume does not attempt to provide a single, unifying general theory of the field; instead, it comprises a wide range of theoretical contributions to the careers field, each examining career from that chapter's own unique angle.

So if the SCF is neither a theory of career nor a metatheory that requires an underlying theoretical body that "interrogate[s] the presuppositions of any theory" (Hesketh and Fleetwood, 2006: 683) and has to "advise us ... on how to choose what problem we ought to be solving, ... on how to specify the detailed structure of the problem we have chosen to solve, and ... on which criteria to accept or reject a proposed solution" (Mitroff and Betz, 1972: 12), yet theory is central to this book, what is our claim vis-à-vis careers?

Frameworks and Models

In this book we distinguish between three things: theory, model, and framework. Not everyone does. For example, in their book on models, Lave and March (1975: 3–4) say that

[w]e construct models in order to explain and appreciate the world. Sometimes we call our simplifications theories, paradigms, hypotheses, or simply ideas. In a more formal treatise we might make distinctions among some of the labels; but we will not do so here. We will talk simply of models as a generic term for any set of conjectures about real world observations.

It is by no means uncommon for authors to use the terms "model" and "framework" interchangeably (e.g. Upton and Egan, 2010; Sydow *et al.*, 2009; Matten and Moon, 2008; Gundlach, Douglas, and Martinko, 2003; Crossan, Lane, and White, 1999). Marquis and Tilcsik (2013), however, show how the distinction can be useful. They begin by devising an organizing *framework* for their topic (imprinting research) that classifies the literature along two dimensions and then show how this can become the basis of a multilevel process *model* of imprinting. Framework, for them, is something that organizes in order to clear the ground for modeling.

On the other hand, the same authors (Marquis and Tilcsik, 2013) conflate model with theory, describing their *model* as "a multilevel *theory* of imprinting" (227; emphasis added). Indeed the distinction between theory and model can be as difficult to discern as that between framework and model:

Scientists are usually quite vague as to the relationship between theory and model, or even between model and empirical law; they use these second-order terms in a vague and often inconsistent manner that would play havoc in their science were it to be extended to the first-order terms also. (McMullin, 1968: 386)

That said, those who do look for a distinction typically do so by arguing that models interpose between theory and reality. They are often described, in a variety of ways, as abstractions of the real world, with the aim of making it easier to understand what is happening in that real world. Clarke and Primo (2012) cite Black (1962) as the source of modern treatments of scientific models. Black begins with scale models – physical representations of objects scaled down or up – and then moves on to

analogue models in which an object is represented in some new medium. Whereas a scale model shares features with its original, an analogue model shares only a structure or pattern of relationships. A subset of analogue models are mathematical models

through which structures are represented in the new medium of mathematics ...
Theoretical models ... [represent] the structure of the original. Black describes such
models as metaphors with the power to bring "two separate domains into cognitive
and emotional relation" by using the language of one as "a lens for seeing the other"
(236–237). (Clarke and Primo, 2012, Section 1.2, paras 2–5)

Faye (2005: 2) echoes this notion of models as representations of reality:

It will be argued that a theory is not a representation of reality but first and foremost an
explicitly defined language which enables us to express various representations of the
world. What has the power to act as representations are models of concrete systems. It is
these models that supply us with the material for telling the causal stories.

Nurmi (2013) introduces a multiple-stage view of the relationship between
theory and model. He describes a hierarchy with metatheories at the highest
level of abstraction, followed by "more concrete" theories, then modeling
derived from theory that is "typically detailed and concrete enough to be tested
and falsified on the basis of empirical data" (p. 183), next leading to measurement models (to do with "investigating whether a certain theoretical construct
can be measured in reliable and valid ways"; ibid.), and finally operationalization in actual empirical studies. However, to muddy waters again that seemed to
have been clearing, Grüne-Yanoff (2013: 197) notes that

Nurmi's distinction between theory and model closely matches the distinction in
economics between theoretical and empirical (or econometric) model. Typical purposes
of theoretical models in economics are the illustration of underlying theoretical principles or hypotheses, and checking the results of their interactions. Econometric models,
in contrast, specify the concrete functional forms for estimation.

The only common theme that seems to emerge from this brief review is that a
model is something that represents something else. The something else can be
many things. An empirical model is based on reality, for example, a scale model
of an aircraft or an econometric model of a large data set. A theoretical model
works forward from theoretical concepts, laying them out in a form, possibly
graphic or mathematical and perhaps by combining more than one theory, that
allows them to be tested empirically. But the essence of this view of model is
that it must always be seen in relation to something else; it is a model *of*
something. And if that something is a theory, it can be very hard in practice to
differentiate between the model and the theory it is derived from. For example,
most textbooks of organizational behavior include a model of Vroom's expectancy theory (Vroom, 2005). Is that the theory, or is the theory the set of
propositions underlying the model? In a sense it doesn't matter; what does
matter is that the model leaves no room for ambiguity about where the ideas
represented by the boxes and arrows come from. Are they from Vroom's
theoretical work? Do they come from elaborations of the theory provided by

other writers? Once this is made clear, the relationship of the model as represented in the textbook to Vroom's theory becomes evident.

One writer's theory, therefore, is another writer's model, and frameworks bounce uncomfortably between and around them. The conclusions we draw from this are twofold. First, in the absence of any overwhelming consensus on how theory, model, and framework differ, we shall adopt an approach that seems to be consistent with what many writers are suggesting and that, we shall argue, helps make sense of the field of career studies. But second, we know that in so doing we shall offend some, if not many, others who have thought about these matters. In the next section, we explain the senses in which we use the terms "framework," "theory," and "model." To that we add "theorizing" as an essential concept pointing toward the process of generating theories and models.

The SCF as a Framework

Here is how we use the terms "model," "theory," "theorizing," and "framework":

• *Theory* is used in the traditional sense we describe previously: something that connects at least two constructs or variables in order to explain and predict. We shall mainly be concerned with hypothesis-testing, that is, theory about specific empirical phenomena (e.g. theories of career mobility) as opposed to grand theory of the kind developed by, for example, Giddens and Bourdieu or theory of the middle range (Merton, 1957a) that connects the two; we return to these distinctions in Chapter 10.
• *Model* denotes a representation of a set of propositions or theoretical predictions. The model may draw on a range of different theories, or it may not. An example of a model not drawing on specific theories is, of course, our heuristic model of Chapter 4, which is based on propositions that lack the specificity of theory. But there will be times when the distinction between theory and model is fuzzy at best.
• *Theorize* is used to describe the process of developing theory or models.
• *Framework* is reserved as a term for the entire enterprise on which this book is based: an organizing device for approaching the study of career.

Applying this organizing device, the SCF, typically goes through five distinct stages (Figure 5.1). The first stage comprises its foundation, namely the set of three basic perspectives – spatial, ontic, and temporal – we describe in Chapter 3. In the second stage, three core constructs (and the related guiding differences and operations) are drawn from the basic perspectives: boundaries (in/out; mapping) from the spatial perspective, condition (Ego/Alter; comparing) from the ontic perspective, and chronology (precedes/follows; sequencing) from the temporal. In the third stage this is combined with career actors to

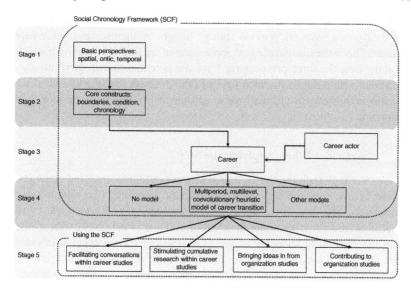

Figure 5.1 The stages of the SCF and its applications

yield a concept of career as a pattern of a career actor's positions and condition within a bounded social and geographic space over their life to date. In the fourth, this view of career is expanded to develop models that can be used to apply theory to career phenomena. In Chapter 4, we develop one such model, a heuristic model of career transitions that provides the basis for either applying existing theory to these transitions or developing new, more detailed theory and more specific models to account for specific features of the career. But that is just our suggestion for a fourth-stage model. There is plenty of scope for others to provide other foci for research, e.g. an interest in the subjective construction of career narratives or the changing career aspirations of different age cohorts of business school graduates. These different approaches will most likely lead to other heuristic models.

The first four stages comprise the SCF. In the fifth and final stage, it is put to work on concrete applications, using the SCF for specific issues in OMC studies and beyond.

The key to the fifth stage is the purpose for which the career scholar wishes to use it, which is the theme for Part III of this book. The "framework" quality of the SCF implies an invitation to the career scholar to find different ways of modeling career based on the very general precept of the third stage, namely the definition of career that emerges from the SCF's three perspectives and their related core constructs, guiding differences, and operations. It may be that no model is required: in any given situation, it might be that the three perspectives and their core constructs provide enough insight by themselves to stimulate thought. This is the case for the first application of the SCF (Chapter 6) in which we show how the three perspectives have the potential to help generate conversations within the fragmented field of OMC studies. But the ideas that we develop in subsequent chapters make greater use of the heuristic model of Chapter 4.

Activities When Applying the SCF

Various ways of applying the SCF require a set of four interrelated activities: reconstructing, equivalizing, understanding, and importing (we explain these terms later). The first of the activities, reconstructing, is fundamental to all kinds of usage since it addresses the creation and interpretation of career reality using the theoretical language of the SCF. The other three become relevant when the SCF is used for what is arguably its most far-reaching contribution: offering a language and a framework for making connections between organizational and career studies by drawing attention to analogous areas of organization studies that also examine condition, boundaries, and time and making them useful for career-related research. In this chapter, we will outline these activities. In Part III we build on these ideas when demonstrating various ways of making use of the SCF.

Before elaborating on the four activities in greater detail, however, we will raise an issue that is an important prerequisite for applying the SCF and, for that matter, at the heart of doing research: selecting your field of study.

Selecting: Focusing on an Area of Interest

Applying the SCF requires, first of all, the selection of a career-related area of interest. Of course, this is nothing specific to the SCF. All research efforts, be they theoretical or empirical, require such a choice. One could even argue that focusing one's efforts is at the heart of science, since a "discipline may be called a science only if it has a definite field to explore. Science is concerned with things, realities. If it does not have definite material to describe and interpret, it exists in a vacuum" (Durkheim, 1960: 3). If there are not "at least some mental horizons that would help scholars curb their curiosity, organize their intellectual attention in a more 'focused' manner, and essentially separate the relevant from the irrelevant, for example, it would be absolutely impossible to establish any coherent scholarly agenda at all" (Zerubavel, 1995: 1098). At first glance, this seems to be a no-brainer. A closer look, however, reveals that this is a decision laden with suppositions.

First, there are numerous and vastly different reasons for choosing an area. They include, for example, personal interest, one's own research history and considerations about recycling one's own texts, the degree of research deficit in a certain area, expected contributions in the light of the often called for cumulative knowledge creation where research efforts relate to and build on each other, perceived reputational gain, opportunistic behavior looking at chances to get published or cited, assumed potential societal impact, responding to grant money competitions by institutions with their open or vested interests, and ad hoc coalitions with colleagues for personal or micro-political reasons. We could extend this list considerably.

Second, as inevitable as it is that one has to make a decision and have a personal reason for it, others will place their own interpretation on one's decision. Their conclusions might or might not be in line with what one actually views it to be. The individual researcher has very little control over this. Imagine the case in which a male researcher starts working with a female colleague from a different department on a new conference paper. Their reasons might be entirely based on a combination of personal interest in the topic, the importance of the conference in their respective fields, and a strong sense of supporting collaboration across disciplines. Yet the social environment, both private and professional, might come to entirely different conclusions. They can range from presumptions about a romantic affair, via assumed preferences for attractive conference locations, to micro-politically founded suspicions of one of them changing departments or of being vanguards for a merger of both departments that has long been heralded by the university's top brass.

Third, beyond individual repercussions, the individual decision for or against dealing with a certain research area and/or a specific theoretical angle also has an effect on the broader field. While these effects, to a certain extent, also depend on the relative prominence of the person in the field, they are basically pervasive. Take, for example, the case of the boundaryless career as one dominant view on careers. It started with the publication of the influential edited volume by Arthur and Rousseau (1996a) in the aftermath of a symposium at the US Academy of Management Meeting 1993 in Atlanta, GA, with its conference theme of "Managing the Boundaryless Organization." When both prominent and great numbers of scholars started to refer to the boundaryless career and use it in their research, it became a quasi-standard for nearly two decades that one should relate one's work to this kind of thinking. At the time of writing, the voices increasingly questioning some of its assumptions and the empirical evidence and arguing for alternatives (e.g. Kattenbach *et al.*, 2014; Inkson *et al.*, 2012; Rodrigues and Guest, 2010) not only reflect a personal choice of research interest by these scholars. They also shape the field and what will go on in the field in the future.

The selection of one's area of interest is part of a broader debate on what makes topics attractive (Davis, 1971) and how dominant paradigms in science evolve at a more general level. While we do not go into the matter in depth here, there is certainly ample literature available about the change and life cycle of scientific paradigms (e.g. Lakatos, 1984; Toulmin, 1972; Kuhn, 1970); the value and dangers of dominant views in an area such as management research (see, for example, the debate between Pfeffer, 1995 and Van Maanen, 1995 to which we return in Chapter 6); the extent to which performativity affects competition among the various management sciences (Abrahamson, Berkowitz, and Dumez, 2016); or the role of management gurus in pushing a topic (e.g. Huczynski, 2006; Jackson, 2001; Clark and Salaman, 1998) as well as what constitutes fads and fashion in management research (e.g. Benders and Van Veen, 2001; Weick, 2001; ten Bos, 2000; Abrahamson and Fairchild, 1999; Abrahamson, 1996; for a different and critical view, see Sokal and Bricmont, 1998).

As outlined earlier, the selection of an area of interest and/or a theoretical lens is not specifically tied to the SCF, nor is it easy and self-evident, but it has massive consequences for both the individual researcher and the whole field. Having said that, we now turn to the four activities guiding some of the applications of the SCF. We will concentrate on their basic description and give brief examples. In Part III we go into more detail when putting the SCF to work.

Reconstructing: Using the SCF to Look at Career Issues

As outlined previously, the selection of an area within career research for exploring is the starting point. To illustrate reconstructing as a basic activity when applying the SCF, we select an area within the career field based on our previous common interest: the role of macro-factors and contextual boundaries for career phenomena (e.g. Briscoe *et al.*, 2012b; Inkson *et al.*, 2012; Mayrhofer *et al.*, 2007a; Gunz, Peiperl, and Tzabbar, 2007b).

We have argued elsewhere "that research exploring the broad context within which work careers are lived helps us understand better the nature of career in an Internet-based, globalized economy and how these careers, in turn, influence developments in the context" (Gunz, Mayrhofer, and Tolbert, 2011: 1614). This account entails five different aspects among others (ibid.):

• the influence of national differences in terms of social structures, economic situation, and labor force policies on concepts of careers that individuals from varying social backgrounds hold and on emerging career patterns within a variety of occupations;
• the widely assumed highly dynamic environment in contemporary societies and economies;

- the changing forms of personal relationships and living together as well as the role of women in WEIRD (Western, educated, industrialized, rich, democratic) societies;
- the need for grounding career research in sound concepts of person and personality but also going beyond this current emphasis – a one-sided bias in our view – to integrate social and political phenomena and their respective theories in the description and explanation of individual careers, thus working toward multilevel analyses of careers; and
- the consequences of different forms of emerging global cooperation between companies and the role of internationally operating organizations beyond the for-profit sector such as the World Bank, the International Monetary Fund, or the UN for the career landscape and international careers.

Reconstructing this account in the language and thinking of the SCF requires identifying the career actor. Normally, we are talking about individuals and their careers, which is the most frequent instance in career research. Alternatively, as we outline in Chapter 3, collective actors of varying degrees of social complexity such as a dyad, a group, or an organization can also have a career and are, as part of the social environment, relevant for individual careers.

The ontic perspective focuses on the condition of the career actor in question. Remember that condition addresses what we see of a career actor at any given moment in time. In our example, a number of different aspects of condition emerge such as the individual conceptualizations of careers people have or the personality of the respective career actors from different social backgrounds. The spatial perspective directs us to the social context within which careers take place and important issues such as social structures, economic policies, and labor force policies. It also alerts us to position as a primary element of the social space. However, in the previous account, there is no clear indication of what kinds of positions are addressed. Implicitly, positions are involved in the ontic idea of career concepts that career actors have because the conceptualization of careers seems necessarily to entail the idea of people moving from one position to another. Likewise, referring to a career landscape influenced by large, internationally operating organizations seems to indicate that within this landscape there are specific locations – positions – that individuals can occupy, which might be changing or emerging in a new way. The social background of career actors mentioned in the preceding account clearly addresses the ontic perspective. The temporal perspective is visible in a number of ways when looking at the account. Not only is time – this is both inevitable and constitutive – an integral part of talking about careers. Talking about the specific environmental dynamics points toward change and different rates of change in various contextual settings such as so-called tiger states or emerging economies.

Reconstructing the account through the three perspectives of the SCF – spatial, ontic, and temporal – allows us to apply a certain order to the

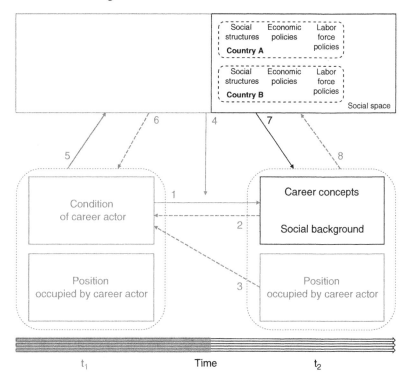

Figure 5.2 Reconstructing contextual perspectives on career in terms of the SCF

reconstruction. Using the basic building block (Chapter 4) and its proposed relationships takes reconstructing one step further and invites us to look for the suggested causal relationships in the model and their relative importance. In the previous account, social structures, economic situation, and labor force policies influence the career concepts of individuals from varying social backgrounds providing a framework for understanding the origin of national differences in careers. Reconstructing this along the SCF leads the line of argument shown in Figure 5.2.

One can clearly see that from the rich possible array of factors and relationships, only a few of them are addressed. However, the structure of the argument has become quite obvious. To be sure, the example only illustrates the basic procedure in the first step in applying the SCF (reconstructing). It allows one to apply a joint language and way of thinking to career problems. Of course, what you get is only as good as the underlying premise. In the preceding case, the insight is general. As we show in Chapter 7, if you apply the activity of reconstructing to a concrete and more elaborate study, the picture becomes sharper and also allows some further developments through systematically guiding the researcher to new research questions.

Equivalizing, Understanding, and Importing: Reaching outside Career Studies

The SCF is applicable not only within career studies. When trying to make use of insight gathered outside the field, it can be helpful, too. In such a case, a set of three further activities beyond reconstructing are necessary: *equivalizing* looks for similar theoretical discussions outside the career field that address similar problems, *understanding* focuses on getting at the core of the major theoretical arguments in these discussions, and *importing* applies the arguments found outside to career research using the SCF. Again, we will use an example to illustrate how these activities work.

Continuing with our area of interest in the role of contextual issues for careers, there is a well-established debate about the extent to which various professions and their contextual specifics influence individual careers. Longstanding examples include musicians (e.g. Dobrow, 2013; Kirschbaum, 2007; Faulkner, 1973), nursing (e.g. Wei and Taormina, 2014; Long and West, 2007; Murrells and Robinson, 1998), and information technology (e.g. Joia and Mangia, 2015; Lee, 2002; Igbaria, Meredith, and Smith, 1995). The various contributions use a wide array of frameworks and theories to analyze this issue. Hardly surprisingly, there are a number of unresolved questions in this debate – for example, how to conceptualize the contextual specifics of these professions and what underlying mechanisms govern individual career actors' moves.

Based on this brief reconstruction of our area of interest, we can now look outside career studies for potentially fruitful insight, which is where *equivalizing* becomes relevant. This entails searching outside career studies for discussions that are "equivalent," i.e. that deal with similar problems but in different contexts. In our case we look at organization and social studies and the discourse around Bourdieu's theory of practice (Bourdieu, 1977). In this theory one major question concerns how actors in a specific field, bound by its specifics, move around and strive for certain, more precisely dominant positions in the field using their capitals and habitus. In the language of the SCF, there is a focal actor – an individual – that moves within the bounded social space and tries to reach a certain position based on the conditions, e.g. competencies, they are equipped with.

This leads us to the next activity, *understanding*. It requires us to get at the heart of the discussion identified, which means pinpointing major lines of the argument in the "outside" discussions, here Bourdieu's theory of practice. In particular we are interested in what it says about actors and their relationships, how the social space is structured, and what mechanisms are relevant for actors' moves. In brief and through the lens of practice theory, fields are "a network, or configuration, of objective relations between positions. These positions are objectively defined ... by their present and potential situation (*situs*) in the structure of the distribution of species of power (or capital) whose possession commands access to the specific profits that are at stake in the field, as well as by their objective relation to other positions" (Bourdieu and Wacquant, 1992: 97; emphasis in the original). As a result of power and domination (König and Berli, 2013), each field has a specific hierarchy, an embodied stratification (Krais and Gebauer, 2002: 73ff.). Actors (or, in the theory's terminology, agents) with their specific habitus play/fight over advancement and use economic, cultural, and social capitals to do so. Based on the doxa of the field (i.e. the dominant views) the field acknowledges different aspects of these capitals as symbolic capital (i.e. the valid currency or, speaking in theoretical terms, the field-dependent amalgamation of the three forms of capital). This yields prestige and reputation, and it enables as well as limits actors' mobility within the field. Those actors who are equipped with a lot of symbolic capital fit well into the structures of the field and have a good basis for the games of entry, survival, and advancement played within the field.

The final activity when using insight gained outside the career field is *importing*. Based on an understanding of the external discussion, one looks for ways to make these insights fruitful for the career discussion – to import them into the career discussion. In the questions we raised previously, a first insight we can import is a more fine-grained view of how to conceptualize professions when trying to understand their influence on careers and career advancement. Interpreting professions as a field, one has to identify relevant actors in the profession; look for power-based rules that are relevant for acknowledging different forms of capitals as symbolic capital (i.e. as a valid currency in the field); and pinpoint games played in the field relevant for different kinds of career moves such as field entry, survival, and advancement. A second insight concerns the interplay between field, habitus, and capitals that allows career studies to transcend the classic structure versus agency division and enable an integrated multilevel perspective. Not surprisingly, given the weight of the outside concept, this type of thinking has begun to make its mark on career studies at both a conceptual and empirical level (e.g. Schneidhofer, Latzke, and Mayrhofer, 2015; Duberley and Cohen, 2010; Iellatchitch *et al.*, 2003; Lindh and Dahlin, 2000).

Note that as was the case with reconstructing, the preceding account is not meant to provide in-depth answers to the questions we raised. Nor does it represent a claim that the theoretical discussion targeted, Bourdieu's theory of practice, has the, relatively speaking, best answers. What we are trying to do in this chapter is illustrate how a set of four interrelated activities – reconstructing, equivalizing, understanding, and importing – can be a systematic guide to the application of the perspectives and the models of the SCF to discussions outside career studies and make these discussions useful to the field. In Chapter 8, we make fuller use of these activities when illustrating in more detail how the SCF supports the importation of ideas from other areas of studies, in particular organization studies.

Summation

In this chapter, we explain the nature of the theoretical claim we are making for this book. We start by saying what the SCF is not: it is not a general theory of careers. We discuss the different treatments in the literature of the terms "theory," "model," and "framework," showing how confused the situation is. Rather than taking sides on which version is "correct," we set out the approach we take in this book. Given the meaning that is generally attached to the term "theory" by scholars working within the currently dominant North American paradigm of organizational research, which probably excludes the kind of grand theory developed by writers such as Giddens and Bourdieu, we argue that it is highly unlikely that any such general theory of careers is possible: there is no unitary phenomenon to be explained in the way required by conventional understandings of what theory is. Indeed, career theory, as it is found in the literature, is invariably about some specific aspect of career, not career as a whole.

So rather than being a general theory of careers, the SCF provides a *framework for theorizing* about careers. It provides an approach to the task of making sense of the nature of careers and of what constitutes career research. It suggests ways of providing broad heuristic models of careers that can, in turn, be used to apply specific theories to specific career phenomena or develop new such theories. In this way we set the scene for Part III of the book, the task of which is to explore how the SCF can be used to further develop the field of OMC studies.

Part III

Putting the SCF to Work

6   Facilitating Conversations within Career Studies

This chapter starts Part III of the book, which is where we put the SCF to work, so to speak. Using its three perspectives and the models described in Part II, we discuss different ways in which both career and organization studies can benefit from the SCF, by facilitating conversation across disciplinary boundaries. When we speak of career studies, we mean all scientific efforts across the broad range of disciplines that we describe in Chapter 1 as falling within the proto-field of career studies (Figure 1.1). This comprises fields dealing with career (or an obvious synonym) as their primary object of study, even though scholars working within these fields may not necessarily think of themselves as working on a common project with scholars in other fields within the proto-field (or even agree that this proto-field exists). Examples of these fields include life-course research, migration research, vocational psychology, and studies on organization and management careers (OMC). As we note in Chapter 1, we devote most attention here to OMC studies.

In this chapter, we focus on the potential of the SCF for supporting conversations across different scientific boundaries within the proto-field of career studies. The SCF, in particular its three perspectives, constitutes a means for creating common ground in such conversations. By relating different types of empirical and theoretical work to the ontic, spatial, and temporal perspectives, we suggest, the SCF highlights typical characteristics of different kinds of career research and shows commonalities and differences between various streams of work.

We begin the chapter by outlining the importance of conversations between partially disconnected discourses and actors. We then demonstrate how the SCF supports conversations across different fields of career studies. Using ideal types in the Weberian sense, we show how different studies address the basic issues linked to the three SCF perspectives to differing degrees and how that provides possible starting points for conversations about similarities and differences between them. The final step in this chapter illustrates the potential of the SCF for facilitating a different type of conversation that touches the identity of the field of OMC studies. It traces the development of the OMC field – to be sure, one of many possible accounts – from its origins in sociological, vocational, and developmental literatures, which stretch back to the nineteenth century in some cases and to the classical period in others (Moore *et al.*, 2007), and focuses on developments since the 1950s. So using the SCF we reconstruct the history of the OMC field.

The Importance of Conversation

As we note in earlier chapters, prominent voices over a number of years have raised the issue of the lack of contact between different fields of career studies (e.g. Collin and Patton, 2009; Arthur, 2008; Peiperl and Gunz, 2007; Collin and Young, 2000). Again as we note in Chapter 1, the field of OMC studies can be described as a fragmented adhocracy (Whitley, 1984), being highly differentiated internally with a large number of discourses, a complex set of conversations around a common theme that are, at best, mutually politely acknowledged and, at worst, only marginally aware of each other. Two questions follow from this: Does any of this matter, and if yes, what is to be done? We address these issues next.

Fragmentation and Its Consequences

Fragmentation is by no means unique to the field of OMC studies in particular or the proto-field of career studies in general. For decades, influential figures in the field of management studies have been regularly pointing out the state of disarray of the field. As early as 1962, Koontz, for example, writes that

the varied approaches to management theory have led to a kind of confused and destructive jungle warfare. Particularly in academic writings, the primary interests of many would-be cult leaders seem to be to carve out a distinct (and hence, original) approach to management. To defend this originality, and thereby gain a place in posterity (or at least to gain a publication which will justify academic status or promotion), these writers seem to have become overly concerned with downrating, and sometimes misrepresenting, what anyone else has said, or thought, or done. (Koontz, 1962: 25)

By 1984 not much has changed:

We have recently argued . . . that the organizational sciences are severely fragmented, and that this fragmentation presents a serious obstacle to scientific growth of the field. For example, topics in introductory textbooks are so loosely interconnected that virtually any of them can be arbitrarily dropped without damaging the flow of the course . . . This is not the fault of the textbook writers but of the field itself: most research issues and themes develop, flourish, or die in essential isolation from one another. Each may speak to the very general concern of "behavior in organization," but few have much to say to one another. (Zammuto and Connolly, 1984: 30)

Pfeffer returns to the theme in 1993 in a paper setting out the benefits of paradigm development within a field, which he enumerates in considerable depth before turning to organization studies:

The study of organizations has numerous subspecialties, and these certainly vary in terms of the level of paradigm development. Nevertheless, it appears that, in general, the field of organizational studies is characterized by a fairly low level of paradigm development, particularly as compared to some adjacent social sciences such as psychology, economics, and even political science. (Pfeffer, 1993: 607)

It does not stop there. Fast-forward twenty years to 2013, to find Shepherd and Challenger (2013) writing about what they describe as the "paradigm wars" that still, they argue, sweep the field of management research. While observing that

[a]round the millennium, calls increased for the dissolution of the paradigm wars [that] . . . sought to bring discursive closure to two decades of debate surrounding the notion of paradigm(s) and incommensurability . . . [and] the paradigm wars have abated somewhat over the past 10 years, the concept of paradigm(s) remains in widespread use across a range of disciplines. (226)

A tacit assumption of many of these laments is that, ultimately, fragmentation is detrimental to the development of the field. Rather, it should be organized around a common paradigm, albeit acknowledging that the term is used in many different ways, at least twenty-one of which come from Kuhn (1970; critically and with more emphasis on gradual change: Lakatos, 1984), the *spiritus rector* of the idea of science as developing along different paradigms and their revolutionary change, himself (Masterman, 1970).

However, there is a contrary view to that notion. Perhaps Van Maanen's response to Pfeffer's plea for more paradigmatic consensus within organization and management studies puts it most succinctly:

In simple moral terms, the idea that we should somehow look toward paradigmatic consensus for our salvation is wrong. Even if such a world were possible (which it is not, see below), it would be a most uncomfortable place to reside. It would be a world with little emancipatory possibilities, a world with even tighter restrictions on who can be published, promoted, fired, celebrated, reviled than we have now. *Sturm und Drang und Tenure.*[1] The image of a large research community characterized by the kinds of traits

[1] In response to our request for illumination of this intriguing remark, Van Maanen replied: "I think what I meant [by *Sturm und Drang und Tenure*] was the anxiety and turbulence (storm and stress), both personal and collective, that the US system of tenure creates would be even further focused around a rigid view of what constitutes acceptable (tenure-able) work. The tenure system is always an uncertain and potentially blackball(able) process that no one seems altogether comfortable and satisfied with but are at wits end to find a substitute. Paradigmatic consensus – should it be possible to obtain (I think not) – would make mechanics out of us; it might make tenure slightly more predictable and easier to get over the bar if one does conventional work (the more convention the better) but less likely to reward novelty and invention. That's a 2016

Jeff [Pfeffer] associates with paradigm consensus is that of a clean California research park where nothing is out of place and all is governed by a corporate logic focused on productivity, competitive advantage and the good old bottom line. This is not scholarship. On normative grounds alone, paradigm consensus can be rejected. (Van Maanen, 1995: 689)

That said, favoring a plurality of viewpoints does not preclude an emphasis on the importance of mutual exchange and conversations across boundaries. Van Maanen recognizes that "it is pernicious and beside the point to suggest we stick to our own claustrophobic ways with each of us camped by our own totem pole. We need ways of talking across research programs and theoretical commitments" (1995: 691). This theme is echoed by Czarniawska:

After all, there are much more serious dangers in life than dissonance in organization theory. Crossing the street every day is one such instance. We may as well abandon this self-centered rhetoric and concentrate on a more practical issue: it seems that we would like to be able to talk to one another, and from time to time have an illusion of understanding what the Other is saying … What we need, I think, is not commensurability but plenty of translation. Not "translatability" as a property of a text, but "translation" as an action, in a meaning coined by Michel Serre and circulated by Michel Callon and Bruno Latour. Such translation has a meaning far beyond the linguistic one, as it concerns anything taken from one place and time, and put into another – an act which changes both the translator, and what is translated. There is no question of 'faithfulness': by definition, what has been translated is never the same again. Plenty of translation makes the field vibrant and lively, it energizes it, rather than putting it to a (commensurate) sleep." (Czarniawska, 1998: 274)

To sum up, in this chapter we are in territory that is familiar to anyone who has been following the progress of the field of management studies (and others; for a thoughtful analysis of similar issues in the field of management information systems, see Banville and Landry, 1989). One set of voices points to the disorganization of the field and the harm that this does to scientific progress; another set argues that, even if it could be done, this would result in the field being put in a straitjacket with catastrophic loss of creativity. A third set of voices argues for an intermediate position between what Knudsen (2003) calls the "specialization" trap, in which all that happens is that researchers work unimaginatively on safe, established paradigms, and the "fragmentation" trap, in which new theories proliferate faster than anyone can evaluate or compare them. However, regardless of the position one takes in terms of the need or danger of a common paradigm, it seems to be a common denominator that conversation is needed between the fragmented parts of the field and beyond (Czarniawska, 1998). But what exactly is conversation, and how can it help?

interpretation of a 1995 paper but probably close to what I might have said at the time." (John Van Maanen, personal communication, November 7, 2016)

Conversation as a Way Forward

We subscribe to the notion that scientific progress requires the free exchange of ideas, talking to each other across disciplinary, theoretical, methodical, methodological, epistemological, geographical, and ideological boundaries. Fragmentation is an obstacle to this, regardless of whether the ultimate goal is a unified paradigm or a field where a thousand flowers bloom. But is conversation, put forward by major voices (e.g. Arthur, 2008) as an important way of communicating across boundaries, a suitable candidate for this? We now address this question.

Conversation is a specific kind of communication. Three of its major characteristics important here (for a more general discussion on features of conversations, see, e.g. Thornbury and Slade, 2006; Warren, 2006) are (1) the need for establishing common ground, (2) the absence of predefined goals other than reaching understanding and strengthening social ties, and (3) the equal status of participants.

1 Need for Establishing Common Ground There are some basic requirements for achieving common ground when conversations are to unfold, none of them necessarily easy to achieve, such as a common language, the availability of time resources, or the willingness and capability of individuals to participate in a conversation (sometimes called an art in itself; see Miller, 2008). Beyond that, a crucial and arguably basic requirement for having a conversation about an object is the existence of "a temporary agreement about how they [the speakers] and their addressees are to conceptualize that object" (Brennan and Clark, 1996: 1491). Called a *conceptual pact*, this helps the partners in a conversation to reach a basic understanding about what they are talking about. In addition, situation models, i.e. "multi-dimensional representations containing information about space, time, causality, intentionality and currently relevant individuals" (Garrod and Pickering, 2004: 8; see also Zwaan and Radvansky, 1998), help to structure the situation and advise participants in the conversation about relevant dimensions and elements. In so doing, the participants potentially aim for different forms of coordination, in particular *semantic* coordination in terms of the mental models employed by the participants in the conversation; *lexical* coordination with regard to the expressions they use to refer to entities in their models; and *syntactic* coordination, which refers to the grammatical form during a conversation. Note that by no means do the coordination efforts have to be intentional. "It is important to stress that such convergence in behavior may be implicit; it need not involve any conscious or deliberate intent on the part of participants" (Branigan, Pickering, and Cleland, 2000: B14). Yet, as Conversation Theory puts it, to have an "agreement of an understanding" (Pask, 1984: 13) is crucial in order to understand each other.

2 Absence of Predefined Goals Other Than Reaching Understanding and Strengthening Social Ties Conversations have little, if any, transactional function for reaching predefined goals but are open for different types of outcome, which often emerge in the course of the conversation. Two implicitly important results, though, are understanding and strengthening social ties. Regarding the former, conversation builds strongly on communicative action, with reaching understanding located at its center. As Habermas (1981) puts it: "*Verständigung wohnt als Telos der menschlichen Sprache inne* [Reaching understanding is the inherent telos (aim) of human speech]" (387; for the English version: Habermas, 1984: 287). This is a substantial difference from, for example, strategic action where achieving individual goals that actors bring to the situation is most important. Of course, this does not preclude the possibility that conversations between career scholars from different areas of the field can later turn into a discourse (Howarth, 2010), i.e. "processes of argumentation and dialogue in which the claims implicit in the speech act are tested for their rational justifiability as true, correct or authentic" (Bohman and Rehg, 2014), where "right/wrong" rather than "understand/not understand" is the guiding difference. Yet in essence "[c]onversations have no pre-defined goal(s) and the negotiation of topical coherence is shared between participants" (Warren, 2006: 13). The interpersonal function of conversation crucially involves establishing and maintaining social ties rather than achieving individual goals for one's own benefit (Thornbury and Slade, 2006). Having a conversation with others mutually acknowledges that one regards the other as a person worthy of devoting time and energy to and, for better or worse, that the conversation can lead to new insights about the conversation partner. This strengthens the relationship as it provides a basis for future exchange, even in the case that at an emotional level bonding has not been strengthened.

3 Equal Status of Participants A symmetrical relationship between participating interlocutors, i.e. actors taking part in the exchange, is a further constitutive characteristic of a conversation (Thornbury and Slade, 2006). In contrast to other communicative situations such as bureaucratic encounters, nurse–patient consultations, or court hearings where hierarchical, asymmetrical relationships are an integral part of the situation, conversations have little or no structurally prescribed asymmetries. Of course, there will be power differentials emerging from inevitable differences in knowledge about a subject, conversational skills, interpersonal attraction, or physical appearance. However, these differentials are more ad hoc and fluid and not an essential characteristic. Basically, the status of the participants in a conversation is perceived to be equal, and they share responsibility for successful outcomes and progress (Warren, 2006).

These three important characteristics of conversations – conceptual pacts, strengthening social ties, and a symmetrical relationship – make this form of exchange well suited for communicating in a fragmented field. Putting interlocutors on an equal footing, detecting conceptual pacts, and jointly defining situation models are all about discovering common ground. This view of conversation is of an exchange among equals and not a parochial endeavor in which the major agenda is discrediting deviant ways and conquering theoretical and empirical territory. In addition, the emphasis on building and sustaining social ties rather than achieving an interest-related outcome makes a fruitful exchange of ideas more likely.

Because conversations typically take place in complex situations and because the situations in which conversations take place across scientific boundaries are especially complex, it is helpful for a conversation to happen in such a situation to have some kind of simplifications that are accepted by both interlocutors. Ideal types are widely used to provide this kind of simplification, and we turn to them next.

Ideal Types Facilitating Conversation

One of the benefits of examining the field of career studies through the SCF is that, as we show later in this chapter, it allows us to construct a number of ideal types of single career studies. These ideal types help career researchers see where the foci of studies are by simplifying their complexity. Ideal types experienced their breakthrough in the social sciences through the work of German sociologist Max Weber (1968 [Original 1922]: 190 ff.). The term is used in a variety of senses, but the one we use here is an idealized representation of a concept, of a kind that does not exist in the real world but that helps us make sense of that real world. It can be used to denote an abstraction of something that is empirically observable. So, for example, Barley (1996) describes how new models of work and of the relations of production allow us to construct new ideal-typical occupations:

An ideal-typical occupation is an abstraction that captures key attributes of a cluster of occupations. As Weber noted, ideal types are useful not because they are descriptively accurate – actual instances rarely evince all of the attributes of an ideal type – but because they serve as models that assist in thinking about social phenomena. (pp. 406–407)

More commonly, however, ideal types are used in connection with taxonomies of social constructs. Van de Ven, Ganco, and Hinings (2013) list a number of ideal types from the literature, including March and Simon's (1958) and Thompson's (1967) types of programs for organizing, Burns and Stalker's (1961) distinction between organic and mechanistic structures, Mintzberg's

(1979) five organizational designs, and Miles and Snow's (1978) types of organizational design (prospector, analyzer, defender, reactor). Nelson and Nielsen (2000) describe three ideal types of inside counsel (lawyers employed by commercial operations, the types being cops, counsels, entrepreneurs); Swanson (1999) distinguishes between two ideal types of corporate social interactions, value neglect and value attunement. Arguably, the rational decision-making model is another ideal type, one that has provided a useful straw person for decision theorists for many years.

Ideal types have been widely used in the career literature, too, to denote various kinds of career taxonomies. For example, Nicholson (1996) describes traditional and new paradigms of career as being ideal types because they have a

mythical and unreal quality … The traditional model was only rarely found in a fully articulated form. AT&T's elaborate career system is a much quoted example. Yet even in such classic cases there were always people who would find the model did not apply–for example, specialist professionals, plateaued managers, and many women. (p. 42)

Similarly, King, Burke and Pemberton (2005: 982) talk about traditional and boundaryless careers as ideal types in the sense that "neither adequately captures the complex interaction between individual agency and structural constraints that circumscribes a person's career"; Mayrhofer (2001) describes four ideal type organizational international career logics; Inkson *et al.* (2012) also consider describing the boundaryless career as an ideal type but dismiss the idea because the construct's boundaries are too fuzzy.

It is important for present purposes to emphasize that the "ideal" in the term "ideal type" does not mean to imply desirability, as Weber himself wryly remarked in a letter to a colleague:

That you have linguistic doubts about the "ideal type" distresses me in my paternal vanity. But my view is that, if we speak of Bismarck not as the "ideal" among Germans but as the "ideal type" of [being] German, we do not mean anything "exemplary" as such but are saying that he possessed certain German, essentially indifferent and perhaps even unpleasant qualities … (letter to Heinrich Rickert from April 28, 1905, in Hübinger and Lepsius, 2015: 470; English translation in Radkau, 2009: 260)

So the ideal types we list here do not describe specific forms of career scholarship as ideals against which all real career scholarship will emerge wanting and inadequate. Because the SCF talks in broad terms about condition, social space, and time, it is easy to draw the erroneous inference that an ideal type career research project would examine all aspects of the condition of the career actor, within a global and multifaceted social space, against a background of historic time approached in any way that time can be conceived of in a social setting. It would also be easy to draw the, again erroneous, inference that any career research that fails to address each of these in its fullness is inadequate. Of course, for practical reasons no single study can do that. Every researcher must make choices about what to focus on and what to leave out; otherwise nobody would ever get anything done. The ideal types serve here a different purpose, namely to help identify distinctions between different types of career scholarship in order, as we note previously, to facilitate conversation within and between them.

The ideal types we derive from the SCF emerge from the observation that although, as we argue, career scholarship involves the application of all three perspectives, not all such scholarship necessarily places equal emphasis on all three. Depending on the focus of any given topic area, studies within it are likely to place greater emphasis on only one or two of the perspectives. That is not to say that the other perspectives are ignored, but simply that they play a more background role. In rather the same way that Mintzberg (1979) constructs a set of ideal types of organization based on the varying degree of emphasis the different types place on elements of his basic model of organization, we distinguish between three ideal typical forms of career research that we call focused, bivalent, and balanced. While in the following we will illustrate these ideal types with examples of single studies, they also can apply to larger discourses such as fields within career studies.

Focused Focused career research concentrates primarily on one perspective of the SCF while placing lesser emphasis on the other two dimensions. Two examples at the level of individual studies may suffice. Career studies focusing on the link between personality and different types of career success are examples of focused career research emphasizing the ontic aspect of careers. While they vary in the importance they give to factors located in the social space and to the dimension of time in which careers are embedded, their primary interest lies in personality and/or factors closely linked with the person.

A well-cited piece by Seibert and Kraimer (2001) examines the relationship between the Big Five personality dimensions and extrinsic as well as intrinsic career success, measured as promotion and salary, and career satisfaction, respectively. Their focus clearly is on the effects of the Big Five on career success. However, in controlling for what they call "other career related variables," they acknowledge the importance of the other perspectives for their research interest. Indeed, they find, among other things, that the negative effect of agreeableness on salary was moderated by occupation, in SCF terms an element of the social space.

Arguably, the analysis by Hesketh (2000) looking at time-discounting principles in career-related choices and focusing on the temporal perspective also reflects this ideal type of focused career research. It speaks to the discussion about job choices and their anticipated future consequences, how individuals discount the value of a delayed outcome, and the role that time and probability information plays in career-related decisions. The two experimental studies in the paper look at choices related to student union fees and scholarships and at the differences in time discounting between career counseling novices and experts when giving advice about job options. Clearly, the interest is the temporal dimension, using the concrete issues – partly ontic, partly spatial – only as a vehicle.

Bivalent Bivalent career research gives roughly equal weight to two perspectives and lesser emphasis to the third. A good example of putting a dual emphasis on the spatial and temporal aspects can be found in studies of career timetables (Lawrence, 1984), examining the rate (temporal) at which people move through hierarchical levels within organizations or professions (spatial). This points to various forms of intra-organizational mobility analysis focusing on structural characteristics of the organization and career trajectories, a classical topic of career research.

A highly influential contribution by White (1970) looks at promotions from within and ponders the consequences of an internal promotion. He argues that the subsequent set of transitions is not a set of vacancies, but, in effect, is one single vacancy, triggered by the original job move, propagating through the organization. Developing mathematical models to analyze mobility within organizations and to measure vacancy chains, understood as chains of contingent events, he empirically demonstrates the relevance of his considerations by using data from three churches as organizational settings.

Focusing on the temporal and ontic aspect, a classic study by Staw *et al.* (1986) argues for a more dispositional approach, explicitly countering calls for greater situationalism in organizational research. The study uses three waves of a longitudinal sample (Guidance Study, Berkeley Growth Study, Oakland Growth Study) coming from the Intergenerational Studies effort following individuals over a span of fifty years with five time periods under scrutiny (early adolescence, twelve to fourteen years; late adolescence, fifteen to eighteen years; and three adult periods more or less evenly distributed between thirty and fifty years of age). The study shows that dispositional measures predicted job attitudes over a span of fifty years and is an excellent example of a temporal/ontic study.

Balanced Balanced career research gives roughly equal weight to all three perspectives of the SCF. While there might be – and often is – a primary focus, the other perspectives are prominently present and do play a major role in the design of studies and in explaining the findings. Again, two illustrations may suffice.

The widely cited study by Rosenbaum (1979b) analyzes intra-organizational mobility patterns in a large corporation. Covering a thirteen-year time span, this study builds two conflicting conceptual viewpoints: a basically ahistorical path independence model with contest and sponsored mobility and a tournament model that takes into account the historical, i.e. developments over time where careers are seen as a sequence of competition, with each competition having consequences for the next round, usually putting the winners and losers on different tracks from then on. From a spatial perspective, the organization and the various tournament rules provide the social context; the temporal perspective emphasizes the historical, path dependent quality – or the lack of it – of career trajectories; the ontic perspective emphasizes status, the prestige assigned to people based on their position and operationalized as level category that shows the linkages between the spatial and the ontic perspective.

Going beyond organization, Higgins (2005) looks at the effects that career imprints have on the careers of these individuals. Imprints are the cumulative outcome of strategy, structure, and culture of employers for their executives' connections, capabilities, cognition, and confidence. These career imprints, an ontic element, travel with the individuals across different contexts such as other firms or industries (spatial) and not only affect the career trajectories of the individuals over time (temporal) but can also have effects on other organizations or even whole industries, e.g. by transferring certain views or practices from one context to another.

Graphically, one can depict these ideal types as follows. The inner circle indicates that in all career studies, the three perspectives are present at least as a nucleus. The outer circle indicates where the actual emphasis lies (Figure 6.1).

In principle, we could have specified seven rather than three ideal types: three focused ideal types, one for each perspective; three bivalent, one for each possible pairing of perspectives; and one balanced. However, loosely applying one version of Ockham's razor – enough but not too much or, more precisely, *numquam ponenda est pluralitas sine necessitate* (plurality is never to be posited without necessity; Ockam, 1962: Book 1, page 391, column A, line 42 [Original 1495: Book 1, Dist. 27, Qu. 2, K]) – leads us to the three basic ideal types that serve best for our purpose, facilitating conversation in a fragmented field.

Up to now in this chapter we have identified the need for exchange across various boundaries of fragmented fields such as career studies. We have proposed that conversation with some of its major requirements and characteristics – establishing common ground, emphasis on mutual understanding and strengthening social ties rather than reaching predefined goals, and equal status of participants – is a suitable candidate for such an exchange and have outlined three ideal types of career research following from the SCF. We now show how the SCF supports different kinds of conversations. We start with conversations between interlocutors pursuing different research interests, using examples from the OMC field.

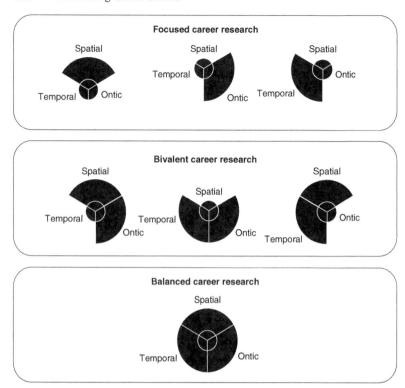

Figure 6.1 Ideal types of career research

Conversations between Career Fields

Conversation between fragmented areas boxed in by specific boundaries is facilitated by a framework that allows researchers from different traditions and fields to talk to each other and frame their ideas in ways that make it easier for others to understand (Newman, 2006). The SCF offers such a common language and framework that can serve as a crystallizing point for shared conceptual pacts and situation models and the starting point for an exchange on an equal footing. As such, it rattles the cage of fragmentation. The SCF is specific enough to allow researchers from different fields with different interests and approaches to find common ground. At the same time, it is generic enough that it does minimal preformation in terms of theoretical perspective and epistemological, methodological, and methodical assumptions, and it emphasizes the symmetrical relationships between different members in the field.

The SCF acknowledges that insight into careers, in the broadest sense in which we use the term, is distributed between many pockets of research across a large number of disciplines, fields, and discourses as well as the regulative, cognitive, and cultural achievements that disciplines and fields provide. As with a discipline, it instils those using it "with what the sociologists [sic] Johan Asplund calls 'aspect vision,' which allows them to see certain dimensions of a phenomenon [and] offers its members a particular set of lenses, which enables them to see the issue more sharply" (Buanes and Jentoft, 2009: 450). As a tool of "interactional expertise" (Collins and Evans, 2007), the SCF opens up the road for not putting too narrow a limit on issues such as the subject focus, assumptions about the issues one studies, models and methods used, and the audience addressed (Lélé and Norgaard, 2005: 972).

Of course, very different types of conversation can and will come up. Imagine conversations between researchers working broadly within the same ideal type using the same perspectives. If we are both doing bivalent work, with an interest primarily in the ontic and spatial perspectives, then we are likely to share some basic definitions about the kinds of things we are interested in. The main problems we are likely to face are, first, that we are interested in different aspects of each perspective and, second, that we may have different words for them – we speak different sociolects.

Conversations between scholars working with different sets of perspectives, or different ideal types, introduce additional complications. Beyond the problems just mentioned to do with being interested in different aspects of a perspective and different sociolects, the interlocutors here face the difficulty that one or both will regard as fundamental something that simply does not figure in the other's thinking.

Facilitating conversation across fields is not the universal remedy or even the most important enabler for exchange across various kinds of boundaries. "Institutional impediments related to incentives, funding, and priorities given disciplinary versus interdisciplinary work [and p]rofessional impediments related to hiring, promotion, status, and recognition" (Brewer, 1999: 335; see also Youngblood, 2007) remain largely untouched. Likewise, while the SCF tries to avoid any kind of conceptual imperialism, the issue of power is always present since "[t]he search for 'the perfect language' or a 'meta-orientation system' is a search for power rather than comprehension" (Czarniawska, 1998: 273). Yet we argue that the SCF *helps*; it does not reveal things that would otherwise be invisible, but it makes them easier to see.

Following up on this general argument, we now illustrate the potential of the SCF with regard to establishing and supporting conversation in more detail.

Establishing Common Ground

The three perspectives and the ideal types offer a conceptually founded view of seemingly very different activities, allowing participants to detect a new kind of order and common ground at a more abstract level beyond discussing research questions and objects, theories, and methods. Researchers getting into such a conversation can easily identify their relative emphases and basic interests and detect commonalities despite profound differences with regard to constructs, theories, and methods used. This can lead to a shared conceptual pact and situational model that provides the basis for exchange.

A good example of this is a stream of research examining the topic of personality and career success from the perspective of I/O psychology (Judge and Kammeyer-Mueller, 2007) and another one looking at occupational choice from the perspective of vocational psychology (Savickas, 2007). Although the latter field is much broader than the former, in the sense that it also deals with the decision-making process that the individual goes through in making an occupational choice and the counseling interventions that can help this choice process, it is still fundamentally concerned with the same thing as the personality and career success field. Each attempts to predict career success on the basis of the career actor's personality. Yet the way they conceptualize career success is markedly different. The OMC topic area linking personality and career success takes a clearly ontic perspective and uses dependent variables such as income or career satisfaction. In contrast, the vocational discussion emphasizes crossing spatial boundaries, in particular into specific vocations, and the individual–job fit. Consequently, they represent different ideal types, the OMC approach being ontic focused and the vocational ontic-spatial bivalent. The temporal does play a role, in the sense that career success is always subsequent to personality measurements, but it does not emerge as an issue of primary importance to either.

Perhaps not surprisingly, then, out of the 147 unique references in total cited by the two chapters listed previously that appear in the same handbook (Gunz and Peiperl, 2007a), only one is common to both. In the face of this evidence, there does not seem to be much conversation between the two. A more detailed analysis using the SCF leads to a structured and analytically detached diagnosis suggesting why this might be the case, as we see next.

Leaving aside for the moment the different role that the spatial perspective plays in the two approaches, the ontic perspective provides the most obvious points of contrast between them. To oversimplify in order to make the point, conversation between these two is complicated by superficially similar but actually different applications of the ontic perspective. They are superficially similar in the sense that they are both interested in predicting career success from a knowledge of the actor's personality. But the two literatures differ strikingly in the constructs that they use to examine the condition of career actors, i.e. how they conceptualize personality and career success.

Targeting personality, the personality/career success literature typically works with personality variables such as the five-factor model (FFM: Judge, Heller, and Mount, 2002), proactive personality, agentic and communal orientation, and core self-evaluations such as locus of control, self-esteem, and self-confidence (Judge and Kammeyer-Mueller, 2007). The vocational literature employs a large variety of instruments based on varying approaches to establishing person–environment fit (Savickas, 2007). Some assess the qualifications of the person for a particular job (complementary fit), while others assess their similarity to people who are doing the job (supplementary fit). Examples of these instruments include the Campbell Interest and Skills Survey, the Strong Interest Inventory, and the Kuder Occupational Interest Inventory (Savickas and Taber, 2006). Holland's (1959) RIASEC model has become extremely influential in assessing both personality and positions in the vocational literature, and the instruments in common use now typically use its framework.

Turning to career success, the personality/career success literature normally uses standard constructs for viewing objective and subjective success (Judge and Kammeyer-Mueller, 2007). The most commonly used objective career success criteria are income, number of promotions, and occupational status, while subjective success is most often measured in terms of the actor's satisfaction with their career (ibid.). The vocational literature, by contrast, as noted earlier, looks for person–environment fit: how well the person fits either with the requirements of the job or with other people doing it (Savickas, 2007). In a 2013 review of the vocational field, for example, career success does not figure prominently in the topics of interest to vocational scholars and not at all in practice articles (Sampson et al., 2014).

To summarize, then, the SCF allows us to identify with some precision basic characteristics of a conversation between members of the topic area/field. On the one hand, the two we have been discussing here do indeed have a great deal in common. For each, their real interest lies in the ontic. In addition, their use of the ontic reflects the aims of the respective topic area/field. The conceptual pact, then, involves agreeing that each is interested broadly in personality and career success, and the conversation can then proceed by examining why each views these constructs as it does.

On the other hand, the SCF also helps us understand why such a conversation might be difficult. While they are both interested in the link between personality and different forms of career success, applying the SCF reveals that their operationalization of two features of the ontic perspective is incommensurable, that the words and concepts each topic area/field uses have different meanings, and that there is very little connection between them in this regard. By being able to see familiar "facts" in a new light through the SCF, it supplies additional grounds for the conceptual pact between interlocutors from the two areas/ fields. Rather than asking the bland question of why is it that two sets of researchers working on similar aspects of careers have so little in common, the SCF provides a conceptual framework that leads the interlocutors to focus in a nonthreatening way on where they are different and what they have in common.

In a similar vein, the SCF can also help establish common ground in cases of more segregated fields of research. While the break between the personality/ career success and vocational literatures is one of the more remarkable within career studies, that between OMC and life-course studies is, if anything, an even more remarkable example of a lack of conversation. Until recently, work on the life course went to considerable lengths to avoid the use of the term "career," and when it did so it did it in a way that made it clear that life-course researchers regarded the career as a subset of the life course. For example, Volume I of the authoritative *Handbook of the Life Course* (Mortimer and Shanahan, 2003a) has just one reference to "career" in its index, in which career is defined as "an individual's sequence of jobs held across the socioeconomic life cycle" (Pallas, 2003: 167). Volume II (Shanahan, Mortimer, and Kirkpatrick Johnson, 2016) has many references to the term "career" throughout but almost no reference to the OMC literature. The life course, by contrast, is "the age-graded, socially-embedded sequence of roles that connect the phases of life" (Mortimer and Shanahan, 2003b: xi). The two concepts are distinguished by the comparatively restricted sense in which life-course scholars appear to think of career:

The concept of "career" was another way of linking roles across the life course. These careers are based on role histories in education, work, or family. Though readily applicable to multiple domains of life, these models most often focused on a single domain, oversimplifying to a great extent the lives of people who were in reality dealing with multiple roles simultaneously. Moreover, much like the family cycle, the concept of career did not locate individuals in historical context or identify their temporal location within the life span. In other words, the available models of social pathways lacked mechanisms connecting lives with biographical and historical time, and the changes in social life that spanned this time. (Elder, Johnson, and Crosnoe, 2003: 7)

Perhaps as a result, not only do life-course researchers hardly ever refer to the OMC literature (and many to the term "career"), but career researchers return the compliment by being, on the whole, oblivious of the life-course literature. For example, two major handbooks of career theory/studies (Gunz and Peiperl, 2007a; Arthur *et al.*, 1989b) identify the life course solely with life-course psychologists such as Levinson *et al.* (1978), who examined the stages of lives of men in the USA, or the developmental models of writers such as Alderfer (1972) or Vaillant (1977).

Table 6.1 *Life-course theory paradigmatic principles (from Elder, Johnson, and Crosnoe, 2003: 11–13) and the SCF*

Principle	SCF interpretation
1. The principle of life-span development: human development and aging are lifelong processes	Ontic and temporal
2. The principle of agency: individuals construct their own life course through the choices and actions they take within the opportunities and constraints of history and social circumstance	Ontic, temporal, and spatial
3. The principle of time and place: the life course of individuals is embedded and shaped by the historical times and places they experience over their lifetime	Temporal and spatial
4. The principle of timing: the developmental antecedents and consequences of life transitions, events, and behavioral patterns vary according to their timing in a person's life	Ontic and temporal
5. The principle of linked lives: lives are lived interdependently and sociohistorical influences are expressed through this network of shared relationships	Extended heuristic model (Chapter 4)

Yet a strong case could be made for the life-course field to be an excellent example of what we call here balanced career research. Elder, Johnson, and Crosnoe (2003: 10ff.) identify five "paradigmatic principles in life-course theory," which map on to the SCF remarkably well (Table 6.1).

Indeed the life course as defined in the life-course literature resembles at its core the career as we define it in Chapter 3: quite simply, its canvas is the actor's entire lifetime to date and all of the social and geographic space occupied by the actor during that time. So, to follow the logic of our argument in that chapter, "career" as typically conceived of particularly in the OMC literature is pretty much exactly as it is seen by life-course theorists: a subset of the life course, over a limited time (the time span where one is part of the workforce) and involving only that part of the social space occupied by the actor's work roles, possibly extended to those (e.g. home life) that interfere with work roles.

Using the language of the SCF, we tend to see more clearly why life-course scholars show little interest in the careers literature: they seem to see it as unduly constrained in its application of the three perspectives. It also explains why career scholars apparently show little interest in the life-course literature. The life-course literature talks about things – early childhood, disadvantaged or unemployed people – who are outside the temporal zone or social space defined by the conventional (post-Chicago) careers literature (see later in this chapter for a fuller account of what we mean by post-Chicago). Yet the temporal zone of interest to careers scholars is creeping forward in time, now encompassing, for example, retirement (Sargent, Lee, Martin, and Zikic, 2013) or interest in work-life balance (Williams, Berdahl, and Vandello, 2016). So the intellectual boundaries that career scholars work with are becoming more permeable than previously, suggesting that they may well find conversation with life-course scholars profitable. If only, that is, the conversation could be established.

For this to happen, a conceptual pact needs to be established, and the SCF-based analysis we have just conducted makes it obvious what that pact should be. By framing both fields in terms of the three perspectives, the interlocutors establish conceptual agreement about what it is that they do: each applies the three perspectives to the study of people, but one (life course) has a broader definition than the other (career) of the social space and time that are of interest. So the life-course scholar may help the career scholar by suggesting additional constructs that might be of use in understanding what is going on, while the career scholar might help the life-course scholar by providing more detail about the constructs that the life-course scholar is trying to apply, particularly those to do with organizations.

Overall, the theme connecting our examples with regard to the role of the SCF in establishing common ground can be summarized as follows. In order to establish conversation between career scholars working in different fields of a fragmented proto-field (Chapter 1) or between scholars working in ostensibly different fields that have a great deal in common, it is necessary to establish a conceptual pact between interlocutors. The SCF provides an approach to doing this by offering a way of moving to a more abstract level so that the particularities of each topic area or field's discourse cease to be an obstacle to communication. That is not to say that everyone needs to abandon their normal way of describing the concepts and constructs with which they work. But by mapping the concepts and constructs on to the SCF perspectives, they can establish the common ground – the conceptual pact – that helps connect their conceptual framework with that of their interlocutor.

Emphasizing Understanding, Evenhandedness, and Social Ties

Beyond establishing common ground, the SCF also pushes conversations between researchers with an interest in various ideal types of career research toward understanding the ideas of others. As a broad heuristic framework, the SCF neither requires nor allows one to judge specific studies to be better or worse than others. Rather, it helps participants in such a conversation to establish a common frame for description and clarification of what they do, thus generating the possibility of mutual understanding. This explicitly discourages the standard academic game of deploring other research only because it either emphasizes different perspectives or uses different constructs and operationalizations within the same perspective or ideal types. Rather, it provides generic categories for mutual, descriptive exchange. There is not per se a right/wrong or better/worse way of exploring the relative emphases of the three perspectives. The joint search concentrates on descriptive information and, hopefully, mutual understanding of what the other does and deems important.

Take the example of two researchers with a clearly bivalent career research interest. Let us assume one is a member of the Cross-Cultural Collaboration on Contemporary Careers (5C; www.5C.careers) looking at the role of various contextual settings differentiated by cultural and institutional characteristics for careers and pointing toward a qualitative eleven-country study (Shen *et al.*, 2015a) that shows how different contexts bring forth differences in what individuals view as career success and how this relates to organizational HRM policies and practices. Its emphasis, then, is clearly ontic-spatial. The other belongs to a group investigating the relationship between general mental ability (GMA), human capital, and career success. She admires a study that draws on data from the National Longitudinal Survey of Youth, covers a time span of twenty-eight years, follows the development of individuals based on yearly (1979–1994) or biannual (from 1995 onward) interviews, and proposes a crucial role for GMA in the form of more intelligent individuals not only reaching higher levels of extrinsic career success by getting earlier promotions but also achieving steeper career success trajectories that, in turn, constitute the basis for a self-reinforcing cycle where skills are amplified and contribute to greater career success (Judge *et al.*, 2010). The emphasis of this work is evidently ontic-temporal.

In such a situation, it is not uncommon for academic conversations to head toward a contagious self-enhancing exchange bordering on boasting and openly or tacitly leading to an evaluative, implicitly or explicitly judgmental comparison along the lines of academic superiority and astuteness. Sample sizes, sophistication of methods of analysis, publication channels, and reputation of coauthors fuel a debate that, sooner or later, is likely to end in an implicit "winner-loser" division between the participants in the exchange. This is clearly less likely to happen within the realm of the SCF. As a framework, it does not qualify very well for a conversational turn toward "winning-losing." Within the SCF, it is hard to imagine building a credible claim that "ontic-spatial," as is the case with 5C, is a better form of bivalent research than the "ontic-temporal" emphasis of the study on general mental ability. The SCF also does not imply that one of these bivalent approaches or even balanced studies constitute the "ultimate coronation" of career research. Sure enough, these claims can be made. But they have to come from outside the SCF and require additional arguments, assumptions and – often implicit – value judgments. At its core, the SCF invites systematically guided inquiry to better understand what the other does, to dig deeper and to get a better map about the respective efforts with regard to condition, boundary, and time on different levels of social complexity.

Focusing on understanding rather than proving one's own superiority and being relaxed about various kinds of outcomes of the conversation also shifts the focus toward the personal relationship. Not only are such an exchange and its tacit evenhandedness compatible with the rhetoric of science being a joint effort of equals. They also at least implicitly convey the basic notions of esteem and acceptance. "Here we are, two professionals interested in partly similar, partly different aspects of careers, having an informed conversation detecting commonalities and differences while referring to a framework that constitutes a starting point for common ground, generic enough to capture our views and classify our emphases while not in itself promoting better/worse or right/wrong judgments" – this or a similar inner image of individuals participating in such a conversation has the potential to strengthen social ties by providing common-alities and strengthening self-esteem.

Identity-Related Conversations: A Narrative of the OMC Field's History

"Who are we and where do we come from?" – this is a topic not only of melancholic late-night bar conversations dealing with the mysteries of personal life but also of ongoing debates in scientific fields. Attributing roles, causality, and influence to scholars deemed important in the field, schools of thought, and publications are but a few ways of making sense of what has happened in the past and what that means for today's scientific endeavors. Of course, there is no objective truth to be reached. History is always in the making, told as a result of various narratives offering different interpretations, and usually overtly or subtly driven by a political agenda or by personal or scientific interest.

In this section, we provide a narrative of the OMC field that informs these kinds of conversations. Using the SCF and the related ideal types, we invoke the notion of a present-day careers researcher reading earlier work, trying to connect with it through the medium of an imaginary conversation with the authors of that work, and making sense of what has happened in the past. Given obvious space limits as well as the fact that we are part of the field, this narrative is a very partial account. Our purpose is simply to show how the SCF and, related to it, the ideal types provide a useful analytical tool when constructing a narrative about the OMC field.

The Chicago School

It has been suggested that the current field of career studies has its roots in three intellectual traditions coming from, respectively, sociology, vocational psychology, and developmental psychology (Moore *et al.*, 2007). These differing traditions have left their mark on the field, most notably in what is sometimes described as the almost unbridged gulf between organizational and vocational career studies to which we refer in Chapter 1 (Collin and Patton, 2009). The story we shall be telling here, which we acknowledge is a partial one leaving out a lot of interesting threads, focuses on the seminal role of the Massachusetts Institute of Technology (MIT) school in the 1970s. It ignores career research happening elsewhere in the USA, most notably at Cornell (Vardi, 2006; Dyer, 1976), and outside North America (for one national example, Germany, see, e.g. Domsch and Gerpott, 1986; Gerpott, Domsch, and Keller, 1986; Berthel and Koch, 1985; Eckardstein, 1971). In order to do so, we need to take one further step back in time to examine another school of thought, coming from the Chicago Department of Sociology, that plays a key role in the way that the MIT group's ideas developed (Barley, 1989).

The 1930s were a difficult time in both Europe and North America, both economically and politically. They also saw the rise of large industrial bureaucracies on both sides of the Atlantic and, with that trend, an increase in the number of people making their careers in these bureaucracies (Hughes, 1937). The sociologist Everett C. Hughes returned to his PhD alma mater, the Department of Sociology at the University of Chicago, in 1938, where there was a tradition of producing "ethnographies of deviant subcultures based on the life histories of people who partook of the subculture. Notable among these were Anderson's (1923) study of hobo life, Cressey's (1932) description of taxi-dance halls, and Sutherland's (1937) work on professional thieves" (Barley, 1989: 43). Hughes, as a student of his mentor, Robert E. Park (whom he quoted "all the time" to his students; Becker, 1999: 7), developed his interest in the effect on the person of moving through and between what he termed "institutional offices" (Hughes, 1937). The so-called "Chicago school," a term much criticized by one of its members, Howard S. Becker, who tells the story (Becker, 1999) of a typical academic department in which colleagues are at loggerheads about their various theoretical and methodological approaches, produced a long stream of research on careers, where the career is seen as encompassing the person's entire life (as we note in Chapter 3).

In SCF terms, it is a classic example of balanced research. The ethnography is rich, describing the people, their contexts, and the stages through which their careers progress. As we see in Chapter 2, Hughes views careers both subjectively and objectively. Subjectively and from an ontic perspective, the Chicago sociologists are interested in the meanings that the people they study attribute to their careers (Barley, 1989). Objectively and spatially, they are interested in the institutional forms in which their subjects make their careers and how they move through these forms. And temporally, they are fascinated by the stages through which their subjects pass as their careers progress (perhaps the best-known of these studies being Roth, 1963); the concept of status passage (Glaser and Strauss, 1971) is central to their thinking.

1960s and 1970s: The Age of the Organization

Societal and Economic Developments Both the 1960s and the 1970s were turbulent times in the Western industrialized world, which, at least at that time, dominated the societal and economic developments across the globe. At the societal level, many countries of the Western industrialized world in the 1960s still felt the aftermath of World War II, which had raged until 1945. However, new developments were starting to develop in the early 1960s and were seeing full daylight at the end of this decade. Most notably, three developments have to be mentioned. First, the 1968 movement emerged. Self-realization and self-development, the importance of the individual as part of a more communitarian society, the so-called sexual revolution including the emergence of the birth control pill, and skepticism of the establishment and the long-standing order emphasizing well-established hierarchies are but major cornerstones of a societal movement that laid the groundwork for many developments in later years. Second, and linked to the developments just mentioned, the civil rights movement gained momentum. Rosa Parks and her "transgression" when refusing to be seated in the colored section of a bus in Montgomery, Alabama, on December 1, 1955, ignited a freedom movement in the USA that lasted well into the 1960s. Third, the Cold War between the Soviet Union and its satellite states and the Western democratic world, in particular the USA – more broadly between a communist and a capitalist view of the world – was in full swing in the 1960s. Major occurrences such as the Cuban Missile crisis in 1962 and the invasion of Czechoslovakia by the armies of the Warsaw Pact in 1968 are two primary examples. In addition, the Vietnam war, which continued until the fall of Saigon in April 1975, testifies to this basic tension. In the 1970s, the women's movement gained great momentum, paving the way for various waves of feminism still having large effects on society today.

Economically, the 1960s and '70s were the heyday of large multinational companies impacting business around the globe. Industry icons such as Unilever, IBM, General Motors, and British Petroleum were global players. Basically, optimism regarding postwar growth and economic prosperity dominated. However, the first signs of skepticism emerged. Most notably, these included first doubts about the positive aspects of growth voiced in a widely acclaimed report of the Club of Rome conjuring up the new concept of limits of growth (Meadows, Meadows, Randers, and Behrens, 1972) and the oil shock in

1973. The latter also introduced renewed doubts about Keynesian politics and offered an inroad for neoliberal economic theory and politics due to fears of stagflation.

Two themes from these macro-developments are relevant for understanding what happened in the career discourse. First, organizations, in particular large organizations, were a major element of the economies. Spreading across national and cultural boundaries, they seemed to be the role model for a new and bright future. Second, the individual and their development, often linked to self-realization and agentic determination of one's life course as opposed to being organization men and, increasingly, women, received new attention in the societal discourse. As we shall argue later on, these themes were instrumental for the focus on organizations and on time in much of the career discourse of this period.

Social Science Discourse The period of the mid-1960s to the mid-1970s was not only a time of substantial change in the societal and economic fabric of the Western industrialized world. It was also a time when major theoretical breakthroughs of the 1950s bore fruit and new seminal works emerged on organizations, individuals, and their relationship, influential far beyond the decade. These include "radical" new ways of theorizing organizations, the role of the social/individual in organizations, and individual behavior. Many of these insights were theoretical cornerstones of current work and serve as benchmarks until today. It is hardly pure coincidence that both the Carnegie Foundation's report on university-college programs in business administration (Pierson, 1959) and the Gordon and Howell report (Gordon and Howell, 1959) on higher education for business point out a number of substantial weaknesses in the contemporary educational system in the USA. Among other things, they recommend a stronger anchoring of organization studies in social science and mathematics. Although not causal, these calls are at least partly reflected in the major theoretical steps within the scientific discourse that follow.

In a nutshell, the major works in this area get rid of an overly simplistic, machinelike model of individual actors and organizations. They emphasize the social element, at least partially questioning an unbroken belief in objective insight and truth, and underscore the manifold individual and social filters when constructing reality. From a management theory perspective, the relationship between the individual and the organization and the organization-individual-(mis)fit are prominent themes. While space prohibits a full account, a few examples may suffice.

Conceptualizing Organizations In the footsteps of earlier landmark publications summarizing, critiquing, and synthesizing the respective state of affairs in previous decades (in particular Barnard, 1971 [Original 1938]; Simon, 1957

[Original 1947]), March and Simon (1958) published their seminal work on organizations. They go beyond the view that hierarchy is simply a chain of command and emphasize its information processing function as well as point toward the limits of rationality ("bounded rationality") when it comes to decision making. Other early works published in Anglo-Saxon countries address the difference between mechanistic and organic organizations (Burns and Stalker, 1961); pick up the issues of charisma, power, and compliance (Etzioni, 1961); or discuss the tensions between hierarchy and competence or authority and ability/specialization (Thompson, 1961). Works like these pave the way for a stream of ideas about theorizing organizations in the 1960s and the 1970s. By means of example rather than completeness, these include the role of structure (Blau and Schoenherr, 1962) and formal organization (Blau and Scott, 1962); rethinking organizational decision making and moving it further away from the realm of pure rationality toward uncertainty avoidance, quasi-resolution of conflicts, and organizational learning (Cyert and March, 1963) or comparing it to a garbage can with retrospective rationality applied in organized anarchies (March and Olsen, 1976); the limits of classical management principles along Tayloristic lines and the role of production technology for explaining structure and leadership (Woodward, 1965); discarding the concept of organization as a solid block and favoring organizing as a dynamic process along the lines of evolutionary theory with a focus on the double interact between Person and Other (Weick, 1969); viewing hierarchy or internal organization as the superior mode of allocation under conditions of market failure and where trust is required for exchange to occur (Williamson, 1975); focusing on how organizations, viewed as open systems operating under the dictum of rationality and needing determinedness and certainty, reduce uncertainty coming from their environment and the technology they use (Thompson, 1967); diving into the peculiarities of an open system view and trying to connect sociological and psychological views of organizations (Katz and Kahn, 1966); understanding organizations and their relationship to employees and customers in times of concern and conflict through the three basic options of exit, voice, and loyalty (Hirschman, 1970); and pointing out the importance of power relations and the dependence of the organization on the external environment and important stakeholders (Pfeffer and Salancik, 1978).

Works like these have turned out to be classics and triggered numerous streams of research and publications. Among others, they have also influenced more regional scientific debates about how to conceptualize organizations. For example, in the German language area, the 1970s were characterized by a sometimes furious debate about what organizations, in particular companies, "really are" and how they can be theorized. Departing from the classical views linked to production factors (Gutenberg, 1958) or techno-economic views (Kosiol, 1972), new approaches emphasized decisions in organizations

(Heinen, 1972), the systems-quality of organizations (Ulrich, 1970), behavioral aspects of organizations (Schanz, 1977) or the importance of social aspects when managing organizations (Staehle, 1980).

Overall, there is a clearly discernible undercurrent linking these works and their ideas. Organizations and the individuals working in them are a far cry from machinelike entities. Rather, they teem with life and power. Conflicts and contradictions, uncertainties, decisions, and the like play an important role alongside formal structures and processes. As such, they are a social universe in their own right with specific characteristics, in particular formalized internal structures and processes and the embeddedness in their broader environment with special ties to the economic and legal sphere.

Behavior and Organizations As with the major new developments in theorizing organizations in general, the 1960s and '70s witnessed substantial works focusing on organizational behavior at the collective level as well as individual behavior in general and behavior in organizations in particular. Again a few, highly selective examples must suffice. Various views of organizational behavior were put forward (e.g. Schein, 1965; Argyris, 1960); theorizing on motivation in general included dissonance theory (Festinger, 1957), need hierarchy (Maslow, 1962) and the structure of human needs (Alderfer, 1972), achievement motivation (Atkinson, 1966; McClelland, Atkinson, Clark, and Lowell, 1953), or intrinsic motivation (Deci, 1975); theoretical considerations about motivation at work comprise, e.g. theory X/Y (McGregor, 1960), the interplay between satisfiers and hygiene-factors (Herzberg, 1966), or the role of expectancy (Vroom, 1964). Later on and with a clearly different starting point and line of argumentation, the economic calculus turned more prominently to the analysis of human behavior (Becker, 1976).

Again, a common thread runs through these viewpoints. No longer is "economic man" the only legitimate point of reference whose behavior is guided by rational decisions linked to materialistic preferences. Other issues such as basic motives and needs, a broad array of goals from different areas of life, and economic considerations constitute a unique mix for understanding what drives individuals and how they deal with their immediate and long-term concerns in life in general and work life in particular. As such, taking a broad, multidisciplinary view of individuals becomes essential for every thorough analysis looking at behavior and organizations.

Learning and Development Both at the individual and the organizational level, development and learning became an area where new concepts emerged. They addressed important issues, offered a solid theoretical background, and became the basis for much subsequent research. A few examples can illustrate this. At the individual level, the importance of model learning going beyond relying solely on the feedback of one's own action (Bandura, 1977b) greatly added to the existing views on learning and built on the notion that individuals are cognitive beings and active processors of information. At the organizational level, an elaborate view of types of learning differentiated between single- and double-loop learning, the latter questioning the given frameworks and learning systems of the status quo, which also made clear that organizations as a whole can learn (Argyris and Schön, 1978). Looking at various transitions across different areas and stages of life, a model with universally applicable dimensions of transitions – reversibility, temporality, shape, desirability, circumstantiality, and multiple status passages – emerged (Glaser and Strauss, 1971).

What holds these approaches together is a strong awareness of and emphasis on the dynamic quality of life in general and work life in particular. The developmental aspect underscores the importance of taking a long-term view and being sensitive to different stages or phases of life with their respective idiosyncrasies. Learning focuses on the relationship between the entity of interest, e.g. an individual or an organization, and its environment and the continuously ongoing and required processes of reaction and adaption to the environment and its changes.

Career Studies Against the backdrop of these developments at the societal and scientific level, it is little wonder that career studies during the 1960s and 1970s addressed a number of themes matching the scholarly *zeitgeist*. A first theme addressed organizations as an important element of social space when looking at careers. While this stream of research does not necessarily assume that careers are only taking place within organizations, organizations were a central point of reference. A number of well-known works from this area dealt with various facets of careers in organizations (e.g. Van Maanen and Schein, 1977; Hall, 1976), their theoretical underpinnings (e.g. Glaser, 1968), the relationship between individual and organization when it comes to careers (e.g. Schein, 1978; Dyer, 1976), the types of persons found in organizations (e.g. Maccoby, 1978), or the specifics of moving in the organizational hierarchy (e.g. Rosenbaum, 1979b; Jennings, 1971; White, 1970).

A second theme partly zoomed in on organizations and, at the same time, went across organizations and revolved around careers of specific groups, professions, and occupations (e.g. Sarason, 1977; Strauss, 1975; Slocum, 1966). Examples include scientists (Glaser, 1964), scientists and technical engineers (Zaleznik, Dalton, Barnes, and Laurin, 1970), managers (e.g. Guerrier and Philpot, 1978; Bray, Campbell, and Grant, 1974; Lorsch and Barnes, 1972; Eckardstein, 1971), technical specialists (e.g. Sofer, 1970), school superintendents (e.g. Carlson, 1972), minorities (Picou and Campbell, 1975), or medical students (e.g. Becker, Geer, Hughes, and Strauss, 1961). Here the underlying assumption is that the specifics of these groups, i.e. the individuals attracted by and selected through the respective field as well as the characteristics of the field, provide "standardized," "universal" insights related to careers.

A third theme was the developmental aspect with a strong emphasis on time as expressed in ideas of cycle, stages, or phases. Work on general timetables of career (e.g. Roth, 1963) or on different stages of life (e.g. Levinson *et al.*, 1978) explicitly related to the time aspect. The issue of career development, from both an organizational and an individual angle, touched on both the learning and development issue and the time aspect (e.g. Van Maanen and Schein, 1977). Reflecting the changing role of women in society and in working life, various issues related to the individual and joint development of couples where both partners work and pursue a career of their own emerged (e.g. Derr, 1980; Hall and Hall, 1979; Rice, 1979; Rapoport and Rapoport, 1976, 1971). With regard to vocational development and drawing on the idea of life-stage concepts, career patterns and factors influencing these patterns stemming from the economic, psychological, and sociological realm as well as from chance generated considerable interest (Super, 1970). More closely related to occupational choice during one's personal development, issues of self-selection (i.e. choosing adequate environments), socialization (i.e. specific environments (dis)rewarding certain talents), and congruence (i.e. positive effects of fit between the person and the environment) became crucial (Holland, 1973).

Reconstruction through the SCF Using the SCF, in particular the ontic, spatial, and temporal perspectives, the following picture emerges with regard to the relative importance of the three perspectives. Career works during the 1960s and '70s clearly emphasize spatial aspects. Far from being tempted to overemphasize individual agency, careers are squarely put into context. By and large, the organization constitutes this context. Issues such as organizational socialization after entering the organization, internal career paths and logics, and developmental aspects play a major role. In a similar vein, the ontic perspective has considerable prominence. Not only do professions and occupations play an important role. The emphasis on development and the strong focus on reaching a fit between the individual and the organization as a primary characteristic of the individual context add to the importance of the ontic perspective during this period. Finally, the temporal perspective arguably is the strongest one during this period. Many of the seminal contributions take time not only as a latent factor underlying all analyses of career. On the contrary, timetables, stages/phases, and the interest in the development of careers over extended periods of time signal the strong use of the temporal perspective.

Overall, then, a picture emerges that shows a balanced use of the three perspectives. The spatial, ontic, and temporal perspective are prominent when looking at the overall picture. While there is substantial heterogeneity in terms of the specific emphases and interest within the various perspectives, e.g. which professional groups are at the center, there seems to be a clear understanding within the field that all three perspectives deserve roughly equal attention.

1980s: A Period of Transition

The 1980s began on an uncertain note. The USSR became bogged down in Afghanistan in much the same way that the Americans got bogged down in Vietnam some ten or more years earlier. The Iran-Iraq war continued inconclusively but at hideous cost in human lives. The USA's President Carter continued to lose face as a result of a failed attempt to rescue hostages from the US embassy in Tehran. The post-Mao confusion in China carried on with the prosecution of the "Gang of Four" who had attempted to succeed Mao. A global recession set in during the late 1970s.

The uncertainties and strife of the 1970s led to sweeping changes to the government of a number of countries, many moving to the political right. Margaret Thatcher's government achieved power in the UK at the end of the decade after a disastrous series of public sector strikes accompanied by worrying levels of stagflation. Ronald Reagan was elected as President of the USA and raised the temperature of US Cold War rhetoric against the Soviet Union. The global recession eased, led by the USA, which was hailed as a victory for supply-side economics. Meanwhile, Mikhail Gorbachev became a member of the USSR Politburo, and Lech Walesa, leader of the Solidarity Movement in Poland, began to win advances for the workers he represented. Indira Gandhi and Anwar Sadat were assassinated by ethnic and religious insurgents. Following a series of short-lived leaders, Gorbachev became General Secretary of the Communist Party of the USSR and attempted to warm relations with the West as well as to open up to greater visibility ("glasnost") and restructure ("perestroika") the government of his country. Economic and political change began to sweep through Eastern European countries, and the decade ended with the collapse of the Soviet bloc as an economic, political, and military entity, amid extraordinary political change in Europe.

At the same time, globalization became much more evident. For example, Di Giovanni, Gottselig, Jaumotte, Ricci, and Tokarick (2008) pointed toward increases in:

- The value of trade (goods and services) as a percentage of world GDP . . . from 42.1 percent in 1980 to 62.1 percent in 2007.
- Foreign direct investment . . . from 6.5 percent of world GDP in 1980 to 31.8 percent in 2006.
- The stock of international claims (primarily bank loans), as a percentage of world GDP, . . . from roughly 10 percent in 1980 to 48 percent in 2006.

- The number of minutes spent on cross-border telephone calls, on a per-capita basis, ... from 7.3 in 1991 to 28.8 in 2006.
- The number of foreign workers ... from 78 million people (2.4 percent of the world population) in 1965 to 191 million people (3.0 percent of the world population) in 2005.

These massive changes were accompanied by the gradual abandonment of the conglomerate corporate structure (the account that follows draws on Davis, Diekmann, and Tinsley, 1994). Conglomerates, in the form that dominated much of the latter part of the twentieth century in the USA, were the result of anti-trust legislation of the mid-century (particularly the Celler-Kefauver Act of 1950). Because the ability of corporations to grow by buying firms to support horizontal and vertical integration thus became curtailed, the firms sought other methods of growth and hit on the conglomerate – a corporation consisting of businesses that have little if any relationship with each other – as the solution. The concept is that of the firm-as-portfolio (Fligstein, 1991), in which the head office acts "as an internal capital market, allocating resources among the units" (Davis *et al.*, 1994: 552). By the early 1980s the conglomerate form dominated the USA's large corporations. "Only about 25 percent of the 1980 *Fortune* 500 operated exclusively in a single 2-digit SIC industry, while over half operated in three or more" (Davis *et al.*, 1994: 553). But also by the beginning of the 1980s, it had become evident to anyone who looked at the numbers that, at least in terms of stock market valuation, the concept was a failure: conglomerates were typically worth less than their component parts would be separately. This led to an industry of "bust-up takeovers," aided by a change in policy by the US federal government that "reduced the barriers to acquisition in the same industry" (ibid.: 554). These takeovers, often financed by junk bonds that were repaid with the proceeds of the breakup sales, argue Davis *et al.* (1994: 549), over time had a radical impact on the way that organizational boundaries were viewed:

... perhaps the most radical concomitant of the deconglomeration movement was the undermining of the notion of organizations as primordial social units in favor of a radical individualist view in which corporations were simply "financial tinker toys" which could be rearranged at whim, without regard for organizational boundaries (Gordon 1991). Ironically, it was the firm-as-portfolio model itself that made this imagery credible. (Espeland and Hirsch 1990)

In the mid-1980s, business process reengineering was presented as a rational solution to the problems of organizing (Kleiner, 2000). Neoliberal thinking in public policy was reflected in a growth in interest in transaction cost economics (Williamson, 1975) and the firm as the outcome of decisions to minimize these costs. Organization theorists were changing the level of their analysis from the organization itself to populations of organizations. Two themes emerge in the literature, one based on population ecology (Hannan and Freeman, 1977) and the other on neo-institutional theory (DiMaggio and Powell, 1983). If anything connects these disparate initiatives, it is the notion of organizations as the product of their circumstances: the cost of their transactions, the nature of the ecological niche they occupy, or the mimetic forces to which they are subject.

Research within the OMC field delved into these changing organizational structures and processes that provide the context for, particularly, managerial careers. There was interest in, among many other topics, career exploration (Greenhaus and Sklarew, 1981), the nature of work role transitions (Nicholson, 1984; Louis, 1980a), the structure of internal labor markets and what causes them to function as they do (Gunz, 1989a; DiPrete, 1987; Forbes, 1987; Baron, Davis-Blake, and Bielby, 1986; Lawrence, 1984; Anderson, Milkovich, and Tsui, 1981; Grandjean, 1981; Jacobs, 1981; Stumpf and London, 1981; Rosenbaum, 1979a) and how they relate to corporate performance (Feldman, 1988; Sonnenfeld and Peiperl, 1988; Pfeffer and Davis-Blake, 1986; Gupta and Govindarajan, 1984; Szilagyi and Schweiger, 1984; Scholl, 1983; Brown, 1982; Snow and Hrebiniak, 1980), organizational demography (Stewman, 1986; Wagner, Pfeffer, and O'Reilly, 1984, McCain, O'Reilly, and Pfeffer, 1983), the backgrounds of CEOs (Useem and Karabel, 1986; Kerin, 1981; Lee, 1981), mobility and the structure of managerial careers (Nicholson and West, 1988; Kanter, 1984; Veiga, 1983; Poole, Mansfield, Blyton, and Frost, 1981), and mentorship (Kram, 1985; Hunt and Michael, 1983).

If there is a theme linking these approaches to OMC, it is that the organization remains as a critical contextual factor. It is not that careers are seen as remaining within organizations exclusively, let alone that they take place within a single organization, a myth that seems to have grown up as part of the OMC discourse during the next period we examine. It is simply that organizations, although partly changed in comparison to the 1970s, still provide a major context for careers and that OMC researchers are interested in exploring the implications of this observation. There is therefore a strongly spatial element to the work reflecting the equally strong structural element to organization theory of the period, although the ontic, as represented for example by the growing interest in career exploration and mentorship, is becoming evident. The temporal is present in the work of, for example, Lawrence's (1984) study of age grading, the dynamic modeling of Stewman and Konda (1983), and continuing surveys of managerial careers (e.g. Nicholson and West, 1988), but it does not play quite such a strong role as it did in the 1960s and '70s because of the strong structural interest of career researchers during this period.

At the same time, there is consciousness growing of the existence of OMC as a field. Works begin to appear developing the theme that there is a theoretical foundation for the study of careers (Collin and Young, 1986; Sonnenfeld and Kotter, 1982). This culminates in the 1989 *Handbook of Career Theory* (Arthur *et al.*, 1989b), an influential work that declares: "In a word (or two), career theory has 'gone legitimate.' We (people who study careers) have become established. We have become a *field*" (Arthur *et al.*, 1989c: xv; emphasis in the original). The volume is both retrospective and prospective, summarizing the achievements of the field but also speculating on the directions in which it could move. It provides both a focus and a rallying point for the field to gather around and grow from.

1990 to Date: Boundarylessness and Beyond

The beginning of the 1990s marked a significant transition in the way that the North American and European worlds viewed national boundaries and hege-monies. It was a period of imperial transition that was close to home, as opposed to that of the dissolution of the European empires that had, by and large, affected only people in distant countries whom the imperialists had spent a century or two subjugating and exploiting. The Soviet empire collapsed at the turn of the decade, upsetting a great many assumptions about how national boundaries work in Central and Eastern Europe and removing the USA's Cold War enemy. The Treaty of Maastricht, forming the European Union (EU), was ratified in 1992–1993 by the then twelve member states of the EU. The entire decade witnessed the disintegration of the former Yugoslavia and a brutal war between its ethnic groups. The rise of Islamism as a major international force began coming into focus with the Iranian revolution at the end of the 1970s and continued through the ascendency of the Taliban in Afghanistan in the mid-1990s. Meanwhile another great rearranger of boundaries, the World Wide Web, began unobtrusively in a CERN office in 1989 and started becoming a factor in people's thinking with the release of the first graphical web browser, Mosaic, in 1993.

This turbulence in international boundaries was reflected in parallel changes in the business world. In the early 1990s, a new rhetoric was becoming evident in managerial discourse in the USA; new, that is, to anyone who had not read Burns and Stalker's (1961) work on the organic organizational form:

New technologies, fast-changing markets, and global competition are revolutionizing business relationships. As companies blur their traditional boundaries to respond to this more fluid business environment, the roles that people play at work and the tasks they perform become correspondingly blurred and ambiguous. (Hirschhorn and Gilmore, 1992: 105)

This, it was argued, had an impact on corporate forms:

"Business schools and management consultants preach a unanimous gospel: make it lean, mean and centred on a core business" (*Economist* 1989: 75). Under such circum-stances, producing complete products often entails forming temporary alliances with several other specialists and results in a network, or "virtual corporation," composed of formally separate entities rather than a single bounded organization. (Davis *et al.*, 1994: 563)

The upshot, argue Davis *et al.*, was a new rhetoric of boundarylessness, citing two examples of how it was being written about in the business press:

Today's joint ventures and strategic alliances may be an early glimpse of the business organization of the future: The Virtual Corporation. It's a temporary network of companies that come together to exploit fast-changing opportunities ... It will have neither central office nor organization chart. It will have no hierarchy, no vertical integration. (Byrne, 1993: 98–99)

Companies are replacing vertical hierarchies with horizontal networks; linking together traditional functions through interfunctional teams; and forming strategic alliances with suppliers, customers, and even competitors ... For many executives, a single metaphor has come to embody this managerial challenge and to capture the kind of organization they want to create: the "corporation without boundaries." (Hirschhorn and Gilmore, 1992: 104)

Ironically, as Davis *et al.* put it, the one remaining large US corporation that continued to operate as a conglomerate, General Electric, also started using this rhetoric. Arguably, its CEO Jack Welch became the leading proponent of the so-called boundaryless organization. In a widely cited manifesto for boundary-lessness, Welch writes:

Our dream for the 1990s is a boundaryless company ... where we knock down the walls that separate us from each other on the inside and from our key constituencies on the outside. (Jack Welch in GE's 1990 Annual Report, cited in Hirschhorn and Gilmore, 1992: 104)

The Academy of Management got swept up in this fevered atmosphere and dedicated its 1993 annual meeting to "Managing the Boundaryless Organization." This provided the stimulus for Michael Arthur and Robert DeFillippi to organize a symposium at the meeting on the topic of what they labeled the boundaryless career, which led in turn to a journal special issue (Arthur, 1994) and, subsequently, an influential edited book in which many authors expand on the idea (Arthur and Rousseau, 1996a). While not rejecting the influence of organization on career, the boundaryless career is presented as the outcome of changes to employment practices, themselves the conse-quences of the changes to corporate structures including those that we have just been reviewing as well as the substantial changes happening to careers in Western economies as a result of globalization of business operations, includ-ing increasing offshoring (Feldman and Ng, 2007). The boundaryless career is presented as "the opposite of 'organizational careers' – careers conceived to unfold in a single organizational setting" (Arthur and Rousseau, 1996c: 5).

In a thoughtful retrospective and prospective article on the boundaryless career, Arthur (2014) points out that the definition of career we cite in Chapter 3 from Van Maanen and Schein (1977: 31), namely "a series of separate but related experiences and adventures through which a person passes during a lifetime," says nothing about organization despite the fact that the MIT school is very well known (as we, too, note earlier) for its work on organizational careers. So boundarylessness was not a new concept in 1996 despite the focus in the careers literature during the 1970 and '80s on organizational careers. But the appearance of the boundarylessness concept nevertheless had a profound effect on the rhetoric of the careers field. During the late 1990s and early 2000s, and despite the occasional skeptical voice being raised to question the extent to which careers had indeed become boundaryless (e.g. Jacoby, 1999), it became almost de rigueur to begin any paper with a reference to "today's boundaryless world" or the equivalent, albeit with its critics (e.g. Inkson *et al.*, 2012; Rodrigues and Guest, 2010). Mobility, both geographic and interorganizational, became an important theme in the careers literature (Feldman and Ng, 2007), but so did employability (De Vos, De Hauw, and Van der Heijden, 2011), identity (Arthur, 2014), and psychological mobility ("the perception of the capacity to make transitions"; Sullivan and Arthur, 2006: 21). At the same time Hall's protean career, introduced in his 1976 book (Hall, 1976), enjoyed a resurgence. Although Hall was critical of the extent to which people muddled the boundaryless and protean concepts (Briscoe and Hall, 2006), the two concepts clearly share a sense of agency and self-reinvention that was consonant with the zeitgeist. At the same time, a considerable amount of research was published on mentorship, a concept that has a strong temporal basis in early work such as Kram's (1983) process model but that, in the 1990s and 2000s, tended to focus much more on what makes for a successful mentoring relationship (Chandler, Kram, and Yip, 2011), giving it more of a contemporary agentic flavor.

So although it would be easy to identify the driving force behind these changes as spatial – mobility within and between organizations implies an interest of some kind in social and geographic space, and indeed the very term "boundaryless" implies spatiality, while mentorship involves working across and crossing organizational boundaries – it is clear that this period is also marked by a strong interest in the ontic perspective.

Another indication of the ontic emphasis can be seen in the difficulty structural approaches had in gaining a foothold in the OMC field. Attempts to interest careers scholars in the structural forces behind careers did not meet with a great deal of success, for example, those that connect career, structures, and strategy (e.g. Higgins and Dillon, 2007; Higgins, 2005; Gunz and Jalland, 1996; Sonnenfeld and Peiperl, 1988). This approach had more luck outside the careers field (e.g. Dokko and Gaba, 2012; Broschak, 2004; Burton, Sorensen,

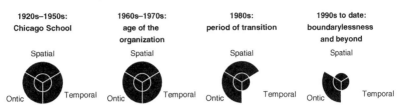

Figure 6.2 Development of the OMC field

and Beckman, 2002; Sorensen, 1999; Boeker, 1997; Haveman and Cohen, 1994). Another approach involved attempts to bring grand sociological theory to the careers table (e.g. Mayrhofer, Meyer, Steyrer, and Langer, 2007b; Iellatchitch et al., 2003), but again it does not appear to hit the careers mainstream.

Career research from this period, then, has a spatial feel to it coming from writing on boundarylessness but is fundamentally ontic: it is about people, their reactions to the "boundaryless world," their beliefs about their mobility, and the people (mentors) who might be able to help them. The temporal perspective, despite its centrality to the mentorship concept, is, with a few exceptions (e.g. Koch et al., 2016; Bidwell and Mollick, 2015; Kattenbach et al., 2014; Schneidhofer, Schiffinger, and Mayrhofer, 2012; Bidwell and Briscoe, 2010) surprisingly absent, at least in part because longitudinal research is both too expensive and risky for junior faculty trying to establish a foothold in the academic world.

The OMC Field's History: Conclusion

We broadly summarize the story we have been telling in Figure 6.2. The story is one of increased focus: of starting with a balanced approach to studying careers, moving to a bivalent one in which the temporal perspective takes something of a back seat, ending up with a more focused approach on the ontic, not, of course, to the complete neglect of the other two perspectives.

The progressive change of emphasis is intriguing. The first, Chicago, period is clearly the outcome of a particular group of scholars trained to do a particular kind of research, namely very detailed ethnographic studies of particular populations. It resulted in a rich approach to studying careers that has rarely been emulated since. As time moves forward to the 1960s and 1970s, we see the influence of advances in organization theory and a growing interest in developing theories of career that reflect these advances. Organizations become objects of considerable interest, and career theorists in turn become interested in organizations as major influences on careers. Through the 1980s, the world of organizations moves into a period of turbulence that lasts for quite some time. Initially it has little effect on career research, which continues to concentrate on organizations as the primary home for careers, although interest in the temporal perspective begins to wane. This trend continues into the last of our four periods, during which the emphasis in the world of practitioners on boundarylessness appears to cause career researchers to lose interest in the social space within which careers are made. Somehow, many writers interpret boundarylessness as meaning an irrelevance of boundaries rather than careers involving boundary-crossing as those who introduced the concept intended. In addition, interest in the temporal perspective diminishes. We have come a long way from Hughes and his Chicago sociologists.

What are we to make of this gradual focusing of research in the OMC field? Does it, for example, reflect the unsurprising focus of OMC research within business schools as opposed to, for example, sociology departments? After all, in business schools, particularly North American ones, psychology is more commonly represented than sociology or anthropology among the faculty who study people. And is it in part a reflection of the nature of academic careers now, which, because of the need for young scholars to rapidly build up their CV with publications in "good" journals and the increasing scarcity of research funds, makes field research that is more complex than questionnaire studies of their students, let alone longitudinal research, increasingly risky and unaffordable (Miller, Taylor, and Bedeian, 2011; De Rond and Miller, 2005)?

These speculations are just that: speculations. But the difference between the focused research of the 1990s and beyond and the more balanced research of earlier years speaks to the difficulty of learning from the past. It also speaks to why it might be that Schein notes such a striking disconnect between the career research that originated in the 1950s and that was picked up by the MIT school he was part of, and that of more recent times:

... there seems to be a strong bias toward treating careers as an individual phenomenon to be analyzed psychologically rather than as a social phenomenon involving economics, political science, anthropology, and sociology. (2007: 573)

Summation

This chapter explores the contribution the SCF can make to encouraging conversation between scholars working in different subfields of OMC studies, in particular where there is little, if any, acknowledgment that the subfields have any relationship to each other. It also uses the SCF to tell a particular – there are many possible – version of the history of OMC studies, partly to review the sense of identity that comes from working in the field and partly to show how it has changed over the years, set against a canvas of historical events. Using the device of an ideal type taxonomy, we see a curious narrowing of focus since the days of the pioneering Chicago school, which may be traceable to changes in the institutional framework within which OMC studies are now typically done.

The chapter, then, responds to the call, echoed in Chapter 1, for finding ways of establishing conversation within the field. Next, we examine ways in which the SCF might help OMC researchers find new questions to ask.

7   Stimulating Cumulative Research within Career Studies

In Chapter 6, we explore some of the richness of the field of career studies, showing how the SCF helps with making sense of OMC studies and establishing conversations between interlocutors with different research interests. In the next two chapters, we continue to examine the benefits that the SCF provides for research in the field, demonstrating how it can generate ideas for research. In this chapter, we look at how it can help identify new research questions within established areas of research in the field by reconstructing familiar areas of research using ideas from the SCF. The emphasis here is on cumulative research: building on existing work. In Chapter 8, we bring in three additional contributions the SCF makes: looking outside the careers field for analogues of existing areas of career research (equivalizing), identifying the major theoretical arguments in these discourses (understanding), and importing these ideas to the careers field in order to showcase how applying the SCF constitutes a systematic way of making theoretical ideas and empirical insight that have been developed outside the field fruitful for career studies. That chapter, then, is much more about reframing career research.

As we emphasize elsewhere in this book, we are using the SCF as a heuristic, a guide to thinking. Any of the ideas that emerge in these chapters could have been arrived at without the aid of the SCF. However, unless we note otherwise, to the best of our knowledge they have not so emerged thus far in a simple, transparent, and noncomplicated way, and that is not, in our view, because they are uninteresting questions. Their nonappearance could simply be because nobody has yet gotten around to investigating them or, in our view more probably, because the fragmented nature of the field means that their absence from the literature has not yet been noticed or there has hitherto been no comparatively simple heuristic to arrive at conclusions like these.

To use an epidemiological analogy, it is well known to experts in that area that John Snow's 1854 map of the geographical clustering of cholera cases around London's infamous Broad Street pump provided striking evidence to support the hypothesis that cholera was spread by contaminated drinking water rather than, as the prevailing view had it at the time, by bad air. Yet there is some question about the role that the map played in Snow's thinking; it appears from his account (Snow, 2008 [Original 1855]) that he was already sure that he knew what the source of the problem was and that the map may well have been a means of trying to convince others of his idea. So although the map in this specific instance may not have provided the answer to this particular question, nobody is in any doubt that the mapping technique used by Snow has proven invaluable in helping later generations of epidemiologists to ask the right questions about the means of propagation of other diseases.

We describe three distinct kinds of reconstructing in this chapter, although in practice they can blur into each other at times. Their common point of departure is the model defining a particular area of interest in career scholarship: the set of constructs that define it and the hypothesized causal connections between them. As we shall show by means of a number of illustrative examples, the SCF, through a common language built into the spatial, ontic, and temporal perspectives and the heuristic model building on this language (see Chapter 4), provides a template for setting out the model for the area of interest in a way that allows us to explore it from novel directions.

First, the process of mapping an existing study and the underlying model onto the SCF can be revealing in itself. The process of deciding where the different constructs might fit if mapped onto the SCF heuristic model can sometimes encourage one to see them, or the way that they relate to others in the model, in a somewhat different light. In particular, as we note in Chapter 4, it can sometimes be trickier than it first appears to decide whether a particular construct is related to the spatial or ontic perspectives, i.e. on which side of the person–environment boundary it falls or if it emerges as being right at the interface of both. The difficulty can sometimes lead to the discovery that what appears in the original model as a single construct is really more than one and that unpacking these constructs is in itself a useful exercise. This, in turn, encourages one to review the constructs and their interrelationships, including the ways in which career actors are defined, to see whether there are any more constructs underlying the ones currently appearing in the model, whether any implied relationships between the constructs have not yet been made manifest, and whether there is anything to be gained by broadening the view of the career actor, for example, from a focus on individuals to include collectivities, or vice versa.

The second and third forms of reconstructing build on the study and model as reconstructed. The second involves looking for missing connections in the reconstructed model. Inevitably, any study or theory will focus on certain causal linkages while ignoring others, perhaps because they are the ones with no interest when using a specific theory, it is impractical or too expensive to investigate every possible pathway in the model, or space and time simply do not allow everything to be examined. But that, of course, opens the possibility of building on the original ideas by examining the links that they did not. As such, this constitutes an opportunity for the kind of cumulative research that career studies too often lacks.

The third form of reconstructing deliberately steps outside the existing study and model, extending it beyond its current bounds. Whereas the second form looks for missing connections between existing constructs, this third form asks: What connections does the model suggest with constructs or theories (i.e. networks of constructs) that do not appear in the model as currently formulated? To a greater extent than the first two forms, the third form acts as a springboard for more freewheeling creativity, for making connections with hitherto apparently unconnected areas of scholarship within the careers field.

We illustrate these forms of reconstructing by drawing mostly on established, typically much admired and seminal works from the literature, mostly empirical even though two in particular have developed new areas of theory as well. It is important also that we emphasize that this endeavor is not meant as a cheap critique of the chosen studies. We do not mean to second-guess the authors: to suggest what they "should" have done. We are well aware of the theoretical, methodological, and pragmatic restrictions on doing and publishing empirical research: there is only so much one can do in any given study, and its authors are usually the ones most aware of its limitations. Rather, we want to show how the SCF can help others to systematically build on good existing research by looking for areas within and beyond its chosen framework. In this way, we hope to show how applying the SCF supports cumulative research.

We begin with the first form of reconstructing: mapping studies to the SCF and reviewing the constructs and their relationships with each other.

Mapping and Reviewing Constructs and Their Relationships

In order to reconstruct an existing study in terms of the SCF, we obviously begin with the model underpinning the study. Sometimes the model is described explicitly in the paper, and sometimes it is implicit in the way that the authors write about their research. The model is bound to have a particular focus, constructed by the authors for their particular purposes. It will identify the constructs and relationships that are needed and inevitably ignore others. So the first step in applying the SCF is to redraw the model in terms of the SCF.

This involves examining each of the constructs to see how the model would be viewed variously from the spatial, ontic, and temporal perspectives. Often the quickest way to do this is to try to map the model onto the SCF heuristic model that we derive in Chapter 4. This is not meant to imply that the process is necessarily an easy one, however. First, it is vital to ensure that the original authors' arguments have been correctly interpreted. For example, the same term can mean different things in different disciplinary traditions, and the interdisciplinary nature of career research means that one often encounters contributions from unfamiliar disciplines. For example, one of the papers that we review later works with social capital, which has many different meanings across different fields. At this stage, the task is not to take issue with some or all of these meanings – that can come later if necessary, which in this case it is not – but to make sure that we understand what the authors mean by the term so that we reconstruct *their* model, not our distortion or parody of it. In practice, as we note previously, the trickiest decisions typically involve constructs that have elements of condition and of social space about them, which makes them hard to place in the SCF model (see Chapter 3 for a discussion on the links between, in particular, ontic and spatial perspectives). As we show with our first example, the process of trying to decide how to position such constructs can be very generative of new ideas.

This example is drawn from a pair of influential papers published in 1981 by Betz and Hackett (Betz and Hackett, 1981; Hackett and Betz, 1981). They were interested in trying to understand the reasons for the underrepresentation of women in many professional and managerial occupations, and both works generated a large literature on the effect of career self-efficacy on occupational choice. Subsequently, Lent, Brown, and Hackett (1994) developed the model underpinning the two papers into what they termed "social cognitive career theory (SCCT)," the empirical evidence for which they summarized in a relatively recent meta-analysis (Sheu *et al.*, 2010). We show here how reconstructing the original model in terms of the SCF anticipates some of the developments that followed and suggests one that, so far as we are aware, has not received attention in this particular literature.

The first of the two 1981 papers is theoretical and the second empirical. In the theoretical paper, Hackett and Betz (1981) draw on Bandura's (1977a) suggestion that self-efficacy is developed from four information sources: the actor's performance accomplishments, vicarious experience, verbal persuasion, and emotional arousal, the last being not a source of information in itself but something that modifies the way that people absorb information. These affect people's socialization experiences, which in turn develop or constrain the development of their self-efficacy. In the empirical paper, the authors extend this chain of causality to suggest that someone who does not feel capable of performing well in a particular occupation is unlikely to consider that occupation. They give the example of differences in sex-role socialization, with the stereotypic masculine role involving primarily instrumental qualities such as assertiveness and competitiveness, and stereotypic feminine roles involving a combination of emotionally expressive characteristics and passive-submissive qualities. These are enhanced, they argue, by boys being more likely to gain experience of activities outside the home such as carpentry, mechanical skills, and sports and girls being more focused on activities in the home. Furthermore, they cite evidence "that feminine sex-typed persons generally report higher levels of anxiety than do masculine-typed

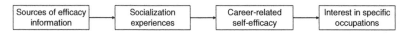

Figure 7.1 Betz and Hackett's model of career-related self-efficacy

individuals (e.g. Biaggio & Nielsen, 1976; Gall, 1969)" (Hackett and Betz, 1981: 332), which affects the way in which they absorb information. The first three steps in Figure 7.1 summarize the arguments in the theoretical paper, based on the labels the authors use for each step; the empirical paper extends the model to the fourth box.

Empirically, Betz and Hackett (1981) show that a sample of female undergraduates had significantly lower self-efficacy with regard to a group of what at the time were seen as traditionally male occupations (e.g. engineer, physician, highway patrol officer) than they did with regard to a group of traditionally female occupations (e.g. elementary school teacher, medical technician, social worker). An equivalent sample of male students showed no such differences. The female students were also significantly more likely to consider the traditionally female occupations than they were the traditionally male ones; the male students, again, did not differentiate between the groups. The differences could not be explained by the students' intellectual capacity: there was no significant difference between them in terms of their scores in a standard test of academic ability (American College Test Math and English subtests).

As a first step in reconstruction, we redraw Figure 7.1 in terms of the SCF, based on the heuristic model of Chapter 4. The second, third, and fourth constructs are relatively straightforward to interpret: they all make sense from the ontic perspective. That is not to say that they do not include spatial references. Interest in specific occupations, for example, refers to occupations, which are in the actor's social space. We return to this point later. The information construct in the first box, sources of efficacy information, has, however, a much more obvious problem. The first of the four sources of self-efficacy listed in the theoretical paper (Hackett and Betz, 1981) is evident from the ontic perspective, namely the state of the actor's arousal. But performance accomplishments relate more to position, in the sense that performance is something that happens in role. One may be a fast keyboard typist, for example, but the significance of this capacity to perform varies with the reason one is typing. It may be extremely relevant for someone who transcribes audio material and much less important for someone who writes novels. Finally, the other two sources of efficacy – other role models and verbal persuasion – are by definition in the actor's social space. All of this implies that mapping Betz and Hackett's model on to the SCF implies splitting the first box of Figure 7.1 into three, between the actor's social space, their position, and their condition (Figure 7.2).

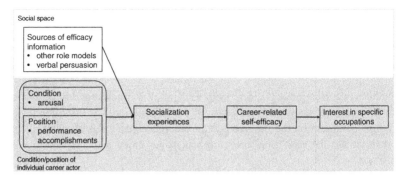

Figure 7.2 Reconstructing Betz and Hackett's model within the SCF

What do we gain from this redrawing? At first sight, the original model appears to be about the individual. Figure 7.2, however, immediately draws attention to the social nature of the primary drivers of interest in occupations. The examples the authors give of sources of efficacy information make it clear that this is the case. Yet they do not develop their model in such a way as to make a set of analytical distinctions between social space, condition, and position as an element of the social space tightly linked with condition. When the model is collapsed into the four boxes of Figure 7.1, it is easy to lose sight of these distinctions. In this way the SCF reconstruction anticipates developments that came some thirteen years later in the Social Cognitive Career Theory (SCCT; see Lent *et al.*, 1994), the model of which explicitly recognizes the contribution that context makes to what Lent *et al.* call "learning experiences" rather than socialization experiences. More recently, the context appears in a different form in the model of Sheu *et al.*'s (2010) meta-analysis, as "supports" and "barriers," which are shown as affecting self-efficacy.

Our second example, which we shall follow through all three types of reconceptualization, is another extremely well-cited study, that of Seibert, Kraimer, and Liden (2001) on the effect of social capital on career success. The authors chose three social capital theories, namely Granovetter's (1973) strength of weak ties theory, Burt's (1992) structural holes theory, and social resources theory (e.g. Lin, Ensel, and Vaughn, 1981; Lin, Vaughn, and Ensel, 1981). Their argument is that various aspects of someone's network structure, namely the number of weak ties they have and the extent of structural holes in their network, affect the social resources available to them, specifically the number of contacts they have in other functions and at higher levels, both in the same organization. These social resources lead to network benefits, namely access to information and resources that will help them in their career and career sponsorship from people who can help their career. Finally, these benefits affect their career success, operationalized

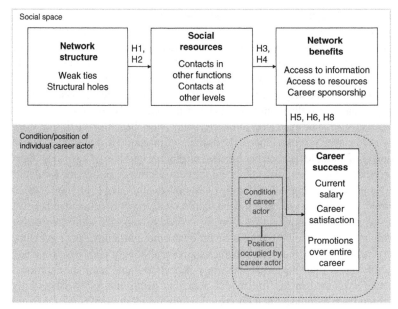

H1...8: Hypotheses proposed in the study

Figure 7.3 Reconstructing the Seibert *et al.* (2001) model within the SCF

objectively as their current salary and the total number of promotions they have had and subjectively as their career satisfaction. We can reconstruct this as shown in Figure 7.3.

At first sight, the model is a straightforward, albeit theoretically sophisticated, examination of the effect of context, represented by the first three groups of constructs, on an element of condition, i.e. career success. However, as soon as one frames the study in this way, it becomes evident that the situation is more complex than the figure shows.

First, although social networks are certainly part of the actor's social context, they are also very much the creation of the actor. Most obviously, the number of weak ties is of course a network property, but the ties do not come about by themselves: they are created by the actor in their dealings with their social context. Similarly, structural holes are sometimes a given, an element of the social structure in which the actor is embedded, and sometimes the creation of the actor when they choose, for example, nonredundant contacts over linked contacts. After all, a good tactic for anyone who is politically astute is to make sure that they are the sole bridging contact between two organizational entities that need to deal with each other. So the reconstruction shown in Figure 7.3 draws attention immediately to a further set of interactions between condition and context.

Second, although the study is understandably cross-sectional – longitudinal or retrospective network data would be nice to have but very expensive to collect – showing it as a process model potentially enriches it. For example, while the social resources are a facet of the network structure, in the sense that they identify contacts that the networks make available so that no time dimension is implied, the network benefits they give rise to follow later in time. Career sponsorship, for example, happens as the sponsor gets to know the actor and opportunities arise for the sponsorship to be exercised. Similarly, the network benefits take time to work through to career success. Indeed, the number of promotions is a cross-sectional summary of a full, lengthy career process, raising the question of how soon in the actor's career the network was built and the network resources became available.

So although a longitudinal study was outside the scope of the research reported by Seibert *et al.*, and indeed would be a very difficult and expensive thing to do, the SCF reconstruction nevertheless suggests some interesting questions from viewing the actor's career over time. The study does not evince a very strong effect on objective career success, although, given its scope and difficulty it is perhaps remarkable that any effect was found at all: the additional variance explained in the full model over that using control variables only increased from 42 percent to 47 percent for salary and 29 percent to 34 percent in number of promotions. By contrast, variance explained in career satisfaction increased from 5 percent to 36 percent. It is presumably possible that the reason for the difference between objective and subjective effects lies in the timing of the network benefits. Tournament models of careers (Rosenbaum, 1984) place considerable emphasis on early promotion success – winning early rounds in the tournament – in determining long-run objective career success. If so, then the current state of someone's networks is less important than the state of the networks *early* in one's career. To take an extreme example, someone who works hard at building good networks and acquiring influential career sponsors at a very early stage in their career is doing their later career a great favor by being spotted as a young high flier. Career satisfaction, on the other hand, is a measure of how the actor feels about their career at the same time as the other measures are being taken. If someone is happy with their networks, their contacts, and the benefits they are currently gaining from their networks, perhaps it is to be expected that they will also be satisfied with their career. The proposed lagged effect of network structure on objective career success is shown in Figure 7.4.

We note previously that it may also be of value to consider the way in which the career actor is defined in the study under consideration. To continue with our example of the effects of social capital on career success (Seibert *et al.*, 2001), the SCF directs our attention to the chosen career actors and their level of social complexity. In the study, this is pretty straightforward. The focal career actors are individuals employed in organizations. But through the lens of the SCF, one can

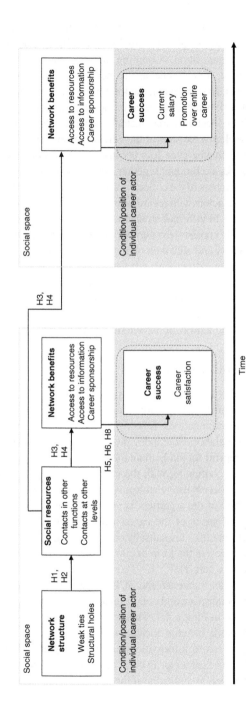

Figure 7.4 Reconstructing Seibert *et al.* (2001) to show a lagged effect on objective career success

H1...4: Hypotheses proposed in the study

additionally raise the question of the extent to which the proposed constructs, relationships, and outcomes would also apply to a collective actor such as a department within the organization. Assuming that the career success of such a collective actor, measured, for example, as the increase in its relative importance within the organization, also depends on the kind of network structure, the social resources, and the network benefits included in the study, a number of interesting questions arise. Is the collective career actor's network structure in terms of structural holes and weak ties the sum of the network properties of its individual members? Is it more or maybe even less because some adverse effects emerge when individual networks are brought together, for example, because of negative competition between members of the collective social network? Are the arguments used for individual career actors with regard to contacts in other functions, contacts at higher levels, or access to information also valid when it comes to a collective career actor that internally consists of a number of individuals with their own way of interpreting social reality and with their own agenda? Would the members of the collective career actor's social network consist of individuals and of collective actors, and what effects does that have on the network characteristics?

While this first approach to reconstructing largely stays within the frame of the study in question, the second approach expands this to some extent and explicitly pursues missing connections. We turn to this next.

Looking for Missing Connections

Besides clarifying the structure of the argument and the constructs used and analyzing implicit relationships in a study, the SCF also facilitates a systematic search for meaningful connections missing in existing studies. The basic building block and the elaborated model propose a number of relationships that can serve as a blueprint for such an analysis.

We first show this by continuing with the study on the relationship between social capital and career success used in the previous section (Seibert et al., 2001). There, the basic structure of the argument is very clear: three sets of constructs located within the social space of the career actor – network structure, social resources, and network benefits – are causally chained and influence an element of condition (i.e. career success in the form of current salary, career satisfaction, and promotions over the entire career).

Adding to this argument, however, the SCF suggests that some anticipatory effects exist between social space and condition as indicated by relationship 8 in the basic model outlined in Figure 4.1. This is relevant for the link between all three elements of network benefits located in the focal actor's social space (access to resources, access to information, and career sponsorship) and their promotions over their entire career as an ontic construct. An actor's past promotion record can be viewed as an indicator of their potential for future hierarchical advancement in the organizational world. From this point of view, it is not just that these promotions are, as a dependent variable, the *result* of network benefits, as rightly argued in the paper. A focal actor's career history of advancements within the hierarchy and, based on this, expected future promotions also create a reverse effect: other career actors in the social space, be they individual or collective, will create *anticipatory effects* regarding access to information, access to resources, and career sponsorship based on what they expect of the focal actor's entire career in the future.

For career sponsorship, there are some arguments that the possibility for attaining it will increase when individuals are regarded as potentially very successful within the concrete setting, as is the case for high potentials: for example, mentors typically prefer to select high-ability protégés (Allen, 2004; Olian, Carroll, and Giannantonio, 1993; Kram, 1985). In terms of access to information and resources, one could argue both ways. One line of argument sees a positive relation. To follow the kind of reasoning used earlier, one can claim that a strong promotion record will increase the likelihood of access because individuals in the social space like to associate with successful career actors. On the other hand, it could also be argued that if individuals are or seem to be very successful, they are potentially dangerous to other people in the social space, for example, colleagues or supervisors in the organization with whom they might be competing for promotion and/or positions. Hence, these people will try to shut the successful individuals out from the information flow. To sum up these arguments, at a general level, the logic of the SCF suggests a supplementary hypothesis (sH1), namely that a focal actor's promotions over their entire career influence their network benefits (see Figure 7.5, which for simplicity builds on Figure 7.3). This very brief formulation does not, in the interests of being concise, get into the issue of which elements of network benefits are affected, and in which direction.

Next, we turn to a second example to illustrate the usefulness of the SCF for supporting cumulative research by detecting additional relationships between constructs in an existing study. An empirical analysis of CEO succession (Boyer and Ortiz-Molina, 2008) focuses on current top managers' stock ownership in the company and its role in the CEO succession process. The authors argue

that a top manager's stock ownership in the firm signals to the board information about his or her privately known ability to run the company. As a consequence, the outcome of a CEO succession is affected by the managers' ownership choices, which therefore depend on their career concerns. (178)

They link two different classes of individual career actor, the newly appointed CEO and current managers, and develop six hypotheses about the relationships between internal/external CEO succession, current managers' ownership

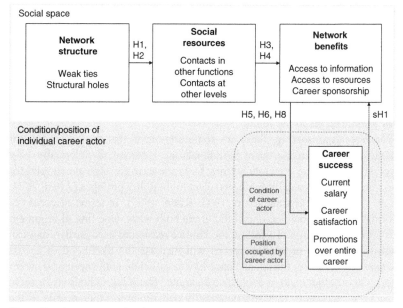

H1...n: Hypotheses proposed in the study; sH1: supplementary hypothesis building on the SCF

Figure 7.5 Career success and social capital (Seibert *et al.*, 2001):
supplementary hypothesis

stakes in the firm, and the resignations of current managers who did not get appointed as CEO. A couple of hypotheses look at the importance of having ownership stakes for the appointment of an internal or external CEO. A growing degree of insider ownership stakes, i.e. current managers having a stake in the company, reduces the likelihood of an outside CEO appointment (H1) and increases the chances of becoming the new CEO when the CEO is chosen from among insiders (H2). The other hypotheses focus on nonappointed internal managers. The greater their ownership stake when another person than they themselves is appointed as CEO, the more they reduce it once passed over (H3) and the greater the likelihood that they will leave the company (H5). Finally, a CEO appointment from outside makes it more likely that nonappointed inside managers reduce their ownership stakes (H4) or resign (H6). Overall, the study confirms these hypotheses. Figure 7.6 illustrates the underlying logic, framed in terms of the SCF's heuristic model (Chapter 4).

As is apparent from Figure 7.6, seen through the lens of the SCF, this study neatly maps on the SCF's basic building block: it examines a change in condition of career actors between at least two points in time while crossing

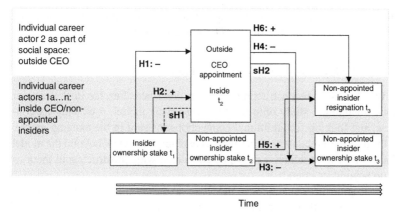

Time

H1...6: Hypotheses proposed in the study; sH1...2: supplementary hypotheses building on the SCF

Figure 7.6 Reconstructing CEO succession and non-appointed managers (Boyer and Ortiz-Molina, 2008)

a boundary in social space. It also uses some elements of the multilevel coevolutionary model, in particular integrating other career actors in the social space of the focal career actor. Using the SCF for complementing the existing study, additional or alternative relationships emerge. For example, hypothesis 2 predicts that the greater the ownership stake held by insiders, the greater their chances of becoming CEO. The SCF, however, also suggests the possibility of a reverse causality: the valence of the potential reward of becoming CEO is likely to encourage insider executives to increase their ownership stakes in an attempt to make themselves more attractive as candidates (Vroom, 1964). In this sense, internal candidates who anticipate positive results from becoming CEO will have a higher ownership stake than those whose anticipation is less positive (sH1).

Hypothesis 4 proposes that an outside CEO appointment has a direct negative effect on the ownership stakes of insiders who are not appointed to the position. Hypothesis 3 proposes a direct effect between ownership stakes of nonappointed internals at the time of the external succession (t_2) and a consequent reduction of these stakes at t_3. Looking at the basic model of the SCF, we could argue that such an outside appointment also has a moderating effect on the relationship. We suggest that insiders' disappointment is likely to be greater when they have been passed over in favor of an external successor since they may deduce that internal promotion also will be blocked in the future. Hence, the kind of CEO succession (internal/external) has a moderating effect on the relationship between ownership at t_2 and t_3 such that the reduction in the stake will be greater in case of a CEO coming from outside (sH2).

Moving beyond the Current Bounds

The two forms of reconstruction we have described thus far in the chapter involve mapping a study onto the SCF's heuristic model, reviewing its constructs, and looking for additional connections missing in the existing model. The third form of reconstruction involves extending the view beyond the model to look for ways in which it might be connected with constructs and theories that lie beyond its bounds.

We will give three examples to demonstrate the contributions of the SCF in this respect. Note that these are just illustrations of the potential usefulness of the SCF; they certainly do not paint a comprehensive picture of all possible developments beyond the existing study. Also, to repeat, they are not a negative critique of the existing study but, rather, are intended to show the potential of the chosen studies to serve as the basis for future research.

First, we return to the Betz and Hackett studies that we began analyzing earlier (Figures 7.1 and 7.2). As we show in Figure 7.7, the SCF allows us to further refine the model reconstructed in Figure 7.2. We introduce two aspects of the social space that are not explicitly considered in the earlier models – socialization processes and the perceived labor market – and begin to chain the model of Figure 7.2 over time in the manner of the first elaboration, chaining over time, of the basic building block (Figure 4.2).

Socialization *experiences*, located at the level of condition, are the product also of socialization *processes*, which by definition are contextual (arrow 1). By identifying the role of socialization processes in modifying career self-efficacy (for simplicity we shall refer to it here just as self-efficacy), the reconstructed model draws attention to the possibility of broadening the examination of these processes. This leads to further questions, for example: How might these socialization processes vary across different strata of society within any one country, or indeed across national cultures? These questions do not figure in, for example, the 2010 meta-analysis of the Social Cognitive Career Theory (SCCT; Sheu *et al.*, 2010).

Everyone starts with some kind of view of the labor market, however unsophisticated (at t_4 in Figure 7.7). Although Betz and Hackett focus on what they describe as the relationship between their subjects' self-efficacy and the occupations they would consider, what they seem to be describing is the way that self-efficacy *modifies* their subjects' view of the labor market (arrow 2). Where might this view come from?

In order to know which occupations I have an interest in, I have to know about them. Similarly, if I am going to dismiss an occupation as something I cannot do,

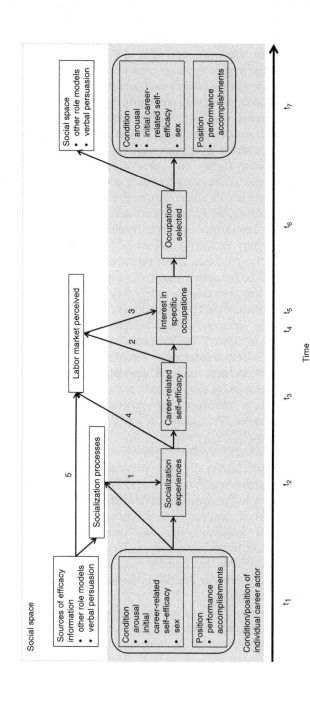

Figure 7.7 Refinement of the reconstruction of Betz and Hackett's model

I have to be aware of it even if I do not know much about it (cf. Gunz, Peiperl, and Tzabbar's [2007a] concept of awareness in the development of subjective career boundaries). Both of these require me to have some perception of the labor market, however flawed, which we show at t_4 in Figure 7.7. This perception affects the actor's interest in specific occupations via arrow 3.

An actor's original view of the labor market does not come from nowhere. In addition to being modified, as we note previously, by the actor's self-efficacy (arrow 2), it is presumably also the product of the actor's socialization processes and experiences, which define much of who they see themselves to be and how they connect with the labor market (arrow 4). These perceptions are influenced by a great many factors, only some of which are shown in Figure 7.7. They also come from the social context such as other role models and the verbal persuasion of people with whom the career actor interacts (arrow 5).

In essence, then, two things are happening in relation to individuals' views of the labor market. The first involves a simple bounded rationality model: the labor market as it actually is, i.e. the full set of available opportunities, is filtered by many cognitive processes. These filters can include the obvious, for example, eliminating from the actor's knowledge anything about jobs in other countries or parts of their own country unless they are actively considering moving. They can also include the kind of mechanism described in the Betz and Hackett model, namely filtering out anything that the actor does not feel capable of doing (t_3–t_5 in Figure 7.7). The second mechanism is one in which the actor sees opportunities to construct their own part of the labor market. An example of this is an entrepreneur seeing an opportunity to generate a business that in turn creates a position for them, as well, perhaps, as positions for many others, or an employee detecting an opportunity to craft their job (Wrzesniewski and Dutton, 2001) in such a way that they can create a new position for themselves.

This perceptual point has been referred to briefly in the literature building on Betz and Hackett's work. Lent at al. (1994: 106) cite earlier writers who note that what matters is the context as the actor sees it, for example, what they refer to as "perceived aspects of the environment (Huebner and Corazzini, 1984)." Shue *et al.* (2010: 261) note that "early adolescents may not anticipate encountering barriers to their choice behavior because of their more limited knowledge of career requirements or workplace conditions." Yet the full implications of the idea, in the sense that an individual's socialization experiences shape perceptions of the labor market as described previously, do not seem to have been considered in this literature.

The reconstructed model also brings out the time-based nature of the process. Hackett and Betz (1981) clearly argue that a person starts with a given level of self-efficacy that changes over time as the result of a series of socialization experiences. As self-efficacy changes, so does the person's perception of the labor market. Time appears obliquely in the developed models (Sheu *et al.*, 2010; Lent *et al.*, 1994), as a recognition that they are cyclic: people go through cycles of experience, developing as they do. We can duplicate this in the SCF version of the model by chaining it over time, which directs the researcher's attention to a more fine-grained examination of time spans. In Figure 7.7, we begin the chaining by showing at t_7 the social space, condition, and position of the actor, all of which will be affected by the occupation that they have chosen at t_6 following the t_1-t_5 process.

Consider the example of a young woman brought up in a local culture in which sex-role stereotyping is strong and who goes to university to encounter a very different atmosphere. She will probably arrive with a strong belief that there are parts of the labor market virtually closed off to her, so she has a very limited set of occupations in which she has an interest. During her time at university, her socialization experiences lead her to realize that this is not the case and that there are a good many occupations that she could well consider; her labor market perceptions change drastically. But she then joins one that still suffers from a misogynistic culture, and her perceptions of the labor market change yet again. A chained model makes developments such as these more evident than a parsimonious (in terms of the number of boxes and arrows that must be drawn) cyclic one because the chain explicitly links particular stages in the model to particular stages in life, thereby showing the pattern of condition and position that is the actor's career.

The temporal perspective also enriches the model in other ways. If the initially perceived labor market does not include any occupations that are subject to gender influences or that are much less subject to these influences, then the change in self-efficacy postulated by the model between t_1 and t_3 will have little, if any, effect. For example, let us imagine that the same study was being conducted on a twenty-first-century sample of North American students. It is much less likely that occupations such as engineer, physician, or highway patrol officer would be seen as mostly sex-stereotyped, especially physician.

Our second example is the study on social capital and career success we discuss earlier (Seibert *et al.*, 2001). The network structure constructs and the social resources constructs imply further links in the model between condition and social space beyond SH1 in Figure 7.5 (connecting promotions over the career to network benefits). This, in turn, addresses two major aspects, i.e. how *individuals* build and maintain social networks and how an individual's *position* is involved in the process of building and maintaining social networks.

In the language of the SCF, the former aspect addresses the relationship between condition and social space, in particular the different ways in which individuals with varying characteristics build networks of weak ties, networks with structural holes, and how that affects contacts in other functions and at higher levels. An example can illustrate what we mean. We concentrate here on two of the five-factor model personality constructs (see the overviews in Barrick, Mount, and Judge, 2001; Barrick and Mount, 1991; Digman, 1990), namely extraversion (i.e. engagement with the external world) and agreeableness (i.e. concern for social harmony). It seems plausible that these two characteristics of condition of the individual career actor do not only influence the building and maintaining of social networks (sH2 in Figure 7.8, which again for simplicity builds on Figure 7.3 rather than on Figure 7.5). More importantly in the context of this study, extraversion and agreeableness also are likely to moderate (sH3) the proposed relationship between social resources (such as contacts in other functions and contacts at higher levels) and network benefits (such as access to information, access to resources, and career sponsorship). A very extraverted and agreeable person might be able to exploit the same network structure and available social resources more profoundly than a highly introverted and only marginally agreeable individual.

Looking at the current relationships in the study also raises the question of how important position is. In line with the basic argument used with respect to the moderating effects of personality traits, positional characteristics are likely to play a role in the processes outlined in the study, too. The importance of positional characteristics for acquiring power in organizations is well established (Hickson, Hinings, Lee, Schneck, and Pennings, 1971). For example, Pfeffer (1992) identifies internal significance, the availability of internal allies, and positioning in the communication network as important power bases for a collective actor such as an organizational department. Against this backdrop, some questions with regard to the relationships between the variables emerge. Are some kinds of position – for example, those that bring the actor into contact with others across the organization, such as perhaps product management – more favorably disposed toward networking than others? How sensitive to the organizational level of the actor is their ability to make contact with senior members of the organization? Following from this, might there be some kind of threshold value you have to reach before senior people will talk to you in any given organization? Position, therefore, may moderate the relationship between network structure and social resources (sH4).

Finally, does the internal organizational context such as organizational structure or culture affect this? For example, do you have to be much closer in level to the senior person in mechanistic structures than in more free-flowing, organic structures for the proposed relationships to work out as suggested (sH5)?

Figure 7.8 illustrates both sets of supplementary hypotheses, linking the individual career actor as well as their position more closely with the causal chain in the social space proposed by the study and showing potentially interesting avenues for building future research, in terms both of theory building and of empirical research.

Another route for moving beyond the current bounds uses the multilayered and multifaceted view of the social space proposed by the SCF. The authors

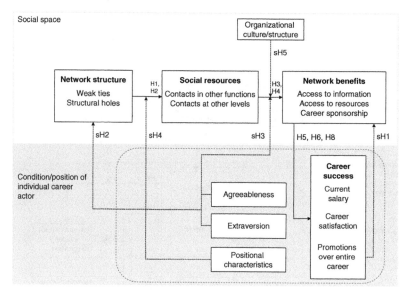

H1...8: Hypotheses proposed in the study; sH1...5: supplementary hypotheses building on the SCF

Figure 7.8 Further extension of Seibert *et al.* (2001) model

confine their network measures to the organization because the career outcomes they are interested in are organizational in order to be consistent with
previous social network and promotion research. However, if one were to
extend the model beyond the actor's employing organization, further interesting questions arise. Assuming that successful people in their own organizations
are likely to have a good network of external contacts – for example, among
businesses in the same industry or geographical region, the financial world,
local and regional government, community organizations, and so on – this
introduces a new range of possibilities to study, including: Which types of
external contacts and resulting networks are more effective for the three forms
of career success addressed in the study? Do the types of networks and the
resulting effects vary with the kind of industry? What is the influence of
cultural and institutional differences between countries on the proposed links
between network structure, social capital, and network benefits as well as the
effect on career success?

Our third example is the study on CEO succession from the previous section
(Boyer and Ortiz-Molina, 2008). It looks at the consequences of internal
managers possessing stock in the company on the type of succession (i.e.
external or internal) and the consequences of different types of succession

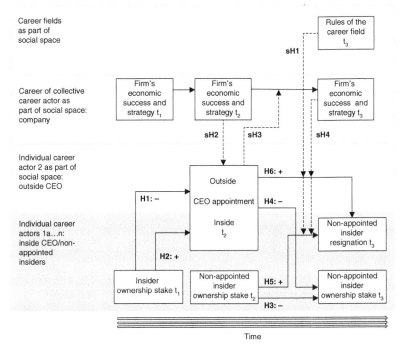

Figure 7.9 Extended model of reconstructing CEO succession and non-appointed managers (Boyer and Ortiz-Molina, 2008)

and the stock ownership of nonappointed insiders on their future behavior in terms of resigning from the company or changing their stock (see also Figure 7.6). Locating these ideas within the SCF allows us to develop them further, reaching outside the scope of the existing study. Figure 7.9 shows these extensions to the study recast in terms of the SCF. Locating these ideas within the SCF allows us to develop them further, reaching outside the scope of the existing study.

A few examples for going beyond the current bounds may suffice. Including the social space more fully and taking a career field perspective (Iellatchitch *et al.*, 2003), one could argue that the decision processes about leaving the company and, ultimately, resigning are strongly influenced by the rules of the career field and what a certain move would signal in the field (sH1). Imagine that the nonappointed insider, thinking about leaving the company in the wake of a new CEO arriving from outside, has been with the company for only a short time. If she is in a career field such as certain parts of the IT industry that requires a comparatively frequent change of company as a sign of being flexible, in demand, and willing to enlarge one's horizons, this will support leaving the company. By contrast, if she is in a career field that puts a lot of weight on seniority, as is the case in some law firms, and has been there for just two years, this will reduce the probability of leaving. Therefore, one could argue that the decision to leave the company after being passed over for promotion because an outside CEO is hired is moderated by mean rates of executive turnover in the industry, such that the decision is more likely in an industry with high mobility expectations. However, the vaguer the anticipated rules of the career field, the less they influence the decision process about leaving the organization.

Another step in developing the thoughts of the current study picks up the SCF's idea about including both individual and collective career actors and addresses the social space beyond the outsider CEO. As we note in Chapter 4, coevolutionary processes are not limited to other individuals but can also include entities of higher social complexity such as, for example, organizations. It is very plausible that the economic and strategic condition of the firm, understood as a collective career actor, plays an important role during the processes described in the study. In particular, the size of the company's performance gap in the light of stakeholders' expectations, a possible change in the company's overall strategy, and its assumed future economic performance do relate to the decision about appointing an insider or outsider CEO and to the consequences of this decision. A substantial literature looks at the effects of hiring a new CEO on various aspects of organizations, for example, turnover in the top management team (see Karaevli, 2007, for an overview; Kesner and Dalton, 1994). Firm performance receives plenty of attention, either as a cause for CEO turnover (Brickley, 2003; Farrell and Whidbee, 2003; Bommer and Ellstrand, 1996; Fizel and Louie, 1990) or as a measure of a new CEO's success, for example, by analyzing firm performance effects of interim CEOs (Ballinger and Marcel, 2010), of inside and outside CEOs (Zhang and Rajagopalan, 2010; Rhim, Peluchette, and Song, 2006; Lausten, 2002; Zajac, 1990; Beatty and Zajac, 1987) or state-controlled versus independent CEOs (Kato and Long, 2006), and of delayed naming of successors (Behn, Dawley, Riley, and Ya-wen, 2006).

Relating this to the Boyer and Ortiz-Molina study, we can build on findings that show that outsider CEOs bring about greater strategic change than insiders (Boeker, 1997) and that the impact of the change on performance is more exaggerated for outsider CEOs (Zhang and Rajagopalan, 2010). This, in turn, is likely to have an effect on the probability of existing managers staying with the firm. Therefore, not only could one argue that strong deviation from expected firm performance increases the probability of appointing an outsider CEO willing and able to change organizational policies and strategies (sH2). It is also plausible that the performance of a firm is moderated by succession type such that an outsider appointment results in greater changes in strategy and greater changes in economic success than an insider appointment (sH3). In addition, an improvement in the firm's economic success reduces the likelihood of departure of insider executives (sH4).

Overall, the expansion in terms of the effects of the rules of the career field and the role of the company as a collective career actor in the social space of the individual show interesting ways for future research building on this study.

Summation

This chapter builds on its predecessor by showing how the SCF can be used to reconstruct good career research in order to build on it by suggesting new questions to ask. The starting point for all of this reconstruction is to map the constructs and variables used in the original study in terms of the basic building block of Chapter 4.

Sometimes, just doing this suggests alternative ways of viewing the constructs, for example, by separating those based on the ontic perspective from those based on the spatial perspective. This in turn can lead to interesting questions about the relationships among these reconstructed constructs and variables. But sometimes the process also suggests connections that are not apparent in the original formulation of the problem, leading to further interesting issues for investigation. And sometimes the reconstruction process leads one to look outside the boundaries of the original approach to see relationships with new constructs and variables.

Once again it is important to revisit our caveats. First, this chapter is not a critique of the studies we chose. Instead, we use the studies to build on, in the way that cumulative research should. One does not wisely build anything on a shaky foundation. Second, we are not claiming that any of our suggestions absolutely requires the SCF to arrive at. The SCF facilitates the process, but, like any good facilitator, it can be dispensed with. Nevertheless, life is usually harder without facilitators. To take another example, catalysts typically speed the process of a chemical reaction, but they are by no means always required for the reaction to take place. What we do claim is that the reconstruction process that the SCF encourages the researcher to perform is, surprisingly often, a useful one. It shows relationships and connections that were not obvious hitherto, suggesting new ways of framing research questions. It has the potential to get the researcher somewhere interesting in shorter order than might otherwise have been the case.

Thus far in Part III we have confined ourselves to the literature based on OMC studies. In the next chapter, we step outside these boundaries and see how the SCF might help us make use of ideas within organizational studies more generally.

8 Bringing Ideas In from Organization Studies

In this chapter we continue the process of examining the applications of the SCF by seeing how it facilitates the importation of theories and models from outside what we call in Chapter 1 the proto-field of career studies (Figure 1.1), here looking at the broader field of organization studies. We are exploiting what might perhaps be the most far-reaching contribution of the SCF: it provides a language and a framework for making connections between apparently disconnected phenomena and areas of research both within career research, as we discuss in Chapter 7, and between organizational and career research.

To anticipate, we select two examples of established areas of career research, mentorship and career success, reconstructing them in terms of the SCF. This brings out certain features of both areas that suggest analogous areas of scholarship in the organizational literature. These, in turn, propose novel approaches to studying mentorship and career success.

We follow the systematic step-by-step procedure outlined in Chapter 5 in greater detail. It consists of four interrelated activities: reconstructing, phrasing the problem within the language of SCF; equivalizing, looking for similar theoretical discussions outside the career field that, compared to the reconstruction, address similar problems; understanding, focusing on the major theoretical arguments in these discussions; and importing, applying these arguments in career research through the SCF. We use these activities to go through the two areas, mentorship research and research on career success, in turn.

To repeat the point made at the end of the previous chapter, we are not claiming that the SCF provides the only route to the outcomes of this process. Nothing that appears in this chapter *requires* the SCF. But what we do claim is that the SCF appears to be very helpful in making the kind of connections that we describe later. We found the process of doing so both intuitive and straightforward, and – so far as we know – the suggestions that emerged for tackling research on mentorship and career success seem novel.

Coevolutionary Theory, Complementarity Theory, and Mentorship

Mentoring – the process by which "individuals with advanced experience and knowledge ... are committed to providing support and upwards mobility to their protégés'[1] careers" (Ragins, 1999: 349) – has been a matter of abiding interest in the career literature for many years (Allen and Eby, 2007; Ragins and Kram, 2007a). There is, of course, nothing exactly new about the idea: in Homer's *Odyssey*, Mentor was teacher and overseer of Odysseus's son Telemachus, and senior figures have advised junior figures probably since people were able to communicate at the necessary level of sophistication. Chandler, Kram, and Yip (2011: 520) trace interest in mentorship within the field of OMC studies to Levinson *et al.* (1978) and their observation that a mentor is "developmentally critical in early adulthood." However, Kram's (1985) pioneering work, establishing the phases through which these relationships pass, triggered a major expansion of research on the topic.

The bulk of this body of research addresses the Homeric notion of mentorship as a dyadic phenomenon: a mentor advises and provides support to a protégé. Mentorship support broadly falls into two categories (Kram, 1983): career support and psychosocial support. Career support involves such things as sponsorship, exposure-and-visibility, coaching, protection, and challenging assignments; it is to do with "those aspects of the relationship that primarily enhance career advancement" (ibid.: 614). Psychosocial support, involving for example role modeling, acceptance-and-confirmation, counseling, and friendship, is to do with "those aspects of the relationship that primarily enhance sense of competence, clarity of identity, and effectiveness in the managerial role" (ibid.: 614).

More recently interest has grown in more complex sets of relationships, viewing mentorship not just as a bilateral relationship, but also in terms of multiple mentors in groupings variously called relationship constellations (Kram, 1985) or developmental networks (Dobrow, Chandler, Murphy, and Kram, 2011; Higgins and Kram, 2001). This allows more complex sets of relationships to be studied. In a review of the field of mentorship research, Chandler, Kram, and Yip (2011: 526) bring to the subject an ecological perspective, "situat[ing] the phenomenon of mentoring at the intersection of complex social and psychological systems." They present an onion-skin model showing mentorship as what they label an "ontological" system to do with the focal protégé. It is embedded within layers, starting with a dyadic microsystem, within a developmental network/multiple microsystem, within an organizational microsystem, which finally is within a macrosystem encompassing social contexts, cultural differences, and technological advances.

---

[1] There is some controversy over whether "protégé" or "mentee" is the more appropriate term. We follow Chandler, Kram, and Yip (2011) in using the former.

Mentorship in the Language of the SCF

If that is the territory, how do we reconstruct it in terms of the SCF? We begin by identifying the protégé as the focal career actor and their mentor(s) as important components of their social space. The social space within which the mentors and protégé operate is likely to be structured by a variety of boundaries. For example, mentors are usually senior to protégés, meaning that hierarchical and social boundaries are part of the relevant structure. It may well be that some or all of the mentors are in different parts of the organization, implying perhaps functional or divisional boundaries separating them. It is also possible that some mentors may be from another organization entirely. For example, people may stay in touch with their teachers or professors (especially if they remain in academic life); as professionals, they may have mentors with whom they have worked in the past and who have maintained an interest in their career; and so on. The social space becomes important, too, for tracking the progress of the protégé's career, as they move across the boundaries that mark their development and growth.

The ontic perspective directs our attention to the protégé's condition. Age, for example, is in all probability going to be a key variable as a proxy for experience, both in terms of the protégé's life span and in relation to their mentors. So, for example, the kind of mentoring a protégé receives may well vary at different stages of their career. When they are young, it is likely to be about things like who in the organization is helpful and who should be avoided, which kinds of assignment are good for a career and which aren't, or which kinds of behaviors are helpful to getting ahead and which are career-limiting. When they are older, it is more likely to be about whether to accept a promotion or an offer of a position in another organization or when it makes sense to retire. Mentors are probably older than protégés when the protégés are young but of similar ages later.

Other aspects of condition that figure in research on mentorship include personality, gender, race, human capital, and, of course, career success measured in its many modes (Chandler *et al.*, 2011). Again, it is not just the protégé whose condition is of interest. Because mentorship is a relational phenomenon, the relationship between particular aspects of condition matter. To take the example of gender, cross-gender mentoring brings up issues that are different from within-gender mentoring (O'Brien, Biga, Kessler, and Allen, 2010).

So far in this account, time has appeared only in terms of the age of the actors. But mentorship becomes interesting, of course, when it is mapped over time: the mentor's advice today affects the condition and position of the protégé at some stage in the future. Furthermore, as the relationships develop, the mentors' condition and position are likely to be affected by what happens to the protégé. For example, a young woman acquires a more senior figure as mentor, from whom she learns the ropes in terms of how things work in the organization. As the protégé gains in experience and confidence and begins to get noticed, her mentor benefits not just in terms of the satisfaction he gains from the experience (Allen, 2007) but perhaps because the projects that the protégé is working on are yielding results that benefit his own career. As his career flourishes, he brings his protégé along with him, and so the cycle potentially repeats itself.

In this example, we have adopted the first elaboration of the basic building block of the SCF heuristic model by chaining events forward in time (see Figure 4.2). Mentors affect the protégé's condition in some way; the protégé, in the next step along the chain, affects the condition of the mentors, which in a further step along the chain affects the protégé, and so on. Although this is an obvious way of viewing the mentoring relationship, Chandler *et al.* (2011) note that it – they use the term "relational mentoring," a concept from Positive Organizational Scholarship denoting a broad form of "mutual learning and growth" (Chandler *et al.*, 2011: 537) – has had little empirical attention in the literature.

Reconstructing mentorship in this way makes at least two things evident. First, we are describing here a form of coevolution: the careers of mentors and protégé coevolve over time. But it is, potentially, a complex form of coevolution, especially if more than one mentor is involved. There are many variables that can come into play when we are trying to predict how a given mentorship relationship or relationship constellation will develop over time because there are many facets of each actor's condition that could be important when seen in relation to those of the others. We have already touched on two – age and gender – but there are many more. In countries in which race figures prominently in people's thinking, it can have an important influence on mentorship relations (Thomas, 1993). In others, religion might be equally, if not more, influential (although, curiously, it does not seem to have been much studied in the mentorship context; for examples of exceptions, see Dworkin, Maurer, and Schipani, 2012; Opayemi, 2012). So, second, the ways in which *combinations* of variables may interact are clearly important.

We now come to the equivalizing step: Are there theoretical approaches in organizational studies more generally that deal with similar kinds of issues? We have already given the game away with the first point in the previous paragraph, of course, because there is indeed a literature on coevolution (Lewin, Long, and Carroll, 1999) on which it may be fruitful to draw. The second point is about combinations of properties, and it turns out that there is a literature on this, too, or, rather two connected literatures, configuration and complementarity theory (Whittington, Pettigrew, Simon, Fenton, and Conyon, 1999). The configuration literature looks at organizations holistically, arguing that certain archetypes or ideal types emerge that form "coherent ensembles" (Van de Ven *et al.*, 2013:

404). Complementarity extends this view by opening the black box of config-uration and examining how the properties that define it interact. Here we focus on complementarity theory because it has the potential to address the question: How might the complex sets of variables involved in describing a mentorship relation interact and influence that relation? We address each of these – coevolution and complementarity – in turn.

Challenging Conventional Wisdom: Coevolutionary Theory

Coevolution as a concept has been of interest to organizational scholars for the past two decades at least (Lewin *et al.*, 1999), but it has not always been used with care:

"Evolution" is a widely used but ambiguous term. Many organizational researchers (Huygens, Baden-Fuller, van den Bosch & Volberda, 2001; Jenkins & Floyd, 2001; Jones, 2001; Lewin & Volberda, 2003; Rodrigues & Child, 2003) refer to "evolution" or "co-evolution" while being insufficiently clear what they mean. There is no established, common meaning for these terms. In some academic disciplines "evolution" evokes Darwinism, but in other quarters (notably in current evolutionary economics) it refers more vaguely and broadly to change. Terms such as "evolution" or "co-evolution" are often used with gravitas, as if they signify something important; but without further specification they actually mean very little. One is left asking what kind of evolutionary theory or meta-theoretical framework is intended. (Hodgson, 2013: 973–974)

We follow Heylighen and Campbell (1995: 184), who define it as follows:

[t]he environment [of an evolving entity] changes in part because it also often consists of evolving systems that try to optimize their fitness. This interdependency, where the change in fitness of one system changes the fitness function for another system, and vice-versa, is called co-evolution.

Fitness "is a complex function of the system and its environment, an index of the likelihood that the system would persist and replicate. Those systems will be selected that have the highest fitness" (ibid.: 184). So fitness is an index of the evolutionary success of the entity in question.

In the case of mentorship, the evolving entities/systems in which we are interested are the protégé and their mentor(s). We can visualize fitness in any way that is helpful to our purpose. Suppose, for example, we think of it as career success. This is, of course, a very complex construct (Heslin, 2005; see, too, later under "Neo-institutionalism and Career Success") that has been approached in the mentorship literature from both objective (e.g. promotions, salary) and subjective (e.g. career satisfaction, career commitment, and job satisfaction) angles (Ragins and Kram, 2007b). Again, for simplicity, let us assume that each actor (system) strives to increase their career success in order to be able to achieve what it is that they are looking to achieve in life – fame and fortune, personal growth, a flourishing family, or whatever it might be. That is, after all, what most people at least try to do. Life, of course, places many obstacles in the way.

At this point we need to introduce the concept of "fitness landscapes," something devised by evolutionary biologists to depict the relationship between genotype and reproductive success (Kauffman, 1993; for an introduction to their applications to organizations, see Van de Ven *et al.*, 2013). Initially we shall use fitness landscapes purely descriptively, as an alternative way of conceptualizing fitness in the context of mentoring. But later we shall need them to understand what lies behind the various suggestions that coevolutionary theory potentially can make for handling some of the consequences for mentorship relations that are predicted by the theory.

In fitness landscapes as used by evolutionary biologists, genotype is represented by the horizontal dimensions of the landscape and reproductive success by its vertical dimension. Organisms with similar genotypes are close to each other in the landscape and probably have similar reproductive success, while organisms with significantly differing genotypes, at different locations in the landscape, may have differing reproductive success. The landscape has peaks of organisms with similar genotypes and high reproductive success and valleys of organisms with similar genotypes but low reproductive success. It may be smooth, with perhaps a single peak, or rugged, with many smaller peaks, ridges, and valleys. Evolution is imagined as a process of genotypes climbing the peaks (increasing their fitness and therefore reproductive success), and the topography of the landscape describes how that evolutionary process might unfold for that particular genotype.

To return to mentorship, i.e. to import ideas from coevolutionary theory, the analogy we use here for genotype is condition, so that provides the horizontal dimensions of the fitness landscape we are imagining, with career success as the vertical dimension. We can envisage career actors with similar combinations of condition being close to each other on an imaginary career success landscape and actors with different combinations of condition being far away. We can also imagine certain combinations of condition – perhaps high intelligence, agreeability, social capital – being associated with peaks in the landscape and other combinations of condition, perhaps the opposite of that list, being associated with valleys. Our assertion that the actors are trying to increase their career success translates here into them trying to change their condition, perhaps by improving their social capital, so that they can climb a nearby success "peak."

Now let us add in the coevolutionary component. Coevolution, as explicated by Heylighen and Campbell, comprises systems/entities interacting so that a change in the fitness of one affects the fitness of others. We previously described ways in which the success of a protégé might affect the success of their mentor(s), which in turn may have a further impact on the protégé's success. To put it in terms of fitness landscapes, as one actor moves up a fitness peak, they affect the fitness landscapes of the actors in their social space. If, for example, the protégé's actions improve things for a mentor, we visualize the mentor's landscape moving upward so that they achieve greater success without changing other aspects of their condition, rather like geological processes might push upward the land on which one is standing (albeit faster, unless the geological process is an earthquake). To give another example, as the protégé learns from his mentors about who needs to be impressed when putting forward a proposal within the organization, the mentors' careers in turn may benefit from their association with their protégé's increased proposal acceptance rate. So the protégé climbs a fitness (success) peak, pushing the "ground" up beneath the feet of their mentors.

Thus far we have simply restated the mentorship relationship in coevolutionary terms. In order to demonstrate the benefits of so doing, we need to address a basic assumption of the current mentorship literature. It is that, despite work on dysfunctional aspects of mentoring (e.g. Feldman, 1999; Scandura, 1998), mentoring is normally seen as a synergistic relationship that results in the greater good for the collectivity. This is not particularly surprising given that mentorship is about providing "support and upward mobility to . . . protégé's careers" (Ragins, 1999: 349), an obvious reference to the Homeric origins of the word to which we refer earlier. Indeed it is probably not much of an exaggeration to say that the practical (and laudable) aim of research on mentorship is, by and large, to come up with ways of supporting people in the development of their careers.

Yet coevolutionary theory suggests that coevolutionary relationships may not be stable over time and that less rosy outcomes are possible or even likely. Building on insight into regularities of social behavior, Heylighen and Campbell (1995) derive a five-way classification of coevolutionary systems. At one end of the scale are synergistic systems in which each member benefits from the actions of the others. The paradigmatic examples of this are lichens, in which cyanobacteria and/or algae and fungi cooperate (although recent research shows that a yeast is involved as well; Ash, 2016), the former extracting carbon dioxide from the atmosphere, converting it to organic matter that the fungus lives off and converts to other resources that the cyanobacteria and algae need. At the other end of the scale is super-competition, in which self-interested actions of some members cause losses for all, in the manner of the so-called tragedy of the commons (Hardin, 1968) in which the need for all grazing animals to gather as much grass as they can leads to famine for all. Heylighen and Campbell (1995: 190) argue that, over time, synergistic systems have a built-in tendency to change to competitive systems in a variant of the "nice guys finish last" scenario:

The problem is that everybody profits from cooperation, but that noncooperators profit more, since they reap the additional resources produced by synergy, while investing nothing in return. This is the classical "free-rider" problem: everyone benefits from a public transport system funded by individual contributions, but the one who does not pay benefits most. Since evolution never stops, variation will sooner or later produce "free riders" in an otherwise optimized social system, and it is the latter that will be selected, not the earnest cooperators, resulting in the erosion and eventual collapse of the cooperative system.

Baum (1999) extends this view of the risks associated with coevolution, building on the work of Heylighen and Campbell (1995) using Kauffman's (1993: Chapter 6) *NK[C]* simulations of coevolving systems. Following Kauffman, he "conceive[s] *coevolution* as a process that couples the *NK* fitness landscapes of different agents" (Baum, 1999: 121; emphasis in the original). *N*, *K*, and *C* refer to critical parameters used in the models to specify the "conditions under which agents composing a coevolving system are able to adapt successfully" (Baum, 1999: 121):

In the *NK[C]* model, *N* refers to the number of traits of an agent; *K* refers to internal complexity, the number of traits that are interdependent; and *C* refers to external complexity, the number of traits of one agent that coevolve with the traits of another agent. Each trait, *K*, makes a fitness contribution that depends on that trait and on *K* other traits among the *N* that compose the agent.

Kauffman's simulations show how the ruggedness of fitness landscapes changes as *N*, *K*, and *C* vary, ranging from a Kilimanjaro-like single peak that can be reached by climbing upward from anywhere in the landscape to multiple peaks, ridges, and valleys in which it is easy when climbing to get stuck on a minor peak. Baum's point is that, at a general level, coevolutionary systems cannot be relied on to evolve into a state of optimal fitness. This he describes as a Nash equilibrium, in which no entity has anything to gain by changing its strategy given the strategies of the other entities with which it interacts. Depending on the complexity of the relationships governing the coevolutionary process, Kauffman's simulations demonstrate that systems may not reach Nash equilibrium atop the highest peak in the landscape but can get trapped in less than optimal states, which we can view as getting stuck at the top of lesser peaks in the fitness landscape.

These two lines of argument – degrading relationships (Heylighen and Campbell, 1995) and getting stuck in suboptimal states (Baum, 1999) – suggest two counterintuitive predictions that challenge the conventional wisdom in the mentorship literature: that on the whole it is a beneficial process. Next, we use some hypothetical examples to show what these predictions might look like in practice.

Degrading Relationships An example of a synergistic, developmental relationship degrading in the way that Heylighen and Campbell describe might be one in which the developmental relationship between mentor and protégé turns into an exploitative one on the part of the mentor as she takes advantage of her power to appropriate the benefits of projects initiated by the protégé. Alternatively the protégé might take advantage of his mentor[s] being busy and distracted and therefore unaware of all he is up to, which could include using their names to his benefit but not to theirs. The more destructive the political maneuvering, the more likely it is that the situation moves from a synergistic to a zero-sum or net negative overall benefit. As soon as one party starts taking advantage of the relationship, it becomes very hard to reverse the situation to move back to its original synergistic tone: trust, once broken, is not easy to restore.

It is important to note that this is a different kind of argument from that used by, for example, Scandura (1998) to describe the development of dysfunctional mentorship relationships. Scandura's model (ibid.: 461) shows how dysfunctional mentoring can be the result of what the SCF would label the condition (demographics, personality, relationship skills) of mentor and protégé. Heylighen and Campbell's argument, by contrast, is that dysfunction is the result of *the way that protégé and mentors' careers are likely to coevolve*; it has nothing to do with the actors' condition (which still has the potential to exacerbate the situation in the manner that Scandura describes).

Suboptimality To return to the example of the protégé being helped by their mentors with their proposals, the success of the developmental network in gaining resources may be suboptimal for the organization as a whole because it could, in time, turn into a self-serving clique. Each – or, at least, some – of the clique may do nicely out of the arrangement for the time being, but if the clique is self-serving enough, as cliques have a tendency to be, in the extreme providing "the social support that allows employees to engage in workplace deviance while at the same time avoiding the stigmatization and guilt that often accompanies misconduct" (Litzky, Eddleston, and Kidder, 2006: 99), it is likely to be bad for the fitness of the organization of which they are members and, eventually, for them. Alternatively, a mentor might provide the protégé with less than optimal advice, perhaps about whom to avoid when putting a particular proposal together based on the mentor's ongoing feud with that person. If the protégé does so and reaps the consequences in terms, for example, of a less-than-successful proposal presentation, the chances are that the mentors may lose ground as well because the knowledge that the advice came from them strengthens the hand of their enemies. So mentor and protégé suffer, but so, too, may the organization, given the general destructiveness of political infighting.

To summarize, coevolutionary theory makes two predictions about how developmental networks can be expected to deteriorate over time: first, cooperative mentorship relationships are likely to degrade to competitive ones over time, and second, the complex relationships that may arise particularly in developmental networks may result in the development of the actors getting "stuck" in suboptimal states, either because cliques can form that are suboptimal for the organization or because things that happen to one actor in the network can hold back the development of another.

If that is what coevolutionary theory predicts for mentorship relations, does it have any suggestions for what might be done to ameliorate the outcomes? What does the theory say about managing these systems?

Here we return to the work of Baum (1999), who describes a number of system-level policies, which he refers to as "tuning," that might help coevolving organizational systems approach Nash equilibrium, i.e. an optimal state. The basic aim of the strategies is to avoid what Kauffman (1993) calls complexity catastrophe: the consequence of systems getting trapped in suboptimal states on very rugged fitness landscapes. As we have seen, the ruggedness of these landscapes depends on the internal complexity of the agent K:

Thus, Kauffman's $NK[C]$ framework affords a dynamic model of coupled fitness landscapes whose ruggedness and richness of coupling can be *tuned*. Increasing K [the system's internal complexity] tunes the landscape toward … more ruggedness (increased numbers of less-fit local optima) and increased likelihood of agents becoming stranded on local (sub)optima – a complexity catastrophe. Increasing C [the connectedness of the system with others with which it is coevolving] prolongs the "coupled dancing" (Kauffman, 1993) in which agents' moves alter one another's fitness landscapes, preventing stabilization. (Baum, 1999: 122–123, emphasis in the original)

The greater K, the internal complexity of the system that is coevolving with other systems (i.e. one of the agents in the overall coevolving system), the more rugged its fitness landscape. The greater the number of connections between the coevolving agents, C, the longer it takes for the system to reach Nash equilibrium because there is so much more "coupled dancing" going on between the agents. So Baum's tuning involves adjusting both K and C, the tuning techniques depending on, and varying with, the particular pattern of the parameters (N, K, and C) for a given system.

Can we apply Baum's analysis to mentorship systems? First, let us translate the N, K, and C parameters into terms that apply to such a system. *Agents* are our career actors: mentors or protégés. N is the number of traits we consider for the actors, and K is a measure of internal complexity, of how interconnected these traits are within any one actor. Finally, C depicts how interconnected the actors are: the more connections and the more complex the connections, the higher C becomes. For present purposes, we can think of K as an indication of the complexity of an actor, which includes the complexity of their connection with, for example, the organization's reward system because their motivations are part of their condition, and these motivations are activated by the reward system(s). We can think of C as an indication of how complex the connections are *between* actors – mentor(s) and protégé(s).

Applying Baum's analysis to mentorship systems suggests, for example, that when connections between mentors and protégés are complex (C is large), as might happen in an organization with many strong ties between mentors and protégés especially in complex developmental networks, it might be advisable to reduce C by reorganizing the mentor–protégé linkages every so often in order to reduce the possibility of cliquishness within the networks. Alternatively, one could increase K in order to increase ruggedness and thereby the number of local peaks on which people can get stuck, perhaps by adopting many different ways of rewarding performance across the organization. This sounds paradoxical, but multiple lower peaks mean that the returns to individuals from their developmental networks are lower, so the incentives pulling them toward the dysfunctions of these networks are correspondingly lower. In doing so, we are using a complexity catastrophe to avoid other catastrophes. Finally, if the aim is to *avoid* multiple sub-peaks for people to get stuck on, i.e. if the overriding concern is to allow people to develop as much as they can, then either K can be reduced to reduce ruggedness or C can be increased to slow down the rate at which networks can settle down and get stuck in suboptimal states, giving more time for experimentation with different and potentially more advantageous arrangements. We might reduce K by introducing more uniform policies and procedures concerning mentorship, thereby reducing the possibility of protégés, for example, being mis-advised by their mentors, or increase C by encouraging the formation of larger and more tightly interconnected developmental networks.

Our point is not that this application of these tuning methods is necessarily correct. We do propose, though, that importing coevolutionary thinking from the broader organizational literature at the organizational level of analysis introduces fresh approaches to analyzing the behavior of mentorship systems as a whole. It suggests a set of new research agendas such as looking at degrading mentorship systems over time or systems-based interventions into sets of mentorship networks, and it leads to a number of concrete propositions. For example, following the argument of Heylinghen and Campbell (1995) that cooperative relationships are likely to degrade:

Proposition 1: The longer a coevolutionary developmental network exists, the more its members will show self-serving behavior at the expense of other network members.

Proposition 2: The more successful developmental networks become in obtaining resources, the greater will be the tendency for self-serving behavior on the part of some or all of the developmental network members.

Following Baum's (1999) predictions of clique development as an example of a sub-optimal state:

Proposition 3: The greater the uniformity with which mentorship is rewarded within a given organization, the greater the possibility that developmental networks will demonstrate self-serving behavior.

Specifically targeted at reward practices:

Proposition 3a: Standardized organizational reward practices for mentorship reduce organizational commitment of mentors and protégées in developmental networks.

Proposition 3b: Standardized organizational reward practices for mentorship reduce organizational citizenship behavior of mentors and protégées in developmental networks.

Finally, addressing the observations concerning the quality of mentorship relations:

Proposition 4a: Greater uniformity in the way mentorship is rewarded across an organization results in higher-quality developmental relations.

Proposition 4b: Larger, more tightly interconnected mentorship networks result in higher-quality developmental relations.

Asking New Research Questions: Complementarity Theory

The relationships between mentors and protégé also lead to interesting questions about fit: How do different combinations of the condition of mentors and protégé affect the relationship? Thus far, this has been addressed from two directions: studies of dyadic heterogeneity mostly in terms of gender and race and studies that examine the quality of the relationship in terms of properties such as agreement or developmental support (Chandler *et al.*, 2011). Yet, as we have seen, the literature on mentorship has moved beyond dyads to support networks. Reconstructing it in SCF terms, we can frame it not only as a coevolutionary system in which the condition of protégé, mentors, and their social context change over time but also as a question of fit within the complex cluster of individual and contextual properties, properties of actor condition and of social space.

In order to equivalize, we focus on the overall fitness of the system. This leads us to well-studied areas in the organizational literature. In particular, the related configurational (Miller, 1987a) and complementarity (Whittington *et al.*, 1999) literatures address this issue with respect to organizations (Van de Ven *et al.*, 2013). Understanding these literatures is the next stage. Configurational theory looks at organizations as ensembles of properties and examines whether there are particular configurations of organizational and environmental properties that are more viable than others. Complementarity theory climbs inside the black box of configuration by looking to see how the combinations of properties work together to produce a payoff that is either greater or less than the sum of its parts. In short, complementary properties increase the marginal benefit of other properties:

As we show, these ideas give substance to previously elusive notions such as "fit" or "systems effects," provide some basis for interpreting claims such as the need for strategy and structure to fit one another, give an approach to modeling such issues formally, clarify some ambiguities and enrich our understanding concerning directions of causation, and also suggest reasons why fit may be hard to achieve and change may be slow, painful, and uncertain. (Milgrom and Roberts, 1995: 180)

But the complementarities may not necessarily be positive: complementarity theory also recognizes the possibility that "changing only a few of the system elements at a time to their optimal values may not come at all close to achieving all the benefits that are available through a fully co-ordinated move, and may even have negative payoffs" (Milgrom and Roberts, 1995: 191).

Siggelkow (2001) provides an example of just such a negative payoff. He describes how the fashion apparel manufacturer Liz Claiborne in the early 1990s changed one aspect of its operations, which unexpectedly had a seriously negative impact on its profitability. It had many small suppliers in the Far East, which gave it a complex supply chain to manage. One of the ways in which it had managed this complexity hitherto was its long-standing policy of not allowing retailers to reorder, which meant that it had not needed to spend much on information systems, nor had it needed a production-to-order system. Together these would have added cost and delays to its supply chain. However, changes in the retailing and competitive landscape in the 1990s meant that it was forced to abandon its no-reordering policy, which it did without changing any other aspects of its business processes ("playing an incomplete game": Siggelkow, 2001: 851). The result was a buildup of inventory, loss of sales, and inventory writeoffs, which was only corrected by a change of management and a substantial overhaul of all of the company's business practices. The case is an illustration of how the complementarities of one factor – here, the no-reorder policy – can lead to disproportionate effects on the overall system when it is changed.

Complementarity theory, then, recognizes that the impact on a system of any one property depends on how that property interacts with other properties. Something that is relatively ineffectual under some combinations of properties may turn out to have an important effect – positive or negative – under other combinations. The theory leads to an approach that is new to the mentorship literature. Instead of examining the impact of properties such as gender or ethnicity one by one on mentorship relations, it points toward examining how different *combinations* of the properties of the condition of protégé, mentors, and their social context work together to affect the performance of mentorship systems. To express this in terms of the elaborated SCF model, complementarity theory directs attention to the ways in which subsets of various characteristics of the social space and of career actors may interact in order to affect the full set of relationships shown in in the heuristic model (Figure 4.3).

One example of importing the thinking of complementarity theory in terms of mentorship theory is to consider research on formal mentoring programs, those based on organizationally sanctioned relationships that involve some kind of standardized matching process. The literature on these programs is largely anecdotal, although there are some indications of the factors associated with more successful programs (Baugh and Fagenson-Eland, 2007). These include program goals that match the company's strategic objectives, linking the program to career development rather than socialization, a program in which participation is voluntary and participants have input to the matching process, dyad similarity, frequent dyad interaction, and good quality training. However, a complementary perspective immediately makes one wonder whether there might be other sociocultural factors that might influence the relationship. To take one example, voluntary participation and participation in the choice process needs to be matched to the organization's culture. It is hard to imagine it succeeding in a rigidly hierarchical culture with large power distances; nothing is likely to feel "voluntary" to a junior member of such an organization.

To take a second example, mixed-ethnicity dyadic mentoring appears to be most effective when the preferred strategies of mentor and protégé to handling matters of race – whether they prefer to engage directly with race-related information and racial differences or to deny and suppress any race-related discussion – are "complementary" (Thomas, 1993), i.e. matching. If they are not, then the person whose preferred strategy is not being used "will feel race to be an obstacle to developing a close personal bond" (ibid.: 177). Thomas argues that denial/suppression arises from a liberal assimilationist perspective in which minorities are assumed to "develop the tastes and sensibilities of the majority, race ceases to be a salient dimension of difference (Park, 1950), and 'color blindness' becomes the ideal psychological state (Will, 1990)" (ibid.: 178). The alternative perspective, pluralism, is presented as a healthier, more mature attitude (without using those terms). It

suggests that individuals seek to maintain a positive sense of racial identity and connectedness while adopting aspects of the dominant culture that enable them to be

effective (Greeley, 1974; Hraba and Hoiberg, 1983). According to this view, relationships are facilitated by acknowledging and valuing differences and committing to work
against inequalities (Jackson and Holvino, 1988). (ibid.: 174)

This framing is very understandable in a country such as the USA (where this
study was conducted) with race looming large as a social issue. However, how
might this change in other jurisdictions? What role might other factors, such as
the complementarity of educational backgrounds, the nature of HR policies,
informal sociocultural practices, political or religious affiliation, or the legislative
environment, play in determining how these sets of relationships develop over
time? Are there particular factors that are unimportant by themselves but become
significant when combined with certain other factors? Political affiliation, for
example, may have little effect on a mentorship relationship other than, perhaps,
a mild positive one if both share the affiliation. However, suppose that the shared
affiliation is to a party that is noted for strong stands on certain issues: race as in
the case of the South African ANC, nationality as with the Scottish National
Party or the Parti Québécois, or socioeconomic issues such as taxes or government influence with any strongly left-wing or right-wing party. It is not beyond
question that such a situation might swamp the ethnicity effect described by
Thomas, not to mention the influence of other attributes that have been studied in
the mentorship literature, notably gender. This is likely to be even more the case
if religious affiliations are under consideration, as for example with a Muslim
protégé–mentor pair in a strongly Christian country or vice versa.

These speculative examples are of complementarities between aspects of the
condition of a mentor–protégé dyad. The situation becomes potentially more
complex when we consider a relationship constellation. For example, the
effectiveness with which a multifunctional group of mentors, perhaps chosen
by a protégé who is interested in developing useful contacts across an organization, operates is likely to be markedly affected by the permeability of the
internal organizational boundaries. A fluid, organic structure, for example, is
likely to be much more supportive of such a constellation than a more rigid,
mechanistic one.

Again, we introduce these possibilities not because they are necessarily
correct but simply to illustrate the direction that the complementarities perspective takes thinking on mentorship, in turn a consequence of following the
direction in which the SCF points. Each suggests a potential study and illustrates the potential of the complementarity perspective (Chandler et al., 2011).

Neo-institutionalism and Career Success

Our second example of how to use the SCF encompasses career success, a
central topic in career studies. We start with outlining major lines of thinking

and insight in the area, in particular conceptualizing career success and looking for influencing factors as well as reconstructing the basic issues in the language of the SCF. We then turn to equivalizing, i.e. looking outside for areas in organization studies dealing with similar problems where the debates about the ultimate goals of organizations (e.g. Simon, 1964) and about the role of contextual elements for organizational goal achievement (critically March and Sutton, 1997) come to mind. In the stage of understanding, we use new institutional theory (see, e.g. Scott, 2014; Greenwood, Oliver, Sahlin, and Suddaby, 2008b; Powell, 2007; Powell and DiMaggio, 1991) and outline some major answers to the question of basic organizational goals and influence of the context on organizations. In a final step we import these insights to show how they help career research in terms of challenging conventional wisdom in career success research, asking new research questions and develop the current research methodology.

Dimensions and Influencing Factors

Career success is a major issue in career studies and the focus of a great number of both theoretical and empirical studies. Two major streams within this literature deal with what career success actually "is," i.e. how different individuals across various contextual settings conceptualize it, and what factors influence it. We will deal with these issues in turn before reconstructing career success in the language of the SCF.

Conceptualizing Career Success Career success is often referred to as psychological success and "the experience of achieving goals that are personally meaningful to the individual, rather than those set by parents, peers, an organization, or society" (Mirvis and Hall, 1994: 366). Arguably the most basic differentiation is between objective and subjective career success, a distinction drawn long ago by Hughes (1937) between what he labels the objective and the subjective career.

Objective careers denote those aspects of careers that are visible to others, usually objectively measurable. They are linked to positions in a social space, often with an emphasis on organizations and the jobs they can offer. Consequently, measures of objective career success typically include hierarchical advancement, number of promotions (sometimes within a given time period), or income. The subjective career can be regarded as the way that individuals construct and perceive their own career. It is seen as "the moving perspective in which the person sees his life as a whole and interprets the meaning of his various attributes, actions and the things which happen to him" (Hughes, 1958: 63). Individuals' idiosyncratic construction of their career and career outcomes is crucial here. Building on this view, early concepts such as the protean career

(Hall, 1976), career anchors (Schein, 1985), and career orientations (Derr, 1986) unfold the various dimensions of subjective career success. More recent conceptual efforts also analyze variations within subjective career success (e.g. Dries, Pepermans, and De Kerpel, 2008b; Arthur, Khapova, and Wilderom, 2005; Heslin, 2005). Subjective career success normally is operationalized as job or career satisfaction (e.g. Greenhaus, Parasuraman, and Wormley, 1990; for a more elaborate view see Dries, Pepermans, Hofmans, and Rypens, 2009).

Against the backdrop of this basic differentiation, a number of further approaches toward unfolding the concept of career success exist (see an overview of empirically derived dimensions in Dries, Pepermans, and Calier, 2008a). From a conceptual perspective, Heslin (2005) elaborates on the simple subjective–objective divide. He argues that the evaluation of career success depends "upon the standards against which they are evaluated. Career outcomes may be evaluated relative to personal standards (i.e. self-referent criteria), or the attainments and expectations of others (i.e. other-referent criteria)" (ibid.: 118). He suggests that these two different types of criteria stem from the objective and the subjective domain, which leads to a two-by-two matrix, one dimension distinguishing between self-referent and other-referent domains and the second between objective and subjective domains. Examples include promotion aspirations (self-referent and objective), goals for fulfillment (self-referent and subjective), one's social standing (other-referent and objective), and fun relative to peers (other-referent and subjective). In addition, more recent considerations partly challenge the distinction between objective and subjective career success, arguing that this differentiation is at least partly misleading (Heslin and Mayrhofer, 2016).

Gunz and Heslin (2005) draw a distinction between what they call subjectivist and objectivist approaches to studying career success. They point out that the word "success" is ambiguous, meaning a favorable outcome but also quite simply an outcome, i.e. the consequences, neither necessarily good nor bad, of an event or succession of events. So a key question about studying career success, they argue, concerns who it is that defines what constitutes success. Is it the researcher (the objectivist approach) or the people being studied (subjectivist)? Most studies described thus far here have taken the objectivist approach; the subjectivist approach is relatively rare (exceptions include, e.g. Heslin, 2003; Juntunen et al., 2001; Gersick, Bartunek, and Dutton, 2000; Hofer, Stallings, Reynolds, Cliff, and Russell, 1994). More recently, two interesting studies further strengthen the subjectivist approach to conceptualizing career success.

In a study of twenty-two managers in Belgium, Dries et al. (2008a) use both objectivist and subjectivist elements. They derive forty-two superordinate career success operationalizations that are the input for a Q-sort study in which thirty subject matter experts evaluated these views. Based on multidimensional scaling, they extract a two-dimensional space with affect versus achievement and intrapersonal versus interpersonal as the poles, defining a space that broadly combines subjective (affect, intrapersonal) with objective (achievement, interpersonal). Within this configuration, they identify nine regions of meaning: performance, advancement, self-development, creativity, security, satisfaction, recognition, cooperation, and contribution.

The Dries *et al.* study is, of course, of a small sample of subjects from one occupation in one national context. More recently, in a much larger-scale, cross-national study, Briscoe *et al.* (2014, 2012b) rely solely on individuals' views of their own career success. They analyze the dimensions of career success across individuals from different age and professional groups and cultural contexts. In a large-scale qualitative study, they interview nurses, business school graduates, and blue-collar workers in the early and late stages of their careers across eleven countries. Building on this, in a second round, they enlarge the sample of participants and countries. After an online card sort exercise with 360 participants from thirteen countries along GLOBE's (House, Javidan, Hanges, and Dorfman, 2002) ten sampled cultural regions and a confirmatory factor analysis study across 4,438 survey respondents in sixteen countries (Austria, Belgium, Brazil, China, France, Greece, India, Italy, Malaysia, Nigeria, Norway, Philippines, Slovenia, South Korea, Turkey, and the United States), they develop a new scale measuring career success along seven dimensions. Perhaps not surprisingly given the difference in scales of the two studies, the factors that emerge from the larger study are partly different from those from the smaller one: learning and development, entrepreneurship, work-life balance, positive impact, positive work relationships, financial security, and financial achievement (Mayrhofer *et al.*, 2016).

Influencing Factors A second or even, as some would argue, the major stream of career research is the identification of influencing factors on career success. There is a substantial amount of empirical research trying to identify the link between both objective and subjective career success and a wealth of influencing factors at various levels, ranging from the individual to macro-factors such as globalization or virtualization.

Conceptually structuring the myriad of influencing factors on career success and career patterns, Mayrhofer *et al.* (2007a) present a multilayer model with four contextual layers beyond the individual. The context of work contains factors such as the labor market situation, social relationships at work, and new forms of work and organizing. In the context of origin, there are factors such as class and strata, educational socialization, and the individual's work history. The context of society and culture relates to regional and/or national culture and points toward factors such as national demographic and ethnic diversity, institutions such as labor law and trade unions, and the role of women in society. In the final global layer, there are factors from the global context such as virtualization and globalization.

Ng, Eby, Sorensen, and Feldman (2005) conduct a meta-analysis of influencing factors with regard to studies looking at promotion and salary level as objective career success measures and career satisfaction indicating subjective career success. They differentiate between four groups of influencing factors. Human capital indicates an individual's personal, educational, and professional experiences. Related predictors include, for example, job and organization tenure, international work experience, or the number of hours worked. Organizational sponsorship relates to "the extent to which organizations provide special assistance to employees to facilitate their career success" (371). Examples of predictors are training and skill development opportunities or supervisor support. Sociodemographic factors include indicators such as sex, ethnicity, age, or marital status. Finally, stable individual differences relate to dispositional traits such as the five-factor model or locus of control. At a general level, stable individual differences and organizational sponsorship had a stronger relationship to subjective career success, whereas sociodemographic and human capital predictors were more strongly related to objective career success.

This stream of work continues in the current decade. Examples with regard to objective career success include mediating effects of cognitive ability and conscientiousness when looking at the relationship between human capital and objective indicators of career success (Ng and Feldman, 2010), the role of psychological contract breach on career success (Restubog, Bordia, and Bordia, 2011), or the effect of interorganizational mobility (Sammarra, Profili, and Innocenti, 2013). Examples focusing on subjective career success include methodological considerations about measurement (Pan and Zhou, 2015), the effects of objective on subjective career success (Stumpf and Tymon, 2012), or the role of gender orientation (Ngo, Foley, Ji, and Loi, 2014). With a broader perspective covering both objective and subjective career success, recent studies address, for example, commonalities and differences of career success views in different countries (Shen *et al.*, 2015b), time-related effects of self-efficacy (Spurk and Abele, 2014), or the effects of narcissism (Hirschi and Jaensch, 2015).

The point has often been made (e.g. Judge and Kammeyer-Mueller, 2007) that there is little correlation between the objective and subjective side of career success. People who appear to have had very successful lives do not necessarily feel successful, and people who are happy with their lives are by no means necessarily those with the greatest wealth or social status (as captured nicely in the song "I've Got Plenty o' Nuttin" from Gershwin's opera *Porgy and Bess*). The point has also been made, however (Nicholson and De Waal-Andrews, 2005), that subjective success could result from rationalizing objective failure.

Evidently, then, career success has been much studied both as a construct and as an outcome. Broadly speaking, it is something that has meaning both objectively, as a visible index of achievement, and subjectively, as a personal interpretation of that achievement. How might the SCF add to our understanding by rephrasing these research efforts in its language and, consequently, help to make use of insight gained in organization studies elsewhere? We will first briefly reconstruct the activities in the language of the SCF before we look outside for an equivalent discussion – here neo-institutionalist theorizing – and try to understand basic lines of argument relevant for the discussion on career success. In a final step, we will then import this thinking back to career studies, showing how career research can learn from it.

Career Success in the Language of the SCF

The language of the SCF allows us to reconstruct the core concerns of both streams of study: defining the career success construct and understanding what influences it. Reconstructing the career success construct is about identifying relevant single or multiple elements of the condition and position of career actors. This quest for identifying relevant dimensions of career success involves examining a specific element of the career actor's condition and position embedded in a social context, trying to unfold various dimensions of this element, and analyzing its relative importance vis-à-vis other elements for the career actors and their environment. Examples include ontic elements such as career satisfaction or joy; elements of the social space such as hierarchical advancement; and a combination of ontic and spatial elements such as satisfaction with one's income level in the light of societal norms and social benchmarks such as, for example, colleagues, parents, or supervisors.

Understanding what influences career success (i.e. looking for relevant influencing factors of career success) involves, in the language of the SCF, analyzing the relative importance of various elements of an individual career actor's condition, position, and social space, including their interplay as mediators or moderators, for relevant single or multiple elements of condition at a later point in time. Potentially, this zooms into all parts of the SCF model.

Such an account provides not only something of a simple robustness check on the SCF to see whether the framework is actually capable of representing one central construct of career studies: career success. It also lays the foundation for the next stage – equivalizing – by formulating the basic structure of the problem: What do actors strive for, and how do they deal with a complex set of internal and external factors in order to be successful?

A Neo-institutionalist View

When looking outside career studies to find a theoretical area dealing with a similar constellation as outlined in the language of the SCF, neo-institutional theorizing comes to mind. In this section, we first will briefly outline the basic ideas in this line of thinking. A primary characteristic of neo-institutional theorizing is that it seeks a rationale for the behavior of organizational actors that cannot be sufficiently explained by the dominant view of rational actor-hood. We then go on to discuss three major aspects in more detail – institutional context, legitimacy, and institutional complexity – because of their potential fruitfulness for highlighting crucial aspects of careers as seen through the SCF. They address both the internal makeup of a complex set of influencing factors and how the actors deal with them.

Foundations Organizational institutionalism (e.g. Suddaby, Elsbach, Greenwood, and Meyer, 2010; Greenwood *et al.*, 2008b; Powell and DiMaggio, 1991), along-side resource-dependence views and population ecology approaches, provides a counterpoint to the organization theory of the 1960s and '70s that was dominated by rational choice and structural-contingency views of organizations (see Chapter 7; in the following we draw on the developmental account in Greenwood *et al.*, 2008a). Broadly speaking, its basic works rest upon five theses (Greenwood *et al.*, 2008a: 11, emphasis in the original):

1. organizations are influenced by their *institutional* and *network* contexts. The institutional context consists of rationalized myths of appropriate conduct;
2. institutional pressures affect all organizations but especially those with unclear technologies and/or difficult to evaluate outputs. Organizations especially sensitive to institutional contexts are *institutionalized organizations;*
3. organizations become isomorphic with their institutional context in order to secure social approval *(legitimacy)*, which provides survival benefits;
4. because conformity to institutional pressures may be contrary to the dictates of efficiency, conformity may be ceremonial, whereby symbolic structures are decoupled from an organization's technical core;
5. institutionalized practices are typically taken-for granted [sic], widely accepted and resistant to change.

Behind these theses lurks a more fundamental question: "Why and with what consequences do organizations exhibit particular organizational arrangements that defy traditional rational explanation?" (Greenwood *et al.*, 2008a: 7). The answers developed in the neo-institutionalist camp build on conceptualizing the relationship between organizations and their context in a new way by at least partially departing from the importance of the technical environment that includes elements such as information flows, resources, or technology. Instead, "the new formulation stresses the role played by cultural elements – symbols, cognitive systems, normative beliefs – and the sources of such elements" (Scott, 1987: 498) by requirements and rules "to which individual organizations must conform if they are to receive support and legitimacy" (Scott and Meyer, 1983: 149).

Institutional Context The institutional context plays a major role in what happens with and in organizations. On the one hand, it encompasses all regulatory policies and agencies that are important for an organization and are usually provided by the state, for example, labor laws, tax regimes, and immigration laws. On the other hand, institutional context relates to the role of institutions. The importance of institutions has been acknowledged throughout much theorizing about the embeddedness of individuals and organizations in a broader context, in modern times arguably most prominently with the Weberian interest in the rationalization of society (Weber, 1980 [Original 1921]). In a nutshell, Weber argued that the rationalization of society, in particular of economics, and the related value changes put significant pressure on individuals to adapt – or resist, for that matter – to these developments by how they lead their life. *Methodische Lebensführung* (methodical lifestyle) takes a holistic approach and orders one's life toward the maxims of the rational society. Likewise, Hughes expresses interest in the concept of institution which "is applied to those features of social life which outlast biological generations or survive drastic social changes that might have been expected to bring them to an end" (Hughes, 1939: 283).

Building a differentiated view of the institutional environment, Scott (1995) argues that "[i]nstitutions consist of cognitive, normative, and regulative structures and activities that provide stability and meaning to social behavior. Institutions are transported by various carriers – cultures, structures, and routines – and they operate at multiple levels of jurisdiction" (ibid.: 33). He differentiates between three "pillars" that make up or support institutions: normative, regulative, and cognitive. The normative pillar stresses that normative rules, for example, legal quotas, introduce a prescriptive, evaluative, and obligatory dimension into social life. Normative systems include values and norms and they define goals and appropriate ways to pursue them. The regulative pillar makes clear that institutions such as social obligations constrain and regularize behavior that involves, in an attempt to influence future behavior, the capacity to establish rules, inspect others' conformity with them, and sanction deviant behavior. The cognitive pillar of institutions points out that internalized symbolic representations of the world, for example, taken-for-granted values, mediate the response of individuals to the external world of stimuli. Institutions of the respective pillars are embedded in three types of repositories or "carriers" (Jepperson, 1991: 150), i.e. cultures, social structures, and routines (Table 8.1).

Table 8.1 *Institutional pillars and carriers (Scott, 1995: 52)*

	Institutional pillars		
Carriers	Regulative	Normative	Cognitive
Cultures	Rules, laws	Values, expectations	Categories, typifications
Social structures	Governance systems, power systems	Regimes, authority systems	Structural isomorphism, identities
Routines	Protocols, standard procedures	Conformity, performance of duty	Performance programs, scripts

Cultures rely on interpretative schemes as codified patterns of meaning and rule systems that constrain and reinforce behavior but can also be changed by behavior. Social structures build on role systems, i.e. patterned expectations connected to networks of social positions. Finally, routines address patterned actions reflecting deeply ingrained habits and procedures based on unarticulated knowledge and beliefs of actors.

There is no agreement on the exact meaning of institutions. On offer are, among other possibilities, "normative and cognitive belief systems" (Scott, 1983: 163), "common understandings of what is appropriate and, fundamentally, meaningful behavior" (Zucker, 1983: 105), "the rules, norms, and ideologies of the wider society" (Meyer and Rowan, 1983: 84), and, with the benefit of hindsight, "more-or-less taken-for-granted repetitive social behaviour that is underpinned by normative systems and cognitive understandings that give meaning to social exchange and thus enable self-reproducing social order" (Greenwood *et al.*, 2008a: 5, in the original all in italics). Yet there seems to be some common understanding that it is the institutional context that is pivotal for explaining the deviation of organizational actors from rational behavior. Since organizations are seen "as dramatic enactments of the rationalized myths pervading modern societies" (Meyer and Rowan, 1977: 346), regulatory elements as well as taken-for-granted, widely shared ideas and social values play an essential role. In this light, "the institutional explanation is not derived from the calculated self-interest of organizational actors, nor from the imperatives of instrumental functionality. Instead, the institutional explanation emphasizes that organizations seek legitimacy and survival not efficiency, and highlights the role of cognition and obligation, not self-interest" (Greenwood *et al.*, 2008a: 7).

Legitimacy Legitimacy, then, becomes one of the core issues in institutional views of organizational actors. Substantial variety in terms of its meaning exists (see, e.g. the account by Suchman, 1995). It is important to note that in the line of institutional thinking, legitimacy is a set of constitutive beliefs rather than an operational resource:

> Organizations do not simply extract legitimacy from the environment in a feat of cultural strip mining; rather, external institutions construct and interpenetrate the organization in every respect. Cultural definitions determine how the organization is built, how it is run, and, simultaneously, how it is understood and evaluated. Within this tradition, legitimacy and institutionalization are virtually synonymous. Both phenomena empower organizations primarily by making them seem natural and meaningful; access to resources is largely a by-product. (Suchman, 1995: 576)

Since organizations are expected to be rational, conforming to myths of rationality such as "training and development is beneficial" or "expertise beats intuition" helps gain legitimacy and contributes to survival (Meyer and Rowan, 1977).

However, the questions emerged early on of what exactly happens if efficiency and legitimacy demands do not go in parallel and how to handle this. Decoupling emphasizes that "elements of structure are decoupled from activities and from each other" (Meyer and Rowan, 1977: 357). Organizational hypocrisy emphasizes that organizations use different processes, structures, and ideologies for internal and external use in order to secure legitimacy when facing conflicting or inconsistent demands and norms (Brunsson, 1989). Surface isomorphism argues that organizations use loose coupling to detach superficial change due to environmental demands from task activities (Zucker, 1987: 673) and "to buffer their formal structures from the uncertainties of technical activities by becoming loosely coupled, building gaps between their formal structures and actual work activities" (Meyer and Rowan, 1977: 341). As a result, concrete organizational activities are based on efficiency requirements, whereas formal structural elements relate to institutionalized expectations and become a legitimation façade. An example for this would be organizations establishing units such as corporate social responsibility departments or diversity managers in order to appear more legitimate without being convinced about their contribution to efficiency. However, actors in the institutional context might not be satisfied with some kind of "cynical Goffmanesque façade" (Powell, 1985: 565) and demand deeper restructuring.

Institutional Complexity To complicate matters further, efficiency demands can become institutionalized themselves, making the differentiation between efficiency and legitimacy tricky (Meyer, 1994). Demands from within the institutional context are by no means straightforward, either. There can be massive institutional complexity arising from potentially ambiguous, contradictory, tacit, and changing demands of various actors in the institutional environment.

One way of conceptualizing institutional complexity is to assume the existence of institutional logics (see, e.g. Thornton, Ocasio, and Lounsbury, 2012; Thornton and Ocasio, 2008). These guide actors on the interpretation and proper action in social settings and "constitute a set of assumptions and values, usually implicit, about how to interpret organizational reality, what constitutes appropriate behavior, and how to succeed" (Thornton, 2004: 70). Multiple logics at the level of society and of fields usually lead to incompatibilities and conflicting demands and to institutional complexity. This triggers organizational responses. For example, when hospitals have to deal not only with the health-related expectations of healing and caring but also with the market logic of making money, they have to find ways to deal with these partly contradictory expectations. Organizational attributes such as size or governance structure moderate the link between institutional complexity and organizational responses. To continue the example, a hospital will have more leeway in responding to a market-based logic introduced by the government and linked to the public financing of the hospital if it is a highly respected institution in the field (Greenwood, Raynard, Kodeih, Micelotta, and Lounsbury, 2011: 324 f.). It is important to note that "the dynamic patterns of complexity that confront organizations . . . [arise] from the multiplicity of logics to which organizations must respond, and the degree of incompatibility between those logics" (ibid.: 334).

What Career Studies Can Learn

For career studies, two major elements of institutionalist thinking as outlined earlier emerge: the tension between striving for legitimacy and efficiency and how actors deal with institutional complexity, i.e. the varied and partly contradictory demands from their environment. We will deal with these issues in turn.

Handling the Tensions between Legitimacy and Efficiency To begin with, the importance of legitimacy in institutional theory suggests that career actors do not just strive for a specific set of conditions related to the efficiency imperatives in the career fields they are operating in. Of course, in these fields goals such as hierarchical advancement, increase of income, or a certain level of career satisfaction are basic rational tenets following the fields' efficiency dictum. To simplify grossly: organizations follow the efficiency myth in order to make the most of the resources they put in when producing their output, following the requirements of their respective operations; career actors do it by following what their job demands.

However, organizations as well as career actors also have to take into account legitimacy. At the organizational level, take the example of various forms of official procedures such as ISO certification (www.iso.org) for products and services, AACSB (www.aacsb.edu) and EQUIS (www.efmd.org/accreditation-main/equis), both certification bodies for certain educational organizations. We are erring on the safe side when we say that there are some discrepancies between what helps efficient production and what is required in these certification processes. Yet organizations must bow to these processes since they are indispensable for appearing to be a legitimate member of the field. Large manufacturers only select suppliers if they are certified according to specific standards; prominent universities only accept partner universities when they are accredited at a certain level.

A similar situation emerges when looking at career actors. The social space of the career actor contains a number of institutions that formulate demands in terms of legitimacy going beyond what is required from an efficiency angle. A few illustrations may suffice.

In many societies it is not enough simply to have certain skills such as being able to do a thorough financial check of corporate finances, treat children's illnesses, or do the right kind of massage for lymphatic drainage. In order to be officially allowed to do this and be a legitimate member of the respective career field, you have to "go legitimate." By and large, this requires some form of official approval, for example, becoming a certified public accountant (CPA) or a licensed pediatrician or getting an education as a medical masseur. While some of this also helps you to do your job efficiently, part of it follows other ideas like efforts of professional bodies to accumulate power and define who is entering the field or make money by offering courses that help you get the official certificate. Therefore it is not enough for a career actor to know their trade. They also have to follow legitimacy-enhancing rules that sometimes closely, sometimes hardly at all, relate to the competencies required for their jobs. In addition to such official rules, career fields also contain a number of informal rules that address legitimacy issues. To continue the examples used previously: teaching courses for incoming CPA candidates, taking part in scientific conferences, and having a well-equipped practice in a nice part of town are hardly career goals for CPAs, pediatricians, and medical masseurs, respectively. Yet they clearly contribute to enhancing legitimacy. Examples from other areas include the frequency of job offers that you get in the field of IT, the number of top-tier journal articles that are needed for you to be accepted as a valuable partner for an international research project, or the required firm-specific habitus for making you a member of the inner circle within a large sales team. Again, while not directly a goal in themselves or necessary for doing a job efficiently, they enhance the legitimacy of the career actor.

In our view, we add a very basic perspective to career success studies by accepting that *legitimacy* is a crucial feature of a career actor's condition and their social space. It has to be taken into account for the actor to become and stay a legitimate field member entitled to future career moves. This has the potential for new lines of thinking within career studies.

Let us assume that career actors do indeed simultaneously strive for both legitimacy and efficiency outputs. The latter is reflected in traditional career success constructs such as advancement or satisfaction. However, by including the former, we challenge these dominant career success constructs at a conceptual level. The existing constructs primarily reflect the efficiency dimension but seem to underestimate the legitimacy aspect of career success. This raises the conceptual issue of whether legitimacy and survival are new to the career success discourse or at least grossly underestimated in their importance and whether they are fundamentally different from existing career success constructs in the field. If so, and we tend to yes on both counts, further fascinating questions emerge at the conceptual level: How do legitimacy and survival relate to existing career success constructs such as subjective and objective career success? Can one build them into these constructs, or do we have to develop constructs in their own right? Do the existing constructs suffice, but does one have to relate them more to the legitimacy angle and put the dimensions of these constructs such as advancement or income into a spatial perspective, relating them to the institutions in the respective career field and analyze to what extent they support a career actor's legitimacy in the field without necessarily contributing to classical efficiency goals? If new constructs are required, how can they be theoretically developed and operationalized, and how do typical influencing factors such as personality or social origin conceptually relate to these new constructs?

Beyond that, there is the empirical question whether the data back up the conceptual difference between legitimacy- and efficiency-related career goals and behavior. This makes salient the question: When and how do career actors become legitimate members of a career field? Entering into and staying in a field as a legitimate member is, we suggest, quite different from advancing within the career field because the former involves establishing legitimacy and the latter maintaining it. This assumption leads to further lines of empirical inquiry: Do career actors differentiate between these two profoundly different types of goals and respective behavior? How does the difference between establishing oneself as a legitimate player in the field and the ongoing process of upholding one's legitimacy play out in manifest career aspirations and one's relationship to the social environment? How do individuals detect which institutions in their context are relevant for them and to what degree? Under which circumstances and to what extent can legitimation façades contribute not only to legitimacy but also to classical efficiency-related goals?

Addressing the relationship between legitimacy- and efficiency-oriented goals and behavior, the following propositions constitute examples for empirical lines of research that follow the type of thinking outlined previously. Being regarded as a legitimate member of the field is a basic requirement for all kinds of career behavior. Therefore, even when it costs in terms of typical career goals, career actors will make sure that they do not endanger their legitimacy.

Proposition 1a: Career actors show legitimacy-enhancing behavior even to the detriment of reaching financial goals.

Proposition 1b: Career actors show legitimacy-enhancing behavior even to the detriment of reaching advancement goals.

Of course, showing too much legitimacy-enhancing behavior and not investing in career behavior contributing to the "real," i.e. task-related requirements of the job can lead to reduced career prospects. Major decision makers might see the career actor as spending too much energy on "window-dressing" – however important that may be – and not investing enough in getting the job done.

Proposition 2: Legitimacy-enhancing behavior above the contextually specific norm reduces the prospect for objective career success.

This raises the interesting research question of where such norms requiring legitimacy might come from. Of course, we are not indicating that there is no existing research dealing with issues related to this. For example, in research about impression management and its reasons as well as outcomes we do find evidence that reenacting oneself as a modest member of the organization in the eyes of one's supervisors and colleagues is an important facet of individual behavior and related to future career success (Blickle, Diekmann, Schneider, Kalthofer, and Summers, 2012). In a similar vein, the literature on organizational socialization (e.g. Fisher, 1990; Van Maanen and Schein, 1979) rests on the assumption that individuals are looking for or at least responsive to signals about what the relevant organizational normative and cognitive belief systems are and how one has to accommodate.

Nevertheless, what we are indicating is that institutionalist thinking offers a larger frame for this type of research. It not only provides more fine-grained nuances about different aspects of these phenomena but also allows one to tell a bigger story. These kinds of career-related behavior are part of a more general quest on the part of individual and organizational actors to deal with profoundly different requirements than those that come from the part of their environment related to legitimacy and efficiency demands. In the language of the SCF, this urges us to take a theoretically grounded look at specific aspects of the interplay between the social space and its individual and collective actors as well as at the effects this interplay has on a variety of aspects of the condition of the career actor.

Dealing with Institutional Complexity The institutionalist account also raises the issue of institutional complexity. Actors dealing with their institutional context often experience substantial institutional pluralism leading to institutional complexity, i.e. greater numbers of institutions with mutually differing degrees of compatibility. These institutions and the related expectations are inevitably partly incompatible, contradictory, and ambiguous. This raises the question of how the actor, be it individual or collective, deals with this kind of fragmented, unclear, ambiguous, and conflict-laden situation.

In career terms, we provide a few examples that illustrate the potential of the institutionalist discussion when looking at career actors' behavior. At a very basic level, it is yet to be established empirically whether and, if so, how individuals perceive, make sense of, and prioritize different career-related institutional demands and in what respect these decisions are reflected in their actual behavior. Drawing on insight with regard to organizations' reactions such as decoupling, surface isomorphism, or hypocrisy, one can pursue the question at the individual level. The analysis could focus on whether career actors produce a variety of selves and identities in order to respond to respective legitimacy-related requirements existing in their social space while, at the same time, consistently following the evident organizational career logic (Gunz, 1988), which is likely to adhere to rationality and efficiency considerations, for the fast way to the next hierarchical level. When looking at decoupling, i.e. introducing systematically different behavior with regard to the two fundamentally different sets of goals and logics, the question of potential effects of this division arises. For example, do different degrees of decoupling have similar or largely different effects on individual health and long-term ability to show performance, given that this way of constructing realities and various identities for various audiences requires substantial psychological energy? And beyond the individual: Are there typical career-relevant institutional logics in various organizations, industries, and national cultures that lead to typical configurations of institutional complexity?

A few propositions illustrate these points. In strong HRM systems (Bowen and Ostroff, 2004), employees receive consistent, clear, and unambiguous messages about what the organization expects and rewards with regard to expected behavior for achieving organizational goals. Such a situation requires individual career actors to decouple from these standards and show different sets of behavioral patterns in order to also fulfill their individual goals.

Proposition 3: The strength of HRM systems is positively related to decoupling behavior of career actors.

However, such a decoupling can also lead to considerable tensions, in particular when the sets of required behavior are partly contradictory, for example, in terms of dealing with supervisors ("follow their advice versus go over their heads"). While a certain amount of noncongruent behavior is most likely unavoidable, too much might lead to inner tensions and negative health effects.

Proposition 4: Above a certain threshold, decoupling behavior of career actors leads to negative health effects.

Again, research related to this kind of thinking is not unheard of in current efforts. We do see substantial work in the area of work/nonwork on how individuals interpret and cope with the partly conflicting demands from those two spheres of life (Lazarova, Westman, and Shaffer, 2010; Cohen, Duberley, and Musson, 2009; Sturges, 2008; Staines, 1980). Likewise, work on comparative career research looking at national, regional, and cultural specifics of various aspects of careers such as individual conceptualizations of careers and career success, typical career models, or the respective regulatory policies and agencies (Briscoe *et al.*, 2012b) relates closely to these issues, although this work uses neither this theoretical lens nor its vocabulary explicitly.

However, as outlined before in the case of legitimacy and efficiency, the advantage of using an established concept from broader organization studies seems evident: it allows one to profit from the highly differentiated discussion in this area and links insight from the broader discourse about the social fabric of our world to the career area, applying *mutatis mutandis* well-developed arguments, refinements, ways of empirical analysis, and so on.

Gaining a Theoretically Grounded Understanding of Context Understanding career success and its influencing factors also requires a sound conceptualization of the context within which the career unfolds in order to understand the interplay between the various factors. Therefore, we show in a final step how institutional theory introduces a more differentiated view of the social space in career transitions. Going beyond simple and descriptive layer models of career context (e.g. Mayrhofer *et al.*, 2007a), institutionalist thinking offers a theoretically grounded and differentiated view of context, in particular the social space and the demands from the environment that career actors face as well as specific mechanisms that are at work when various elements of the social spaces in which career actors are embedded unfold their effects.

Table 8.1 outlines the relationship between the three institutional pillars (i.e. regulative, normative, and cognitive) and their respective carriers (i.e. cultures, social structures, and routines). This suggests a number of avenues that provide a better understanding of how the relationship between career actors and their respective conditions and position on the one hand and the social space on the other unfolds. A few examples can illustrate this.

A first use of this theoretical lens exploits its potential for charting and identifying relevant elements in the social space of career actors. While the SCF emphasizes the embeddedness of the career actor in the social space, it has to remain silent about what exactly is out there that deserves attention. This, we argued, is integral to its characteristic as a generic framework that has to be supplemented with concrete theoretical assumptions in specific instances. The institutional account allows such a specification. For example, for a professional field such as physiotherapy, one can set out to chart career actors' environments along the three basic categories of regulative, normative, and cognitive pillars of institutional orders. In Austria, as in several other European countries, the regulative elements of the institutional environment legally require future physiotherapists (physical therapists) to acquire an academic degree at a university of applied sciences; in Germany, this is not the case. Related to the normative pillar, the Swiss Association of Physiotherapy (www .physioswiss.ch) has formulated guidelines that address, among other things, legitimate expectations of clients vis-à-vis physiotherapists and respective treatments. With regard to the cognitive pillar, the Austrian Association of Physiotherapy (www.physioaustria.at) identifies seventeen widely different categories of physiotherapeutic theaters of operations covering, for example, pediatrics, hippotherapy, sports, and palliative care.

Already such a comparatively straightforward but highly differentiated analysis of the social space according to various institutional pillars and carriers leads to a number of questions related to several aspects of the condition of a career actor: Do ontic characteristics of career actors such as IQ, social competence, or manual skills systematically vary between Austria and Switzerland with their academic and Germany with its nonacademic system of education, and is there any difference in their satisfaction with their job and careers? How do physiotherapists rising through the ranks and getting into management positions or founding their own companies view the importance of normative (e.g. values) and cognitive (e.g. physiotherapeutic categories) elements of the institutional environment, and to what extent are they relevant for their career choice and for transitions during their career? What effects do different regimes and authority systems in public and private hospitals and rehabilitation clinics, respectively, have on the career goals of physiotherapists working in these organizations? These examples illustrate that an institutionalist view of the social space guides the analysis of the interplay between ontic and spatial elements and encourages taking an in-depth view of the social space and career actors' interactions with it.

A second form of use relates to the systematic analysis of the relationship between relevant elements of the social space and their effects on the condition of the career actor in order to arrive at a better conceptual understanding of these relationships. Basically, three different types of relationship exist. First, the elements of the social space can be at odds with one another, for example, normative and cultural requirements conflict with each other. This is, for example, the case for a promotion that is only possible through bribing business partners – a cognitively shared perception – which is at odds with the regulatory pressure exerted by corporate governance systems of the organization, for example, by the code of conduct, and the normative pressure through professional ethics as outlined in professional standards, both prohibiting bribery. Second, elements can be nested within one another, for example, when normative and cultural requirements support and supplement each other. This would happen when, for example, the organizational expectations for getting a position are in line with, but go beyond, what is legally required, as is the case when becoming a human resource development officer not only requires a British Chartered Institute of Personnel and Development certification but also requires five years of expertise as line manager. Finally, the elements of the social space can apply differentially to different members of a field, as is the case when the various elements apply differently to high potentials and "normal employees."

Again, these theoretically grounded configurations of relationships between elements in the social space lead to a number of questions: Do conflicting institutional requirements enhance or diminish the career opportunities for individuals with a strong entrepreneurial orientation? Do certain types of conflicting arrangements – regulative versus normative, cognitive versus normative, etc. – have different effects on the successful implementation of individual career strategies? Do career transitions between fields with a similar regulative, normative, and cognitive setup provide fewer opportunities for self-development than transitions between fields with a different setup, or does this have no effect at all? Do different configurations of relationships between the elements of institutional pillars affect career satisfaction and future career goals? Which types of careers make conforming career behavior, where deviations seem to be inconceivable ("taken for grantedness"), especially likely? Again, these are only examples illustrating promising routes and demonstrating the potential of these kind of analyses.

A few propositions can be derived from the preceding discussion. As a rule, the social space for career actors does not provide a clear and unambiguous picture but is fraught with uncertainty due to various and partly conflicting institutional requirements. People differ in the extent to which they can make sense of such situations and use this interpretation as the basis for their own behavior. A more adequate interpretation of the social space allows career actors to develop successful career strategies and behaviors for advancing in a given setting.

Proposition 5a: A more adequate view of relevant elements and processes of the institutional environment increases the likelihood of promotion.

Proposition 5b: Successful career actors view conflicts between regulative and normative elements to a greater extent as an opportunity and not as a threat.

Arguably, career actors look for external coaching help in particular in situations of medium complexity. In case of low levels of complexity, they assume that they can deal with it themselves; in high-level situations, they might assume that things are so complicated that even coaching does not help.

Proposition 6: A medium level of conflicting relationships between normative and regulative elements of the social space creates more demand for career coaching than either a low or high level.

Summation

In this chapter, we look outside the field of OMC studies to see how the SCF might facilitate importing ideas from the broader field of organization studies, ideas that have the potential to introduce new approaches to established career research problems. This is, of course, a strong claim to make of the SCF, and we have been careful to note that it is one of facilitation only; there is always more than one route to any goal.

Our claims for this chapter are helped by the observation that the ideas that emerge from applying coevolutionary, complementarity, and institutional theory to OMC studies are by and large novel in the sense that they ask questions about mentorship and career success that, to our knowledge at least, have rarely – if at all – been asked hitherto. And, of course, the examples that we choose are limited by our imaginations and the space that is available in this book. We have no doubt that others could take our ideas considerably further. For example, game theory might well provide a useful framework for exploring interactions over time between focal career actors and others in their social space.

As a final step, which we take in the next chapter, we ask the question: In addition to *taking* from the field of organization studies, is there anything that the SCF can *contribute* to it?

9   Contributing to Organization Studies

In this chapter, we continue with the theme we began working on in Chapter 8, which is about exploring the benefits of developing conversation between the career discourse and those outside what we call in Chapter 1 the proto-field of career studies.

To begin with, we need to bring a little more precision to what we are discussing. As we note elsewhere in the book, writers in many fields use the concept of career, which is no great surprise given how fundamental the notion is to human existence. But for some writers it provides the primary focus of their work, while for others it is incidental, something brought in to help them make sense of their own primary interest. This is a different distinction from that between those who see themselves as working within the organization management career (OMC) discourse and those who do not. While in practice the boundaries are somewhat blurred, these distinctions allow us to differentiate between four types of writing (see Table 9.1).

The first cell, "OMC focus," comprises the classical OMC case in which researchers in the OMC field focus on career issues, for example, when researching factors influencing career success. The cell "OMC as side-interest" is related in that OMC research deals with career as a derivative problem while the main focus lies somewhere else, as is the case, for example, when analyzing mentor–protégé relationships from an OMC angle (e.g. Humberd and Rouse, 2016). In the other two cells, discourses outside the OMC field focus either on careers as their primary interest (cell "Related career focus"), as is the case with work looking at career implications of organizational ecology (e.g. Haveman and Cohen, 1994), or on other issues where career is an important derivative aspect (cell "Incidental career focus"), for example, when strategy or finance scholars interested in organizational performance analyze the respective effects of changes in the top management team or CEO succession (e.g. Karaevli, 2007).

In this chapter, we are interested in the latter two cells: "Related career focus" and "Incidental career focus." It is here we suspect the greatest need exists for benefiting from some of the knowledge available in the OMC discourse. When illustrating the potential of the SCF for contributing to

Table 9.1 *Interplay between discourses and career as a research focus*

		Discourse	
		OMC	Non-OMC
Primary focus	Career	OMC focus	Related career focus
	Noncareer	OMC as side-interest	Incidental career focus

discourses outside the OMC field dealing with career issues, we proceed in two steps. First, we show the potential of the SCF to systematically help further develop *single studies* within discourses outside the OMC field, thus supporting cumulative research in organization studies by showing further routes for research building on existing work. Second, we address how the SCF can contribute to *research fields* outside the OMC field having a noncareer focus – in our examples, organizational succession and professional service firms, respectively – but where career issues play a central role.

Reframing Individual Studies

There are research efforts from a broad variety of different discourses that prominently use the term "career" and refer to some of the concepts and insights generated in the OMC discourse but ultimately do not make substantial use of it. To give four examples:

- Drinkwater (1979) analyzes the careers of local magistracies in the three Gauls of the early Roman Empire, challenging the seemingly straightforward progression of tribal decurions moving "from quaestorship (dealing with finance) to aedileship (dealing with administration) to duumvirate (the chief magisterial office, dealing especially with justice)" (ibid.: 89) and reconstructing their actual objective career patterns based on the Corpus Inscriptionum Latinarum (CIL; Berlin-Brandenburg Academy of Sciences and Humanities, 2016), an edited collection of classical Latin inscriptions.
- Katz (2005) looks at members of the Plateau Tribes, populating an area roughly comprising the high plateau region between the Pacific coastal mountain system of the Cascade Range and the Rocky Mountains in North America, and provides a fine-grained analysis of the decisions leading them into nursing with the goal of providing a basis to develop culturally con-gruent strategies for retention and recruitment.
- Stronach and Adair (2010) examine the retirement experiences of elite indigenous Australian boxers and show that an overly strong focus on their physical capital is present, especially when the transition to the post-sports

career approaches sooner than expected due to a premature, unexpected erosion of their physical capital, for example, because of an injury.

• Shen and Cannella (2002) are interested in the impact of various facets of CEO succession, in particular different types of CEO successors, on organizational performance, reporting that for publicly traded corporations in the USA there is an inverted U-shaped relationship between return on assets (post-succession) and the tenure of the departed CEO.

Studies such as these, while using career as a prominent label or implicitly referring to it, are usually interested primarily in specific sets of career actors, specific segments of the social space, or a certain outcome. They rarely make substantial, if any, references to a general career literature and the respective insights created there. Instead, such studies are firmly rooted in their respective primary discussions, i.e. research on the Roman Empire, nursing/Native Americans, professional sports, or succession and organizational performance. In terms of Table 9.1, they fall outside the OMC discourse, mostly in the cell "Related career focus," although Shen and Canella's study could also be thought of as occupying the cell "Incidental career focus" because, unlike the others, they are less specifically interested in career as a focus.

We suggest that the SCF can provide a systematic and low-threshold way of introducing basic insights of the OMC discourse into these studies. It is systematic in the sense that it involves applying the ontic, spatial, and temporal perspectives to uncover areas of emphasis and neglect; mapping the studies according to the basic or enlarged heuristic models (Chapter 4), thus unearthing potentially fruitful further avenues of further analyzing and interpreting the data; or exploiting the coevolutionary aspect by systematically bringing other career actors into the picture to provide potential "hooks" for developing further studies that have an interest in career issues but might not have a clear understanding of what OMC research has to offer. It is low-threshold in the sense that it does not involve too much preformatting of the issue: it does not require the adoption of a particular theoretical perspective. We demonstrate this potential by analyzing in more detail the well-received (with, as of February 2017, 431 citations on Google Scholar) CEO succession study (Shen and Cannella, 2002).

We introduce the CEO succession literature in Chapter 7 in our discussion of the study of Boyer and Ortiz-Molina (2008), and we return to it later in greater depth. It has wrestled for many decades with the insider/outsider question: Is it better to hire a CEO from within or outside the corporation? No clear answer has emerged, and Shen and Cannella (2002) argue that part of the reason may be that the insider/outsider distinction is an oversimplification. It is necessary, they suggest, to distinguish between two kinds of insiders they label contenders, "those appointed following their predecessors' dismissals" (ibid.: 717), and followers, "those appointed following their predecessors' ordinary

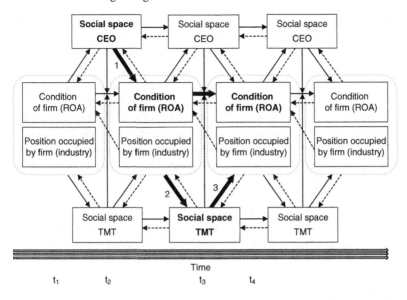

Figure 9.1 Recasting Shen and Cannella's (2002) model in terms of the
SCF – view 1

retirements" (ibid.). Because contenders are appointed after a CEO is dis-
missed, it is assumed that their appointment is a consequence of the board
deciding that change of some kind is needed and that the executive they select
has been in contention with the ex-CEO. Followers are assumed to have been
groomed for the role by the outgoing CEO *because* they are appointed following the normal retirement of the outgoing CEO.

In Figure 9.1, we begin the process of mapping the study onto a more general
SCF model, showing the elements from the study in boldface. We show the
firm, a collective actor, as the focal career actor, thus departing from our
previous exclusive focus on individual career actors and building on the notion
elaborated in Chapter 2 that collectivities, here companies, can be career actors,
too. We separate out two key features of its social space – its chief executive
officer (CEO) and its top management team (TMT) – because the study
examines their coevolution (although that term is not used in the paper).

The firm's condition is the focus of the paper's interest and is primarily what
the authors call operational performance (return on assets), although other
variables such as diversification and restructuring are included as control
variables. The firm's position in its social space is considered in terms of the
industry that the firm occupies.

The model demonstrates how the condition of the firm changes over a series
of time periods, including the succession event at time t_2. In SCF terms, the

study examines the impact of one of the actors in the focal actor's (the firm's) social space, the incoming CEO (outsider/contender/follower), on the condition of the focal career actor (arrow 1); the impact of the condition of the focal actor on another actor in the focal actor's social space (the TMT) in terms of its turnover following the succession event (arrow 2); and the subsequent impact of this condition on the condition of the focal actor (arrow 3). In their analysis, Shen and Cannella also examine the interaction of the condition of the two actors in the focal actor's social space (the incoming CEO and the TMT) on the condition of the focal actor, showing that the impact of post-succession TMT turnover on the firm's condition (i.e. its operational performance) depends on the characteristics of the incoming CEO, specifically whether the CEO is a contender insider or an outsider.

Because of the way that the key variables in the study were operationalized, the situation is not quite as clear-cut as this explanation makes it appear. The succession takes place at t_2, and the pre- and post-succession periods cover three years each. The firm's condition is measured in terms of its average ROA for these two periods (the pre-succession performance appears in their regression models as a control variable), which we label here t_1 and t_4, respectively. We do not know the firm's condition immediately after the event at t_2, so we do not know the direct impact of the succession event on the condition of the firm. Rather, we only know it slightly after changes have taken place in the TMT, which is measured over the two years immediately following the succession event.

Finally, the study also examines the impact of the tenure of the outgoing CEO. It shows that those with very short and very long tenures tend to be hard acts to follow in the sense that the firm's post-succession performance is lower for each than it is for intermediate tenures.

In order to see how the SCF might help researchers develop further the kind of questions addressed by Shen and Cannella, we need to enrich the model. One way of doing so is to include a set of relationships that are not in Figure 9.1, showing how the careers of CEO and TMT coevolve (Figure 9.2, which we show separately from Figure 9.1 in order to avoid the figure becoming overly complex). This also allows us to depict the interaction effect found by Shen and Cannella between the CEO succession type and TMT turnover on the firm's condition (arrow 4 in Figure 9.2 and arrow 3 in Figure 9.1).

The CEO is treated in the Shen and Cannella model as essentially exogenous, in a model that includes the tenure of the outgoing CEO and the origin of the incoming one. However, Figures 9.1 and 9.2 taken together point to a number of useful features of the situation. Most obviously, they make it apparent that CEOs have a history and that the history involves being part of an organization or several organizations over time. In so doing, the CEO's career coevolves

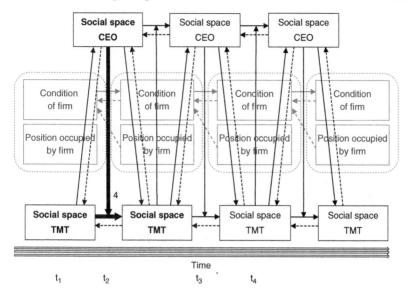

Figure 9.2 Recasting Shen and Cannella's (2002) model in terms of the SCF – view 2

with that of other actors appearing in the model, most notably the members of the TMT.

This analysis could be further enhanced by examining the social space occupied by the CEO in greater detail. Currently it shows the occupant of the CEO position, who changes at the succession event so that the occupant before t_2 is different from the occupant after t_2. But suppose we were to flip the model so that the incoming CEO becomes the focal career actor, and the firm or firms for which they work are shown as part of their social space. But so, too, are the outgoing CEO and other executives who may play a significant role in the career of the focal career actor, for example, the TMT of the firm the CEO assumes control over as a result of the succession event. Without stretching this too far, it would be entirely plausible to model the interconnected roles of incumbent CEO and the various internal candidates to replace the incumbent. For example, for insider incoming CEOs, a range of forms of coevolution between outgoing CEO and candidates' careers can be imagined, from distant and disconnected, even hostile, to one in which the former is the mentor of the latter. How do these differing evolving relationships affect the succession event?

Similarly, the TMT appears in the model as an exogenous influence (TMT turnover), although it is clear from the paper that the authors are aware that this is an oversimplification that they needed to make for the purposes of their study.

But the TMT, too, has a history that coevolves with that of the CEO. Figure 9.2 suggests that examining how this coevolution develops, in particular in terms of the differing kinds of relationship that can be envisaged between different members of the TMT and the CEO, could provide interesting new approaches to studies of the origins of successors. For example, how do differing compositions of the TMT affect (Proposition 4 in the basic building block) the way in which the CEO's career develops?

None of the foregoing, of course, is intended as a criticism of the Shen and Cannella study. As we point out in Chapter 7, our aim is to show how the SCF has the potential to help the researcher build on well-received studies in order to generate high-quality cumulative research. Here, we show how recasting an interesting study in terms of the SCF leads to new questions, many of which focus on the various actors' careers. In so doing, it brings together the OMC and general organizational discourses in a way that is potentially helpful to both. The OMC discourse benefits from new material concerning the careers of top executives, and the organizational discourse benefits from a new focus on career.

Reframing Fields

Going beyond single studies, this section focuses on research topics outside the OMC discourse that might profit from the insight generated in career studies, in particular in OMC studies. We will deal with organizational succession and professional service firms in turn.

Organizational Succession

Changes in the upper echelons of organizations tend to attract a lot of attention from the general public and in the world of practitioners. To cite a few examples of career transitions that gained wide publicity and had potentially far-reaching consequences: Steve Jobs stepping down from his top position at Apple in 1985 after losing the power struggle with former Pepsi manager John Sculley and his return as a successor of Gil Amelio in 1997 as well his final farewell in 2011; Jürgen Schrempp following Edzard Reuter in 1995 as CEO of Daimler-Benz and initiating a substantial strategic change toward refocusing Daimler as a car manufacturer and paving the way for DaimlerChrysler in 1998; or Kim Jong-un following his father Kim Jong-il as supreme leader of North Korea as well as First Secretary of the Workers' Party of Korea in 2012 and intensifying the country's rocket-launch program.

It is therefore no surprise that there has been a long-standing and ongoing interest in succession in the social scientific realm, too. Propelled by discourses such as organization theory, strategy, or organizational behavior, organizational succession research looks at various aspects of succession events. Of particular importance in this area is an extensive literature dating back more than sixty years to Gouldner's (1954) classic study examining the impact of a change of CEO on the firm. As we note in our introduction to our discussion of Shen and Cannella's (2002) study, the question of perhaps the most enduring interest has been simply: Is it better for the firm to hire a CEO from within the firm, the so-called "insider" replacement, or from outside ("outsider")? Findings on the impact of outsider CEO succession events, and indeed on CEO succession events generally, reviewed by Karaevli (2007) have been inconsistent, ranging from negative, through none or mixed, to positive. In addition to Shen and Cannella's (2002) explanation, Karaevli suggests that this is because insufficient account has been taken of influences such as the environment of the firm at the time, the firm's business performance pre-succession, the amount of strategic change going on in the firm, and the post-succession stability of the firm's TMT membership.

At a more general level, much if not all succession research can be mapped upon a succession model presented by Kesner and Sebora (1994) that uses a comparatively generic transition model well known in other areas (e.g. Mayrhofer and Iellatchich, 2005; Nicholson, 1984; Louis, 1980a; Glaser and Strauss, 1971). At the center of the model is the succession event itself. Areas of interest include process issues such as pattern, rate, or stages; candidate issues like experience, character, or competence; and choice issues revolving around, for example, criteria, the process, or justification. Succession antecedents are causal for the succession event. They include, among other things, organizational issues such as voluntary/involuntary departure of the predecessor or the preparation and responsibility for the change; role issues such as expectations or the structural integration of the position; and candidate issues including, for example, the origin (insider/outsider) and the quality of the successor. Succession consequences follow the antecedent–event link. Of particular interest are organizational issues such as strategic change, performance or effectiveness; stakeholder issues including internal stakeholders such as the top management team or external stakeholders such as shareholders; and evaluation issues.

Major reviews look at the succession discourse in total (Giambatista, Rowe, and Riaz, 2005), from a specific theoretical angle such as a practice view (Ma, Seidl, and Guérard, 2015), or with a focus on strategic change as the primary result (Hutzschenreuter, Kleindienst, and Greger, 2012). They offer a pretty coherent picture about the state of affairs. First, organizational succession as a research topic is of continuing interest for a variety of other discourses within the broader realm of social, in particular organization, studies. Primary examples are strategy research with a focus on the consequences of top-echelon succession, in particular CEO succession, for strategic change and strategic alignment; organization theory research applying concepts such as practice theory or circulation of power; or corporate finance and accounting focusing on various forms of organizational performance as primary outcomes of succession. Second, and arguably as a consequence of the broad interest, a substantial heterogeneity exists. This is particularly true for the theoretical angles taken and for the operationalizations of the constructs used. Scholars in this area note that "while succession was pursued across a variety of scientific disciplines, no single, systematic picture emerged across these disciplines" (Kesner and Sebora, 1994: 362) and "[b]ecause there are many facets to the CEO post-succession process and diverse research interests and theoretical perspectives, the existing literature on this process is highly fragmented" (Ma *et al.*, 2015: 461), resulting in "a lack of consistency in perspectives taken" (Giambatista *et al.*, 2005: 965). Third, besides urging the field to further improve in the area of research design and methods, the reviews call for a better link to the respective theoretical underpinnings and a broader theoretical scope, including, for example, game theory, managerial discretion theory, path dependence perspective, institutional theory, and organizational learning. Fourth, there are calls for a more sophisticated, in-depth view of the successor. They include going beyond the focus on cognition and integrating both cognition and affect as well as using established ways of capturing personality – for example, the well-established five-factor model.

Given this overall picture and particularly with respect to the call for a more differentiated actor-related view, it is somewhat surprising that hardly any work in this area uses advanced insight from career studies and that none of the calls sees career studies as a major potential contributor for further advancing the field. At the core of any succession event is a classical career matter: the career transition of a specific career actor, i.e. the incoming person, most often a highly visible and at least symbolically important person when it comes to members of the top management team or the CEO. A number of additional career transitions by other career actors are linked to the incoming person taking their new position. At a minimum, the former incumbent of the position has to leave and go elsewhere, usually but not always outside the current organization. In addition, the other members of the top management team are potentially affected and up for a job change, either from their own choice because of, for example, an insufficient fit with the plans and style of the incoming successor or because the successor asks for a partial or total change in personnel. Overall, then, we usually have a string of career transitions at hand resembling White's (1970) vacancy chains, which we introduce in Chapter 5 and which describe a string of career events and organizational reshuffling triggered by a single career move (see Pinfield, 1995, for an example of how these chains can manifest themselves).

Against this backdrop, we suggest the framing of top management succession coherently as a career transition of a crucial career actor within a specific social space, i.e. the upper echelon of organizations (Hambrick and Mason, 1984) around which other career transitions of members of the top management team are grouped. These positions are important and highly visible, so a lot of influencing factors from the social space within and outside the organization are likely to be involved, and the career transition potentially has major effects on the organization. More specifically, we use the SCF to respond to and further develop the following calls in the succession literature for further developing the field (Hutzschenreuter *et al.*, 2012; Giambatista *et al.*, 2005): strengthening the emphasis on personality and emotions, which relates to the ontic perspective on careers; bringing time into the picture and taking a more dynamic, two-way view of the transition of the successor, which resembles the chaining aspects and anticipatory relationships indicated in the SCF's heuristic model (Chapter 4); and emphasizing the simultaneous development and interlinkages between the successor and other individual and collective career actors around them and the multiple career transitions that are likely to emerge, thus addressing the coevolutionary angle of the SCF. We will deal with these three issues in turn.

Going beyond Personality   The call in the succession literature for a more in-depth understanding of the individual when analyzing organizational succession brings the ontic element of the SCF, in particular the career actor in question, to the forefront. Existing suggestions relate to concepts such as the five-factor model ("Big Five") of personality (Digman, 1990; McCrae and Costa, 1987), temporal personality depicting the characteristic way an individual relates to time (e.g. in terms of perception, interpretation, or allocation) (Ancona *et al.*, 2001), or emotions (Ballinger and Schoorman, 2007; Miller, Steier, and Le Breton-Miller, 2003). Already at a first glance, individual success-factor research within career studies offers a rich field to exploit in this area. There are a number of studies summarizing the state of affairs in this area (e.g. Ng and Feldman, 2014; Fouad and Byars-Winston, 2005; Ng *et al.*, 2005). Research goes far beyond the influencing factors addressed in succession research as areas to expand. They include, for example, individual aspects such as different types of motivation (e.g. Liu, Liu, and Wu, 2010; Wayne, Liden, Kraimer, and Graf, 1999), self-monitoring (e.g. Kilduff and Day, 1994), intelligence (e.g. Garcia and Costa, 2014), or self-efficacy (Abele and Spurk, 2009).

However, the ontic perspective of the SCF points toward characteristics used widely in individual success-factor research, outside the succession literature. As outlined in Chapter 3, it addresses a career actor's condition, i.e. it encompasses everything that we can say about a career actor, and it is assessed as the result of a process of comparison between the career actor (Ego) and any number of other actors (Alter). Of course, what we measure depends on the theoretical foundation and purpose of the study being conducted. This might differ depending on whether one looks at the succession at the top level of an organization or at the case of a career transition at the shop floor. For example, the public image of a successor in their respective social circles might be of greater interest in the case of a CEO succession than when one night clerk follows another. On the other hand, when analyzing the effectiveness of a succession of roofers, the physical sense of balance of an incoming new roofer will be a more interesting variable to look at than when focusing on the replacement of a CEO. Presumably a major reason that the succession literature has not looked at a great variety of ontic variables is that the studies primarily use archival data, which only contain a limited set of variables as well as being focused on people occupying top management positions at some stage in their careers.

In addition, the SCF suggests that one should not look at individual variables in an isolated way. It links the three perspectives and advocates a systematic connection between ontic, spatial, and temporal elements in both the basic and the elaborated models. Therefore, looking at succession inevitably suggests integrating the individual focus with the broader picture, in particular the temporal dimension that alerts one to the dynamic qualities of succession and the social space within which the succession event occurs. This points toward temporal chaining and coevolutionary aspects of succession to which we turn next.

Chaining Events and Anticipatory Linkages   Much of the current succession literature focuses on a single succession event. While this is under-standable in the light of the difficulties in following career actors empirically over time and packing the complexities of a multi-period career study into the standard journal article format and length, it also seems to be the source of various calls for a stronger inclusion of the temporal dimension into succession research (Hutzschenreuter *et al.*, 2012). The SCF clearly seconds this call. The explicit integration of the temporal perspective points toward the fact that there is always a "before" and "after" for each succession event. What happens in a particular succession cannot be fully understood unless one temporally broad-ens the view and looks at linkages to past and potential future career transitions of the actor(s) involved. Therefore, the chaining of career transitions is essential.

Chaining involves two things. First, it requires adding previous and succes-sive career transitions, usually also succession events, to the picture; second, it suggests including anticipatory linkages (i.e. future characteristics of the social space, the career actor's condition, and their position) into the picture in order to get a more fine-grained picture.

We will illustrate this with an example from recent history: Nelson Mandela coming into office as President of South Africa in 1994. While this not only marks a turning point in the history of South Africa and has an impact far beyond South Africa's national boundaries, it is also a remarkable personal career transition. Figure 9.3 roughly outlines major elements of the political life of Mandela, from joining the Transvaal Provincial Executive of the African National Congress (ANC) in 1947 to departing from presidential office in 1999.

In order to gain a better understanding of his succession of Frederik Willem de Klerk, the last South African president under the apartheid regime, we need to look at both preceding and succeeding career transitions of Mandela as the focal career actor. Regarding preceding transitions, three factors stand out that arguably have an influence on the transition of Mandela into the presidency.

First, the career transition into the exclusive circle of Nobel Peace Prize laureates in 1993 changed the available scope of action due to personal and public expectations. Armed struggle, guerrilla warfare, and violent action are obviously part of Mandela's earlier history as indicated by his role in founding and leading Umkhonto we Sizwe ("Spear of the Nation"), the armed wing of the ANC, and his justification of violent action as expressed in his well-known "Statement from the Dock" speech at the beginning of the so-called Rivonia Trial on April 20, 1964 (Mandela, 1964). Becoming a Nobel Peace Prize laureate emphasizes the other side of the spectrum. This personal career transition of the recent past before coming into office evoked, if nothing else, additional public expectations concerning how to live up to this award when in office. Overall, then, it is hard to see how preparing for and then actually exercising the presidential office cannot have been shaped by this preceding career transition. In SCF terms, past personal condition and past characteristics of the social space influence the current transition.

Second, the release from prison in 1990 after more than a quarter of a century in prison marked the transition from a convicted criminal sentenced for life to a free citizen and a legitimate political player. Having ample insight through the career transitions into and out of the prison system led to unique experiences compared to a "normal" political career. Arguably, this influenced Mandela's transition into office with regard to agenda and form. In this light, it is hardly surprising, then, that introducing the Truth and Reconciliation Commission investigating incidents between 1960 and 1994, establishing a "Government of National Unity," and propagating a "rainbow nation" where different parts of society live together in unity were high on the list of priorities when Mandela entered office. Likewise, playing both *Nkosi Sikelel' iAfrika* ("God Bless Africa"), the then anthem of the ANC, and *Die Stem van Suid-Afrika* ("The Voice of South Africa"), South Africa's national anthem, during the

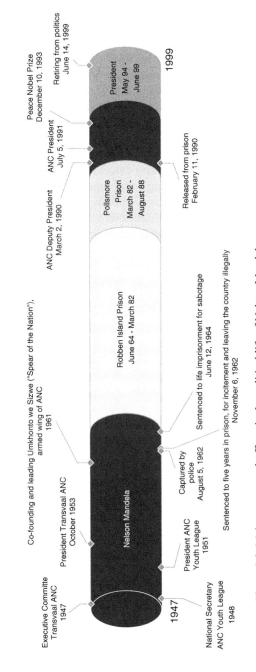

Figure 9.3 Major events and offices in the political life of Nelson Mandela

Executive Committe
Transvaal ANC
1947

Co-founding and leading Umkhonto we Sizwe ("Spear of the Nation"),
armed wing of ANC
1961

President Transvaal ANC
October 1953

Peace Nobel Prize
December 10, 1993

Retiring from politics
June 14, 1999

ANC President
July 5, 1991

ANC Deputy President
March 2, 1990

Released from prison
February 11, 1990

President
May 94 -
June 99

1999

Pollsmore
Prison
March 82 -
August 88

Robben Island Prison
June 64 - March 82

Nelson Mandela

1947

President ANC
Youth League
1951

Captured by
police
August 5, 1962

Sentenced to life imprisonment for sabotage
June 12, 1964

National Secretary
ANC Youth League
1948

Sentenced to five years in prison, for incitement and leaving the country illegally
November 6, 1962

inauguration and, in his inaugural address, appealing to a time when healing the wounds, bridging chasms, and rebuilding are central reflected his past firsthand experience with vastly different aspects of life in South African society. Again, through chaining, the SCF emphasizes the importance of past transitions with their respective condition and characteristics of social space for understanding succession events.

Third, the international support for final successful demands to release Mandela from prison lasted many decades. In the language of the SCF: the influence of the social space on a particular career transition arguably had a significant influence when Mandela succeeded de Klerk in office. While de Klerk experienced the international community as hostile to the National Party's cause as expressed, for example, in the effects of economic sanctions from the mid-1980s onward (Levy, 1999) or the various forms of sports boycott, Mandela had a different experience. For him, the international community had a largely positive influence. The efforts ranged from the UN campaign against apartheid starting with Resolution 134 in 1960 in the wake of the so-called Sharpeville massacre (United Nations, 2016) to many grass-roots groups around the world calling for an end to apartheid and the release of Mandela. Such previous international support opened many doors on the international scene for the incoming president and allowed him to use this long-standing previous support as a resource for rebuilding the country in political, economic, and symbolic terms. Again, understanding the succession into office and its outcomes would be incomplete without considering the previous career transition – here the change from state enemy to political leader and its enabling circumstances.

Overall, then, the SCF provides a clear rationale for extending the angle backward in time and chaining the current with previous career transitions. As any historian would say, to understand the present one needs to understand the past. It also points toward the potentially rich and diverse set of past career transitions' factors in terms of condition, position, and social space that are relevant for a current succession event.

In addition to taking into account previous career transitions, a more detailed look into succession events also suggests including potential future career transitions and potential anticipatory linkages. In the case of Mandela succeeding de Klerk and opening a new era in South African history, this is true for a number of reasons. When Mandela came into office, he was seventy-six years old and had been diagnosed with early stage tuberculosis at the age of seventy. While this did not automatically limit his capacity for a multi-term presidency, it clearly made the illusion of "open-ended reign" – sometimes turned into harsh reality through changing the constitutional regulations and/or using violent measures as has been the case with close-by Robert Mugabe in Zimbabwe, who announced in late 2016 that he would be running for a new term of president in 2018 at the age of ninety-four, or Mobutu Sese Seko in Zaire – harder to maintain. In addition, it was obvious to all astute observers that tremendous tasks lay ahead and that the transition period from the apartheid era to a new, reconciled, and functioning South Africa would require more years than were available in even the most optimistic estimates about Mandela's political lifetime. The new president demonstrated remarkable farsightedness by, from the beginning of his presidency, preparing for his own succession and starting a number of initiatives that would form the basis for his country's long-term development but that would continue long after he left office. In combination with the tremendous tasks ahead, the new president would have demonstrated substantial shortsightedness were he not to have, from the beginning of his presidency, prepared for his own succession and started a number of initiatives to form the basis for a long-term development.

Compared to other succession events as heads of state, this is a somewhat unique situation. Overall, it demonstrates the importance of including anticipatory linkages for understanding career succession events. In the case of Mandela, the often-announced "one term only" prospect, combined with its anticipated long-term requirements in the social and political arena when rebuilding the country, arguably were part of considerations when planning for how – and how long – to run the presidency. "His parting comments were, 'Don't call me, I will call you,' reflecting the need for the development of others to take the helm of the South African Government" (Williams, 2014: 109). To this issue – the importance of other actors in the social space for one's own career moves – we turn next, continuing the example of Mandela coming into office.

Coevolutionary Development The SCF suggests that not only chaining career transitions but also integrating the coevolving careers of other actors in the social space of the focal career actor support an in-depth analysis of succession events. In illustrating this by continuing our example of Nelson Mandela taking office as president of South Africa in 1994, we limit ourselves to two other prominent individual career actors relevant in his social space: his predecessor Frederik Willem de Klerk and his successor Thabo Mbeki, both also serving as deputies during his presidency. Of course, this is a gross simplification since there were a number of other individuals crucial for the succession event such as his separated wife Winnie Mandela or Walter Sisulu, a close confidant of Mandela over many years. In a similar way, for an extensive analysis one would have to include relevant collective social actors and their development such as the African National Congress (ANC) and its various factions, the National Party (NP) with its internal wrangling about the future course that eventually led to its demise by the end of the decade, the multiparty

Transnational Executive Council (TEC) preparing the ground for the first elections, and, as a broader aspect of the social space, the collapse of classical Eastern Bloc communism after 1989. However, this brief list of examples of relevant individual and collective actors already shows the complexity of the social space within which the succession event happened. Since our main goal is to illustrate – and not fully exploit – the capacity of the SCF to guide an in-depth succession analysis by pointing toward coevolving actors in the social space of the focal career actor, we limit ourselves to two individual actors, de Klerk and Mbeki.

Adding de Klerk and Mbeki to the picture results and again focusing on major events and transitions in their political life result in the overview shown in Figure 9.4.

The development of both actors and their previous and planned future career transitions provide important input for analyzing Mandela's succession of de Klerk. Given Mandela's initial plan to serve for only one term as president, his presidency from the beginning was linked to the question of his successor. While Mbeki was by no means uncontested, he was Mandela's choice over Cyril Ramaphosa, General Secretary of the ANC, and became the first deputy and later president in 1999. Several factors should have created a strong joint basis for a relationship between Mandela and Mbeki. Among them were their common roots in the ANC Youth League, the long-standing involvement of Mbeki in the ANC, and his outstanding role in the negotiations between the ANC and the apartheid regime of the ruling NP paving the way for the power change (Meersman, 2012). Indeed, Mbeki was being described as a de facto prime minister handling national affairs. However, the relationship between Mandela and Mbeki was also a difficult one. In particular, their view on racial reconciliation differed. Mbeki emphasized the need to induce a fundamental socioeconomic change in South African society as a prerequisite for reconciliation. Its delay was a constant source of irritation and failure for him (Gevisser, 2007). In addition, for Mbeki the stardom of Mandela and his self-orchestration as "one-good-native" damaged good governance and favored personality over process (Nutall and Mbembe, 2014). Clearly both the immediate transition into office and how Mandela conducted his office were influenced by Mbeki as an important actor in his social environment with a career of his own. His particular capacities allowed and maybe even partly forced Mandela to focus on international relations and the reconciliation issue from the very beginning. At the same time, the differing views and the long-term prospect for transitioning into presidency after Mandela's term in office also required heightened attention on the part of Mandela in order not to endanger crucial achievements, in particular in the area of reconciliation across racial boundaries. Through the lens of the SCF: Mbeki's past and potential future career was an important factor for Mandela to take into account during his own succession

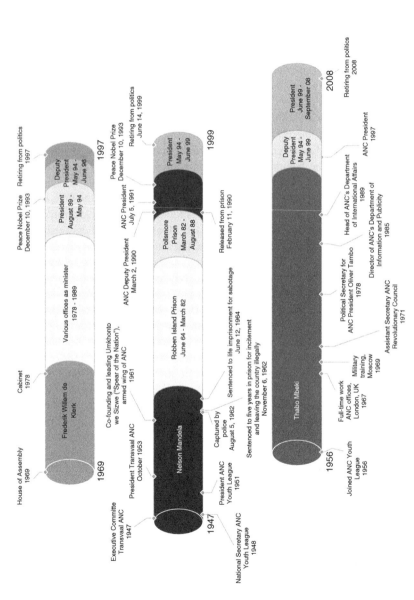

Figure 9.4 de Klerk, Mandela, and Mbeki – major events and offices in their political lives

and his presidency, illustrating both the chaining aspect addressed previously and the coevolutionary angle.

Of similar yet fundamentally different importance was de Klerk. As predecessor and second deputy, he was another crucial individual actor in Mandela's social environment when taking office. At first sight, de Klerk's personal background and political career showed no sign of producing a moderate reformer willing to abandon the apartheid policy. Because he was a traditional Afrikaner politician, his move toward unbanning the ANC in early 1990 and having elections came as somewhat of a surprise (Herbst, 1997). Yet there is some consensus that the South African transition to a multiparty democracy stands out as an overall positive example, in particular compared to similar efforts in Rwanda or Burundi, and de Klerk, by and large, played a key and positive role in this process. He was a congenial counterpart to Mandela; both were "[c]omplementary enemies, to be sure, yet willing to jettison the ballast when the circumstances required, [and] they deserve all the credit bestowed upon them by the media for 'making it happen'" (Lemarchand, 1994: 594). Analyzing the succession event bringing Mandela into office and its results without including the career of de Klerk as a major actor in the relevant social space tends to miss out on important aspects. De Klerk's credibility within the White minority, his formal position of president, his comparatively clear negotiation strategy, and the formulation of a (more or less) nonnegotiable bottom line for calling elections were both limitations and resources for Mandela. While it partly limited his options, it was also a source of justification for a more moderate course vis-à-vis the hardliners in the ANC. In addition, the symbolic capital of de Klerk reflected positively on Mandela, increasing his legitimization also in the White minority.

In summary, the coevolutionary angle of the SCF reminds succession research that the integration of individual and collective actors in the social space of the focal career actor and the temporal, dynamic view of these actors not being static entities but having careers of their own brings potential new insight. This strengthens a facet of the overall picture of organization succession that currently exists only in embryonic form.

We now move from succession research as a topic area to professional service firms, another issue addressed in organization studies.

Professional Service Firms

Professional service firms (PSFs) form a significant sector of developed economies:

Over the past three decades the Professional Service Firm (PSF) sector has emerged as one of the most rapidly growing, profitable, and significant sectors of the global economy. In 2013 the accountancy, management consulting, legal, and architectural sectors alone generated revenues of US$1.6 trillion and employed 14 million people (IBISWorld 2014a, 2014b, 2014c; MarketLine 2014). If sectors such as engineering services and advertising are included, the figure rises to US$2.5 trillion and US$18 [sic; presumably people, not dollars] million respectively (IBISWorld 2014d, 2014e). (Hinings, Muzio, Broschak, and Empson, 2015a: 1–2)

Partly for this reason, and partly because of sociologists' long-standing fascination with the professions, PSFs are attracting growing interest among organization theorists (Hinings, Muzio, Broschak, and Empson, 2015b). A review (Brock, 2006) examines their development since the 1960s and identifies a number of "forces for change" – deregulation, competition, technological developments, and globalization of services – that are leading to the emergence of organizational forms that differ notably from the traditional P^2, i.e. professional partnership, structure (Greenwood, Hinings, and Brown, 1990). For present purposes we identify two threads in this literature.

The first thread concerns the effects of these changes in terms of a shift from what has been called social trustee professionalism (Brint, 1994), in which the professional acts primarily in the public interest when serving clients, to something variously called commercial (Hanlon, 1996), expert (Brint, 1994), or entrepreneurial (Rittenberg and Covaleski, 2001) professionalism, in which

the entrepreneurial profession could be seen as too closely aligned to the vested interests of the client thereby undermining the professional claim of neutrality and independence in that the exercise of expertise is not objectified by a wholly codified knowledge base. (Rittenberg and Covaleski, 2001: 621)

The term "client capture" has been used to describe the potential consequences of this shift:

Under client capture the consumers of professional work gain the ability to control the activities, timing, and costs of professional work. In effect the "consumer becomes sovereign" much as consumers search for (and price) other consumer goods and services. (Leicht and Fennell, 2001: 106)

This capture effect can reach the professional from many directions: directly from an influential client or directly or indirectly from colleagues within the PSF who also have an interest in not upsetting the client (Dinovitzer, Gunz, and Gunz, 2014b). For example:

[Arthur] Andersen team members routinely succumbed to demands for certification from Enron management. Where the local auditors did not succumb directly, they were told to do so by their Chicago peers. When they refused, their advice was ignored. (Macey and Sale, 2003: 1179)

This shift to commercial professionalism (as we shall call it here) has been accompanied by interesting shifts in socialization practices within PSFs:

This dimension is also highlighted in an emerging body of research that explores PSFs as sites "where professional identities are mediated, formed and transformed" (Cooper and Robson 2006: 416). ... The emphasis therefore is on how organizations have become increasingly prominent actors in the socialization of professions as a means of control to promote their own commercial priorities and how this may be undermining a wider, collective, sense of professional identity. This process in turn, [sic] may be reshaping the priorities of professionals, eroding older commitments to social trustee-ship in favor of logics that stress more the values of technical expertise and commercial objectives (Hanlon, 1998; Reed, 2007; Suddaby et al., 2007). (Kirkpatrick and Noordegraaf, 2015: 10)

This seems to have been accompanied by an interesting change, at least in the case of accounting firms, in the meaning attached by members of PSFs to the concept of professionalism. The change is from a traditional one to do with expertise acquired from a lengthy training certified by a professional body, a disinterested service to client, and autonomy to decide in the interests of the client but within the policies and ethical rules of the profession, and so on, to being

seen primarily as a way of behaving: accountants view the idea of "professional" as referring to ways of acting, particularly in front of clients. Attention is given to matters of appearance, dress sense, and personal grooming (Coffey, 1993). Relatedly, appear-ance in terms of ways of talking and writing are important. Time management, eager-ness and other forms of overt commitment also mark the aspirant professional (Anderson-Gough, Grey, & Robson, 2001; Coffey, 1994). (Cooper and Robson, 2006: 432)

So the shift toward commercial professionalism and the rise in concern for client capture noted by a number of authors have apparently been accompanied by a shift in the socialization that young professionals experience, from one that is based within the profession to one that is, to a much greater extent, controlled by the PSF in which they work. And the socialization has a much greater emphasis than hitherto on meeting the needs of the client on the client's terms.

The second thread concerns the role that PSFs have played in diffusing "new and often radical business practices and structures" (Hinings et al., 2015a: 2). The examples that Hinings et al. give "include the 'M' form of business promoted by consulting firm McKinsey (Kipping 1999), the poison pill defense developed by law firm Wachtell Lipton (Starbuck 1993), and the business risk audit associated in particular with KPMG (Robson et al. 2007)" (ibid.). This thread concerns the dynamics of the relationships between PSFs and their clients. On the one hand, PSFs are the agents of change in their clients that Hinings et al. identify. On the other, the clients, through the various complex mechanisms of client capture, affect the PSFs that advise them. Furthermore, in Anglo-Saxon societies, the professions are dominated by their professional bodies, while in European societies, the state plays a much more central role in the regulation of professionals (Smets, Morris, and Greenwood, 2012; Collins, 1990). So PSFs presumably interact with the professional bodies of which their professional staff are members and that, therefore, play an important role in regulating the behavior of those staff. In turn, we can expect the firms, especially large ones, to have some kind of influence over their professional bodies, although these interactions have not, apparently, received much attention in the literature (Hinings *et al.*, 2015a: 18).

The picture that emerges from these two threads is a complex one (and, of course, in the space we have available here we have only scratched the surface of an extensive and long-running area of inquiry). Hinings *et al.* (2015a: 19) suggest an integrative perspective for viewing the situation of PSFs with respect to the worlds with which they interact. From the point of view of the SCF, their approach is interesting because they emphasize that each of the actors they consider – the PSF, its professionals, its clients, its competitors, and the profession's regulators – influence each other in a symmetrical series of reciprocal relations. They present a simple model with the PSF at the center and the four other sets of actors (professionals, clients, competitors, and regulators) at the periphery, each interacting with the PSF and each other. This, of course, is familiar to us from the SCF heuristic model (Figure 4.3), with one obvious exception, namely that the Hinings *et al.* model has no temporal aspect. And it is here that recasting the model in SCF terms may be illuminating because by adding a time base to the model, we have the potential for generating a model of strategic change in PSFs linked to career considerations of crucial actors.

Professional Service Firms and the SCF   The components of such a model of strategic change are all present in the literature, albeit scattered across it. The overall shapes of careers in PSFs are reasonably well understood (Cohen, 2015). The "up or out" model, in which professionals are hired on the assumption that they will be reviewed for partnership at some appropriate time and that if they do not make partner (in the terms of Malos and Campion, 1995, the firm fails to exercise its option on the individual) they are likely to have to leave the firm or, at least, be confined to a second-class rank in the firm, is widely encountered in PSFs, particularly in law and accounting. Parenthetically, we should note that in some jurisdictions – for example, the United Kingdom – resistance from junior professionals seeking better work-life balance resulting in a greater variety of career paths has also, argue Malhotra, Smets, and Morris (2016), coincidentally enhanced the innovation capacity of PSFs. This puts junior professionals in such firms under great pressure to demonstrate that they have what the firm is looking for in its partners. In part this involves learning the behaviors of the professional as defined in the firm (Cooper and Robson, 2006) as part of the process of imagining oneself in one's future (Costas and Grey, 2014; Ibarra, 1999). It represents a manifestation of the impact on their present condition of the career actor's beliefs about their possible future condition and the social space within which they hope to work.

We are thus describing the influences on an individual's career coming from their social context. Yet this picture has the potential to take us considerably further, suggesting a possible approach to explaining the kinds of change in PSFs that we describe earlier. Thus far these changes have typically been discussed in terms of the environmental pressures to which PSFs are subject:

We have examined three mechanisms of institutional change in organizations. Institutional entrepreneurs introduce institutional change and mediate the influences of structural overlap and historical events when they transpose the organizing principles of different societal sectors. Thus, a shift in institutional logics is more likely to occur when institutional entrepreneurs and structural overlap expose the discontinuities in the meaning and opportunities of institutional logics of different societal sectors. These discontinuities are amplified by the sequencing of historical events when institutional entrepreneurs pick up and use these discontinuities to frame their actions and alter cognitive perceptions in the process. (Thornton, Jones, and Kury, 2005: 162)

Yet Thornton *et al.* (2005) recognize that this tells only part of the story, concluding with the comment: "More research is needed to understand the micro-processes of how these three meso-level mechanisms work" (ibid.: 162). Potentially, the SCF provides the bridge that these authors are looking for. This observation hinges on the particular nature of PSFs, namely fundamentally as partnerships, even though the precise nature of the governance structure may vary (Leblebici and Sherer, 2015) and new corporate forms such as the limited liability partnership can affect the extent to which individual partners are responsible for the actions of their colleagues (Macey and Sale, 2003). As a partnership, the strategy of a PSF is determined by the collective will of its partners (Greenwood *et al.*, 1990). So the individual careers of the partners are intimately bound up with the "career" of the firm. This means that the process by which PSFs change – for example, in the ways described previously – is closely connected with the careers of the partners, themselves interconnected in the sense that each provides context for the others.

In order to adapt the Hinings *et al.* (2015a) model to the SCF, we expand on the interconnections between its elements (Figure 9.5). Rather than showing the PSF as the nexus of the model, which Hinings *et al.* do to display its relationships with the main elements with which it interacts (professionals, clients, competitors, and regulators), we show the key inter-relationships between all of the elements, including the firm, so that these elements can appear as actors in an extended SCF model. In order to do this, we need to make three key adaptations. First, the SCF model requires a focal career actor, and we show this as the "focal professional" rather than collectively as "professionals." This actor is arbitrarily selected so that

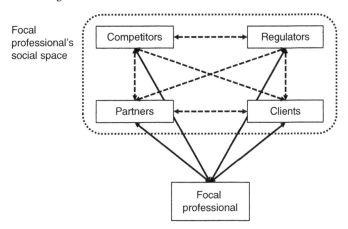

Figure 9.5 Interconnections between the PSF's principal actors (based on Hinings *et al.*, 2015a: 19)

we can show the relationships between the individual and their social space. Second, the "PSF" is shown as the "partners" because later we concentrate on the key people in the firm (the partners) with whom the focal professional interacts. Third, the clients are the set of clients of the focal professional, not of the PSF overall. The firm will, of course, have many other clients, so that there are as many versions of Figure 9.5 as there are professionals working in the firm.

All of the actors may interact at one time or another. Some of these interactions are of an everyday nature, such as the connection between the focal professional, their partners, and their clients. In the cases of other pairings, the interactions are less straightforward. For example, the link between client and competitor may be a real one or a potential one. Any given client may retain more than one PSF, so the connection may be real if both the professional and one or more of their competitors are retained by the same client. But if it is not, then the professional is always aware that it could be and that this could result in the professional losing the client. Given that the competitors are in the same profession, there are bound to be interactions between them, the focal professional, and their partners, if only at meetings of their professional society. But competitors can hire professionals away from other firms, too, leading to so-called lateral moves between firms (Mawdsley and Somaya, 2015; Rider and Tan, 2014; Galanter and Henderson, 2008), creating a potentially complex set of relationships between professionals, partners, and competitors. Finally, regulators certainly have a relationship with professionals in all groups in the model, but complaints to them typically come from clients because professionals are notoriously reluctant to turn in their professional colleagues (e.g. Abel, 1989).

We convert the map of interconnections shown in Figure 9.5 into the extended SCF model – that is, by putting it on a time base – in Figure 9.6. We again select one "focal professional" and map their social space in terms of their partners, their clients, their competitors, and the regulators.

Clients may have a particularly complex relationship with the professional. They can be either individuals or collectivities, and the two can be confused in practice. For example, the corporate client of a law or accounting firm is not the person (or people) with whom the focal professional interacts at the client but is the corporation, i.e. the employer of the people with whom the focal professional interacts. Even experienced professionals can confuse the two: in a study of 106 corporate lawyers given a vignette in which this distinction was an important issue, fewer than 25 percent identified it as something that they should take into account (Dinovitzer et al., 2014b). It was also a trap that Enron's lawyers fell into too often for the liking of Enron's court-appointed bankruptcy examiner, who criticized them for doing what Enron's executives wanted them to do rather than what was in the best interests of their real client, namely the overall corporation Enron (Batson, 2003: 28).

We depict the rest of the focal professional's social space in terms of partners, competitors, and regulators. Each may form a complex social network, the most salient of which is that composed of the other partners in the PSF. There are, of course, many other actors in the focal professional's social space who are not shown here, most notably members of the firm who are not partners, for example, the focal professional's associates – i.e. junior professionals – and staff who are not members of the PSF's profession. But here we concentrate on the other partners because of their central role in determining the PSF's strategy.

In essence, as we note previously, the model in Figure 9.6 puts the model of Hinings et al. (2015a), adapted in Figure 9.5, on a time base. To reiterate, the model arbitrarily selects one member of the firm as the focal career actor and depicts "the firm" as the other partners. The focal actor's social space comprises the clients, the other partners, the focal professional's competitors, and the profession's regulatory body (which may or may not be statutory, depending on the profession and the jurisdiction). It defines the "intimate ecological relationship" (Suddaby and Muzio, 2015: 37) between the firm and the institutions that surround it.

Strategic Change in PSFs: The SCF View   We are now able to return to the question of how the SCF can help make sense of strategic change in PSFs. The model in Figure 9.6 depicts the way in which the career of a professional coevolves with those of the other career actors in their social

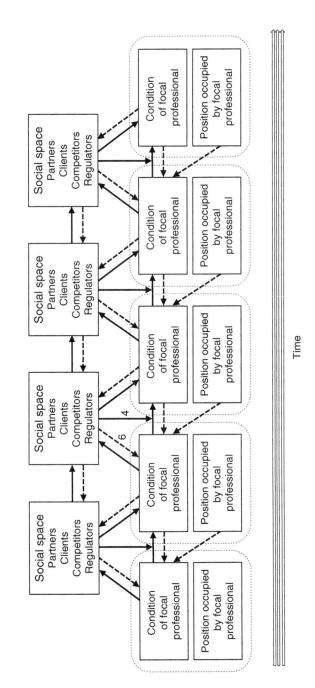

Figure 9.6 Model of the career of the focal professional, chained over time

space, some of whom are individuals (partners) and some of which may be either individuals or collectivities. The model, then, takes what is originally framed in the literature as a problem of organizational strategic change and reframes it as one of coevolving careers. Although, as we have noted, the model in Figure 9.6 is highly simplified in the sense that it shows only the main conceptual levels in play but not the complexities within each, it nevertheless makes clear that the coevolution is of a complex kind. What observations can we make from it?

A useful starting point is the study of Beckman and Phillips (2005), who find that clients with more women in top executive positions (general counsel, CEO, and board director) increase the probability of women being promoted to partner in the law firms that service them. Combining arguments based on bargaining power, legitimacy, and homophily, they invoke two main mechanisms for explaining their findings. First, clients with women in senior positions may intervene directly to increase the number of women associates in their law firm who are promoted to partner, an illustration of Proposition 4 from our heuristic model (Chapter 4) at work, shown as arrow 4 in Figure 9.6:

Proposition 4: The change in career actors' condition and position is moderated by the characteristics of the social space in which the transition takes place.

Second, Beckman and Phillips propose that PSFs anticipate the reaction of clients with women in senior positions by adding more women to their partnership ranks. This argument, which is to do with the PSF taking steps to retain its client, is an illustration of Proposition 6 (arrow 6 in Figure 9.6):

Proposition 6: The condition of a career actor before a career transition will reflect their anticipation of the characteristics of the social space in which the career transition will take place.

These propositions explain change in a PSF in terms of the influence of a client. They illustrate the point we shall develop next, namely that change in PSFs can be explained by examining the way that individual members of the firm seek career benefit because both explanations are based on the assumption, not made particularly explicit in the paper, that partners will take the actions described because they see their own career benefiting from retaining their clients.

The model in Figure 9.6 is somewhat deceptive in the sense that it shows the focal professional's social space as a box containing several different classes of actor but without showing how they interact between themselves and with the focal professional. But the social space is a very complex affair. It comprises many actors, some of which are individuals and some collectivities, whose careers coevolve in complex ways. The Beckman and Phillips study shows, for example, how the career of a corporate client, which over time appoints women to senior positions, coevolves with the careers of the women in the law firm serving it.

This process, by means of which changes in the condition and position of actors change the social space of the other actors, potentially generates a condition of path dependence in the sense that once these changes in the focal actor's social space take place, the route forward is shaped in ways that place constraints on the entity's future. For example, the partners in the Panamanian law firm Mossack Fonseca who were responsible for acquiring clients allegedly looking for ways of evading tax in their home jurisdictions created a set of professional–client linkages that directed the firm down a path toward worldwide notoriety in the 2016 Panama Papers affair from which it will not prove easy to escape (Obermayer and Obermaier, 2016). Similarly, the Arthur Andersen partners responsible for acquiring Enron as a client set the firm onto a seemingly irreversible slide to destruction, climaxing in Enron's Chapter 11 bankruptcy in 2001 and being instrumental in Arthur Andersen's demise in 2002.

For our present purposes, we look on the strategy followed by a PSF as being evidenced by, for example, the clients they choose, the extent to which they tend to be "captured" by their clients, and where the services they provide to their clients come on the continuum we describe earlier between social trustee-ship and commercial professionalism. We view it as an emergent process (Mirabeau and Maguire, 2014; Mintzberg and Waters, 1985) coming from the individual decisions made by professionals in their dealings with their clients and leading to a coordinated approach between the professionals: "Coordination also means that practitioners work under the same organiza-tional strategy and share the realization that they, and their careers, are impli-cated by that strategy's successful implementation" (Smets *et al.*, 2012: 896).

This view of strategy, of course, draws on Mintzberg's (1978: 934) definition of strategy, which we encountered in Chapter 3 as "a pattern in a stream of decisions" and which echoes strongly our definition of career as a pattern of a career actor's positions and condition within a bounded social and geographic space over their life to date.

At the level of the career actor, these decisions are influenced by the actors' beliefs about where their actions will take them in terms of their careers and their beliefs about the future condition and position of the actors comprising their social space after they have taken their actions. However, as we note earlier, the model in Figure 9.6, despite its simplifications, defines an extraordinarily com-plex set of changing relationships, which is probably too much for any actor within the system it defines to make sense of. This means that each actor in the system has to take part in a very complex game of prediction, of imagining their future (Costas and Grey, 2014), which may involve a lot of guessing about individual outcomes and how those outcomes will affect other outcomes of the kind: "If I do this, X will probably do that, which Y won't like, so Y may do the following, which is likely to bite me back in the following way ... "

A common response to "wicked problems" (Rittel and Webber, 1973) of this nature – wicked problems "are ill-formulated, where the information is confusing, where there are many clients and decision makers with conflicting values, and where the ramifications in the whole system are thoroughly confusing" (Churchman, 1967: B141) – is to rely on the advice of someone else, often called an opinion leader. These figures emerge in the classic study by Lazarsfeld, Berelson, and Gaudet (1944) of electors taking part in the 1940 US presidential election and ubiquitously since. In order to simplify things, each actor is likely to choose one or a few other actors on whom to rely for help in making their predictions. "In general, opinion leadership is considered to be the informal influence that recognized peers have on the attitudes, opinions, beliefs, and decisions of others" (Chen, Brown, O'Donnell, and Huning, 2015).

One cannot predict who the opinion leaders will be without knowing the specifics of the system in question; these people are not necessarily in positions of formal authority (and authority typically takes a distributed form in PSFs anyway). Opinion leadership may be limited to a relatively restricted area of expertise (Chen *et al.*, 2015). Certainly, in the context of a PSF, a professional's actions in relation to a client will be influenced by other partners who have dealings with the same client, especially the so-called relationship partners who are primarily responsible for maintaining the PSF's relationship with the client (Dinovitzer *et al.*, 2014b). In order to understand how the opinion leaders and seekers interrelate, one needs to understand the structure of the social network comprising the actors in the system.

The account we have just given suggests strongly that the missing link referred to by Thornton *et al.* (2005) – the micro-processes that connect their three meso-level mechanisms of change – can be found at least in substantial part in the career decisions taken by the actors within the system of Figure 9.6. In brief, what the SCF focuses on is the way in which strategic change at the firm level comes about because of the decisions of individual partners to do things differently, which they do because they believe that it will help their careers. We refer previously to Mintzberg's concept of strategy as a pattern in a stream of decisions, and here we focus on the decisions.

The hypothetical example we shall use for our analysis goes as follows. A partner in a particular firm in which the dominant approach falls within the social trusteeship model finds themselves dealing with a client who is pressing them to adopt a more commercial approach. Should they do so? If they do, then they have taken a decision that does not fit the pattern of decisions typical of their firm and their own professional practice to date. It would be the first step in a potential process of strategic change for the firm. The question arises: Under what circumstances might this first step happen, and under what circumstances might it propagate through the firm so that a change of firm strategy can be said to have taken place? If they do not take the step, they risk losing the client (an example of the pressures that may result in client capture), which may be harmful to their career if it leads to loss of income and status within the firm, or helpful if their partners see it as a positive move to support the status quo. Next, we examine this example more closely using the language of the SCF.

Analyzing Strategic Change **The Initial Decision** Our starting assumption is that the focal career actor – the partner faced with the problem outlined in the previous section – is more likely to adopt the new approach if they believe that it will help their career. This enhancement to their career could come about in one of two main ways depending on whether their partner colleagues approve of the new approach. The other partners might approve if they decide that the new approach will help *their* careers, too, by bringing more clients to their door, helping them keep the ones they have, or generating additional business with the existing ones. If so, then the focal career actor is likely to be rewarded in the short term informally within the firm's reputational system by being treated as an opinion leader on that issue and perhaps more formally through the firm's profit-sharing scheme. In the longer term, their career may benefit because their reputation as innovator spreads beyond the firm within the profession or they become seen by their colleagues as a potential managing partner or equivalent.

The other partners might *not* approve if they believe it to be harmful to their careers. They might, for example, be concerned that the new approach will draw unfavorable attention from the regulator or be the subject of concern from their other clients, who have stayed with them because they like their more traditional approach. Or they might simply feel that their own competencies are devalued by or insufficient for the new situation or that this is not the way that their profession should be practiced. If so, then the focal career actor has a choice: they might abandon the idea, or they might seek out and attempt to move to a competitor firm that is known for being favorably disposed to the new way of doing things. This, in turn, may be a disincentive to their partner colleagues to oppose the change, depending on the focal career actor's reputation within the firm (there are some colleagues one can afford to lose and some one cannot).

This brief outline of a process by means of which strategic change might be initiated within a PSF is based on the precept that professionals tend to be motivated to a great extent to do things that they think will benefit their careers (Proposition 2 from the basic building block of Chapter 4, also shown as arrow 2 in Figure 9.7):

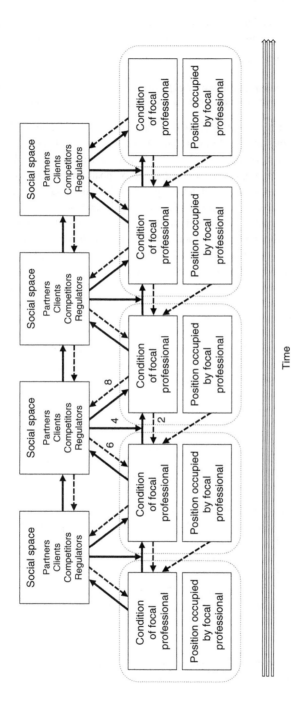

Figure 9.7 Elaborated model of focal professional's career, showing propositions

Proposition 2: The condition of a career actor at the beginning of a career transition is affected by their anticipation of their condition at the end of the career transition.

For example, in this case:

Proposition 2a: The more resistance a focal professional anticipates to their proposals to change current practice, the more open they will be to offers from a competitor.

But it also implies a great deal of guessing and second-guessing about the outcome of various actions. For example: What will the focal actor's partners' response be to the new approach in terms of the focal actor's career? Will their actions result in an improved condition and/or position for the focal actor (Proposition/arrow 4)? The focal actor's guesses about their partners' reactions will affect the focal actor's approach to handling the decision about whether to adopt the new approach (Proposition/arrow 6). Of course, the focal actor is likely to discuss the matter with their partners, although professionals vary in the extent to which, despite being partners in a PSF, they appear to think of themselves as collaborative members of the collectivity that is the partnership as opposed to "lone rangers" (Dinovitzer, Gunz, and Gunz, 2014a) who operate almost as if they are independent practitioners. A "lone ranger" may just tell their colleagues what they're doing without consulting them or allow them to find out after the fact.

The focal actor also has to guess at the likely response of the client if the focal actor decides *not* to adopt the new approach (i.e. the focal actor does *not* comply with the client's wishes). Will the client move to a competing PSF, or will a moral stand on the part of the focal actor (if indeed it appears to the focal actor like this) result in the client accepting the situation and staying? Losing the client is very likely to result in a loss of income and/or reputation for the focal actor (Proposition/arrow 2), but keeping the client and thereby reinforcing the firm's existing strategy might be seen by the focal actor's partners as worthy of reward (Proposition/arrow 4). This difficult choice, based on the focal actor's guesses about the mutual responses of client and partners, will affect the focal actor's approach to the decision (whether to adopt the new approach; Proposition/arrow 6). And if the focal actor makes the change and it is not accepted by the partners, is the focal actor's professional reputation strong enough that they will find it easy to move to a competitor? If they were to threaten to do so, is their reputation in their current firm strong enough that their colleagues will adjust their view of the new approach because they do not wish to risk losing the focal actor from the firm (Proposition/arrow 8 from the basic building block)?

Proposition 8: Individual and collective actors in the social space are directly affected by anticipated characteristics of position and condition at the end of the career transition.

For example,

Proposition 8a: The higher the risk to the firm of the focal professional leaving, in the perception of their partners, the lower their resistance to changes proposed by the focal professional.

Finally, the focal actor may find themselves wondering about the response of the regulator and whether that will affect their future, in the sense that a disciplinary hearing is never a good thing. As we note earlier, this is not very likely; more likely is their concern that the client, if displeased by the way that the focal actor handled the file, may complain to the regulator themselves, which might have the same ultimate effect (Proposition/arrow 4).

The account so far is about the pressures surrounding the decision on the part of the focal career actor, a partner within the PSF, to adopt a new approach to their practice. It is about the preliminary stages of a possible change in strategy for the firm. Nothing has happened yet at the firm level; all we have been considering is the thought process of the focal actor faced with the decision about whether to adopt a new way of providing service to a client. The pressures acting on the focal actor derive from uncertainties about how the decision will affect the focal actor's career, deriving in turn from further uncertainties about the potential responses of their partners and their client to the focal actor's decision. The pressures are structured around the propositions of the basic building block (Figure 9.7).

Let us assume that the focal actor decides to adopt the new practice and stays with the firm. Under what circumstances does the SCF suggest that this practice is adopted throughout the firm, so that we can say that there has been a change in firm strategy?

Propagating the Decision through the PSF The question we have posed is: If one partner in a PSF adopts a practice that is new to the firm – for example, taking a more commercial approach rather than the firm's current social trustee-ship approach – what might affect the likelihood of their colleagues adopting it as well, so that it can be said that a new pattern has emerged in the stream of the firm's decisions? If it can, then, following Mintzberg (1978), we can say that there has been a change in the PSF's strategy.

In order to answer this question, we need to imagine that we are redrawing Figure 9.7 for each of the PSF's partners in turn because each partner has to go through a similar exercise to that of the original focal actor in order to decide whether they, too, will adopt the new approach and decide whether it is in the interests of their career to adopt the change. For each successive partner, the process becomes somewhat easier because some uncertainty will have dissipated. They will have more information on the actual responses of their other partners and of their competitors, although each individual client is likely to respond in their own way such that it may not be easy to learn from the experience of others. And indeed it may reach a point at which a meeting of the partners comes to a collective decision about how to respond to the new approach. However, that is unlikely to happen unless either a considerable proportion of the partners have adopted it already, the firm's managing partner(s) have recognized the significance of the change to the firm and decided to put the matter to the partnership, or the firm has some kind of practice committee to which matters like these are delegated and it recommends adopting the new approach.

The process we have described is, in essence, an iterative application of the SCF to frame the decision processes followed by individual partners in the PSF as they analyze how their career interests should shape their response to a potential change in their professional practice. We have shown just how "wicked" the problem can be, which implies that they are likely to seek the advice of opinion leaders within or possibly outside the firm. This, in turn, means that in order to understand just how the change process either will or will not propagate throughout the PSF, emerging as a recognizable change in the pattern of the stream of decisions taking place within it, we also need to understand the structure of the social network that links the firm's partners.

Strategic Change in PSFs: Summary   The change process we have been exploring is a pretty dense one, with many branches to it leading to different outcomes. It is nevertheless based on a simple precept: that individual professionals working within the PSF will take decisions that they believe will benefit their careers. The simplicity of the precept is deceptive, however, because as the model makes clear, the professionals' beliefs depend on their predictions about how other actors in the system will react to their actions, how others will react to those reactions, and so forth, in an almost infinite chain of predicted events. Except that nobody can do that, so the actors simplify the situation by relying on opinion leaders for advice and, presumably, either consciously or unconsciously limiting the number of guesses they make about future events.

In sum, the SCF heuristic model provides an architecture for examining strategic change in PSFs from a career perspective. In order to make use of the architecture – to apply it to specific examples, for example, to predict the nature of strategic change in the accounting profession in response to concerns about conflict of interest between auditing and consulting functions (Lisic, Myers, Pawlewicz, and Seidel, 2016) – one would need to know more about the careers of the respective partners and the structure of the profession, as well as the corporate forms of the firms themselves, in the jurisdiction of interest. That would begin to provide the specificities that would, potentially, allow predictions about the likelihood and nature of strategic change to be made.

Summation

In this chapter we examine in some depth how the SCF helps reframe both individual studies and more general topic areas in fields outside the proto-field of career studies, so that the view provided by the SCF and concepts from the field of OMC studies yield a different way of seeing the study or the topic area that, in turn, may lead to new ways of studying both. We have worked in the opposite direction to that of Chapter 8. There, we used the SCF to import ideas from the world outside OMC studies to find new approaches to existing career research problems. Here, we use the SCF to export ideas from OMC studies to discourses that have nothing to do with OMC, hopefully helping these discourses by systematically offering OMC insights.

This completes our Part III journey through some of the ways that the SCF can be put to work. In the final chapter, we review where the book as a whole has taken us and where it might lead.

Part IV

Conclusion

10   Taking the SCF Forward

We introduce this book by saying that our aim is not merely to celebrate the richness of career – that has been done many times before – but to find a way of putting a structure on the richness in order to facilitate conversation between the many scholarly discourses in which career appears. The discourses in question range from those in which career plays a central role to those in which it plays a supporting role. Scholars working in the former discourses think of themselves as career scholars (or scholars of an obvious synonym of career), while those in the latter do not, and our assumption is that all of us, whether self-described career scholars or not, have an interest in learning from each other's work. We offer the SCF as a framework for facilitating these conversations.

In this chapter, we reflect on what we see as the main messages that emerge from our exploration of the SCF and its implications for career studies and areas of study related to it. First, we review the SCF itself and our account of its implications and applications.

Main Messages of the Book

"Career," as we and many others point out, is a word with a great many meanings. That is the first and most obvious obstacle to conversation: if you cannot agree on what a word means, it is hard to find common ground in order to be able to communicate usefully. That would be tricky enough if the word is sufficiently obscure that everyone had to look it up in their dictionary. Ironically, the very commonplace nature of "career" adds to the problem because one has to listen very carefully to realize that it is indeed being used in different senses in different – sometimes even the same – discourses. It is rather like the difference between American and British English. There are certain words and phrases that have different, sometimes startlingly different meanings, as witness the panic experienced by an apocryphal English passenger on a US airliner when the captain announces that the aircraft will be taking off "momentarily" (US English: "soon"; British English: "for a very short time, fleetingly").

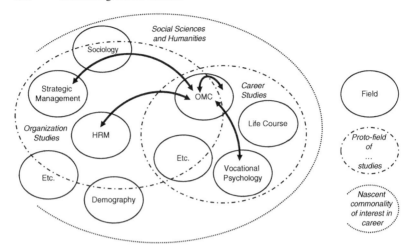

Figure 10.1 Conversations between fields, proto-fields, and nascent commonalities of interest

In order to map the territories in which career appears, we distinguish in Chapter 1 between fields, proto-fields, and nascent commonalities of interest (Figure 10.1). While fields within the proto-field of career studies vary in the nature of their internal coordination, even loosely coordinated fields such as OMC studies, to which we apply Whitley's (1984) label of fragmented adhoc-racies, have a sense of who they are and, within very broad terms, what they do. We call career studies a proto-field because there is no real indication that those working within the fields that we have put within it see themselves engaged in any kind of common endeavor, even though in each field "career" or an obvious synonym for it provides its primary focus. Yet if a means could be found, and we suggest that the SCF provides just such a means, for conversations to be struck up across these field boundaries, perhaps a mutual recognition of the links between the fields may grow to the point at which scholars in each of the fields identify a common project in which they are all engaged and the proto-field becomes a field.

Within the broader area of the social sciences and humanities, there are many scholars who use the concept of career in their work. However, they certainly do not think of themselves as career scholars, nor do they normally cite the work of those who do in their writing. For example, a historian writing a biography of a major historical figure sees themselves entirely understandably as a historian; they would probably be most surprised to be told that their study could alternatively be described as being about careers even though they may well refer to the "career" of their subject.

In terms of fields, our focus is mainly on OMC studies, but the conversations that we refer to in the book, shown schematically in Figure 10.1 as curved double-headed arrows, connect all three levels of analysis. We offer the SCF as a basis for these conversations because, we suggest, it provides a discipline-independent view of career that, we hope, anyone working with the concept in any of the fields in Figure 10.1 should recognize.

We introduce our view of career as an actor's social chronology, i.e. a chronology that traces the "path" of a career actor through a given social (as well as geographical) space over a given time. This implies – and we show how the implication derives from most, if not all, well-received definitions of career – that examining careers involves the simultaneous application of spatial, ontic, and temporal perspectives. These, in turn, suggest basic constructs for viewing career: boundary for the spatial perspective, condition for the ontic, and chronology for the temporal. The operations that lie behind the characterization of each of these constructs are, respectively, mapping, comparing, and sequencing. Putting it this way – that a career is a pattern of a career actor's positions and condition within a bounded social and geographic space over their life to date – gives us, we claim, a means of viewing career that is abstract enough to be recognizable to anyone working with the concept. Obviously it needs to be translated into the language of particular fields, so that, for example, OMC researchers would require the definition to be modified to refer to work-related social and geographic space and working life to date.

The three perspectives of the SCF form the foundation of a model of career that takes as its unit of analysis the career transition and takes the form of a multi-period, multilevel coevolutionary heuristic. We work with this heuristic model for the rest of the book, showing how it can be used to facilitate conversation within the OMC field and between fields within the proto-field of career studies, suggest new pathways to cumulative OMC research, point to ways of importing ideas from fields outside the proto-field of career studies, and suggest approaches to problems within those noncareer fields using ideas from career studies. In brief, then, the SCF offers five key elements.

A Tri-perspective View of Career Career is viewed as a social phenomenon that becomes apparent when social actors are examined from the perspectives of space, being, and time – what we call here the spatial, ontic, and temporal perspectives. It is therefore not the property of any one discipline: any discipline or art (although this book does not consider the treatment of career in art) can take an interest in it, and most do at some stage. The work of a career researcher (a researcher studying career, not someone who makes a career out of doing research) studying the careers of young people making choices about their occupational future examines the social spaces they are leaving (e.g. education and, perhaps, family) and the ones they are entering (e.g. occupations, work organizations), their condition (e.g. educational attainments, social capital, age), and the time over which this is happening. A historian analyzing the development of the US presidency over the past few decades examines the social space in which the presidency plays out, most likely to be a very broad canvas covering both the USA and much of the world, the condition especially of the presidents during the study period, and the time over which each served as president and, quite possibly, the time during which they developed as politicians. Both career researcher and historian are studying career, and we miss out on a lot if we overlook this.

Career as a Pattern of Positions and Condition within a Bounded Geographical and Social Space over Life to Date The pattern is a product of the application of spatial, ontic, and temporal perspectives to a career actor. It is, therefore, a social construct, the appearance of which is entirely dependent on how the three perspectives are applied. An objective career is not a concrete thing but the pattern that someone sees who is interested in, for example, organizational status and how it can change for particular individuals in particular kinds of organizations over their time as a member of those organizations. A different observer who is interested in the feelings of success experienced by the same people will, in all probability, see a very different kind of pattern. The second observer may call this pattern a subjective career, but it, too, is not a concrete thing in itself; it is still just a pattern inferred by the observer. By understanding that career is a socially constructed pattern, we can begin to understand why other scholars might have radically different views of what career "is" and how to begin a fruitful conversation with them.

A Focus on Career Actors That Can Be Both Individual and Collective It is pretty much a statement of the obvious that careers are things that individuals have, and any reference to "career" in the literature, or to one of its synonyms such as "life course," is almost always – but not always – to the career of an individual. However, the statement that examining careers involves applying the spatial, ontic, and temporal perspectives to a career actor does not require the actor to be an individual. It makes just as much sense to say that we can examine the career of Luiz Inácio Lula da Silva through these perspectives as it does to say that we can examine the career of the Federative Republic of Brazil during the time he served in various political roles. In both cases observers can see patterns in the actor's condition and position. Lula, for example, moves in and out of the presidency, while Brazil's economic and political condition, as well as its position within the erstwhile lauded BRICS group, changes.

Career as a Complex Coevolutionary Process across Different Levels of Social Space The social and geographical space occupied by career actors is populated with more career actors, whose lives intermingle and interact with those of the focal career actor. The actors in the social space can be both individual and collective. To return to the Brazilian example in the previous paragraph, Lula's career and that of Brazil, especially during his presidency, are very closely linked, the one affecting the other and vice versa. A career actor's colleagues, especially if the actor sees them as mentors, can equally have a profound effect on the actor's career, just as the actor's career can affect theirs.

Facilitating a Systematic Approach to Key Issues in Advancing Career Studies This includes

building cumulative research within fragmented adhocracies studying careers. For fields such as OMC studies that lack a clear sense of structure and integration, the SCF suggests ways of reframing areas of study that propose new questions for old problems.

building in existing theory to explain career processes. The heuristic model that emerges from the SCF provides a framework for building in theory that can explain specific career phenomena.

structuring conversations between discourses. By providing a common language that describes career in any discourse in which it appears, the SCF facilitates conversation between the discourses. This, of course, is a necessary but not sufficient condition for meaningful conversation.

the process of importing and exporting ideas between discourses. An important outcome of the inter-field-discourse conversation stimulated by the SCF is that it makes it easier to see opportunities for taking ideas from one discourse and applying them to established problems in another. The SCF suggests a structured approach involving reconstructing the problem in the language of the SCF. It consists of equivalizing (i.e. looking for similar theoretical discussions in different fields); understanding (i.e. getting to the core of these other discussions); and importing the arguments to the original problem.

Once again we must emphasize "facilitate" in all this. The SCF does not reveal what otherwise would be invisible; it simply makes it easier to detect such aspects. We turn next to some major future directions of research that we see tightly linked with the SCF.

Some Further Directions

Three areas seem to us to be of particular importance: focusing on the social and on the time-related aspect of careers and, linked to this, the development of career theory. We address these issues in turn, once again focusing mainly on OMC studies.

Taking the Social *Seriously*

It is widely acknowledged that much of the OMC field focuses on person-centered factors related to careers. The SCF, while clearly acknowledging the ontic perspective as a crucial one, warns us against an overemphasis on ontic elements and falling into the micro-trap represented by not sufficiently taking into account the interplay between the career actor and their social space. At the same time, it calls for a systematic integration and exploration of the social space. This has important implications for three aspects of career scholarship: special groups of career actors inhabiting specific segments of the social space; comparative analyses of various national, cultural, and institutional contexts; and social spaces that are key to the future of the planet. We deal with these issues in turn.

Special Groups If we follow Hughes – which we do in this respect – and assume that an analysis of careers (1937: 413) "may be expected to reveal the nature and 'working constitution' of a society," we can expect to learn much about the many and varied institutions to be found in society and their respective social contexts by examining the careers of the people who live their lives in and through them. Looking at careers beyond the mainstream, by which we mean not just careers in and between traditional organizations but careers involving people on whom the organizational and managerial careers literature may not have focused hitherto, will provide a more in-depth understanding of the intricacies of the interplay between individual career actors and their specific social context. Examples of respective topics include but are not limited to careers of members of particular occupations or professions; actors in highly visible segments of society (e.g. athletes, actors, painters, singers, scientists, politicians, judges and lawyers, or clergy and gurus); individuals at the margin of society (e.g. criminals such as drug dealers or money launderers, prostitutes/sex workers, homeless people, low-skilled and/or illegal immigrants or refugees, or long-time unemployed people); and those who work outside traditional work organizations (e.g. one-person entrepreneurs or the self-employed).

A better understanding of careers in these segments of the social space not only sheds light on the specifics and the commonalities of the special groups linked to these segments. Many if not all of these careers also have the potential to increase our understanding of how broader society works. Basic societal phenomena such as social status and prestige, advancement and demotion, power distribution and struggle, or inclusion and exclusion often become more obvious when one goes beyond the mainstream where several layers of protection, obfuscation, or reconciliation have often been installed. This supports our understanding of how societies and their subgroups work. Take, for example, the case of top athletes retiring from their active sports careers, in particular when they were in disciplines such as whitewater slalom or trap shooting with sparse, if any, possibilities for making money beyond the mere necessities of earning a living and paying for your sport. Making a career transition from the sports field to another field, usually some kind of job outside sports, brings up very typical problems linked to this transition reflecting all kinds of societal issues. This includes the value that is placed on the individual when they are top athletes versus "normal citizens"; the half-life of support promises by politicians when they are in the limelight together with the athlete ("Call me anytime if you need anything!," revealing part of the strict give-and-take logic of the political system, here for example: "As long as you are useful for strengthening my position in the political field, I'll try to keep in touch"), and its interplay with the media; or the importance that the labor market places on different forms of career capital when assigning specific entry positions to the athletes making the career transition. A simple career transition like this can reveal much about how a society works.

Comparative Analyses of National, Cultural, and Institutional Contexts
Taking a comparative angle when looking at social space leads pretty straightforwardly to a comparative analysis of various national, cultural, and institutional contexts. Among other things, this inevitably entails a stronger focus on context and structure, counterbalancing the "actor-first" tendency in career research to date. Countries can be small or large, have greater or fewer regional differences, include one or many language groups, and be more or less economically developed. They may have different labor markets and education systems, different employment laws and trade unions, and different cultural expectations. Research has identified different career models that are pertinent for certain countries in terms of, for example, career entry and development, career paths, career success factors, and career transitions within and between organizations (e.g. Andresen and Walther, 2013; Davoine and Ravasi, 2013; Lazarova, Dany, and Mayrhofer, 2012; Evans, Pucik, and Björkman, 2011; Chudzikowski et al., 2009).

While there is an increasing number of single studies looking at commonalities and differences in individual careers and organizational career management between countries, there is little systematic and cumulative research available. In addition, the greater part of career research has been carried out within single countries from the WEIRD region (Western, educated, industrialized, rich, democratic; Henrich, Heine, and Norenzayan, 2010). As a result, there is a lack of understanding about the nuances of career-related concepts and the heterogeneous views of careers possessed by individuals around the world. This clearly is not satisfactory as every country has its own deep-seated values, beliefs, attitudes, and sets of institutional arrangements. They are simultaneously the result of and the reason for the specific ways that the respective economies and societies operate and how actors work and are managed at work. For example, differences in terms of decisions about promotion, individual career decision making, career planning, or career preferences have been linked to various cultural and institutional settings (e.g. Chong, 2013; Dany, Mallon, and Arthur, 2003; Schaubroeck and Lam, 2002; Bian and Ang, 1997).

Future explorations of this kind could include, for example, a comparative analysis of career systems in various countries; a description of how patterns of stasis, convergence, and/or divergence differ between countries in terms of career systems and practices over time; investigating to what extent the concept of career and career success is defined by individual-level factors such as self-directed career behavior or personality as opposed to higher-level factors (e.g. cultures, economies, educational levels, or generations); or the search for context-specific characteristics of careers in individual career management, career expectations, and career mobility.

Beyond these concrete research foci, following the call of the SCF for a more sophisticated and integrated analysis of the social space and its role in careers also has some more basic implications (see also Briscoe, Hall, and Mayrhofer, 2012a). First, it contributes to our understanding of the relative importance of various contextual macro-factors, in particular culture and institutions but also other factors such as differing demographic or economic characteristics of careers. Examples include legal regulations; the political and economic system; a population's age distribution and its link to career opportunities; or generational issues such as the development of a global youth culture, influenced and socialized along similar lines because of social media such as YouTube, Facebook, Instagram, and Snapchat as well as globally available TV series, films, and music. All of these potentially have consequences for the expectations young people have vis-à-vis careers and what they will encounter when entering the labor market.

Second, it is not just the social space but also career itself that is not a monolithic block. Beyond looking for the influence of different elements of the social space on careers, the need arises for more detailed analyses regarding how the various facets of careers are influenced by their context. Take the example of career success, which is far from being a straightforward construct. The simple distinction between objective and subjective career success is increasingly appearing to be an oversimplification: people from different age groups, professions, and countries seem to address seven dimensions – learning and development, work-life-balance, positive impact on the world, positive work relationships, financial security, financial achievement, entrepreneurship – when relating to career success (Mayrhofer *et al.*, 2016). Yet it is far from clear to what extent these dimensions are susceptible to contextual variation, whether some are more invariant than others, and which elements of the social space influence, and to what extent, which of these dimensions.

Social Spaces Key to the Future of the Planet A different way of responding to the call of the SCF to integrate the social space more strongly into career research is by looking at individuals and organizations dealing with crucial issues for the survival and progress of the planet. A better understanding of the careers of these individuals and the career systems of respective organizations helps us to understand the individual and organizational behavior and why some appear to be more effective in gaining traction with their ideas than others. In turn, this allows us to consider how to influence their behavior, such that they might become more effective.

In terms of topics and individual and collective actors involved, this is a broad area. Topics mentioned time and again range from poverty and inequality to food and water issues, climate change, lack of preschool and primary education, infectious agents, infant mortality to global terrorism and world-spanning criminal organizations. Hardly surprisingly, then, a broad range of actors deal with these issues: scientists such as 2016 World Food Prize winners Maria Andrade from Cape Verde, Robert Mwanga from Uganda, and Jan Low and Howarth Bouis from the USA and controversial figures such as Andrew Wakefield from the UK, whose work purporting to link the MMR vaccine to autism has been described as "an elaborate fraud" (Godlee *et al.,* 2011: 64); politicians like Ellen Johnson Sirleaf, President of Liberia and Nobel Peace Prize laureate (with Leymah Gbowee and Tawakkol Karman) and individual donors like USA media mogul Ted Turner or Californian real estate figure Donald Bren; supra-national organizations such as UNESCO and international networks like Médecins Sans Frontières; large trusts such as the Bill and Melinda Gates Foundation and small NGOs like Aggalia ("Embrace"), established by the late Greek Orthodox priest Father Efstratios Dimou ("Papa Stratis") and helping refugees on the Greek island of Lesvos; international organizations such as Frontex dealing with EU borders; or organizations on the dark side of society such as transnational organized crime like Mara Salvatrucha ("MS-13"; Guatemala) or Solntsevskaya Bratva (Russia) as well as international terrorist organizations like Boko Haram (Nigeria) or Islamic State (Daesh or "The Caliphate"; Middle East).

These actors have one thing in common: we do not have any systematic scientific insight into the careers of these individuals, of careers of individuals linked to these organizations, and of the careers of these organizations as collective actors. True, for some of them (e.g. Bill Gates) there is a lot of public information available. However, in other cases, such as organizations on the dark side or large international organizations, we have very little insight into careers of individuals and the career systems of the respective organizations. All of this prevents better insight into individual career behavior and into the functioning of the organizations, both of which are a prerequisite for influencing both individual behavior one way or the other and the efficiency and effectiveness of the organizations.

In addition to the actors outlined previously, another highly influential segment of social space has been emerging over the past three decades: the virtual world. Starting with the possibilities opened up by microprocessors and the emerging Internet, the virtual world has become a digital ecosystem of its own. Among many other manifestations, it includes new social networks, gaming, and digital marketplaces. While this segment of the social space is still in its infancy, it is clearly both evolving rapidly and having a substantial impact on the material world through its means of communication and in its own right. Again, we can use career research in order to better understand and influence what is going on in this area. However, as in the segments of the social space mentioned earlier, we know very little about the career aspects linked with the virtual world. To give a few examples: What drives someone to make a living as a professional in e-sports such as Olof Kajbjer (nickname "olofm") from Sweden in *Counter Strike* (ego shooter), Huang Xiang ("TH000") from China in *Warcraft* (real-time strategy), Dennis ("styla") and Daniel ("hero") Schellhase in *FIFA* (football/soccer), or Jonathan Le Clercq ("Cluck") in *Project CARS* (motorsport racing), what makes them successful, and how do they measure their career success in these fields? How is the field of fashion blogging defined, which career capitals are essential there, do men and women have different career paths in this field, and what are the success factors? How do career actors having simultaneous careers in the material and virtual world deal with the demands and successes of these two spheres? Linked to this emerging segment of the social space are the organizations that are driving these developments, including highly influential corporations such as Facebook, Twitter, PayPal, and Amazon as well as the people working in these organizations. Again, we have very little idea about the respective organizational career systems and the individual careers and to what extent they are similar to or different from the actors located in more traditional segments of the economy.

These are but a few examples of segments of the social space that are important for the quality of our future lives and, in part, our survival. The call by the SCF to emphasize the social aspect of careers not only leads to questions about the careers of people prominent in these segments and, thereby, new insights into how their careers coevolve with the careers of the various institutional actors that play a critical role in determining the future of our world. It also has the potential to give us useful insights into the individual, organizational, and societal mechanisms at work. In turn, this constitutes a contribution that career research can make to actively shaping the future of our planet in crucial areas.

Taking the Chronology *Seriously*

The SCF not only sensitizes us to the importance of social space when looking at careers but also puts time at the forefront. Of course, many calls have been made for a stronger inclusion of time in the design of empirical studies. Frequently, they include the use of longitudinal designs such as cohort, panel, or trend studies (e.g. Boudreau, Boswell, and Judge, 2001) or of concepts including an explicit time dimension for exploring the influence of time-related phenomena on careers and career systems (e.g. Schein, 2007). So far, so good, so well known.

The SCF goes one step beyond these familiar calls. It explicitly addresses the time dimension and uses as a core construct chronology, i.e. the sequential arrangement of our units of analysis such as, for example, career transitions, along the time dimension. It assigns labels to the units of analysis such as "precedes/follows" or "past/present/future." It brings two aspects of career to the fore. First, because it urges the career actor – individual or collective – to look back on their career, it encourages them to impose meaning on that career. Second, because the chronology is a series of events, it underscores the importance of inferring causality when studying careers: What caused what, why, and what for? This suggests a number of potentially fruitful directions for future developments in career research.

Meaning Human beings are "meaning seekers": they seek to find meaning in the world in general and what happens to them in particular. Telling the story of one's career as it unfolds over time is a narrative, and "[c]omposing a narrative is our primary way of making meaning" (Cochran, 1997: 4). The meaning that we construct out of this narrative, in turn, becomes woven into our identity. This is not confined to individual career actors. Collective actors construct meaning from the narrative of their careers, too. Organizations have their creation myths, their stories about their founders and other heroes, and how they have grown and changed over time, all of which play a role in the creation and maintenance of their culture (Bolman and Deal, 2003).

As part of this meaning-creating process, the actor infers causality. Attributing causal linkages to what is available in the chronology is an additional step in creating meaning because it provides the core to a meaningful story about one's career by answering the "why" questions in a double sense, namely what are one's past reasons and what is one's future purpose? Causality in this connection is the causality inferred by the career actor, not causality as attributed by an external observer using a careful methodology designed to ensure scientific validity (we come to that next). It is part of the narrative the career actor constructs to make meaning, so it is subject to all the distortions to which attributions are subject. For example, the fundamental attribution error will tend to exaggerate agency to explain success or structure to excuse failure. In addition, people may completely misunderstand why a particular chain of events happened, perhaps because they were unaware of things going on in the background that had a significant influence on their career. And so on. But the narrative that is constructed by the actor will feel true to them and forms part of their identity.

Taking the creation of meaning seriously has consequences for future research. It recalls that meaning has for a long time had a prominent place not only in organization research but also in career studies. Chronology as understood by the SCF reminds the field that the stream of research dealing with meaning is constitutive of a comprehensive look into careers. At the content level, this calls for analyzing meaning in careers at the level of both individual and collective actors. Looking at individual career actors, intra-individual processes of producing meaning as well as the role of the social space in these processes emerge as important areas of interest. These efforts can build on established insight, in particular from psychology and philosophy (Gendlin, 1997 [Original 1962]). There is much to do here, since it is hard to imagine any aspect of career that is not potentially a target for the creation of meaning. Similarly, there is a broad literature on collective career actors such as organizations as meaning-seekers (e.g. Suddaby *et al.*, 2010; Weick, 1995a). However, such issues as how organizations assign meaning to different types of internal career paths, to career trajectories of applicants, or to their own careers coevolving with careers of specific individuals – for example, CEOs or members of their supervisory board – are far from being satisfactorily researched. There is rich ground for investigation here.

At the level of theory and methods, a focus on meaning urges the field to actively seek – as opposed to grudgingly allow for – a broad spectrum of approaches when studying meaning in careers. Take as an example career success, undoubtedly crucial for applying meaning to one's career and, perhaps, the biggest question for OMC studies. Attaching meaning to career success involves, among other things, identifying and relating to its various dimensions. Of course, career success means different things to different people in various countries, professions, and age groups. Tackling such an issue involves a broad spectrum of approaches. These potentially range from large-scale comparative questionnaires that help to extract globally valid dimensions of career success to in-depth analyses of how people view and feel about various aspects of career success using methodologies such as Interpretative Phenomenological Analysis (IPA; Smith, 2004). This draws on ideas from phenomenology, hermeneutics, and idiography, underscoring the value of, respectively, the concrete experience of individuals, understanding how people view the issues in question, and single cases.

Understanding attributions of causality, as we note here, plays an important role in understanding the creation of meaning and the establishment of identity, albeit a causality that may not bear much relation to that which another observer might infer. We could call this a psychological or, perhaps, a subjective logic to distinguish it from a scientific logic, which focuses on the validity of causal inferences. We turn to that next.

Causality The question of causality in career research is a fundamental issue that the SCF raises by addressing the time dimension and one we address in our discussion of the temporal perspective in Chapter 3. True, the operation of the temporal perspective, the sequencing of career events, supports looking for causal relationships, arguably one of the noblest endeavors of scientific research. We are still left with two fundamental problems related to careers, both derived from Jaques's (1982) warning implicit in his axis of succession (Chapter 3) where events may follow each other in a chronology but this in itself says nothing about causality: How do we establish causality in a chronology (the methodological issue), and how do we understand why it happened that way (the theoretical issue)?

To address the *methodological* issue, we are drawn inevitably to experiments: laboratory or field experiments, natural experiments in a population, even quasi-experiments. There has been a recently revived interest in this form of empirical work in both management (e.g. Perry, 2012) and economics research (e.g. Levitt and List, 2009). Some aspects of career scholarship lend themselves readily to this type of empirical work. Recent such studies include, for example, decisions on whether and how appearance on the web influences the relative attractiveness of employers and, consequently, has an effect on individuals' intention to apply for a job (e.g. Allen, Mahto, and Otondo, 2007) or whether happiness has an effect on career success (e.g. Boehm and Lyubomirsky, 2008). Yet for other and arguably more substantial and comprehensive issues, it is much harder to see how to do this. How to arrange an experimental – or even quasi-experimental – setting for differentiating the relative importance of social origin and personality on career success or the role of mentors on hierarchical advancement within an organization, both quite classic issues in OMC research, is, to say the least, not easy. Still, we suggest that the emphasis of the SCF on time and chronology pushes the field in the direction of using experiments more than hitherto, where it is appropriate. And that poses a fascinating but clearly difficult challenge: Can we find ways of doing it?

The *theoretical* issue linked to establishing causality in career research to which the SCF points us is the never-ending striving for better causal, i.e. theoretically sound, models for explaining the connection between different constructs/variables beyond demonstrating empirically that they are linked. Advances in methods for analyzing various kinds of data, including major steps forward in using large amounts of texts in quantitative analyses (for an example analyzing 4 percent of all books ever printed, see Michel *et al.*, 2011), as well as the increasing availability of various kinds of digitized data (including "big data") have given a new push to sophisticated quantitative analyses of various kinds. While in itself this seems a positive development for empirical research in general and career research in particular, it also carries with it the potential to be overly concerned with data-driven linkages instead of explanations. In figurative speech, it is valuable to be able to establish empirically a link between two or more variables in a "boxes and arrows" model assuming and/ or demonstrating that causality exists. However, unless one is also able to explain *why* this link exists and what mechanisms are at work, we have "only" contributed to a primarily, if not exclusively applied, technological ("what I have to do in order to achieve X") body of knowledge – the kind one uses for building a better mousetrap or, based on biotechnology developments since the 1980s, building a better mouse (McNeill, 2007: 321 f.). While this has its merits, it falls short of giving the full picture. Looking "into the arrows" and reasoning why they link different "boxes" and how they do it provides a fuller understanding of the phenomenon, which allows not only a more well-founded explanation but also better prognosis and practical application. Once again we find ourselves seeking better theory, and this is the issue we turn to next.

Developing Career Theory

What makes good theory in the social sciences is, as we discuss in Chapter 5, a hotly debated topic. There seems to be a general consensus that it has to explain and predict: to explain why things happen as they do and predict what might happen in a given set of circumstances. What career theory meeting these criteria might emerge from the SCF? First, what kind of theory might it be?

We distinguish here between three levels of theory, following Merton (1957a; see also Mearsheimer and Walt, 2013). First comes what Merton calls general theory, more commonly now called grand theory or by Mearsheimer and Walt (2013: 428, for international politics) "the 'isms' . . . [t]he most prominent among them are constructivism, liberalism, Marxism, and realism." Merton puts Talcott Parsons's work in this category; more recent examples in sociology include that of Bourdieu (1977), Giddens (1984), and Foucault (1995). General or grand theory, says Merton of Parsons's work,

aims to state the fundamental variables of social systems, rather than to furnish substantive solutions, all proceeding from the head of one man, to the numerous problems phrased in terms of these variables. A general theory, such as this one, is intended to locate other sociological theories as special cases; it must therefore include variables of a high order of abstractness. As an avowed effort to work towards a comprehensive theory, it is logically akin though obviously not substantively analogical to a theory such as that of classical mechanics. (Merton, 1957a: 108)

Grand theory provides the canvas for theories of the second type, those of the middle range that

consist of sets of relatively simple ideas, which link together a limited number of facts about the structure and functions of social formations and suggest further observations. They are theories intermediate to comprehensive analytical schemes and detailed workaday hypotheses. The conception of this type of theory is of course not new: there are allusions to it in Plato, Bacon made much of 'intermediate or middle axioms' as did John Stuart Mill. (ibid.: 108)

Theories of the middle range "are theories about a delimited range of social phenomena. They can be recognized, in part, by their very labels: one speaks of a theory of reference groups, a theory of prices, or a germ theory of disease" (ibid.: 109).

Finally, following grand theory and theory of the middle range come what Merton calls "detailed workaday hypotheses" (ibid.: 108) and Mearsheimer and Walt (2013) call "simplistic hypothesis testing."[1] Much of Part III of this book is concerned with showing how novel ideas about hypothesis testing can emerge from applying the SCF to specific problems within OMC studies and outside, often by importing ideas into the field in which the problem is found. So, in a sense, we have this aspect covered. But can the SCF move progress in theory building in the opposite direction, toward a robust theory of the middle range?

Thus far we have been somewhat dismissive of the possibility. We explain in Chapter 5 why we do not believe it likely that a general theory of career, or what in Mertonian terms would be a theory of the middle range (in the sense that it can be recognized by its domain-specific label), will emerge any time soon, if for no other reason than the SCF makes it obvious that there are just too many different ways of conceptualizing the constructs that emerge from the three perspectives. But in this last chapter, let us speculate wildly for a moment. Suppose we *did* have such a general, middle-range theory of career. What might it look like? How might we use the SCF to draw on grand sociological theory in order to develop the kind of theory of career that Merton might recognize as theory of the middle range? We do not mean to suggest that we have the answer to this intriguing question; we simply want to suggest possible directions for future theoretical inquiry.

[1] The rather dismissive "simplistic" comes from the aim of their paper, which is to argue that hypothesis testing, which they acknowledge is important, has in their field taken over too much from what they see as the more important theory creating.

The SCF's heuristic model proposes relationships between an actor's condition, the positions they occupy, and their social space in a processual sense, but it is not specific about the aspects of condition, how position is defined, what the nature of the social space is, and, while suggesting specific links, how and why these links occur. It leaves it to the user to specify each in terms that are appropriate for a given situation. As we have just seen, when it is linked to specific situations, the theory that is used to explain the relationships is in Merton's terms hypothesis testing: theory, for example, that connects specific psychological or sociological constructs such as social class, personality as assessed by the five-factor model, and total compensation. What we are seeking now is something that explains the relationships at a higher level of generality in the way, for example, that Bourdieu's theory connects forms of capital with power and social reproduction, albeit (because it is specific to career) as a theory of the middle range.

A possible clue to the direction that might be taken comes from the resemblance of the SCF's heuristic model to Giddens's notion of the mutually constitutive relationship between structure and agency, which has already been used to show "career's role in the structuring process" (Barley, 1989: 54) of institutions. The coevolutionary aspect of the heuristic model is all about a mutually recursive relationship between career actor and social space. So perhaps a general theory of career might be based on a Giddens-type sense of the mutually constitutive relationship between structure and agency; certainly that seems to be where the SCF's heuristic model is headed. But more is needed than that. Structuration theory has proven notoriously difficult to work with empirically, nor is it clear that Giddens ever intended it to be, at least as a whole: "The works applying concepts from the logical framework of structuration theory that Giddens approved of were those that used them more selectively, 'in a spare and critical fashion' (Giddens, 1991b, p. 213, also see 1991b, pp. 213–16; and 1989, p. 294)" (Stones, 2005: 2). Could we use its concepts sparingly and critically with career?

The SCF makes it clear that any theory of career needs to include something about condition and position, which suggests that it may be fruitful to explore the ideas of Bourdieu in addition to those of Giddens. Might Bourdieu's concepts of capital and habitus illuminate the SCF concept of condition, and field similarly illuminate social space? Following the suggestion of Barley (1989), might, too, condition be illuminated by Giddens's concept of the interpretive schemes that mediate between what Giddens calls the institutional realm and the realm of action, interpretive schemes called "career scripts" by Barley? The SCF's heuristic model does not explicitly identify individual agency and the institution, although the latter is certainly implied in the model's depiction of social context and the positions occupied by the career actor while agency is embedded in the focal actor's condition and the action involved in making career transitions. Career scripts may be embedded in condition, too, except that the term has been used rather loosely (Gunz, 2012). If it were to be employed in theory development of this kind, ambiguities such as whether it is about behavior (Barley and Tolbert, 1997; Barley, 1989) or cognition (Dany, Louvel, and Valette, 2011; Cappellen and Janssens, 2010; Duberley, Cohen, and Mallon, 2006; Gioia and Poole, 1984) would need removing.

Whether this combination of Giddens and Bourdieu will provide the necessary route to a general, middle-range theory of career is beyond the scope of our book. Our aim here is simply to suggest a direction for future development of career theory based on the general guidance provided by the SCF. The aim of the theory is to find better ways of looking for meta-patterns in the patterns of condition and position that are careers. Such a theory would almost certainly involve reaching beyond the boundaries of the fields within what we call the proto-field of career studies to draw on ideas that have, in all probability, been used in entirely different contexts.

Coda: Defamiliarization, Imagination, and Conceptual Combination

Concluding this book, it easy to say what the SCF both is and is not. It clearly is neither a panacea nor magic. The SCF provides no cure-all for the many ills in the fields of career research that we and many others have listed. Likewise, it is not magic as it does not lead to ideas that you could not reach in other ways. Yet, much like the catalyst to which we refer at the end of Chapter 7 – something that makes possible or speeds up a chemical reaction without getting used up in the process – it gets you there quicker. Or, to use another analogy, much like yellow snow goggles help you by improving contrast so that you can see humps and hollows in the snow that are nevertheless not invisible without them, just harder to see, the SCF offers a way of looking at careers that allows a new and, at least in our eyes, helpful approach to careers.

To phrase it at a more generic level, the SCF offers career researchers different perspectives on careers in a threefold way. It enables defamiliarization, DiMaggio's (1995) term to describe the process of helping someone see their world with new eyes:

By defamiliarization, I refer to the process of enabling a native – of a society, an organization, or an academic discipline – to see his or her world with new eyes. Arguably, good theory should accomplish this. (DiMaggio, 1995: 392)

The language and framework of the SCF allow for making connections between apparently disconnected phenomena and areas of research both within career research and between organizational and career research.

The SCF also supports imagination,

the capacity to shift from one perspective to another ... to range from the most impersonal and remote transformations to the most intimate features of the human self – and to see the relations between the two. (Mills, 2000 [Original 1959]: 7)

Using basic perspectives, addressing different levels of analysis, and including a variety of different actors ranging from the focal career actor to collective actors in the social space not only support a multi-perspective view of careers but also call for in-depth analyses of relationships, including the clarification of effect mechanisms at work.

Finally, the SCF also allows and calls for conceptual combination (Mobley, Doares, and Mumford, 1992),

the creation of new knowledge structures through a number of ways, in particular through the integration of previously distinct concepts or, alternatively, the rearrangement of elements within an existing concept. (Scott, Lonergan, and Mumford, 2005: 80)

In particular when combining different areas within the career field and reaching out to research discourses outside the career field, the SCF supports building bridges between different theoretical considerations and opens up the road for using established theoretical thinking for issues in career studies that hitherto have not been targeted with these concepts.

The perspectives, the resulting basic model and its elaborations, and their application will hopefully inspire the various scientific fields dealing with careers in one way or other in the same way as they did for us. Whether this leads to a brighter future for career studies is, of course, another matter and will, as so often happens, be decided in hindsight and not by us.

References

Abbott, A. 1995. Things of Boundaries. *Social Research*, 62(4): 857–882.

Abel, R. L. 1989. *American Lawyers*. New York: Oxford University Press.

Abele, A. E., and Spurk, D. 2009. The Longitudinal Impact of Self-Efficacy and Career Goals on Objective and Subjective Career Success. *Journal of Vocational Behavior*, 74(1): 53–62.

Abrahamson, E. 1996. Management Fashion, Academic Fashion, and Enduring Truths. *Academy of Management. Academy of Management Review*, 21(3): 616–619.

Abrahamson, E., and Fairchild, G. 1999. Management Fashion: Lifecycles, Triggers, and Collective Learning Processes. *Administrative Science Quarterly*, 44(4): 708–740.

Abrahamson, E., Berkowitz, H., & Dumez, H. 2016. A More Relevant Approach to Relevance in Management Studies: An Essay on Performativity. *Academy of Management Review*, 41(2): 367–381.

Academy of Management Journal. 2016. Academy of Management Journal: Information for Contributors. Retrieved 2016-09-12 from http://aom.org/Publications /AMJ/Information-for-Contributors.aspx.

Alderfer, C. P. 1972. *Existence, Relatedness, and Growth. Human Needs in Organizational Settings*. New York: Free Press.

Allen, D. G., Mahto, R. V., and Otondo, R. F. 2007. Web-Based Recruitment: Effects of Information, Organizational Brand, and Attitudes toward a Web Site on Applicant Attraction. *Journal of Applied Psychology*, 92(6): 1696–1708.

Allen, T. D. 2004. Protégé Selection by Mentors: Contributing Individual and Organizational Factors. *Journal of Vocational Behavior*, 65(3): 469–483.

   2007. Mentoring Relationships from the Perspective of the Mentor. In B. R. Ragins and K. E. Kram (Eds.), *The Handbook of Mentoring at Work: Theory, Research, and Practice*: 123–147. Thousand Oaks, CA: Sage.

Allen, T. D., and Eby, L. T. (Eds.). 2007. *Blackwell Handbook of Mentoring: A Multiple Perspectives Approach*. London: Blackwell.

Allen, V. L., and Van de Vliert, E. (Eds.). 1984. *Role Transitions*. New York: Plenum.

Ancona, D., and Chong, C.-L. 1996. Entrainment: Pace, Cycle, and Rhythm in Organizational Behavior. *Research in Organizational Behavior*, 18: 251–284.

Ancona, D. G., Okhuysen, G. A., and Perlow, L. A. 2001. Taking Time to Integrate Temporal Research. *Academy of Management Review*, 26(4): 512–529.

Anderson, J. C., Milkovich, G. T., and Tsui, A. 1981. A Model of Intra-Organizational Mobility. *Academy of Management Review*, 6(4): 529–538.

Anderson, N. 1923. *The Hobo. The Sociology of the Homeless Man.* Chicago: University of Chicago Press.

Andresen, M., and Walther, M. 2013. Self-Initiated Repatriation at the Interplay between Field, Capital and Habitus: An Analysis Based on Bourdieu's Theory of Practice. In M. Andresen, A. A. Ariss, and M. Walther (Eds.), *Self-Initiated Expatriation: Individual, Organizational, and National Perspectives*: 160–180. London: Routledge.

Anonymous. 2016. My New Job Is a Giant Over-Promotion and I Am Horrified. Retrieved 2016-09-28 from http://ask.metafilter.com/296664/My-new-job-is -a-giant-over-promotion-and-I-am-horrified.

Argyris, C. 1960. *Understanding Organizational Behavior.* London: Tavistock Publications.

Argyris, C., and Schön, D. 1978. *Organizational Learning: A Theory of Action Perspective.* Reading, MA: Addison-Wesley.

Armstrong, M. 2000. The Name Has Changed but Has the Game Remained the Same? *Employee Relations*, 22(6): 576–593.

Arnold, J. 1997. *Managing Careers in the 21st Century.* London: PCP.

Arthur, M. B. 1994. The Boundaryless Career: A New Perspective for Organizational Inquiry. *Journal of Organizational Behavior*, 15(4): 295–306.

2008. Examining Contemporary Careers: A Call for Interdisciplinary Enquiry. *Human Relations*, 61(2): 163–186.

2014. The Boundaryless Career at 20: Where Do We Stand, and Where Can We Go? *Career Development International*, 19(6): 627–640.

Arthur, M. B., Hall, D. T., and Lawrence, B. S. 1989a. Generating New Directions in Career Theory: The Case for a Transdisciplinary Approach. In M. B. Arthur, D. T. Hall, and B. S. Lawrence (Eds.), *Handbook of Career Theory*: 7–25. Cambridge: Cambridge University Press.

Arthur, M. B., Hall, D. T., and Lawrence, B. S. (Eds.). 1989b. *Handbook of Career Theory.* Cambridge: Cambridge University Press.

Arthur, M. B., Hall, D. T., and Lawrence, B. S. 1989c. Preface. In M. B. Arthur, D. T. Hall, and B. S. Lawrence (Eds.), *Handbook of Career Theory*: xv–xix. Cambridge: Cambridge University Press.

Arthur, M. B., Khapova, S. N., and Wilderom, C. P. M. 2005. Career Success in a Boundaryless Career World. *Journal of Organizational Behavior*, 26(2): 177–202.

Arthur, M. B., and Rousseau, D. M. (Eds.). 1996a. *The Boundaryless Career: A New Employment Principle for a New Organizational Era.* New York: Oxford University Press.

Arthur, M. B., and Rousseau, D. M. 1996b. Conclusion: A Lexicon for the New Organizational Era. In M. B. Arthur and D. M. Rousseau (Eds.), *The Boundaryless Career: A New Employment Principle for a New Organizational Era*: 370–382. Oxford: Oxford University Press.

1996c. Introduction: The Boundaryless Career as a New Employment Principle. In M. B. Arthur and D. M. Rousseau (Eds.), *The Boundaryless Career*: 1–20. New York: Oxford University Press.

Ash, C. 2016. Lichens Assemble in Three Parts. *Science*, 353(6298): 458–460.

Ashforth, B. E., and Kreiner, G. E. 1999. "How Can You Do It?": Dirty Work and the Challenge of Constructing a Positive Identity. *Academy of Management Review*, 24(3): 413–434.

Ashforth, B. E., Kreiner, G. E., and Fugate, M. 2000. All in a Day's Work: Boundaries and Micro Role Transitions. *Academy of Management Review*, 25(3): 472–491.

Ashforth, B. E., and Saks, A. M. 1995. Work-Role Transitions – A Longitudinal Examination of the Nicholson Model. *Journal of Occupational and Organizational Psychology*, 68(Part 2): 157–175.

Atkinson, J. W. 1966. *A Theory of Achievement and Motivation*. New York: Wiley.

Bacharach, S. B. 1989. Organizational Theories: Some Criteria for Evaluation. *Academy of Management Review*, 14(4): 496–515.

Ballinger, G. A., and Marcel, J. J. 2010. The Use of an Interim CEO during Succession Episodes and Firm Performance. *Strategic Management Journal*, 31(3): 262–283.

Ballinger, G. A., and Schoorman, F. D. 2007. Individual Reactions to Leadership Succession in Workgroups. *Academy of Management Review*, 32(1): 118–136.

Bandura, A. 1977a. Self-Efficacy: Toward a Unifying Theory of Behavioral Change. *Psychological Review*, 84(2): 191–215.

1977b. *Social Learning Theory*. Englewood Cliffs, NJ: Prentice Hall.

2002. Social Cognitive Theory in Cultural Context. *Applied Psychology: An International Review*, 51(2): 269–290.

Banville, C., and Landry, M. 1989. Can the Field of MIS Be Disciplined? *Social Aspects of Computing*, 32(1): 48–60.

Barber, B. 1995. All Economies Are "Embedded": The Career of a Concept, and Beyond. *Social Research*, 62(2): 387–413.

Barley, S. R. 1989. Careers, Identities, and Institutions: The Legacy of the Chicago School of Sociology. In M. B. Arthur, D. T. Hall, and B. S. Lawrence (Eds.), *Handbook of Career Theory*: 41–65. Cambridge: Cambridge University Press.

1996. Technicians in the Workplace: Ethnographic Evidence for Bringing Work into Organization Studies. *Administrative Science Quarterly*, 41(3): 404–441.

Barley, S. R., and Tolbert, P. S. 1997. Institutionalization and Structuration: Studying the Links between Action and Institution. *Organization Studies*, 18: 93–117.

Barnard, C. I. 1971 [Original 1938]. *The Functions of the Executive* (30th anniversary ed.). Cambridge, MA: Harvard University Press.

Baron, J. N., Davis-Blake, A., and Bielby, W. T. 1986. The Structure of Opportunity: How Promotion Ladders Vary within and among Organizations. *Administrative Science Quarterly*, 31: 248–273.

Barrick, M. R., and Mount, M. K. 1991. The Big Five Personality Dimensions and Job Performance: A Meta-Analysis. *Personnel Psychology*, 44(1): 1–26.

Barrick, M. R., Mount, M. K., and Judge, T. A. 2001. Personality and Performance at the Beginning of the New Millennium: What Do We Know and Where Do We Go Next? *International Journal of Selection and Assessment*, 9(1/2): 9–30.

Bateson, G. 2000 [Original 1972]. *Steps to an Ecology of Mind*. Chicago: Chicago University Press.

Batson, N. 2003. Final Report of Neal Batson, Court-Appointed Examiner. United States Bankruptcy Court, Southern District of New York. Case No. 01–16034 (AJG).

Baugh, S., and Fagenson-Eland, E. A. 2007. Formal Mentoring Programs: A "Poor Cousin" to Informal Relationships? In B. R. Ragins and K. E. Kram (Eds.), *The Handbook of Mentoring at Work: Theory, Research, and Practice*: 249–273. Thousand Oaks, CA: Sage Publications.

Baum, J. A. C. 1999. Whole-Part Coevolutionary Competition in Organizations. In J. A. C. Baum and B. McKelvey (Eds.), *Variations in Organization Science: In Honor of Donald T. Campbell*: 113–135. London: Sage.

Beatty, R. P., and Zajac, E. J. 1987. CEO Change and Firm Performance in Large Corporations: Succession Effects and Manager Effects. *Strategic Management Journal*, 8: 305–317.

Becker, G. S. 1976. *The Economic Approach to Human Behavior*. Chicago: University of Chicago Press.

Becker, H. S. 1940. Constructive Typology in the Social Sciences. *American Sociological Review*, 5(1): 40–55.

1999. The Chicago School, So-Called. *Qualitative Sociology*, 22(1): 3–12.

Becker, H. S., Geer, B., Hughes, E. C., and Strauss, A. L. 1961. *Boys in White: Student Culture in Medical School*. Chicago: University of Chicago Press.

Beckman, C. M., and Phillips, D. J. 2005. Interorganizational Determinants of Promotion: Client Leadership and the Attainment of Women Attorneys. *American Sociological Review*, 70(4): 678–701.

Beer, M., Spector, B., Lawrence, P. R., Quinn Mills, D., and Walton, R. E. 1984. *Human Resource Management*. New York: Free Press.

Behn, B. K., Dawley, D. D., Riley, R., and Ya-wen, Y. 2006. Deaths of CEOs: Are Delays in Naming Successors and Insider/Outsider Succession Associated with Subsequent Firm Performance? *Journal of Managerial Issues*, 18(1): 32–46.

Benders, J., and Van Veen, K. 2001. What's in a Fashion? Interpretative Viability and Management Fashions. *Organization*, 8(1): 33–53.

Bergmann, W. 1992. The Problem of Time in Sociology. An Overview of the Literature on the State of Theory and Research on the "Sociology of Time," 1900–82. *Time & Society*, 1(1): 81–134.

Berlin-Brandenburg Academy of Sciences and Humanities. 2016. Corpus Inscriptionum Latinarum. Retrieved 2016-09-16 from http://cil.bbaw.de/cil_en/index_en.html.

Bernert, C. 1983. The Career of Causal Analysis in American Sociology. *The British Journal of Sociology*, 34(2): 230–254.

Berthel, J., and Koch, H.-E. 1985. *Karriereplanung und Mitarbeiterförderung*. Stuttgart: Expert Taylorix.

Betz, N. E., and Hackett, G. 1981. The Relationship of Career-Related Self-Efficacy Expectations to Perceived Career Options in College Women and Men. *Journal of Counseling Psychology*, 28(5): 399–410.

Bian, Y., and Ang, S. 1997. Guanxi Networks and Job Mobility in China and Singapore. *Social Forces*, 75(3): 981–1005.

Bidwell, M. 2011. Paying More to Get Less: The Effects of External Hiring Versus Internal Mobility. *Administrative Science Quarterly*, 56(3): 369–407.

Bidwell, M., & Briscoe, F. 2010. The Dynamics of Interorganizational Careers. *Organization Science*, 21(5): 1034–1053.

Bidwell, M., and Mollick, E. 2015. Shifts and Ladders: Comparing the Role of Internal and External Mobility in Managerial Careers. *Organization Science*, 26(6): 1629–1645.

Bird, A. 1996. Careers as Repositories of Knowledge: Considerations for Boundaryless Careers. In M. B. Arthur and D. M. Rousseau (Eds.), *The Boundaryless Career: A*

New Employment Principle for a New Organizational Era: 150–168. Oxford: Oxford University Press.

Black, M. 1962. *Models and Metaphors: Studies in Language and Philosophy*. Ithaca, NY: Cornell University Press.

Blau, P., and Schoenherr, R. 1962. *Structure of Organizations*. New York: Basic Books.

Blau, P. M., and Scott, W. R. 1962. *Formal Organization*. San Francisco: Chandler.

Blickle, G., Diekmann, C., Schneider, P. B., Kalthofer, Y., and Summers, J. K. 2012. When Modesty Wins: Impression Management through Modesty, Political Skill, and Career Success-a Two-Study Investigation. *European Journal of Work and Organizational Psychology*, 21(6): 899–922.

Bluedorn, A. C. 2002. *The Human Organization of Time: Temporal Realities and Experience*. Stanford, CA: Stanford University Press.

Bluedorn, A. C., and Jaussi, K. S. 2007. Organizationally Relevant Dimensions of Time across Levels of Analysis. *Research in Multi-Level Issues*, 6: 187–223.

Blumer, H. 1966. Sociological Implications of the Thought of George Herbert Mead. *American Journal of Sociology*, 71(5): 535–544.

Boadi-Kusi, S. B., Kyei, S., Mashige, K. P., Abu, E. K., Antwi-Boasiako, D., and Halladay, A. C. 2015. Demographic Characteristics of Ghanaian Optometry Students and Factors Influencing Their Career Choice and Institution of Learning. *Advances in Health Sciences Education*, 20(1): 33–44.

Boehm, J. K., and Lyubomirsky, S. 2008. Does Happiness Promote Career Success? *Journal of Career Assessment*, 16(1): 101–116.

Boeker, W. 1997. Executive Migration and Strategic Change: The Effect of Top Manager Movement on Product-Market Entry. *Administrative Science Quarterly*, 42(2): 213–236.

Bogardus, E. S. 1924. *Fundamentals of Social Psychology*. New York: Century.

Bohman, J., and Rehg, W. 2014. Jürgen Habermas. The Stanford Encyclopedia of Philosophy (Fall 2014 Edition), Edward N. Zalta (ed.), http://plato.stanford.edu/archives/fall2014/entries/habermas/.

Bolman, L. G., and Deal, T. E. 2003. *Reframing Organizations: Artistry, Choice and Leadership*. San Francisco: Jossey Bass.

Boltanski, L., and Thévenot, L. 2006 [Original 1991]. *On Justification. Economies of Worth*. Princeton, NJ: Princeton University Press.

Bommer, W. H., and Ellstrand, A. E. 1996. CEO Successor Choice, Its Antecedents and Influence on Subsequent Firm Performance: An Empirical Analysis. *Group & Organization Management*, 21(1): 105–123.

Boniwell, I. 2009. Perspectives on Time. In S. J. Lopez and C. R. Snyder (Eds.), *Oxford Handbook of Positive Psychology* (2nd ed.): 295–302. New York: Oxford University Press.

Boschma, R. 2005. Proximity and Innovation: A Critical Assessment. *Regional Studies*, 39(1): 61–74.

Boudreau, J. W., Boswell, W. R., and Judge, T. A. 2001. Effects of Personality on Executive Career Success in the United States and Europe. *Journal of Vocational Behavior*, 58(1): 53–81.

Bourdieu, P. 1977. *Outline of a Theory of Practice*. Cambridge: Cambridge University Press.

1986. The Forms of Capital. In J. G. Richardson (Ed.), *Handbook of Theory and Research for the Sociology of Education*: 241–258. New York.

1989. Social Space and Symbolic Power. *Sociological Theory*, 7(1): 14–25.

Bourdieu, P., and Wacquant, L. J. D. 1992. *An Invitation to Reflexive Sociology*. Chicago: University of Chicago Press.

Bowen, D. E., and Ostroff, C. 2004. Understanding HRM-Firm Performance Linkages: The Role of the "Strength" of the HRM System. *Academy of Management Review*, 29(2): 203–221.

Boxall, P., and Purcell, J. 2003. *Strategy and Human Resource Management*. Houndsmills: Palgrave Macmillan.

Boyer, M., and Ortiz-Molina, H. 2008. Career Concerns of Top Executives, Managerial Ownership and CEO Succession *Corporate Governance: An International Review*, 16(3): 178–193.

Branigan, H. P., Pickering, M. J., and Cleland, A. A. 2000. Syntactic Co-Ordination in Dialogue. *Cognition*, 75(2): B13–B25.

Bray, D. W., Campbell, R. J., and Grant, D. L. 1974. *Formative Years in Business: A Long-Term AT&T Study of Managerial Lives*. New York: Wiley.

Brennan, S. E., and Clark, H. H. 1996. Conceptual Pacts and Lexical Choice in Conversation. *Journal of Experimental Psychology: Learning, Memory, and Cognition*, 22(6): 1482–1493.

Brewer, G. D. 1999. The Challenges of Interdisciplinarity. *Policy Sciences*, 32(4): 327–337.

Brewster, C. 1991. *The Management of Expatriates*. London: Kogan Page.

Brewster, C., and Mayrhofer, W. 2011. Comparative Human Resource Management. In A.-W. Harzing and A. Pinnington (Eds.), *International Human Resource Management* (3rd ed.): 47–78. London: Sage.

Brickley, J. A. 2003. Empirical Research on CEO Turnover and Firm-Performance: A Discussion. *Journal of Accounting & Economics*, 36(1): 227–233.

Brint, S. 1994. *In an Age of Experts: The Changing Role of Professionals in Politics and Public Life*. Princeton, NJ: Princeton University Press.

Briscoe, J. P., and Hall, D. T. 2006. The Interplay of Boundaryless and Protean Careers: Combinations and Implications. *Journal of Vocational Behavior*, 69 (1): 4–18.

Briscoe, J. P., Hall, D. T., and Mayrhofer, W. 2012a. Careers around the World. In J. P. Briscoe, D. T. Hall, and W. Mayrhofer (Eds.), *Careers around the World*: 3–14. New York: Routledge Taylor & Francis Group.

Briscoe, J. P., Hall, D. T., and Mayrhofer, W. (Eds.). 2012b. *Careers around the World. Individual and Contextual Perspectives*. New York: Routledge.

Briscoe, J. P., Kaše, R., Dries, N., Dysvik, A., Unite, J., Çakmak-Otluoğlu, K. Ö., Adeeye, I., Apospori, E., Bagdadli, S., Cerdin, J.-L., Fei, Z., Gianecchini, M., Ituma, A., Kim, N., Mayrhofer, W., Mishra, S. K., Reichel, A., Saxena, R., Shen, Y., Supangco, V., and Verbruggen, M. 2014. A Cross-Culturally Generated Measure of Career Success: Results of a Three-Stage Study. In J. Humphreys (Ed.), *Best Paper Proceedings of the 74th Annual Meeting of the Academy of Management*. Philadelphia, PA: Academy of Management.

Brock, D. M. 2006. The Changing Professional Organization: A Review of Competing Archetypes. *International Journal of Management Reviews*, 8(3): 157–174.

Broschak, J. P. 2004. Managers' Mobility and Market Interface: The Effect of Managers' Career Mobility on the Dissolution of Market Ties. *Administrative Science Quarterly*, 49(4): 608–640.

Brown, M. C. 1982. Administrative Succession and Organizational Performance: The Succession Effect. *Administrative Science Quarterly*, 27: 1–16.

Brüderl, J., Diekmann, A., and Preisendorfer, P. 1991. Patterns of Intraorganizational Mobility: Tournament Models, Path Dependency, and Early Promotion Effects. *Social Science Research*, 20(3): 197–216.

Brunsson, N. 1989. *The Organization of Hypocrisy. Talk, Decisions and Actions in Organizations*. Chichester: Wiley.

Buanes, A., and Jentoft, S. 2009. Building Bridges: Institutional Perspectives on Interdisciplinarity. *Futures*, 41: 446–454.

Buldt, B. 2008. Genus Proximum. In J. Mittelstraß (Ed.), *Enzyklopädie Philosophie Und Wissenschaftstheorie* (2nd ed., Vol. 3). Stuttgart/Weimar: Metzler.

Burns, T., and Stalker, G. M. 1961. *The Management of Innovation*. London: Tavistock.

Burt, R. S. 1992. *Structural Holes: The Social Structure of Competition*. Cambridge, MA: Harvard University Press.

Burton, M. D., Sorensen, J. B., and Beckman, C. M. 2002. Coming from Good Stock: Career Histories and New Venture Formation. In M. Lounsbury and M. J. Ventresca (Eds.), *Research in the Sociology of Organizations*, Vol. 19: 229–262. Oxford: Elsevier (JAI Press).

Byrne, J. A. 1993. The Virtual Corporation, *Business Week*, Issue No. 3304, February 8, 98–102.

Caligiuri, P. M. 2000. The Big Five Personality Characteristics as Predictors of Expatriate Desire to Terminate the Assignment and Supervisor-Rated Performance. *Personnel Psychology*, 53(1): 67–88.

Cappellen, T., and Janssens, M. 2010. Enacting Global Careers: Organizational Career Scripts and the Global Economy as Co-Existing Career Referents. *Journal of Organizational Behavior*, 31(5): 687–706.

Cappelli, P., and Hamori, M. 2007. The Institutions of Outside Hiring. In H. P. Gunz and M. A. Peiperl (Eds.), *Handbook of Career Studies*. Thousand Oaks, CA: Sage.

Carlson, R. 1972. *School Superintendents: Career and Performance*. Columbus, OH: Chas. E. Merrill.

Carroll, S. 2012. *The Particle at the End of the Universe: How the Hunt for the Higgs Boson Leads Us to the Edge of a New World*. New York: Dutton.

Castilla, E. J. 2005. Social Networks and Employee Performance in a Call Center. *American Journal of Sociology*, 110(5): 1243–1283.

Chan, T. W. 1999. Revolving Doors Reexamined: Occupational Sex Segregation over the Life Course. *American Sociological Review*, 64(1): 86–96.

Chandler, D. E., Kram, K. E., and Yip, J. 2011. An Ecological Systems Perspective on Mentoring at Work: A Review and Future Prospects. *Academy of Management Annals*, 5(1): 519–570.

Charsley, S. 1998. Sanskritization: The Career of an Anthropological Theory. *Contributions to Indian Sociology*, 32(2): 527–549.

Chen, I. C., Brown, S. D., O'Donnell, E., and Huning, T. 2015. The Influence of Opinion Leader Competence, Communication Frequency, Trust and Idealized Influence on

Perception of Organizational Culture, Knowledge Transfer, and Organizational Identification. *Journal of Leadership and Management*, 3(5–6): 75–89.

Chong, E. 2013. Managerial Competencies and Career Advancement: A Comparative Study of Managers in Two Countries. *Journal of Business Research*, 66(3): 345–353.

Chudzikowski, K., Demel, B., Mayrhofer, W., Briscoe, J. P., Unite, J., Bogicevic Milikic, B., Hall, D. T., Heras, M. L., Shen, Y., and Zikic, J. 2009. Career Transitions and Their Causes: A Country-Comparative Perspective. *Journal of Occupational and Organizational Psychology*, 82: 825–849.

Churchman, C. W. 1967. Guest Editorial: Wicked Problems. *Management Science*, 14(4): B141–B142.

Clark, T., and Salaman, G. 1998. Telling Tales: Management Gurus' Narratives and the Construction of Managerial Identity. *Journal of Management Studies*, 35(2): 137–161.

Clarke, A. E. 1991. Social Worlds/Arenas Theory as Organizational Theory. In D. R. Maines (Ed.), *Social Organization and Social Process: Essays in Honor of Anselm Strauss*. New York: A. de Gruyter. 119–158.

Clarke, K. A., and Primo, D. M. 2012. *A Model Discipline: Political Science and the Logic of Representations*. Oxford: Oxford University Press.

Cochran, L. 1997. *Career Counseling: A Narrative Approach*. Thousand Oaks, CA: Sage Publications.

Cochran, L. R. 1990. Narrative as a Paradigm for Career Research. In R. A. Young and W. A. Borgen (Eds.), *Methodological Approaches to the Study of Career*: 71–86. New York: Praeger.

Cohen, L. 2015. Interplay of Professional, Bureaucratic, and Entrepreneurial Career Forms in Professional Service Firms. In R. Hinings, D. Muzio, J. Broschak, and L. Empson (Eds.), *The Oxford Handbook of Professional Service Firms*: 351–373. Oxford: Oxford University Press.

Cohen, L., Duberley, J., and Musson, G. 2009. Work-Life Balance? An Autoethnographic Exploration of Everyday Home-Work Dynamics. *Journal of Management Inquiry*, 18(2): 229–241.

Cohen, L., and Mallon, M. 2001. My Brilliant Career? *International Studies of Management & Organization*, 31(3): 48–68.

Coleman, J. S. 1974. *Power and the Structure of Society*. New York: Norton.

1990. *Foundations of Social Theory*. Cambridge, MA: Harvard University Press.

Collin, A. 1997. Career in Context. *British Journal of Guidance & Counselling*, 25(4): 435–446.

2006. Career. In J. H. Greenhaus and G. A. Callanan (Eds.), *Encyclopedia of Career Development*: 60–63. Thousand Oaks, CA: Sage Publications.

2007. The Meanings of Career. In H. P. Gunz and M. A. Peiperl (Eds.), *Handbook of Career Studies*: 558–565. Thousand Oaks, CA: Sage.

2009. One Step Towards Realising the Multidisciplinarity of Career Studies. In A. Collin and W. Patton (Eds.), *Organizational Perspectives on Career: Towards a Multidisciplinary Dialogue*: 3–18. Rotterdam: Sense Publishers.

Collin, A., and Patton, W. (Eds.). 2009. *Vocational Psychological and Organisational Perspectives on Career: Towards a Multidisciplinary Dialogue*. Rotterdam: Sense Publishers.

Collin, A., and Young, R. A. 1986. New Directions for Theories of Career. *Human Relations*, 39(9): 837–853.

2000. The Future of Career. In A. Collin and R. A. Young (Eds.), *The Future of Career*: 276–300. Cambridge: Cambridge University Press.

Collins, H. M., and Evans, R. J. 2007. *Rethinking Expertise*. Chicago: University of Chicago Press.

Collins, R. 1990. Changing Conceptions in the Sociology of the Professions. In R. Torstendahl and M. Burrage (Eds.), *The Formation of Professions: Knowledge, State and Strategy*: 11–23. London: Sage.

Cooper, D. J., and Robson, K. 2006. Accounting, Professions and Regulation: Locating the Sites of Professionalization. *Accounting, Organizations and Society*, 31(4–5): 415–444.

Costas, J., and Grey, C. 2014. The Temporality of Power and the Power of Temporality: Imaginary Future Selves in Professional Service Firms. *Organization Studies*, 35(6): 909–937.

Cressey, P. G. 1932. *The Taxi-Dance Hall. A Sociological Study in Commercialized Recreation and City Life*. Chicago: University of Chicago Press.

Crossan, M., Lane, H. W., and White, R. E. 1999. An Organizational Learning Framework: From Intuition to Institution. *Academy of Management Review*, 24 (3): 522–537.

Currie, G., Finn, R., and Martin, G. 2010. Role Transition and the Interaction of Relational and Social Identity: New Nursing Roles in the English NHS. *Organization Studies*, 31(7): 941–961.

Cyert, R. M., and March, J. G. 1963. *A Behavioral Theory of the Firm*. Englewood Cliffs, NJ: Prentice Hall.

Czarniawska, B. 1998. Who Is Afraid of Incommensurability? *Organization*, 5(2): 273–275.

Dany, F., Louvel, S., and Valette, A. 2011. Academic Careers: The Limits of the "Boundaryless Career" and the Power of Promotion Scripts. *Human Relations*, 67(4): 971.

Dany, F., Mallon, M., and Arthur, M. B. 2003. The Odyssey of Career and the Opportunity for International Comparison. *International Journal of Human Resource Management*, 14(5): 705–712.

Davis, G. F., Diekmann, K. A., and Tinsley, C. H. 1994. The Decline and Fall of the Conglomerate Firm in the 1980s: The Deinstitutionalization of an Organizational Form. *American Sociological Review*, 59(4): 547.

Davis, M. S. 1971. That's Interesting: Towards a Phenomenology of Sociology and a Sociology of Phenomenology. *Philosophy of the Social Sciences*, 1(4): 309–334.

Davoine, E., and Ravasi, C. 2013. The Relative Stability of National Career Patterns in European Top Management Careers in the Age of Globalisation: A Comparative Study in France/Germany/Great Britain and Switzerland. *European Management Journal*, 31(2): 152–163.

De Rond, M., and Miller, A. 2005. Publish or Perish. *Journal of Management Inquiry*, 14(4): 321–329.

De Vos, A., De Hauw, S., and Van der Heijden, B. I. J. M. 2011. Competency Development and Career Success: The Mediating Role of Employability. *Journal of Vocational Behavior*, 79(2): 438–447.

Deci, E. L. 1975. *Intrinsic Motivation*. New York: Plenum Press.

Derr, C. B. (Ed.). 1980. *Work, Family, and the Career: New Frontiers in Theory and Research*. New York: Praeger.

Derr, C. B. 1986. *Managing the New Careerists: The Diverse Career Success Orientations of Today's Workers*. San Francisco: Jossey-Bass.

Di Giovanni, J., Gottselig, G., Jaumotte, F., Ricci, L. A., and Tokarick, S. 2008. Globalization: A Brief Overview. Retrieved 2016-02-22 from www.imf.org/external/np/exr/ib/2008/053008.htm.

Digman, J. M. 1990. Personality Structure: Emergence of the Five-Factor Model. *Annual Review of Psychology*, 41(1): 417–440.

DiMaggio, P. J. 1995. Comments on "What Theory Is Not." *Administrative Science Quarterly*, 40(3): 391–397.

DiMaggio, P. J., and Powell, W. W. 1983. The Iron Cage Revisited: Institutional Isomorphism and Collective Rationality in Organizational Fields. *American Sociological Review*, 48(2): 147–160.

Dinovitzer, R., Gunz, H., and Gunz, S. 2014a. Corporate Lawyers and Their Clients: Walking the Line between Law and Business. *International Journal of the Legal Profession*, 21(1): 3–21.

2014b. Unpacking Client Capture: Evidence from Corporate Law Firms. *Journal of Professions and Organization*, 1(2): 90–117.

DiPrete, T. A. 1987. Horizontal and Vertical Mobility in Organizations. *Administrative Science Quarterly*, 32(3): 422–444.

DiPrete, T. A., and Eirich, G. M. 2006. Cumulative Advantage as a Mechanism for Inequality: A Review of Theoretical and Empirical Developments. *Annual Review of Sociology*, 32: 271–297.

Dobrow, S. R. 2013. Dynamics of Calling: A Longitudinal Study of Musicians. *Journal of Organizational Behavior*, 34(4): 431–452.

Dobrow, S. R., Chandler, D. E., Murphy, W., and Kram, K. E. 2011. A Review of Developmental Networks: Incorporating a Mutuality Perspective. *Journal of Management*, 38(1): 210–242.

Dokko, G., & Gaba, V. 2012. Venturing into New Territory: Career Experiences of Corporate Venture Capital Managers and Practice Variation. *Academy of Management Journal*, 55(3): 563–583.

Domsch, M., and Gerpott, T. J. 1986. Aufstiegsklima von industriellen F&E-Einheiten und individuelle Arbeitsleistung und -zufriedenheit. *Zeitschrift für Betriebswirtschaft*, 56(11): 1095–1116.

Dougherty, T. W., and Pritchard, R. D. 1985. The Measurement of Role Variables: Exploratory Examination of a New Approach. *Organizational Behavior and Human Decision Processes*, 35(2): 141–155.

Dowling, P. J., Festing, M., and Engle Sr., A. D. 2013. *International Human Resource Management* (6th ed.). London: Cengage Learning EMEA.

Dries, N., Pepermans, R., and Calier, O. 2008a. Career Success: Constructing a Multidimensional Model. *Journal of Vocational Behavior*, 73(2): 254–267.

Dries, N., Pepermans, R., and De Kerpel, E. 2008b. Exploring Four Generations' Beliefs about Career: Is "Satisfied" the New "Successful"? *Journal of Managerial Psychology*, 23(8): 907–928.

References 267

Dries, N., Pepermans, R., Hofmans, J., and Rypens, L. 2009. Development and Validation of an Objective Intra-Organizational Career Success Measure for Managers. *Journal of Organizational Behavior*, 30: 543–560.

Drinkwater, J. F. 1979. A Note on Local Careers in the Three Gauls under the Early Empire. *Britannia*, 10: 89–100.

Duberley, J., and Cohen, L. 2010. Gendering Career Capital: An Investigation of Scientific Careers. *Journal of Vocational Behavior*, 76(2): 187–197.

Duberley, J., Cohen, L., and Mallon, M. 2006. Constructing Scientific Careers: Change, Continuity and Context, *Organization Studies*, Vol. 27: 1131–1151.

Duden Online. 2016. Retrieved 2016-11-09 from www.duden.de.

Durkheim, E. 1951 [Original 1897]. *Suicide. A Study in Sociology*. New York: Free Press. *Montesquieu and Rousseau: Forerunners of Sociology (Translated by Ralph Manheim)*. Ann Arbor: University of Michigan Press.

Dworkin, T. M., Maurer, V., and Schipani, C. A. 2012. Career Mentoring for Women: New Horizons/Expanded Methods. *Business Horizons*, 55(4): 363–372.

Dyer, L. (Ed.). 1976. *Careers in Organizations: Individual Planning and Organizational Development*. Ithaca, NY: New York School of Industrial Relations, Cornell University.

Eckardstein, D. v. 1971. *Laufbahnplanung Für Führungskräfte*. Berlin: Duncker & Humblot.

Ehlers, C. L., Frank, E., and Kupfer, D. J. 1988. Social Zeitgebers and Biological Rhythms: A Unified Approach to Understanding the Etiology of Depression. *Archives of General Psychiatry*, 45(10): 948–952.

Elder, G. H. J., Johnson, M. K., and Crosnoe, R. 2003. The Emergence and Development of Life Course Theory. In J. T. Mortimer and M. J. Shanahan (Eds.), *Handbook of the Life Course*: 3–19. New York: Kluwer.

Ellemers, N. 1993. The Influence of Socio-Structural Variables on Identity Management Strategies. *European Review of Social Psychology*, 4: 27–57.

Emerson, R. M. 1962. Power Dependence Relations. *American Sociological Review*, 27: 31–41.

Emirbayer, M., and Mische, A. 1998. What Is Agency? *American Journal of Sociology*, 103(4): 962–1023.

Erickson, P., Klein, J. L., Daston, L., Lemov, R., Sturm, T., and Gordin, M. D. 2013. *How Reason Almost Lost Its Mind: The Strange Career of Cold War Rationality*. Chicago: University of Chicago Press.

Etzioni, A. 1961. *A Comparative Analysis of Complex Organizations*. New York: The Free Press.

Evans, J. A., Kunda, G., & Barley, S. R. 2004. Beach Time, Bridge Time, and Billable Hours: The Temporal Structure of Technical Contracting. *Administrative Science Quarterly*, 49(1): 1–38.

Evans, P., Pucik, V., and Björkman, I. 2011. *The Global Challenge: International Human Resource Management* (2nd ed.). New York: McGraw-Hill.

Farrell, K. A., and Whidbee, D. A. 2003. Impact of Firm Performance Expectations on CEO Turnover and Replacement Decisions. *Journal of Accounting & Economics*, 36(1–3): 165.

Faulkner, R. R. 1973. Career Concerns and Mobility Motivations of Orchestra Musicians. *Sociological Quarterly*, 14(Summer): 334–349.

Faye, J. 2005. Models, Theories, and Language. Retrieved 2016-09-26 from http://phi lsci-archive.pitt.edu/3749/.

Feenberg, A. 2000. The Ontic and the Ontological in Heidegger's Philosophy of Technology: Response to Thomson. *Inquiry*, 43(4): 445–450.

Feldman, D. C. 1988. Career Plateaus Reconsidered. *Journal of Management*, 14 (March): 69–80.

1999. Toxic Mentors or Toxic Proteges? A Critical Re-Examination of Dysfunctional Mentoring. *Human Resource Management Review*, 9(3): 247–278.

Feldman, D. C., and Ng, T. W. H. 2007. Careers: Mobility, Embeddedness and Success. *Journal of Management*, 33(3): 350–377.

Fernandez-Mateo, I. 2007. Who Pays the Price of Brokerage? Transferring Constraint through Prices Setting in the Staffing Sector. *American Sociological Review*, 72(2): 291–317.

Ferris, G. R., and Rowland, K. M. 1990. *Career and Human Resources Development*. Greenwich, CT: JAI Press.

Festinger, L. 1957. *A Theory of Cognitive Dissonance*. Evanston, IL: Row, Peterson.

Fisher, C. D. 1990. Organizational Socialization: An Integrative Review. In G. R. Ferris and K. M. Rowland (Eds.), *Organizational Entry*: S.163–208. Greenwich, CT: JAI Press.

Fizel, J. L., and Louie, K. K. T. 1990. CEO Retention, Firm Performance and Corporate Governance. *Managerial & Decision Economics*, 11(3): 167–176.

Fligstein, N. 1991. The Structural Transformation of American Industry. In W. W. Powell and P. J. DiMaggio (Eds.), *The New Institutionalism in the Largest Firms, 1919–1979*: 311–336. Chicago: University of Chicago Press.

Fombrun, C. J., Tichy, N. M., and DeVanna, M. A. 1984. *Strategic Human Resource Management*. New York: Wiley.

Forbes, J. B. 1987. Early Intraorganizational Mobility: Patterns and Influences. *Academy of Management Journal*, 30(1): 110–125.

Forcellini, E., and Facciolati, J. 1828 [Original 1771]. *Totius Latinitatis Lexicon*. London: Baldwin and Cradock, Pickering.

Fouad, N. A., and Byars-Winston, A. M. 2005. Cultural Context of Career Choice: Meta-Analysis of Race/Ethnicity Differences. *The Career Development Quarterly*, 53(3): 223–234.

Foucault, M. 1995. *Discipline and Punish: The Birth of the Prison* (2nd ed.). New York: Vintage Books.

Freidman, M., and Kandel, A. 1999. *Introduction to Pattern Recognition: Statistical, Strucgtural, Neural and Fuzzy Logic Approaches*. London: Imperial College Press.

Galanter, M., and Henderson, W. 2008. The Elastic Tournament: A Second Transformation of the Big Law Firm. *Stanford Law Review*, 60: 1867–1929.

Garcia, J. M. D., and Costa, J. L. C. 2014. Does Trait Emotional Intelligence Predict Unique Variance in Early Career Success Beyond IQ and Personality? *Journal of Career Assessment*, 22(4): 715–725.

Garrod, S., and Pickering, M. J. 2004. Why Is Conversation So Easy? *Trends in Cognitive Sciences*, 8(1): 8–11.

Garrouste, P., and Ioannides, S. (Eds.). 2000. *Evolution and Path Dependence in Economic Ideas: Past and Present*. Cheltenham: Edward Elgar.

Garud, R., and Karnoe, P. (Eds.). 2001. *Path Dependence and Creation*. Mahwah, NJ: Erlbaum.

Gell, A. 1992. *The Anthropology of Time: Cultural Constructions of Temporal Maps and Images*. Oxford: Berg.

Gendlin, E. T. 1997 [Original 1962]. *Experiencing and the Creation of Meaning: A Philosophical and Psychological Approach to the Subjective*. Evanston, IL: Northwestern University Press.

Gerpott, T. J., Domsch, M., and Keller, R. T. 1986. Career Events, Communication Activities, and Working Hours Investment among Research and Development Employees. *IEEE Transactions on Engineering Management*, EM-33(4): 188–196.

Gersick, C. J. G., Bartunek, J. M., and Dutton, J. E. 2000. Learning from Academia: The Importance of Relationships in Professional Life. *Academy of Management Journal*, 43(6): 1026–1044.

Geuss, R. 1981. *The Idea of a Critical Theory: Habermas and the Frankfurt School*. New York: Cambridge University Press.

Gevers, J. M. P., Rutte, C. G., and Van Eerde, W. 2006. Meeting Deadlines in Work Groups: Implicit and Explicit Mechanisms. *Applied Psychology*, 55(1): 52–72.

Gevisser, M. 2007. *Thabo Mbeki: The Dream Deferred*. Johannesburg: Jonathan Ball.

GFK Verein. 2016, March 2016. Worldwide Ranking: Trust in Professions. Retrieved 2016-09-17 from www.gfk-verein.org/en/compact/focustopics/worldwide-ranking -trust-professions.

Giambatista, R. C., Rowe, W. G., and Riaz, S. 2005. Nothing Succeeds Like Succession: A Critical Review of Leader Succession Literature since 1994. *The Leadership Quarterly*, 16(6): 963–991.

Giddens, A. 1981. Agency, Institution and Time-Space Analysis. In K. Knorr-Cetina and A. V. Cicourel (Eds.), *Advances in Social Theory and Methodology: Towards an Integration of Micro- and Macro-Sociologies*: 161–174. Boston: Routledge and Kegan Paul.

1984. *The Constitution of Society. Outline of the Theory of Structuration*. Cambridge: Polity Press.

1991. *Modernity and Self-Identity: Self and Society in the Late Modern Age*. Stanford, CA: Stanford University Press.

Gigliotti, J., and Makhoul, N. 2015. Demographics, Training Satisfaction, and Career Plans of Canadian Oral and Maxillofacial Surgery Residents. *International Journal of Oral and Maxillofacial Surgery*, 44(12): 1574–1580.

Gioia, D. A., and Poole, P. P. 1984. Scripts in Organizational Behavior. *Academy of Management Review*, 9(3): 449–459.

Glaser, B. G. 1964. *Organizational Scientists: Their Professional Careers*. New York: Bobbs-Merrill.

1968. *Organizational Careers: A Sourcebook for Theory*. Chicago: Aldine.

Glaser, B. G., and Strauss, A. L. 1971. *Status Passage: A Formal Theory*. Chicago: Aldine, Atherton.

Godlee, F., Smith, J., and Marcovitch, H. 2011. Wakefield's Article Linking MMR Vaccine and Autism Was Fraudulent. *British Medical Journal*, 342(7788): 64–66.

Gordon, R. A., and Howell, J. E. 1959. *Higher Education for Business*. New York: Columbia University Press.

Gouldner, A. W. 1954. *Patterns of Industrial Bureaucracy.* New York: The Free Press.

Gowler, D., and Legge, K. 1989. Careers, Reputations and the Rhetoric of Bureaucratic Control. In M. B. Arthur, D. T. Hall, and B. S. Lawrence (Eds.), *Handbook of Career Theory.* Cambridge: Cambridge University Press.

Grandin, L. D., Alloy, L. B., and Abramson, L. Y. 2006. The Social Zeitgeber Theory, Circadian Rhythms, and Mood Disorders: Review and Evaluation. *Clinical Psychology Review,* 26(6): 679–694.

Grandjean, B. D. 1981. History and Career in a Bureaucratic Labor Market. *American Journal of Sociology,* 86(5): 1057–1092.

Granovetter, M. S. 1973. The Strength of Weak Ties. *American Journal of Sociology,* 78(6): 1360–1380.

Greenhaus, J. H., and Foley, S. 2007. The Intersection of Work and Family Lives. In H. Gunz and M. Peiperl (Eds.), *Handbook of Career Studies*: 131–152. Thousand Oaks, CA: Sage.

Greenhaus, J. H., Parasuraman, S., and Wormley, W. 1990. Effects of Race on Organizational Experiences, Job Performance Evaluations, and Career Outcomes. *Academy of Management Journal,* 33(1): 64–86.

Greenhaus, J. H., and Sklarew, N. D. 1981. Some Sources and Consequences of Career Exploration. *Journal of Vocational Behavior,* 18(1): 1–12.

Greenhaus, J. S., Callanan, G. A., and Godschalk, V. M. 2010. *Career Management* (4th ed.). Thousand Oaks, CA: Sage.

Greenwood, R., Hinings, C. R., and Brown, J. 1990. "P2-Form" Strategic Management: Corporate Practices in Professional Partnerships. *Academy of Management Journal,* 33(4): 725–755.

Greenwood, R., Oliver, C., Sahlin, K., and Suddaby, R. 2008a. Introduction. In R. Greenwood, C. Oliver, K. Sahlin, and R. Suddaby (Eds.), *The Sage Handbook of Organizational Institutionalism.* London: Sage.

(Eds.). 2008b. *The Sage Handbook of Organizational Institutionalism.* London: Sage.

Greenwood, R., Raynard, M., Kodeih, F., Micelotta, E. R., and Lounsbury, M. 2011. Institutional Complexity and Organizational Responses. *Academy of Management Annals,* 5(1): 317–371.

Grey, C. 1994. Career as a Project of the Self and Labour Process Discipline. *Sociology,* 28(2): 479–497.

Grüne-Yanoff, T. 2013. Relations between Theory and Model in Psychology and Economics. *Perspectives on Science,* 21(2): 196–201.

Gubler, M., Biemann, T., and Herzog, S. 2017. An Apple Doesn't Fall Far from the Tree—or Does It? Occupational Inheritance and Teachers' Career Patterns. *Journal of Vocational Behavior,* http://dx.doi.org/10.1016/j.jvb.2017.02.002.

Guerrier, Y., and Philpot, N. 1978. *The British Manager: Careers and Mobility.* London: British Institute of Management.

Guest, D. E. 1990. Human Resource Management and the American Dream. *Journal of Management Studies,* 27(4): 377–397.

Gundlach, M. J., Douglas, S. C., and Martinko, M. J. 2003. The Decision to Blow the Whistle: A Social Information Processing Framework. *Academy of Management Review,* 28(1): 107–123.

Gunz, H. 1988. Organizational Logics of Managerial Careers. *Organization Studies*, 9 (4): 529–554.

2012. A Rose by Any Other Name: Scripts, Fields, Logics, and Systems, Annual Meeting of the Academy of Management. Boston, MA.

Gunz, H., Mayrhofer, W., and Tolbert, P. 2011. Career as a Social and Political Phenomenon in the Globalized Economy. *Organization Studies*, 32(12): 1613–1620.

Gunz, H., and Peiperl, M. (Eds.). 2007a. *Handbook of Career Studies*. Thousand Oaks, CA: Sage Publications.

Gunz, H., and Peiperl, M. 2007b. Introduction. In H. P. Gunz and M. A. Peiperl (Eds.), *Handbook of Career Studies*: 1–10. London: Sage.

Gunz, H., Peiperl, M., and Tzabbar, D. 2007a. Boundaries in the Study of Career. In H. Gunz and M. Peiperl (Eds.), *Handbook of Career Studies*: 471–494. Thousand Oaks, CA: Sage Publications.

Gunz, H. P. 1989a. *Careers and Corporate Cultures: Managerial Mobility in Large Corporations*. Oxford: Basil Blackwell.

1989b. The Dual Meaning of Managerial Careers: Organizational and Individual Levels of Analysis. *Journal of Management Studies*, 26(3): 225–250.

Gunz, H. P., and Heslin, P. A. 2005. Reconceptualizing Career Success: Introduction to a Special Issue of the Journal of Organizational Behavior. *Journal of Organizational Behavior*, 26(2): 105–111.

Gunz, H. P., and Jalland, R. M. 1996. Managerial Careers and Business Strategies. *Academy of Management Review*, 21(3): 718–756.

Gunz, H. P., Peiperl, M. A., and Tzabbar, D. 2007b. Boundaries in the Study of Career. In H. P. Gunz and M. A. Peiperl (Eds.), *Handbook of Career Studies*: 471–494. Thousand Oaks, CA: Sage.

Gupta, A. K., and Govindarajan, V. 1984. Business Unit Strategy, Managerial Characteristics, and Business Unit Effectiveness at Strategy Implementation. *Academy of Management Journal*, 27(1): 25–41.

Gutenberg, E. 1958. *Einführung in die Betriebswirtschaftslehre*. Wiesbaden: Gabler.

Haack, S. 1997. Science, Scientism, and Anti-Science in the Age of Preposterism. *Skeptical Inquirer*, 21(6): 37–42.

Habermas, J. 1981. *Theorie des kommunikativen Handelns. Bd. 1: Handlungsrationalität und gesellschaftliche Rationalisierung*. Frankfurt am Main: Suhrkamp.

1984. *The Theory of Communicative Action, Vol. I. Reason and the Rationalization of Society*. Boston: Beacon.

Hackett, G., and Betz, N. E. 1981. A Self-Efficacy Approach to the Career Development of Women. *Journal of Vocational Behavior*, 18(3): 326–339.

Haden, D. 2012. Realistic Response Times. Retrieved 2016-09-18 from www.firefighingincanada.com/response/realistic-response-times-10985.

Hall, D. T. 1976. *Careers in Organizations*. Santa Monica, CA: Goodyear.

2002. *Careers in and out of Organizations*. Thousand Oaks, CA: Sage Publications.

Hall, E. T. 1989. *The Dance of Life: The Other Dimension of Time*. New York: Doubleday.

Hall, F. S., and Hall, D. T. 1979. *The Two-Career Couple: He Works, She Works, but How Does the Relationship Work?* Reading, MA: Addison-Wesley.

Hall, P. A., and Soskice, D. (Eds.). 2001. *Varieties of Capitalism. The Institutional Foundations of Comparative Advantage*. Oxford: Oxford University Press.

Hambrick, D. C., and Mason, P. M. 1984. Upper Echelons: The Organization as a Reflection of Its Top Managers. *Academy of Management Review*, 9: 193–206.

Hanlon, G. 1996. Casino Capitalism and the Rise of the Commercialized Service Class – an Examination of the Accountant. *Critical Perspectives on Accounting*, 7(3): 339–363.

Hannan, M. T., and Freeman, J. 1977. The Population Ecology of Organizations. *American Journal of Sociology*, 82(5): 929–964.

Hardin, G. 1968. The Tragedy of the Commons. *Science*, 162(3859): 1243–1248.

Harvey, M., and Moeller, M. 2009. Expatriate Managers: A Historical Review. *International Journal of Management Reviews*, 11(3): 275–296.

Haslberger, A., Brewster, C., and Hippler, T. 2014. *Managing Performance Abroad. A New Model for Understanding Expatriate Adjustment*. New York: Routledge.

Haveman, H. A., and Cohen, L. E. 1994. The Ecological Dynamics of Careers: The Impact of Organizational Founding, Dissolution, and Merger on Job Mobility. *American Journal of Sociology*, 100(1): 104–152.

Heenan, D. A. 1970. The Corporate Expatriate: Assignment to Ambiguity. *Columbia Journal of World Business*, 5(3): 49–54.

Heidegger, M. 1962. *Being and Time*. Malden, MA: Blackwell Publishing Ltd.

Heinen, E. (Ed.). 1972. *Industriebetriebslehre. Entscheidungen Im Industriebetrieb* (1. Aufl. ed.). Wiesbaden: Gabler.

Henrich, J., Heine, S. J., and Norenzayan, A. 2010. Most People Are Not WEIRD. *Nature*, 466(7302): 29.

Heracleous, L. 2004. Boundaries in the Study of Organization. *Human Relations*, 57(1): 95–103.

Herbst, J. 1997. Prospects for Elite-Driven Democracy in South Africa. *Political Science Quarterly*, 112(4): 595–615.

Hernes, T. 2004. Studying Composite Boundaries: A Framework of Analysis. *Human Relations*, 57(1): 9–29.

Herr, E. L. 1990. Issues in Career Research. In R. A. Young and W. A. Borgen (Eds.), *Methodological Approaches to the Study of Career*: 3–21. New York: Praeger.
2013. Trends in the History of Vocational Guidance. *Career Development Quarterly*, 61(3): 277–282.

Herzberg, F. 1966. *Work and the Nature of Man*. Cleveland, OH: World Publishing.

Hesketh, A., and Fleetwood, S. 2006. Beyond Measuring the Human Resources Management-Organizational Performance Link: Applying Critical Realist Meta-Theory. *Organization*, 13(5): 677–699.

Hesketh, B. 2000. Time Perspective in Career-Related Choices: Applications of Time-Discounting Principles. *Journal of Vocational Behavior*, 57(1): 62–84.

Heslin, P. 2003. Self- and Other-Referent Criteria of Career Success. *Journal of Career Assessment*, 11(3): 262–286.

Heslin, P. A. 2005. Conceptualizing and Evaluating Career Success. *Journal of Organizational Behavior*, 26(2): 113–136.

Heslin, P. A., and Mayrhofer, W. 2016. When and Why Objective Career Success Deserves a Demotion. Paper presented at the Annual Meeting of the Academy of Management. Anaheim, CA.

Heylighen, F., and Campbell, D. T. 1995. Selection of Organization at the Social Level: Obstacles and Facilitators of Metasystem Transitions. *World Futures*, 45(1–4): 181–212.

Hickson, D. J., Hinings, C. R., Lee, C. A., Schneck, R. E., and Pennings, J. 1971. A Strategic Contingencies' Theory of Intraorganizational Power. *Administrative Science Quarterly*, 16(2): 216–229.

Higgins, M. C. 2005. *Career Imprints: Creating Leaders across an Industry*. San Francisco: Jossey-Bass.

Higgins, M. C., and Dillon, J. R. 2007. Career Patterns and Organizational Performance. In H. Gunz and M. Peiperl (Eds.), *Handbook of Career Studies*: 422–436. Thousand Oaks, CA: Sage Publications.

Higgins, M. C., Dobrow, S. R., and Chandler, D. 2008. Never Quite Good Enough: The Paradox of Sticky Developmental Relationships for Elite University Graduates. *Journal of Vocational Behavior*, 72(2): 207–224.

Higgins, M. C., and Kram, K. E. 2001. Reconceptualizing Mentoring at Work: A Developmental Network Perspective. *Academy of Management Review*, 26(2): 264–288.

Hinings, R., Muzio, D., Broschak, J., and Empson, L. 2015a. Researching Professional Service Firms: An Introduction and Overview. In R. Hinings, D. Muzio, J. Broschak, and L. Empson (Eds.), *The Oxford Handbook of Professional Service Firms*: 1–28. Oxford: Oxford University Press.

Hinings, R., Muzio, D., Broschak, J. P., and Empson, L. (Eds.). 2015b. *The Oxford Handbook of Professional Service Firms*. Oxford: Oxford University Press.

Hippler, T., Brewster, C., and Haslberger, A. 2015. The Elephant in the Room: The Role of Time in Expatriate Adjustment. *International Journal of Human Resource Management*, 26(15): 1920–1935.

Hirschhorn, L., and Gilmore, T. 1992. The New Boundaries of the "Boundaryless" Company. *Harvard Business Review*, 70(3): 104–115.

Hirschi, A., and Jaensch, V. K. 2015. Narcissism and Career Success: Occupational Self-Efficacy and Career Engagement as Mediators. *Personality and Individual Differences*, 77: 205–208.

Hirschman, A. O. 1970. *Exit, Voice and Loyalty: Responses to Decline in Firms, Organizations, and States*. Cambridge, MA: Harvard University Press.

Hodgson, G. M. 2013. Understanding Organizational Evolution: Toward a Research Agenda Using Generalized Darwinism. *Organization Studies*, 34(7): 973–992.

Hofer, S., Stallings, M., Reynolds, C., Cliff, N., and Russell, G. 1994. What Criteria Define a Successful Career in Psychology? It Depends on Who You Ask. *Educational and Psychological Measurement*, 54(2): 447–458.

Hofstede, G. 1980. *Culture's Consequences. International Differences in Work-Related Values*. Newbury Park, CA: Sage Publications.

Holland, J. L. 1959. A Theory of Vocational Choice. *Journal of Counseling Psychology*, 6: 35–45.

  1973. *Making Vocational Choices*. Englewood Cliffs, NJ: Prentice-Hall.

House, R., Javidan, M., Hanges, P., and Dorfman, P. 2002. Understanding Cultures and Implicit Leadership Theories across the Globe: An Introduction to Project Globe. *Journal of World Business*, 37(1): 3–10.

Howarth, D. 2010. *Discourse*. Buckingham: Open University Press.

Hübinger, G., and Lepsius, M. R. (Eds.). 2015. *Max Weber Gesamtausgabe. Abt. 2, Briefe: Bd. 4. Briefe 1903–1905* (Vol. Abt. 2, Briefe). Tübingen: Mohr.

Huczynski, A. 2006. *Management Gurus*. Milton Park: Routledge.

Hughes, E. C. 1937. Institutional Office and the Person. *American Journal of Sociology*, 43: 404–413.

1939. Institutions Defined. In R. E. Park (Ed.), *An Outline of the Principles of Sociology*: 283–288. New York: Barnes & Noble.

1958. *Men and Their Work*. Glencoe, IL: The Free Press.

Humberd, B. K., and Rouse, E. D. 2016. Seeing You in Me and Me in You: Personal Identification in the Phases of Mentoring Relationships. *Academy of Management Review*, 41(3): 435–455.

Hunt, D. M., and Michael, C. 1983. Mentorship: A Career Training and Development Tool. *Academy of Management Review*, 8(3): 475–485.

Hutzschenreuter, T., Kleindienst, I., and Greger, C. 2012. How New Leaders Affect Strategic Change Following a Succession Event: A Critical Review of the Literature. *The Leadership Quarterly*, 23(5): 729–755.

Iacocca, L., and Novak, W. 1986. *Iacocca: An Autobiography*. New York: Bantam.

Ibarra, H. 1999. Provisional Selves: Experimenting with Image and Identity in Professional Adaptation. *Administrative Science Quarterly*, 44(4): 764–791.

Ibarra, H., and Barbulescu, R. 2010. Identity as Narrative: Prevalence, Effectiveness, and Consequences of Narrative Identity Work in Macro Work Role Transitions. *Academy of Management Review*, 35(1): 135–154.

Iellatchitch, A., Mayrhofer, W., and Meyer, M. 2003. Career Fields: A Small Step Towards a Grand Career Theory? *International Journal of Human Resource Management*, 14(5): 728–750.

Igbaria, M., Meredith, G., and Smith, D. C. 1995. Career Orientations of Information Systems Employees in South Africa. *The Journal of Strategic Information Systems*, 4(4): 319–340.

Inkson, K., Dries, N., and Arnold, J. 2015. *Understanding Careers*. Thousand Oaks, CA: Sage.

Inkson, K., and Elkin, G. 2008. Landscape with Travellers: The Context of Careers in Developed Nations. In R. van Esbroeck and R. Athanassou (Eds.), *International Handbook of Career Guidance*: 69–94. New York: Springer.

Inkson, K., Gunz, H., Ganesh, S., and Roper, J. 2012. Boundaryless Careers: Bringing Back Boundaries. *Organization Studies*, 33(3): 323–340.

Isom, G. N. 2006. *Huckleberry Heart: The Boys of Halloran Avenue*. Frederick, MD: America Star Books.

Jackson, B. 2001. *Management Gurus and Management Fashions*. London: Routledge.

Jackson, L. A., Sullivan, L. A., Harnish, R., and Hodge, C. N. 1996. Achieving Positive Social Identity: Social Mobility, Social Creativity, and Permeability of Group Boundaries. *Journal of Personality & Social Psychology*, 70(2): 241–254.

Jackson, S. E., and Schuler, R. S. 1999. Understanding Human Resource Management in the Context of Organizations and Their Environments. In R. S. Schuler and S. E. Jackson (Eds.), *Strategic Human Resource Management*: 4–28. London: Blackwell.

Jacobs, D. 1981. Toward a Theory of Mobility and Behavior in Organizations: Relationships between Individual Performance and Organizational Success. *American Journal of Sociology*, 87(3): 684–707.

Jacoby, S. M. 1999. Are Career Jobs Headed for Extinction? *California Management Review*, 42(1): 123–145.

Jaques, E. 1982. *The Form of Time*. New York: Crane Russak, Heinemann.

Jenner, A. J., Smith III, M., and Burdick, D. S. 1983. Toward a Theory of Construct Definition. *Journal of Educational Measurement*, 20(4): 1–12.

Jennings, E. E. 1971. *Routes to the Executive Suite*. New York: McGraw-Hill.

Jepperson, R. L. 1991. Institutions, Institutional Effects, and Institutionalism. In W. W. Powell and P. J. DiMaggio (Eds.), *The New Institutionalism in Organizational Analysis*: 143–163. Chicago: Chicago University Press.

Johns, G. 2001. In Praise of Context. *Journal of Organizational Behavior*, 22(1): 31–42.
2006. The Essential Impact of Context on Organizational Behavior. *Academy of Management Review*, 31(2): 386–408.

Johnson, V. 2007. What Is Organizational Imprinting? Cultural Entrepreneurship in the Founding of the Paris Opera. *American Journal of Sociology*, 113(1): 97–127.

Joia, L. A., and Mangia, U. 2015. Career Transition Antecedents in the Information Technology Area. *Information Systems Journal*, 27(1): 31–57.

Jones, C., and Dunn, M. B. 2007. Careers and Institutions: The Centrality of Careers to Organizational Studies. In H. Gunz and M. Peiperl (Eds.), *Handbook of Career Studies*: 437–450. Thousand Oaks, CA: Sage Publications.

Joshi, A., and Roh, H. 2009. The Role of Context in Work Team Diversity Research: A Meta-Analytic Review. *Academy of Management Journal*, 52(3): 599–627.

Judge, T. A., Heller, D., and Mount, M. K. 2002. Five-Factor Model of Personality and Job Satisfaction a Meta-Analysis. *Journal of Applied Psychology*, 87(3): 530–541.

Judge, T. A., and Kammeyer-Mueller, J. D. 2007. Personality and Career Success. In H. Gunz and M. Peiperl (Eds.), *Handbook of Career Studies*: 59–78. Thousand Oaks, CA: Sage Publications.

Judge, T. A., Klinger, R. L., and Simon, L. S. 2010. Time Is on My Side: Time, General Mental Ability, Human Capital, and Extrinsic Career Success. *Journal of Applied Psychology*, 95(1): 92–107.

Juntunen, C. L., Barraclough, D. J., Broneck, C. L., Seibel, G. A., Winrow, S. A., and Morin, P. M. 2001. American Indian Perspectives on the Career Journey. *Journal of Counseling Psychology*, 48(3): 274–285.

Kanter, R. M. 1984. Variations in Managerial Career Structures in High Technology Firms: The Impact of Organizational Characteristics on Internal Labor Market Patterns. In P. Osterman (Ed.), *Internal Labor Markets*. Cambridge, MA: MIT Press.

Karaevli, A. 2007. Performance Consequences of New CEO Outsiderness': Moderating Effects of Pre- and Post-Succession Contexts. *Strategic Management Journal*, 28(7): 681–706.

Karcher, M. J., and Nakkula, M. J. 1997. Multicultural Pair Counseling and the Development of Expanded Worldviews. In R. Selman, C. Watts, and L. Schultz (Eds.), *Fostering Friendship: Pair Therapy for Treatment and Prevention*. New York: Aldine de Gruyter.

Karpik, L. 1978. Organizations, Institutions and History. In L. Karpik (Ed.), *Organization and Environment: Theory, Issues and Reality*: 15–68. London: Sage.

Kato, T., and Long, C. 2006. CEO Turnover, Firm Performance, and Enterprise Reform in China: Evidence from Micro Data. *Journal of Comparative Economics*, 34(4): 796–817.

Kattenbach, R., Schneidhofer, T. M., Lücke, J., Latzke, M., Loacker, B., Schramm, F., and Mayrhofer, W. 2014. A Quarter of a Century of Job Transitions in Germany. *Journal of Vocational Behavior*, 84: 49–58.

Katz, D., and Kahn, R. 1966. *The Social Psychology of Organizations*. New York: John Wiley.

Katz, D., and Kahn, R. L. 1978. *The Social Psychology of Organizations* (2nd ed.). New York: John Wiley and Sons.

Katz, J. R. 2005. "If I Could Do It, They Could Do It": A Collective Case Study of Plateau Tribes' Nurses. *Journal of American Indian Education*, 44(2): 36–51.

Kauffman, S. A. 1993. *The Origins of Order: Self-Organization and Selection in Evolution*. New York: Oxford University Press.

Kaulisch, M., and Enders, J. 2005. Careers in Overlapping Institutional Contexts. The Case of Academe. *Career Development International*, 10(2): 130–144.

Kennedy, R. 2008. *Nigger: The Strange Career of a Troublesome Word*. New York: Vintage.

Kerin, R. A. 1981. Where They Come From: CEOs in 1952 and 1980. *Business Horizons*, 24(6): 66–69.

Kesner, I. F., and Dalton, D. R. 1994. Top Management Turnover and CEO Succession: An Investigation of the Effects of Turnover on Performance. *Journal of Management Studies*, 31(5): 701–713.

Kesner, I. F., and Sebora, T. C. 1994. Executive Succession: Past, Present & Future. *Journal of Management*, 20(2): 327–372.

Kierkegaard, S. 1960. *The Diary of Soren Kierkegaard* (G. M. Anderson, Trans.). London: Peter Owen Limited.

Kilduff, M. 2006. Editor's Comments: Publishing Theory. *Academy of Management Review*, 31: 252–255.

Kilduff, M., and Day, D. V. 1994. Do Chameleons Get Ahead? The Effects of Self-Monitoring on Managerial Careers. *Academy of Management Journal*, 37(4): 1047–1060.

King, Z., Burke, S., and Pemberton, J. 2005. The "Bounded" Career: An Empirical Study of Human Capital, Career Mobility and Employment Outcomes in a Mediated Labour Market. *Human Relations*, 58(8): 981–1007.

Kirkpatrick, I., and Noordegraaf, M. 2015. Organizations and Occupations: Towards Hybrid Professionalism in Professional Service Firms? In R. Hinings, D. Muzio, J. Broschak, and L. Empson (Eds.), *The Oxford Handbook of Professional Service Firms*: 92–112. Oxford: Oxford University Press.

Kirschbaum, C. 2007. Careers in the Right Beat: Us Jazz Musicians' Typical and Non-Typical Trajectories. *Career Development International*, 12(2): 187–201.

Kleiner, A. 2000. Revisiting Reengineering. Retrieved 2016-02-05 from www.strategy -business.com/article/19570?gko=e05ea.

Knudsen, C. 2003. *Pluralism, Scientific Progress and the Structure of Organization Studies.* Oxford: Oxford University Press.

Koch, M., Forgues, B., and Monties, V. 2016. The Way to the Top: Career Patterns of Fortune 100 CEOs. *Human Resource Management.* DOI:10.1002/hrm.21759.

König, A., and Berli, O. 2013. Das Paradox der Doxa – Macht und Herrschaft als Leitmotiv der Soziologie Pierre Bourdieus. In P. Imbusch (Ed.), *Macht und Herrschaft* (2nd ed.): 303–333. Berlin: Springer.

Kooij, D. T. A. M., De Lange, A. H., Jansen, P. G. W., Kanfer, R., and Dikkers, J. S. E. 2011. Age and Work-Related Motives: Results of a Meta-Analysis. *Journal of Organizational Behavior*, 32(2): 197–225.

Koontz, H. 1962. Making Sense of Management Theory. *Harvard Business Review*, 40(4): 24.

Kosiol, E. 1972. *Die Unternehmung als wirtschaftliches Aktionszentrum.* Reinbek: Rowohlt.

Krais, B., and Gebauer, G. 2002. *Habitus.* Bielefeld: Transcript.

Kram, K. E. 1983. Phases of the Mentor Relationship. *Academy of Management Journal*, 26(4): 608–625.

1985. *Mentoring at Work: Developmental Relationships in Organizational Life.* Glenview, IL: Scott, Foresman.

Krücken, G., and Meier, F. 2006. Turning the University into an Organizational Actor. In G. Drori, J. Meyer, and H. Hwang (Eds.), *Globalization and Organization: World Society and Organizational Change*: 241–257. Oxford: Oxford University Press.

Krumboltz, J., Mitchell, A., and Jones, G. 1976. A Social Learning Theory of Career Selection. *The Counseling Psychologist*, 6(1): 71–81.

Krumboltz, J. D. 1996. A Learning Theory of Career Counseling. In M. L. Savickas and W. B. Walsh (Eds.), *Handbook of Career Counseling Theory and Practice*: 55–80. Palo Alto, CA: Davies-Black Publishing.

Kuhn, T. S. 1970. *The Structure of Scientific Revolutions* (2nd ed.). Chicago: University of Chicago Press.

Kutner, M. 2014, September 2014. How to Game the College Rankings. Retrieved 2016-06-20 from www.bostonmagazine.com/news/article/2014/08/26/how-north eastern-gamed-the-college-rankings/.

Lakatos, I. 1984. *Philosophical Papers.* Cambridge: Cambridge University Press.

Lamont, M., and Molnar, V. 2002. The Study of Boundaries in the Social Sciences. *Annual Review of Sociology*, 28: 167–195.

Laumann, E. O., and Marsden, P. V. 1979. The Analysis of Oppositional Structures in Political Elites: Identifying Collective Actors. *American Sociological Review*, 44(October): 713–732.

Lausten, M. 2002. CEO Turnover, Firm Performance and Corporate Governance: Empirical Evidence on Danish Firms. *International Journal of Industrial Organization*, 20(3): 391.

Lave, C., A., and March, J. G. 1975. *An Introduction to Models in the Social Sciences.* New York: Harper & Row.

Lawrence, B. S. 1984. Age Grading: The Implicit Organizational Timetable. *Journal of Occupational Behaviour*, 5: 23–35.

Lawrence, P. R., and Lorsch, J. W. 1967. *Organization and Environment: Managing Differentiation and Integration*. Boston: Harvard University Press.

Lazarova, M., Dany, F., and Mayrhofer, W. 2012. Careers: A Country-Comparative View. In C. Brewster and W. Mayrhofer (Eds.), *Handbook of Research on Comparative Human Resource Management*: 298–321. Cheltenham: Edward Elgar.

Lazarova, M., Westman, M., and Shaffer, M. A. 2010. Elucidating the Positive Side of the Work-Family Interface on International Assignments: A Model of Expatriate Work and Family Performance. *Academy of Management Review*, 35(1): 93–117.

Lazarsfeld, P. F., Berelson, B., and Gaudet, H. 1944. *The People's Choice. How the Voter Makes Up His Mind in a Presidential Campaign*. New York: Duell, Sloan, & Pearce.

Leblebici, H., and Sherer, P. D. 2015. Governance in Professional Service Firms. In R. Hinings, D. Muzio, J. Broschak, and L. Empson (Eds.), *The Oxford Handbook of Professional Service Firms*: 189–212. Oxford: Oxford University Press.

Lee, G. L. 1981. *Who Gets to the Top? A Sociological Study of Business Executives*. Aldershot, Hants: Gower.

Lee, P. C. B. 2002. Career Goals and Career Management Strategy among Information Technology Professionals. *Career Development International*, 7(1): 6–13.

Legge, K. 1995. *Human Resource Management: Rhetorics and Reality*. Basingstoke: Macmillan Business.

Leicht, K. T., and Fennell, M. L. 2001. *Professional Work: A Sociological Approach*. Malden, MA: Blackwell.

Lélé, S., and Norgaard, R. B. 2005. Practicing Interdisciplinarity. *BioScience*, 55(11): 967–975.

Lemarchand, R. 1994. Managing Transition Anarchies: Rwanda, Burundi, and South Africa in Comparative Perspective. *The Journal of Modern African Studies*, 32(04): 581–604.

Lent, R. W., Brown, S. D., and Hackett, G. 1994. Toward a Unifying Social Cognitive Theory of Career and Academic Interest, Choice and Performance. *Journal of Vocational Behavior*, 45: 79–122.

Levine, R. 1997. *A Geography of Time: The Temporal Misadventures of a Social Psychologist, or How Every Culture Keeps Time Just a Little Bit Differently*. New York: Basic Books.

Levinson, D. J., Darrow, C., Klein, E., Levinson, M., and McKee, B. 1978. *The Seasons of a Man's Life*. New York: Knopf.

Levitt, S. D., and List, J. A. 2009. Field Experiments in Economics: The Past, the Present, and the Future. *European Economic Review*, 53(1): 1–18.

Levy, P. I. 1999. Sanctions on South Africa: What Did They Do? *The American Economic Review*, 89(2): 415–420.

Lewin, A. Y., Long, C. P., and Carroll, T. N. 1999. The Coevolution of New Organizational Forms. *Organization Science*, 10(5): 535–550.

Lewin, K. 1936. *Principles of Topological Psychology*. New York: McGraw-Hill.

Lewis, D. 1973. *Counterfactuals*. Malden, MA: Blackwell.

Lin, N., Ensel, W. M., and Vaughn, J. C. 1981. Social Resources and Strength of Ties: Structural Factors in Occupational Status Attainment. *American Sociological Review*, 46(4): 393–405.

Lin, N., Vaughn, J. C., and Ensel, W. M. 1981. Social Resources and Occupational Status Attainment. *Social Forces*, 59(4): 1163–1181.

Lindh, G., and Dahlin, E. 2000. A Swedish Perspective on the Importance of Bourdieu's Theories for Career Counseling. *Journal of Employment Counseling*, 37(December): 194–203.

Linton, R. 1936. *The Study of Man*. New York: Appleton-Century-Crofts.

Lipton, P. 2003. Kant on Wheels. *Social Epistemology: A Journal of Knowledge, Culture and Policy*, 17(2–3): 215–219.

Lisic, L. L., Myers, L. A., Pawlewicz, R. J., and Seidel, T. A. 2016. Do Accounting Firm Consulting Revenues Affect Audit Quality? Evidence from the Post-Sox Era. Available at SSRN: https://ssrn.com/abstract=2460102.

Litzky, B. E., Eddleston, K. A., and Kidder, D. L. 2006. The Good, the Bad, and the Misguided: How Managers Inadvertently Encourage Deviant Behaviors. *Academy of Management Perspectives*, 20(1): 91–103.

Liu, Y., Liu, J., and Wu, L. 2010. Are You Willing and Able? Roles of Motivation, Power, and Politics in Career Growth. *Journal of Management*, 36(6): 1432–1460.

London, M. 1983. Toward a Theory of Career Motivation. *Academy of Management Review*, 8: 620–630.

London, M., and Stumpf, S. A. 1982. *Managing Careers*. Reading, MA: Addison-Wesley.

Long, J., and West, S. 2007. Returning to Nursing after a Career Break: Elements of Successful Re-Entry. *Australian Journal of Advanced Nursing*, 25(1): 49–55.

Lorsch, J. W., and Barnes, L. B. (Eds.). 1972. *Managers and Their Careers*. Homewood, IL: Irwin, Dorsey.

Louis, M. R. 1980a. Career Transitions: Varieties and Commonalities. *Academy of Management Review*, 5(3): 329–340.

1980b. Surprise and Sense Making: What Newcomers Experience in Entering Unfamiliar Organizational Settings. *Administrative Science Quarterly*, 25: 226–251.

Luhmann, N. 1984. *Soziale Systeme. Grundriß einer allgemeinen Theorie*. Frankfurt am Main: Suhrkamp.

1991. Die Form "Person." *Soziale Welt*, 42(2): 166–175.

1995. *Social Systems*. Stanford, CA: Stanford University Press.

2000. *Organisation und Entscheidung*. Opladen: Westdeutscher Verlag.

2002. *Das Erziehungssystem der Gesellschaft (Herausgegeben von Dieter Lenzen)*. Frankfurt am Main: Suhrkamp.

Ma, S., Seidl, D., and Guérard, S. 2015. The New CEO and the Post-Succession Process: An Integration of Past Research and Future Directions. *International Journal of Management Reviews*, 17(4): 460–482.

Maaß, C. D. 2010. Afghanistans Drogenkarriere. Von Der Kriegs- zur Drogenökonomie. Berlin: Stiftung Wissenschaft und Politik, Deutsches Institut für Internationale Politik und Sicherheit.

Maccoby, M. 1978. *The Gamesman: Winning and Losing the Career Game*. New York: Bantam.

Macey, J. R., and Sale, H. A. 2003. Observations on the Role of Commodification, Independence, and Governance in the Accounting Industry. *Villanova Law Review*, 48(4): 1167–1187.

Magnusson, L., and Ottosson, J. (Eds.). 2009. *The Evolution of Path Dependence* Cheltenham: Elgar.

Malhotra, N., Smets, M., and Morris, T. 2016. Career Pathing and Innovation in Professional Service Firms. *Academy of Management Perspectives*, 30(4): 369–383.

Malos, S. B., and Campion, M. A. 1995. An Options-Based Model of Career Mobility in Professional Service Firms. *Academy of Management Review*, 20(3): 611–644.

Mandela, N. 1964. Statement from the Dock. Retrieved 2016-11-09 from www.history place.com/speeches/mandela.htm.

March, J. G., and Olsen, J. P. 1976. *Ambiguity and Choice in Organizations*. Bergen: Universitetsforlaget.

March, J. G., and Simon, H. A. 1958. *Organizations*. New York: John Wiley.

March, J. G., and Sutton, R. I. 1997. Organizational Performance as a Dependent Variable. *Organization Science*, 6: 698–706.

Markus, H., and Nurius, P. 1986. Possible Selves. *American Psychologist*, 41: 954–969.

Marquis, C., and Tilcsik, A. 2013. Imprinting: Towards a Multilevel Theory. *Academy of Management Annals*, 7(1): 193–243.

Maslow, A. H. 1962. *Toward a Psychology of Being*. Princeton, NJ: Van Nostrand.

Masterman, M. 1970. The Nature of a Paradigm. In I. Lakatos and A. Musgrave (Eds.), *Criticism and the Growth of Knowledge*: 59–89. Cambridge: Cambridge University Press.

Matten, D., and Moon, J. 2008. "Implicit" and "Explicit" CSR: A Conceptual Framework for a Comparative Understanding of Corporate Social Responsibility. *Academy of Management Review*, 33(2): 404–424.

Maurice, M., and Sorge, A. 2000. *Embedding Organizations: Societal Analysis of Actors, Organizations and Socio-Economic Context*. Amsterdam: John Benjamins Publishing.

Mawdsley, J., and Somaya, D. 2015. Strategy and Strategic Alignment in Professional Service Firms. In R. Hinings, D. Muzio, J. P. Broschak, and L. Empson (Eds.), *The Oxford Handbook of Professional Service Firms*: 213–237. Oxford: Oxford University Press.

Mayrhofer, W. 1996. *Mobilität und Steuerung in international tätigen Unternehmen. Eine theoretische Analyse*. Stuttgart: Schäffer-Poeschel.

2001. Organizational International Career Logics (OICLs): A Conceptual Tool for Analyzing Organizational Expatriation Patterns and Their Consequences for the Management of Organizations. *Thunderbird International Business Review*, 43(1): 121–144.

Mayrhofer, W., Briscoe, J. P., Hall, D. T., Dickmann, M., Dries, N., Kaše, R., Parry, E., and Unite, J. 2016. Career Success across the Globe – Insights from the 5C Project. *Organizational Dynamics*, 45(2): 197–205.

Mayrhofer, W., and Iellatchich, A. 2005. Rites, Right? The Value of Rites de Passage for Dealing with Today's Career Transitions. *Career Development International*, 10(1): 52–66.

Mayrhofer, W., Meyer, M., Iellatchitch, A., and Schiffinger, M. 2004. Careers and Human Resource Management – a European Perspective. *Human Resource Management Review*, 14(4): 473–498.

Mayrhofer, W., Meyer, M., and Steyrer, J. 2007a. Contextual Issues in the Study of Careers. In H. P. Gunz and M. A. Peiperl (Eds.), *Handbook of Career Studies*: 215–240. Thousand Oaks, CA: Sage.

Mayrhofer, W., Meyer, M., Steyrer, J., and Langer, K. 2007b. Can Expatriation Research Learn from Other Disciplines? The Case of International Career Habitus. *International Studies of Management & Organization*, 37(3): 89–107.

McCain, B. E., O'Reilly, C., and Pfeffer, J. 1983. The Effects of Departmental Demography on Turnover: The Case of a University. *Academy of Management Journal*, 26(4): 626–641.

McClelland, D. C., Atkinson, J. W., Clark, R. A., and Lowell, E. L. 1953. *The Achievement Motive*. New York: Appleton-Century-Crofts.

McCrae, R. R., and Costa, P. T. 1987. Validation of the Five-Factor Model of Personality across Instruments and Observers. *Journal of Personality and Social Psychology*, 52: 81–90.

McGrath, J. E. (Ed.). 1988. *The Social Psychology of Time: New Perspectives*. Newbury Park, CA: Sage.

McGregor, D. M. 1960. *The Human Side of Enterprise*. New York: McGraw-Hill.

McMullin, E. 1968. What Do Physical Models Tell Us? In B. van Rootselaar and J. F. Staal (Eds.), *Logic, Methodology and Philosophy of Science III*, Vol. 52: 385–396. Amsterdam: North-Holland Publishing Company.

McNeill, J. R. 2007. Social, Economic, and Political Forces in Environmental Change. Decadal Scale (1900–2000). In R. Costanza, L. Graumlich, and W. L. Steffen (Eds.), *Sustainability or Collapse? An Integrated History and Future of People on Earth*: 301–329. Cambridge, MA: MIT Press.

McTaggart, J. M. E. 1908. The Unreality of Time. *Mind*, 17(68): 457–474.

Mead, G. H. 1934. Play, the Game, and the Generalized Other. In C. W. Morris (Ed.), *Mind Self and Society from the Standpoint of a Social Behaviorist*. Section 20: 152–164. Chicago: University of Chicago.

Mead, S. 2011. *How to Succeed in Business without Really Trying: The Dastard's Guide to Fame and Fortune*. New York: Simon and Schuster.

Meadows, D. H., Meadows, D., Randers, J., and Behrens, W. 1972. *The Limits to Growth*. New York: Signet Books.

Mearsheimer, J., and Walt, S. 2013. Leaving Theory Behind: Why Simplistic Hypothesis Testing Is Bad for International Relations. *European Journal of International Relations*, 19(3): 427–457.

Meersman, B. 2012. The Legacy of Thabo Mbeki. *Safundi: The Journal of South African and American Studies*, 13(3–4): 425–432.

Merriam-Webster. 2016. *Merriam-Webster Dictionary*. Retrieved 2016-11-02 from www.merriam-webster.com.

Merton, R. K. 1957a. The Role Set: Problems in Sociological Theory. *British Journal of Sociology*, 8: 106–120.

1957b. *Social Theory and Social Structure*. New York: The Free Press.

Meyer, J. W. 1994. Rationalized Environments. In W. R. Scott and J. W. Meyer (Eds.), *Institutional Environments and Organizations*: 28–54. Thousand Oaks, CA: Sage.

Meyer, J. W., and Jepperson, R. L. 2000. The "Actors" of Modern Society: The Cultural Construction of Social Agency. *Sociological Theory*, 18(1): 100–120.

282   References

Meyer, J. W., and Rowan, B. 1977. Institutionalized Organizations: Formal Structure as Myth and Ceremony. *American Journal of Sociology*, 83(2): 340–363.

1983. The Structure of Educational Organisations. In J. W. Meyer and W. R. Scott (Eds.), *Organisational Environments: Ritual and Rationality*: 179–197. Beverly Hills, CA: Sage.

Michel, J.-B., Shen, Y. K., Aiden, A. P., Veres, A., Gray, M. K., The Google Books Team, Pickett, J. P., Hoiberg, D., Clancy, D., Norvig, P., Orwant, J., Pinker, S., Nowak, M. A., and Lieberman, E. 2011. Quantitative Analysis of Culture Using Millions of Digitized Books. *Science*, 331(6014): 176–182.

Miles, R. E., and Snow, C. C. 1978. *Organization Strategy, Structure and Process*. New York: McGraw Hill.

Milgrom, P., and Roberts, J. 1995. Complementarities and Fit: Strategy, Structure and Organizational Change in Manufacturing. *Journal of Accounting and Economics*, 19(2/3): 179–208.

Miller, A. N., Taylor, S. G., and Bedeian, A. G. 2011. Publish or Perish: Academic Life as Management Faculty Live It. *Career Development International*, 16(5): 422–445.

Miller, D. 1987a. The Genesis of Configuration. *Academy of Management Review*, 12(4): 686–701.

Miller, D., Steier, L., and Le Breton-Miller, I. 2003. Lost in Time: Intergenerational Succession, Change, and Failure in Family Business. *Journal of Business Venturing*, 18(4): 513–531.

Miller, E. L. 1975. The Job Satisfaction of Expatriate American Managers. *Journal of International Business Studies*, 6(2): 65–73.

Miller, M. 1987b. Selbstreferenz und Differenzerfahrung. Einige Überlegungen zu Luhmanns Theorie sozialer Systeme. In M. Schmid and H. Haferkamp (Eds.), *Sinn, Kommunikation und soziale Differenzierung. Beiträge zu Luhmanns Theorie sozialer Systeme*: 187–211. Frankfurt am Main: Suhrkamp.

Miller, S. 2008. *Conversation: A History of a Declining Art*. New Haven, CT: Yale University Press.

Mills, C. W. 1959. *The Sociological Imagination*. London: Oxford University Press.

2000 [Original 1959]. *The Sociological Imagination* (40th anniversary ed.). Oxford: Oxford University Press.

Mintzberg, H. 1978. Patterns in Strategy Formulation. *Management Science*, 24(9): 934–948.

1979. *The Structuring of Organizations*. Englewood Cliffs, NJ: Prentice-Hall.

Mintzberg, H., and Waters, J. A. 1985. Of Strategies, Deliberate and Emergent. *Strategic Management Journal*, 6(3): 257–272.

Mirabeau, L., and Maguire, S. 2014. From Autonomous Strategic Behavior to Emergent Strategy. *Strategic Management Journal*, 35(8): 1202–1229.

Mirvis, P. H., and Hall, D. T. 1994. Psychological Success and the Boundaryless Career. *Journal of Organizational Behavior*, 15(4): 365–380.

Mitchell, T. R., and James, L. R. 2001. Building Better Theory: Time and the Specification of When Things Happen. *Academy of Management Review*, 26(4): 530–547.

Mitroff, I. I., and Betz, F. 1972. Dialectical Decision Theory: A Meta-Theory of Decision-Making. *Management Science*, 19(1): 11–24.

Mobley, M. I., Doares, L. M., and Mumford, M. D. 1992. Process Analytic Models of Creative Capacities. Evidence for the Combination and Reorganization Process. *Creativity Research Journal*, 5(2): 125–155.

Moore, C., Gunz, H. P., and Hall, D. T. 2007. Tracing the Historical Roots of Career Theory in Management and Organization Studies. In H. P. Gunz and M. A. Peiperl (Eds.), *Handbook of Career Studies*: 13–38. Thousand Oaks, CA: Sage Publications.

Mortimer, J. T., and Shanahan, M. J. (Eds.). 2003a. *Handbook of the Life Course*. New York: Kluwer.

Mortimer, J. T., and Shanahan, M. J. 2003b. Preface. In J. T. Mortimer and M. J. Shanahan (Eds.), *Handbook of the Life Course*: xi–xvi. New York: Kluwer.

Mosakowski, E., and Earley, P. C. 2000. A Selective Review of Time Assumptions in Strategy Research. *Academy of Management Review*, 25(4): 796–812.

Murrells, T., and Robinson, S. 1998. Researching Career Plans and Career Histories of Mental Health Nurses. *International Journal of Nursing Studies*, 35(4): 233–242.

Nature. 2016. Getting Published in *Nature*: The Editorial Process. Retrieved 2016-09-12 from www.nature.com/nature/authors/get_published.

Nelson, R. L., and Nielsen, L. B. 2000. Cops, Counsel and Entrepreneurs: Constructing the Role of inside Counsel in Large Corporations. *Law & Society Review*, 34(2): 457–494.

Newman, D. 2006 Borders and Bordering: Towards an Interdisciplinary Dialogue. *European Journal of Social Theory*, 9(2): 171–186.

Ng, T. W. H., Eby, L. T., Sorensen, K. L., and Feldman, D. C. 2005. Predictors of Objective and Subjective Career Success: A Meta-Analysis. *Personnel Psychology*, 58: 367–408.

Ng, T. W. H., and Feldman, D. C. 2010. Human Capital and Objective Indicators of Career Success: The Mediating Effects of Cognitive Ability and Conscientiousness. *Journal of Occupational and Organizational Psychology*, 83 (1): 207–235.

2014. Subjective Career Success: A Meta-Analytic Review. *Journal of Vocational Behavior*, 85(2): 169–179.

Ngo, H. Y., Foley, S., Ji, M. S., and Loi, R. 2014. Linking Gender Role Orientation to Subjective Career Success. The Mediating Role of Psychological Capital. *Journal of Career Assessment*, 22(2): 290–303.

Nicholson, N. 1984. A Theory of Work Role Transitions. *Administrative Science Quarterly*, 29(2): 172–191.

1996. Career Systems in Crisis: Change and Opportunity in the Information Age. *Academy of Management Executive*, 10(4): 40–51.

2007. Destiny, Drama and Deliberation: Careers in the Coevolution of Lives and Societies. In H. Gunz and M. Peiperl (Eds.), *Handbook of Career Studies*: 566–572. Thousand Oaks, CA: Sage Publications.

Nicholson, N., and De Waal-Andrews, W. 2005. Playing to Win: Biological Imperatives, Self-Regulation, and Trade-Offs in the Game of Career Success. *Journal of Organizational Behavior*, 26(2): 137–154.

Nicholson, N., and West, M. 1988. *Managerial Job Change: Men and Women in Transition*. Cambridge: Cambridge University Press.

1989. Transitions, Work Histories and Careers. In M. B. Arthur, D. T. Hall, and B. S. Lawrence (Eds.), *Handbook of Career Theory*: 181–201. Cambridge: Cambridge University Press.

Norris, W., Hatch, R. N., Engelkes, J. R., and Winborn, B. B. 1979. *The Career Information Service* (4th ed.). Chicago: Rand McNally.

Nurmi, J.-E. 2013. Modeling Development Processes in Psychology. *Perspectives on Science*, 21: 181–195.

Nutall, S., and Mbembe, A. 2014. Mandela's Mortality. In R. Barnard (Ed.), *The Cambridge Companion to Nelson Mandela*: 267–290. New York: Cambridge University Press.

O'Brien, K., Biga, A., Kessler, S., and Allen, T. 2010. A Meta-Analytic Investigation of Gender Differences in Mentoring. *Journal of Management*, 36(2): 537–554.

O'Mahony, S., and Bechky, B. A. 2006. Stretchwork: Managing the Career Progression Paradox in External Labor Markets. *Academy of Management Journal*, 49(5): 918–941.

Obermayer, B., and Obermaier, F. 2016. *The Panama Papers: Breaking the Story of How the Rich and Powerful Hide Their Money*. London: Oneworld.

Ockam, G. 1962. *Opera Plurima Lyon, 1494–1496: Réimpression En Facsimilé Avec Un Tableau Des Abréviations*. London: Gregg Press. Facsimile of: Ockam, Guilielmus (ca. 1288–ca. 1348). Quaestiones et decisiones in IV libros Sententiarum. Centilogium theologicum. Augustinus de Ratisbona and Jodocus Badius Ascensius, editors. Lyons: Johannes Trechsel, 9–10 Nov. 1495.

OED. 2017. *Oxford English Dictionary*. Oxford: Oxford University Press.

Ofori-Dankwa, J., and Julian, S. D. 2001. Complexifying Organizational Theory: Illustrations Using Time Research. *Academy of Management. Academy of Management Review*, 26(3): 415–430.

Olian, J. D., Carroll, S. J., and Giannantonio, C. M. 1993. Mentor Reactions to Proteges: An Experiment with Managers. *Journal of Vocational Behavior*, 43(3): 266–278.

Opayemi, R. 2012. Psychosocial Factors Predisposing University Undergraduates to Mentoring Relationship. *Ife Psychologia*, 20(1): 70–86.

Ortega y Gasset, J. 1914. *Meditaciones del Quijote*. Madrid: Publicaciones de la residencia de estudiantes.

Pallas, A. M. 2003. Educational Transitions, Trajectories, and Pathways. In J. T. Mortimer and M. J. Shanahan (Eds.), *Handbook of the Life Course*: 165–184. New York: Kluwer.

Pan, J. Z., and Zhou, W. X. 2015. How Do Employees Construe Their Career Success: An Improved Measure of Subjective Career Success. *International Journal of Selection and Assessment*, 23(1): 45–58.

Parker, P., Arthur, M. B., and Inkson, K. 2004. Career Communities: A Preliminary Exploration of Member-Defined Career Support Structures. *Journal of Organizational Behavior*, 25(4): 489–514.

Parsons, T. 1960. *Structure and Process in Modern Societies*. New York: Free Press. 1991 [Original 1951]. *The Social System*. London: Routledge.

Parsons, T., and Shils, E. A. 1962 [Original 1951]. Values, Motives, and Systems of Actions. In T. Parsons and E. A. Shils (Eds.), *Toward a General Theory of Action*: 45–275. Cambridge, MA: Harvard University Press.

Pask, G. 1984. Review of Conversation Theory and a Protologic (or Protolanguage), Lp. *Educational Technology Research and Development/ECTJ*, 32(1): 3–40.

Patchett, A. 2016. *Commonwealth: A Novel*. New York: HarperCollins Publishers Inc.

Patton, W. 2008. Recent Developments in Career Theories: The Influences of Constructivism and Convergence. In J. A. Athanasou and R. van Esbroeck (Eds.), *International Handbook of Career Guidance*: 133–156. London: Springer.

Pearce, S. M. 1995. *On Collecting: An Investigation into Collecting in the European Tradition*. London: Routledge.

Peiperl, M., and Gunz, H. 2007. Taxonomy of Career Studies. In H. Gunz and M. Peiperl (Eds.), *Handbook of Career Studies*: 39–54. Thousand Oaks, CA: Sage Publications.

Perlow, L. A. 1999. The Time Famine: Toward a Sociology of Work Time. *Administrative Science Quarterly*, 44(1): 57–81.

Perrow, C. 1961. The Analysis of Goals in Complex Organizations. *American Sociological Review*, 26: 854–866.

Perry, J. L. 2012. How Can We Improve Our Science to Generate More Usable Knowledge for Public Professionals? *Public Administration Review*, 72(4): 479–482.

Peterson, R. B., Sargent, J., Napier, N. K., and Shim, W. S. 1996. Corporate Expatriate HRM Policies, Internationalization, and Performance in the World's Largest MNCs. *Management International Review*, 36(3): 215–230.

Pfeffer, J. 1992. *Managing with Power – Politics and Influence in Organizations*. Boston: Harvard Business School Press.

1993. Barriers to the Advance of Organizational Science: Paradigm Development as a Dependent Variable. *Academy of Management Review*, 18(4): 599–620.

1995. Mortality, Reproducibility, and the Persistence of Styles of Theory. *Organization Science*, 6(6): 681–686.

Pfeffer, J., and Davis-Blake, A. 1986. Administrative Succession and Organizational Performance: How Administrator Experience Mediates the Succession Effect. *Academy of Management Journal*, 29: 72–83.

Pfeffer, J., and Salancik, G. R. 1978. *The External Control of Organizations – a Resource Dependence Perspective*. New York: Harper & Row.

Picou, J. S., and Campbell, R. E. (Eds.). 1975. *Career Behavior of Specific Groups*. Westerville: Merrill.

Pierson, F. C. and others. 1959. *The Education of American Businessmen: A Study of University-College Programs in Business Administration*. New York: McGraw-Hill.

Pinfield, L. 1995. *The Operation of Internal Labour Markets: Staffing Actions and Vacancy Chains*. New York: Plenum.

Poole, M., Mansfield, R., Blyton, P., and Frost, P. 1981. *Managers in Focus: The British Manager in the Early 1980s*. Aldershot: Gower.

Popitz, H. 1967. *Der Begriff der sozialen Rolle als Element der soziologischen Theorie*. Tübingen: Mohr.

Powell, W., and DiMaggio, P. J. (Eds.). 1991. *The New Institutionalism in Organizational Analysis*. Chicago: University of Chicago Press.

Powell, W. W. 1985. The Institutionalization of Rational Organization. *Contemporary Sociology*, 14: 564–566.

2007. The New Institutionalism. In S. R. Clegg and J. Bailey (Eds.), *The International Encyclopedia of Organization Studies*. Thousand Oaks, CA: Sage.

Radkau, J. 2009. *Max Weber: A Biography*. Cambridge: Polity.

Ragins, B. R. 1999. Gender and Mentoring Relationships: Definitions, Challenges, and Strategies. In G. N. Powell (Ed.), *Handbook of Gender and Work*: 347–370. Thousand Oaks, CA: Sage.

Ragins, B. R., and Kram, K. E. (Eds.). 2007a. *The Handbook of Mentoring at Work: Theory, Research, and Practice*. Thousand Oaks, CA: Sage.

Ragins, B. R., and Kram, K. E. 2007b. The Roots and Meaning of Mentoring. In B. R. Ragins and K. E. Kram (Eds.), *The Handbook of Mentoring at Work: Theory, Research, and Practice*: 3–17. Thousand Oaks, CA: Sage Publications.

Rapoport, R., and Rapoport, R. N. 1971. *Dual-Career Families*. London: Penguin Books.

1976. *Dual-Career Families Re-Examined: New Integrations of Work and Family*. London: Martin Robertson.

Restubog, S. L. D., Bordia, P., and Bordia, S. 2011. Investigating the Role of Psychological Contract Breach on Career Success: Convergent Evidence from Two Longitudinal Studies. *Journal of Vocational Behavior*, 79(2): 428–437.

Rhim, J. C., Peluchette, J. V., and Song, I. 2006. Stock Market Reactions and Firm Performance Surrounding CEO Succession: Antecedents of Succession and Successor Origin. *Mid-American Journal of Business*, 21(1): 21–30.

Rice, D. G. 1979. *Dual-Career Marriage: Conflict and Treatment*. London: The Free Press.

Rider, C. I., and Tan, D. 2014. Labor Market Advantages of Organizational Status: A Study of Lateral Partner Hiring by Large U.S. Law Firms. *Organization Science*, 26(2): 356–372.

Rindova, V. 2009. Editor's Comments: Publishing Theory When You Are New to the Game. *Academy of Management Review*, 33(2): 300–303.

Rittel, H. W. J., and Webber, M. M. 1973. Dilemmas in a General Theory of Planning. *Policy Sciences*, 4(2): 155–169.

Rittenberg, L., and Covaleski, M. A. 2001. Internalization versus Externalization of the Internal Audit Function: An Examination of Professional and Organizational Imperatives. *Accounting, Organizations and Society*, 26(7–8): 617–641.

Roberts, B. W., and DelVecchio, W. F. 2000. The Rank-Order Consistency of Personality Traits from Childhood to Old Age: A Quantitative Review of Longitudinal Studies. *Psychological Bulletin*, 126(1): 3–25.

Rodrigues, R., Guest, D., and Budjanovcanin, A. 2016. Bounded or Boundaryless? An Empirical Investigation of Career Boundaries and Boundary Crossing. *Work, Employment & Society*, 30(4): 669–686.

Rodrigues, R. A., and Guest, D. 2010. Have Careers Become Boundaryless? *Human Relations*, 63(8): 1157–1175.

Rose, N. 1989. *Governing the Soul: The Shaping of the Private Self*. London: Free Association Books.

References 287

Rosenbaum, J. E. 1979a. Organizational Career Mobility: Promotion Chances in a Corporation During Periods of Growth and Contraction. *American Journal of Sociology*, 85(1): 21–48.
1979b. Tournament Mobility: Career Patterns in a Corporation. *Administrative Science Quarterly*, 24(2): 220–241.
1984. Career Mobility in a Corporate Hierarchy. London: Academic Press.
Roth, J. A. 1963. *Timetables: Structuring the Passage of Time in Hospital Treatment and Other Careers*. Indianapolis: Bobbs-Merrill.
Rousseau, D. M., and Fried, Y. 2001. Location, Location, Location: Contextualizing Organizational Research. *Journal of Organizational Behavior*, 22(1): 1–13.
Rousseau, D. M., and House, R. J. 1994. Meso Organizational Behavior: Avoiding Three Fundamental Biases. *Journal of Organizational Behavior*, 1: 13–32.
Sammarra, A., Profili, S., and Innocenti, L. 2013. Do External Careers Pay-Off for Both Managers and Professionals? The Effect of Inter-Organizational Mobility on Objective Career Success. *International Journal of Human Resource Management*, 24(13): 2490–2511.
Sampson, J. P., Hou, P.-C., Kronholz, J. F., Dozier, C., McClain, M.-C., Buzzetta, M., Pawley, E. K., Finklea, J. T., Peterson, G. W., Lenz, J. G., Reardon, R. C., Osborn, D. S., Hayden, S. C. W., Colvin, G. P., and Kennelly, E. L. 2014. A Content Analysis of Career Development Theory, Research, and Practice–2013. *The Career Development Quarterly*, 62(4): 290–326.
Sarason, S. B. 1977. *Work, Aging, and Social Change: Professionals and the One Life-One Career Imperative*. New York: Free.
Sargent, L., Lee, M., Martin, B., and Zikic, J. 2013. Reinventing Retirement: New Pathways, New Arrangements, New Meanings. *Human Relations*, 66(1): 3–21.
Savickas, M. L. 2005. The Theory and Practice of Career Construction. In S. D. Brown and R. W. Lent (Eds.), *Career Development and Counselling: Putting Research and Theory to Work*: 42–70. Hoboken, NJ: Wiley.
2007. Occupational Choice. In H. P. Gunz and M. A. Peiperl (Eds.), *Handbook of Career Studies*: 79–96. Thousand Oaks, CA: Sage Publications.
Savickas, M. L., and Taber, B. J. 2006. Individual Differences in RIASEC Profile Similarity across Five Interest Inventories. *Measurement and Evaluation in Counseling and Development*, 38(4), 207–210.
Scandura, T. 1998. Dysfunctional Mentoring Relationships and Outcomes. *Journal of Management*, 24(3): 449–467.
Schane, S. A. 1986–1987. The Corporation Is a Person: The Language of a Legal Fiction. *Tulane Law Review*, 61(3): 563–609.
Schanz, G. 1977. *Grundlagen der verhaltenstheoretischen Betriebswirtschaftslehre*. Tübingen: Mohr.
Schaubroeck, J., and Lam, S. S. K. 2002. How Similarity to Peers and Supervisor Influences Organizational Advancement in Different Cultures. *Academy of Management Journal*, 45(6): 1120–1136.
Schein, E. 1965. *Organizational Psychology*. Englewood Cliffs, NJ: Prentice Hall.
Schein, E. H. 1971. The Individual, the Organization and the Career: A Conceptual Scheme. *Journal of Applied Behavioral Science*, 7: 401–426.

1977. Career Anchors and Career Paths: A Panel Study of Management School Graduates. In J. Van Maanen (Ed.), *Organizational Careers: Some New Perspectives*: 49–64. London: Wiley.

1978. *Career Dynamics: Matching Individual and Organizational Needs*. Reading, MA: Addison-Wesley Publishing Company.

1980. Career Theory and Research: Some Issues for the Future. In C. B. Derr (Ed.), *Work, Family, and the Career: New Frontiers in Theory and Research*: 357–365. New York: Praeger.

1984. Culture as an Environmental Context for Careers. *Journal of Occupational Behavior*, 5(1): 71–81.

1985. *Career Anchors: Discovering Your Real Values*. San Francisco: Jossey-Bass.

2007. Career Research: Some Issues and Dilemmas. In H. Gunz and M. Peiperl (Eds.), *Handbook of Career Studies*: 573–576. Thousand Oaks, CA: Sage.

Schneider, H., and Herbst-Bayliss, S. 2016. Yellen Says "High-Pressure" Policy May Be Needed to Reverse Damage of Crisis, *The Globe and Mail (Toronto)*: B3.

Schneidhofer, T., Latzke, M., and Mayrhofer, W. 2015. Careers as Sites of Power: A Relational Understanding of Careers Based on Bourdieu's Cornerstones. In A. Tatli, M. Özbilgin, and M. Karatas-Özkan (Eds.), *Pierre Bourdieu, Organisation, and Management*: 19–36. New York: Routledge.

Schneidhofer, T. M., Schiffinger, M., and Mayrhofer, W. 2012. Still a Man's World? The Influence of Gender and Gender Role Type on Income in Two Business School Graduate Cohorts over Time. *Equality, Diversity and Inclusion: An International Journal*, 31(1): 65–82.

Scholl, R. W. 1983. Career Lines and Employment Stability. *Academy of Management Journal*, 26(1): 86–103.

Science. 2016. General Information for Authors. Retrieved 2016-09-12 from www.sciencemag.org/site/feature/contribinfo/prep/gen_info.xhtml.

Scott, G. M., Lonergan, D. C., and Mumford, M. D. 2005. Conceptual Combination: Alternative Knowledge Structures, Alternative Heuristics. *Creativity Research Journal*, 17(1): 79–98.

Scott, W. R. 1983. The Organization of Environments: Network, Cultural, and Historical Elements. In J. W. Meyer and W. R. Scott (Eds.), *Organizational Environments: Ritual and Rationality*: 155–175. Beverly Hills, CA: Sage.

1987. The Adolescence of Institutional Theory. *Administrative Science Quarterly*, 32 (4): 493–511.

1995. *Institutions and Organizations: Ideas and Interests*. Thousand Oaks, CA: Sage.

2004. Reflections on a Half-Century of Organizational Sociology. *Annual Review of Sociology*, 30(1): 1–21.

2014. *Institutions and Organizations. Ideas, Interests, and Identities* (4th ed.). Los Angeles: Sage.

Scott, W. R., and Meyer, J. 1983. The Organization of Societal Sectors In J. W. Meyer and W. R. Scott (Eds.), *Organizational Environments: Ritual and Rationality*: 129–153. Beverly Hills, CA: Sage.

Seibert, S. E., and Kraimer, M. L. 2001. The Five-Factor Model of Personality and Career Success. *Journal of Vocational Behavior*, 58: 1–21.

Seibert, S. E., Kraimer, M. L., and Liden, R. C. 2001. A Social Capital Theory of Career Success. *Academy of Management Journal*, 44(2): 219–237.

Seidl, D. 2005. The Basic Concepts of Luhmann's Theory of Social Systems. In D. Seidl and K. H. Becker (Eds.), *Niklas Luhmann and Organization Studies*: 21–53. Malmö: Liber & Copenhagen Business School Press.

Sennett, R. 1980. *Authority*. New York: Norton.

Shanahan, M. J., Mortimer, J. T., and Kirkpatrick Johnson, M. (Eds.). 2016. *Handbook of the Life Course* (Vol. II). Heidelberg: Springer.

Shaw, C. R. 1930. *The Jack-Roller. A Delinquent Boy's Own Story*. Chicago: University of Chicago Press.

Shaw, K. L. 1987. Occupational Change, Employer Change, and the Transferability of Skills. *Southern Economic Journal*, 53(3): 702–719.

Shen, W., and Cannella, A. A. 2002. Revisiting the Performance Consequences of CEO Succession: The Impacts of Successor Type, Postsuccession Senior Executive Turnover, and Departing CEO Tenure. *Academy of Management Journal*, 45(4): 717–733.

Shen, Y., Demel, B., Unite, J., Briscoe, J. P., Hall, D. T., Chudzikowski, K., Mayrhofer, W., Abdul-Ghani, R., Bogicevic Milikic, B., Colorado, O., Fei, Z., Las Heras, M., Ogliastri, E., Pazy, A., Poon, J. M. L., Shefer, D., Taniguchi, M., and Zikic, J. 2015a. Career Success across Eleven Countries: Implications for International Human Resource Management. *International Journal of Human Resource Management*, 26(13): 1753–1778.

Shen, Y., Demel, B., Unite, J., Briscoe, J. P., Hall, D. T., Chudzikowski, K., Mayrhofer, W., Abdul-Ghani, R., Milikic, B. B., Colorado, O., Fei, Z., Las Heras, M., Ogliastri, E., Pazy, A., Poon, J. M. L., Shefer, D., Taniguchi, M., and Zikic, J. 2015b. Career Success across 11 Countries: Implications for International Human Resource Management. *International Journal of Human Resource Management*, 26(13): 1753–1778.

Shepherd, C., and Challenger, R. 2013. Revisiting Paradigm(s) in Management Research: A Rhetorical Analysis of the Paradigm Wars. *International Journal of Management Reviews*, 15(2): 225–244.

Sheu, H.-B., Lent, R. W., Brown, S. D., Miller, M. J., Hennessy, K. D., and Duffy, R. D. 2010. Testing the Choice Model of Social Cognitive Career Theory across Holland Themes: A Meta-Analytic Path Analysis. *Journal of Vocational Behavior*, 76(2): 252–264.

Shipp, A. J., and Fried, Y. (Eds.). 2014a. *How Time Impacts Groups, Organizations, and Methodological Choices*. East Sussex, UK: Psychology Press.

Shipp, A. J., and Fried, Y. (Eds.). 2014b. *Time and Work Volume 1: How Time Impacts Individuals*. East Sussex, UK: Psychology Press.

Sicherman, N., and Galor, O. 1990. A Theory of Career Mobility. *Journal of Political Economy*, 98(1): 169–192.

Siggelkow, N. 2001. Change in the Presence of Fit: The Rise, the Fall, and the Renaissance of Liz Claiborne. *Academy of Management Journal*, 44(4): 838–857.

Simon, H. A. 1957 [Original 1947]. *Administrative Behavior: A Study of Decision-Making Processes in Administrative Organization* (2nd ed.). New York: Free Press.

1964. On the Concept of Organizational Goal. *Administrative Science Quarterly*, 9 (1): 1–22.

Slocum, W. L. 1966. *Occupational Careers: A Sociological Perspective*. Chicago: Aldine Pub. Co.

Smets, M., Morris, T. I. M., and Greenwood, R. 2012. From Practice to Field: A Multilevel Model of Practice-Driven Institutional Change. *Academy of Management Journal*, 55(4): 877–904.

Smith, J. A. 2004. Reflecting on the Development of Interpretative Phenomenological Analysis and Its Contribution to Qualitative Research in Psychology. *Qualitative Research in Psychology*, 1(1): 39–54.

Smith, P. 1998. *Explaining Chaos*. Cambridge: Cambridge University Press.

Snow, C. C., and Hrebiniak, L. G. 1980. Strategy, Distinctive Competence, and Organizational Performance. *Administrative Science Quarterly*, 25: 317–335.

Snow, J. 2008 [Original 1855]. On the Mode of Communication of Cholera (Second Edition). *Hygeia: Revista Brasileira de Geografia Médica e da Saúde*, 3(6): 1–11.

Sofer, C. 1970. *Men in Mid-Career: A Study of British Managers and Technical Specialists*. Cambridge: Cambridge University Press.

Sokal, A. D., and Bricmont, J. 1998. *Fashionable Nonsense: Postmodern Intellectuals' Abuse of Science*. New York: Picador.

Sonnenfeld, J., and Kotter, J. P. 1982. The Maturation of Career Theory. *Human Relations*, 35(1): 19–46.

Sonnenfeld, J. A., and Peiperl, M. A. 1988. Staffing Policy as a Strategic Response: A Typology of Career Systems. *Academy of Management Review*, 13(4): 588–600.

Sonnenfeld, J. A., Peiperl, M. A., and Kotter, J. P. 1988. Strategic Determinants of Managerial Labor Markets: A Career Systems View. *Human Resource Management*, 27(4): 369–388.

Sonnentag, S. 2012. Time in Organizational Research: Catching up on a Long Neglected Topic in Order to Improve Theory. *Organizational Psychology Review*, 2(4): 361–368.

Sorensen, J. B. 1999. Executive Migration and Interorganizational Competition. *Social Science Research*, 28(3): 289–315.

Sparrow, P. R. (Ed.). 2009. *Handbook of International Human Resource Management: Integrating People, Process, and Context*. Chichester: Wiley.

Specht, J., Egloff, B., and Schmukle, S. C. 2011. Stability and Change of Personality across the Life Course: The Impact of Age and Major Life Events on Mean-Level and Rank-Order Stability of the Big Five. *Journal of Personality & Social Psychology*, 101(4): 862–882.

Spencer-Brown, G. 1972. *Laws of Form*. London: Allen and Unwin.

Spurk, D., and Abele, A. E. 2014. Synchronous and Time-Lagged Effects between Occupational Self-Efficacy and Objective and Subjective Career Success: Findings from a Four-Wave and 9-Year Longitudinal Study. *Journal of Vocational Behavior*, 84(2): 119–132.

Staehle, W. H. 1980. *Management: eine verhaltenswissenschaftliche Einführung*. München: Vahlen.

Staines, G. L. 1980. Spillover Versus Compensation: A Review of the Literature on the Relationship between Work and Non-Work. *Human Relations*, 33(2): 111–129.

Staw, B. M., Bell, N. E., and Clausen, J. A. 1986. The Dispositional Approach to Job Attitudes: A Lifetime Longitudinal Test. *Administrative Science Quarterly*, 31(1): 56–77.

Stewart, S. 1993. *On Longing: Narratives of the Miniature, the Gigantic, the Souvenir, the Collection*. Durham, NC: Duke University Press.

Stewman, S. 1986. Demographic Models of Internal Labor Markets. *Administrative Science Quarterly*, 31(2): 212–247.

Stewman, S., and Konda, S. 1983. Careers and Organizational Labor Markets: Demographic Models of Organizational Behaviour. *American Journal of Sociology*, 88(4): 637–685.

Stinchcombe, A. L. 1965. Social Structure and Organizations. In J. G. March (Ed.), *Handbook of Organizations*: 142–193. Chicago: Rand McNally.

Stones, R. 2005. *Structuration Theory*. Houndsmills: Palgrave Macmillan.

Strauss, A. L. 1975. *Professions, Work, and Careers*. New Brunswick, NJ: Transaction Books.

Stronach, M. M., and Adair, D. 2010. Lords of the Square Ring: Future Capital and Career Transition Issues for Elite Indigenous Australian Boxers. *Cosmopolitan Civil Societies: An Interdisciplinary Journal*, 2(2): 46–70.

Stumpf, S. A., and London, M. 1981. Management Promotions: Individual and Organizational Factors Influencing the Decision Process. *Academy of Management Review*, 6(4): 539–549.

Stumpf, S. A., and Tymon, W. G. 2012. The Effects of Objective Career Success on Subsequent Subjective Career Success. *Journal of Vocational Behavior*, 81(3): 345–353.

Sturges, J. 2008. All in a Day's Work? Career Self-Management and Management of the Boundary between Work and Non-Work. *Human Resource Management Journal*, 18(2): 118–134.

Suchman, M. C. 1995. Managing Legitimacy: Strategic and Institutional Approaches. *Academy of Management Review*, 20(3): 571–610.

Suddaby, R., and Muzio, D. 2015. Theoretical Perspectives on the Professions. In R. Hinings, D. Muzio, J. P. Broschak, and L. Empson (Eds.), *The Oxford Handbook of Professional Service Firms*: 25–47. Oxford: Oxford University Press.

Suddaby, R. O. Y., Elsbach, K. D., Greenwood, R., and Meyer, J. W. 2010. Organizations and Their Institutional Environments – Bringing Meaning, Values, and Culture Back In: Introduction to the Special Research Forum. *Academy of Management Journal*, 53(6): 1234–1240.

Sullivan, S. E. 1999. The Changing Nature of Careers: A Review and Research Agenda. *Journal of Management*, 25(3): 457–484.

Sullivan, S. E., and Arthur, M. B. 2006. The Evolution of the Boundaryless Career Concept: Examining Physical and Psychological Mobility. *Journal of Vocational Behavior*, 69(1): 19–29.

Sullivan, S. E., and Crocitto, M. 2007. The Developmental Theories: A Critical Examination of Their Continuing Impact on Careers Research. In H. Gunz and M. Peiperl (Eds.), *Handbook of Career Studies*: 283–309. Thousand Oaks, CA: Sage Publications.

Super, D. E. 1970. *Occupational Psychology*. London: Tavistock Publications.

1992. Towards a Comprehensive Theory of Career Development. In D. H. Montross and C. J. Shinkman (Eds.), *Career Development: Theory and Practice*. Springfield, IL: Charles C Thomas.

Sutherland, E. H. 1937. *The Professional Thief*. Chicago: University of Chicago Press.

Sutton, R. I., and Staw, B. M. 1995. What Theory Is Not. *Administrative Science Quarterly*, 40(3): 371–384.

Svejenova, S., Vives, L., and Alvarez, J. L. 2010. At the Crossroads of Agency and Communion: Defining the Shared Career, *Journal of Organizational Behavior*, 31(5): 707–725.

Swanson, D. L. 1999. Toward an Integrative Theory of Business and Society: A Research Strategy for Corporate Social Performance. *Academy of Management Review*, 24(3): 506–521.

Sydow, J., Schreyogg, G., and Koch, J. 2009. Organizational Path Dependence: Opening the Black Box. *Academy of Management Review*, 34(4): 689–709.

Szilagyi, A. D., Jr., and Schweiger, D. M. 1984. Matching Managers to Strategies: A Review and Suggested Framework. *Academy of Management Review*, 9(4): 626–637.

Tajfel, H., and Turner, A. L. 1986. The Social Identity Theory of Intergroup Behavior. In W. W. G. Austin (Ed.), *Psychology of Intergroup Relations*: 7–24. Chicago: Nelson-Hall.

ten Bos, R. 2000. *Fashion and Utopia in Management Thinking*. Amsterdam: John Benjamins Publishing.

The Free Dictionary. 2016 Retrieved 2016-09-17 from www.thefreedictionary.com.

Thomas, D. A. 1993. Racial Dynamics in Cross-Race Developmental Relationships. *Administrative Science Quarterly*, 38(2): 169–194.

Thompson, J. D. 1967. *Organizations in Action*. New York: McGraw-Hill.

Thompson, V. 1961. *Modern Organizations*. New York: Knopf.

Thornbury, S., and Slade, D. 2006. *Conversation: From Description to Pedagogy*. Cambridge: Cambridge University Press.

Thornton, P. H. 2004. *Markets from Culture. Institutional Logics and Organizational Decisions in Higher Education Publishing*. Stanford, CA: Stanford Business Books.

Thornton, P. H., Jones, C., and Kury, K. 2005. Institutional Logics and Institutional Change in Organizations: Transformation in Accounting, Architecture, and Publishing. *Research in the Sociology of Organizations*, 23: 125–170.

Thornton, P. H., and Ocasio, W. 2008. Institutional Logics. In R. Greenwood, C. Oliver, R. Suddaby, and K. Sahlin (Eds.), *The Sage Handbook of Organizational Institutionalism*: 99–129. London: Sage.

Thornton, P. H., Ocasio, W., and Lounsbury, M. 2012. *The Institutional Logics Perspective: A New Approach to Culture, Structure and Process*. Oxford: Oxford University Press.

Thurstone, L. L. 1947. *Multiple-Factor Analysis*. Chicago: University of Chicago Press.

Tiedeman, D., and Miller-Tiedeman, A. 1985. The Trend of Life in the Human Career. *Journal of Career Development*, 11(3): 221–250.

Tolbert, P. S., and Zucker, L. G. 1996. The Institutionalization of Institutional Theory. In S. R. Clegg, C. Hardy, and W. R. Nord (Eds.), *Handbook of Organization Studies*: 175–190. London: Sage.

Toulmin, S. 1972. *Human Understanding: The Collective Use and Evolution of Concepts*. Princeton, NJ: Princeton University Press.

Tung, R. L. 1988. *The New Expatriates: Managing Human Resources Abroad*. Cambridge, MA: Ballinger.

Ulrich, H. 1970. *Die Unternehmung als produktives soziales System* (2nd ed.). Bern: Haupt.

United Nations. 2016. The United Nations: Partner in the Struggle against Apartheid. Retrieved 2016-09-16 from www.un.org/en/events/mandeladay/ap artheid.shtml.

Upton, M. G., and Egan, T. M. 2010. Three Approaches to Multilevel Theory Building. *Human Resource Development Review*, 9(4): 333–356.

Useem, M., and Karabel, J. 1986. Pathways to Top Corporate Management. *American Sociological Review*, 51: 184–200.

Vaillant, G. E. 1977. *Adaptation to Life*. Boston: Little, Brown and Co.

Van de Ven, A. H., Ganco, M., and Hinings, C. R. 2013. Returning to the Frontier of Contingency Theory of Organizational and Institutional Designs. *Academy of Management Annals*, 7(1): 393–440.

van Gennep, A. 1960 [Original 1909]. *Rites of Passage*. Chicago: University of Chicago Press.

Van Maanen, J. 1977a. Introduction: The Promise of Career Studies. In J. Van Maanen (Ed.), *Organizational Careers: Some New Perspectives*: 1–12. London: Wiley.

Van Maanen, J. (Ed.). 1977b. *Organizational Careers: Some New Perspectives*. London: John Wiley & Sons.

Van Maanen, J. 1995. Fear and Loathing in Organization Studies. *Organization Science*, 6(6): 687–692.

Van Maanen, J., and Schein, E. H. 1977. Career Development. In J. R. Hackman and J. L. Suttle (Eds.), *Improving Life at Work*. Los Angeles: Goodyear.

1979. Toward a Theory of Organizational Socialization. In B. Staw (Ed.), *Research in Organizational Behavior*: 209–264. Greenwich, CT: JAI Press.

Vardi, Y. 1980. Organizational Career Mobility: An Integrative Model. *Academy of Management Review*, 5(3): 341–355.

2006. Personal communication: Personal Recollections of Origins of Cornell Career Group.

Vecera, S. P., Flevaris, A. V., and Filapek, J. C. 2004. Exogenous Spatial Attention Influences Figure-Ground Assignment. *Psychological Science*, 15(1): 20–26.

Veiga, J. F. 1983. Mobility Influences during Managerial Career Stages. *Academy of Management Journal*, 26(1): 64–85.

Vroom, V. H. 1964. *Work and Motivation*. New York: Wiley.

2005. On the Origins of Expectancy Theory. In K. G. Smith and M. A. Hitt (Eds.), *Great Minds in Management: The Process of Theory Development*: 239–258. Oxford: Oxford University Press.

Wagner, W. G., Pfeffer, J., and O'Reilly, C. A. 1984. Organizational Demography and Turnover in Top-Management Groups. *Administrative Science Quarterly*, 29 (1): 74–92.

Waksman, S. 2001. *Instruments of Desire: The Electric Guitar and the Shaping of Musical Experience*. Harvard: Harvard University Press.

Wanous, J. P. 1980. *Organizational Entry*. Reading, MA: Addison-Wesley.

Warren, M. 2006. *Features of Naturalness in Conversation*. Amsterdam: John Benjamins Publishing.

Wayne, S. J., Liden, R. C., Kraimer, M. L., and Graf, I. K. 1999. The Role of Human Capital, Motivation and Supervisor Sponsorship in Predicting Career Success. *Journal of Organizational Behavior*, 20(5): 577–595.

Weber, M. 1968 [Original 1922]. *Gesammelte Aufsätze zur Wissenschaftslehre* (3rd ed.). Tübingen: Mohr.

1980 [Original 1921]. *Wirtschaft und Gesellschaft* (5th ed.). Tübingen: Mohr.

Wei, W., and Taormina, R. J. 2014. A New Multidimensional Measure of Personal Resilience and Its Use: Chinese Nurse Resilience, Organizational Socialization and Career Success. *Nursing Inquiry*, 21(4): 346–357.

Weick, K. E. 1969. *The Social Psychology of Organizing*. Reading, MA: Addison-Wesley.

1979. *The Social Psychology of Organizing*. Reading, MA: Addison-Wesley.

1995a. *Sensemaking in Organizations*. Thousand Oaks, CA: Sage.

1995b. What Theory Is Not, Theorizing Is. *Administrative Science Quarterly*, 40(3): 385–390.

2001. Gapping the Relevance Bridge: Fashions Meet Fundamentals in Management Research. *British Journal of Management*, 12(s1): S71–S75.

Western, M., and Wright, E. O. 1994. The Permeability of Class Boundaries to Intergenerational Mobility among Men in the United States, Canada, Norway and Sweden. *American Sociological Review*, 59(4): 606–629.

Whetten, D. A. 1989. What Constitutes a Theoretical Contribution? *Academy of Management Review*, 14(4): 490–495.

Whipp, R., Adam, B., and Sabelis, I. (Eds.). 2002. *Making Time: Time and Management in Modern Organizations*. Oxford: Oxford University Press.

White, H. C. 1970. *Chains of Opportunity: System Models of Mobility in Organizations*. Cambridge, MA: Harvard University Press.

Whitley, R. D. 1984. The Development of Management Studies as a Fragmented Adhocracy. *Social Science Information/Information sur les Sciences Sociales*, 23(4–5): 775–818.

Whitley, R. D. 2016. Personal Communication.

Whittington, R., Pettigrew, A., Simon, P., Fenton, E., and Conyon, M. 1999. Change and Complementarities in the New Competitive Landscape: A European Panel Study, 1992–1996. *Organization Science*, 10(5): 583–600.

Wilensky, H. L. 1961. Orderly Careers and Social Participation: The Impact of Work History on Social Integration in the Middle Mass. *American Sociological Review*, 26(4): 521–539.

Williams, E. 2014. *The Leadership Traits and Footsteps of Nelson Mandela. How Nelson Mandela Restored a Nation to Its Rightful Owners*. Xlibris Corporation.

Williams, J. C., Berdahl, J. L., and Vandello, J. A. 2016. Beyond Work-Life "Integration." *Annual Review of Psychology*, 67: 515–539.

Williamson, O. E. 1975. *Markets and Hierarchies: Analysis and Antitrust Implications*. New York: Free Press.

Willke, H. 1987. Differenzierung und Integration in Luhmanns Theorie sozialer Systeme. In H. Haferkamp and M. Schmid (Eds.), *Sinn, Kommunikation und Soziale Differenzierung*: 247–274. Frankfurt am Main: Suhrkamp.

Wilson, R. A., and Barker, M. 2014. The Biological Notion of Individual. In E. N. Zalta (Ed.), *The Stanford Encyclopedia of Philosophy* http://plato.stanford.edu/archives/spr2014/entries/biology-individual/.

Wintle, C. 2008. Career Development: Domestic Display as Imperial, Anthropological, and Social Trophy. *Victorian Studies*, 50(2): 279–288.

Woodward, J. 1965. *Industrial Organization: Theory and Practice*. London: Oxford University Press.

Wrzesniewski, A., and Dutton, J. E. 2001. Crafting a Job: Revisioning Employees as Active Crafters of Their Work. *Academy of Management Review*, 26(2): 179–201.

Wu, L. 2000. Some Comments on "Sequence Analysis and Optimal Matching Methods in Sociology: Review and Prospect." *Sociological Methods and Research*, 29(1): 41–64.

Young, R. A., and Collin, A. (Eds.). 1992. *Interpreting Career: Hermeneutical Studies of Lives in Context*. Westport, CT: Praeger.

Young, R. A., and Collin, A. 2000. Introduction: Framing the Future of Career. In A. Collin and R. A. Young (Eds.), *The Future of Career*: 1–17. Cambridge: Cambridge University Press.

Young, R. A., and Valach, L. 1996. Interpretation and Action in Career Counseling. In M. L. Savickas and W. B. Walsh (Eds.), *Handbook of Career Theory and Practice*: 361–375. Palo Alto, CA: Davies-Black.

Youngblood, D. 2007. Multidisciplinarity, Interdisciplinarity, and Bridging Disciplines: A Matter of Process. *Journal of Research Practice*, 3(2): Article M18.

Zajac, E. J. 1990. CEO Selection, Succession, Compensation and Firm Performance: A Theoretical Integration and Empirical Analysis. *Strategic Management Journal*, 11(3): 217–230.

Zaleznik, A., Dalton, G. W., Barnes, L. B., and Laurin, P. 1970. *Orientation and Conflict in Career*. Boston: Harvard University Press.

Zammuto, R. F., and Connolly, T. 1984. Coping with Disciplinary Fragmentation. *Organizational Behavior Teaching Review*, 9: 30–37.

Zerubavel, E. 1981. *Hidden Rhythms. Schedules and Calendars in Social Life*. Berkeley, CA: University of California Press.

1982. The Standardization of Time: A Sociohistorical Perspective. *American Journal of Sociology*, 88(1): 1–23.

1995. The Rigid, the Fuzzy, and the Flexible: Notes on the Mental Sculpting of Academic Identity. *Social Research*, 62(4): 1093–1106.

Zhang, Y., and Rajagopalan, N. 2010. Once an Outsider, Always an Outsider? CEO Origin, Strategic Change, and Firm Performance. *Strategic Management Journal*, 31(3): 334–346.

Zucker, L. G. 1983. Organizations as Institutions *Research in the Sociology of Organizations*, 2: 1–47.

Zucker, L. G. 1987. Institutional Theories of Organization *Annual Review of Sociology*, 13: 443–464.

Zwaan, R. A., and Radvansky, G. A. 1998. Situation Models in Language Comprehension and Memory. *Psychological Bulletin*, 123(2): 162–185.

Index

5C – Cross-Cultural Collaboration on
    Contemporary Careers, 129, 186
actor, 31, 33, 106
"Man" as, 32
agentic, 32
authenticity of, 32
collective, 33, 53
inanimate, 35
individual, 53
organizational, 34
two major characteristics of, 32
actorhood, 32
actors of public interest, collective
AACSB, 194
African National Congress, 183
Aggalia ("Embrace"), 247
Alibaba, 34
Amazon, 248
America Móvil, 34
Apple, 34, 208
Arthur Andersen, 34, 220, 228
Austrian Association of Physiotherapy, 199
Bill and Melinda Gates Foundation, 247
Boko Haram, 247
British Petroleum, 132
Cavendish Laboratory, Cambridge
    University, 91
CERN, 95
Chicago Department of Sociology, 131
    occupations studied by, 25
Chrysler, 34
Club of Rome, 132
Daimler-Benz, 208
DaimlerChrysler, 208
Enron, 220, 225, 228
EQUIS, 194
Exxon, 71
Facebook, 246, 248
Fiat, 34
Financial Times, 35
Ford Motor Company, 83

Frontex, 247
General Electric, 142
General Motors, 132
GlaxoSmithKline, 34
Hewlett-Packard, 34
IBM, 132
ICI, 34
Instagram, 246
International Monetary Fund, 103
KPMG, 221
Liz Claiborne, 181
Mara Salvatrucha ("MS-13"), 247
McKinsey, 221
Médecins Sans Frontières, 247
Mossack Fonseca, 228
National Party (South Africa), 215, 216
Parti Québécois, 183
PayPal, 248
Penguin Random House, 34
Pepsi, 208
PricewaterhouseCoopers, 34
Safaricom, 68
Scottish National Party, 183
Snapchat, 246
Solidarity Movement, Poland, 138
Solntsevskaya Bratva, 247
Swiss Association of Physiotherapy, 199
Taliban, 141
Taobao, 34
Tata Steel, 34
Telesites, 34
Transnational Executive Council, South
    Africa, 216
Twitter, 248
Umkhonto we Sizwe, South
    Africa, 213
UNESCO, 247
Unilever, 132
United Nations, 84, 103
Wachtell Lipton, 221
World Bank, 103
YouTube, 246

actors of public interest, individual
Alice (from *Alice in Wonderland*), 22
Amelio, Gil, 208
Andrade, Maria, 247
Astor, John Jacob, 35
Bouis, Howarth, 247
Bren, Donald, 247
Carter, Jimmy, 138
Crick, Francis, 91
de Klerk, Frederik Willem, 213, 215, 216, 219
Dimou, Father Efstratios ("Papa Stratis"), 247
Gandhi, Indira, 138
Gates, Bill, 247
Gbowee, Leymah, 247
Gershwin, George, 187
Gorbachev, Mikhail, 138
Homer, 170
Humpty Dumpty, 22
Iacocca, Lee, 83
Jobs, Steve, 208
Kajbjer, Olof (Nickname olofm), 248
Karman, Tawakkol, 247
Kim Jong-il, 208
Kim Jong-un, 208
Le Clercq, Jonathan (Nickname Cluck), 248
Low, Jan, 247
Lula da Silva, Luiz Inácio, 242, 243
Mandela, Nelson, 213–19
Mandela, Winnie, 216
Mao Zedong, 138
Mark Anthony, 6
Mbeki, Thabo, 216, 217
Mentor, 170
Mobutu Sese Seko, 216
Mugabe, Robert, 215
Mwanga, Robert, 247
Parks, Rosa, 132
Patchett, Ann, 60
Ramaphosa, Cyril, 217
Reagan, Ronald, 138
Reuter, Edzard, 208
Sadat, Anwar, 138
Schellhase, Daniel (Nickname hero), 248
Schellhase, Dennis (Nickname styla), 248
Schrempp, Jürgen, 208
Sculley, John, 208
Shakespeare, 85
Sirleaf, Ellen Johnson, 247
Sisulu, Walter, 216
Snow, John, 147
Telemachus, 170
Thatcher, Margaret, 138
Turner, Ted, 247

Wakefield, Andrew, 247
Walesa, Lech, 138
Watson, James, 91
Welch, Jack, 142
Wright, Steven, 70
Xiang, Huang (Nickname TH000), 248
Yellen, Janet, 4
agreeableness, 164
Alter. *See* distinction: Ego/Alter
ambition, 6
aspect vision, 123
autocorrelation, 67

basic building block, 78, 104
chaining, 85, 87, 160, 163, 172
choice between transitions, 84
being, 54
domain of, 54
Berkeley Growth Study, 120
big five personality dimensions of personality. *See* five factor model
boundary, 45, 49, 50, 53, 58, 64, 67, 98, 115
constraining, enabling, punctuating, 49
crossing, 50, 51, 58, 159
defining structure, 50
objective, 50
permeability, 50, 80, 82
scholarly, 42
signaling properties, 82
subjective, 50
boundaryless career, 72, 101, 142
bounded rationality, 162
bounded social world, 71
building bridges, 256

Campbell Interest and Skills Survey, 125
capital, 106
career
collective, 88
definition of, 6, 16, 26, 58, 70
by life-course research, 126
by SCF, 75, 95, 99, 241
in the virtual world, 248
managerial, 140
multiple approaches to studying, 4, 12, 22, 23
multiple meanings of, 4, 23, 239
multiple simultaneous, 69
objective, 25, 184, 242
pattern, 203
of
Australian boxers, 204
CEOs, 204, 205

career (cont.)
  collectivities, 6
    magistrates in Roman empire, 203
    members of Plateau Tribes into nursing, 203
    social entities, 15
    societally important actors, 247
    specific groups, professions and
      occupations, 136
  over
    a lifetime, 68
    life to date, 70
  partial, 76
  shared, 88
  subjective, 26, 184, 242
  suffering from "surplus meaning," 4, 24, 37
  timespan for a, 68
  work, 25, 71
career actor, 15, 21, 28, 31, 52, 54, 59, 62, 64,
      66, 67, 70, 71, 98, 103, 125, 194, 224,
      228, 232, 241, 249
  as agent in *NK*/*C*/ models, 178
  becoming legitimate member of career
    field, 195
  collective. *See* career actor, collective
  focal, 56, 78, 87, 154, 230
  in focal actor's social space, 159
  inanimate. *See* career actor, inanimate
  individual. *See* career actor, individual
  level of social complexity, 154
career actor, collective, 15, 29, 34, 72, 87, 103,
      156, 167, 205, 242, 247, 250
  and network structure, 156
  providing context for individual career actor,
    35, 87, 88
career actor, inanimate, 35
  career of, 36
  fields of study and concepts, career of, 36
career actor, individual, 72, 103, 157, 242, 247
career anchor, 185
career as
  complex coevolutionary process, 243
  lifelong sequence of jobs, role-related
    experiences, 24
  linking levels of social complexity, 27
  narrative, 249
  particular occupation, i.e. partial career, 25
  path through space and time, 27
  pattern, 242
  product not process, 27
  profession, 24
  progress, getting ahead, 24
  retrospective sense-making, 26
  self-construction, 27
  simultaneous application of spatial, ontic,
    temporal perspectives, 241

  social construct, 242
  something restricted to
    interesting people, 6
    professional and managerial people, 24
  subset of life course, 127
  tri-perspective phenomenon, 241
  vertical mobility, 24
  whole-life phenomenon, 7, 69
  whole-working-life phenomenon, 25, 69
career choice, 119
career counseling, 120
career discourse, 12, 17, 122, 123, 124, 129,
    130, 133, 202
career field, 166
  rules of, 167
career imprint and career trajectory, 121
career logic, 49, 67, 118, 197
career orientation, 185
career path, 67
career research by noncareer researchers, 11
career research ideal types, 119, 121
  as ideal to be aspired to, 118
  balanced, 120, 127
  bivalent, 120
  focused, 119
  purpose, 119
career satisfaction, 119, 153, 156
  as subjective career success, 185
  timescale of precursor influence, 154
career scholar, 23, 239
career script, 254, 255
career self-efficacy, 160
career sponsorship, 152, 154, 157, *see also*
    promotion record
career stages, 137
career studies
  as
    embryonic field, 11
    field, 11, 92
    perspective on social enquiry, 15
    proto-field, 11, 12, 14, 19, 111, 112, 169,
      240, 241
    process for becoming a field, 240
  comparative. *See* comparative career studies
  contributing to understanding of society, 245
  developmental, 7
  origins of, 7
  sociological, 7
career success, 129, 173
  conceptual issues, 195
  conceptualizing, 184
  criteria, self-referent and other-referent, 185
  decoupling, 197
  dimensions, 185
  global views, 186

extrinsic, 119
in vocational psychology literature, 125
influencing factor
  cognitive ability, 187
  context, 186
  dispositional traits, 187
  five factor model of personality. *See* five
    factor model of personality: and
    career success
  human capital, 187
  inter-organizational mobility, 187
  locus of control, 187
  narcissism, 187
  organizational sponsorship, 187
  personality, 119, 124
  psychological contract breach, 187
  self-efficacy, 187
  social capital, 152, 163
  sociodemographic factors, 187
influencing factors, 186
intrinsic, 119
meta-analysis of influencing factors, 187
objective, 62, 125, 154, 184, 187, 195
  effect of network structure, 154
  measures, 187
  timescape of precursor influence, 154
SCF equivalizing, 193
SCF reconstructing, 188
subjective, 125, 185
  as career satisfaction, 119, 185, 187
subjective/objective distinction, 185
  correlation, 187
subjectivist and objectivist approaches, 185
career success and neo-institutionalism, 193
  efficiency/legitimacy tension, 193
  empirical support, 195
  establishing legitimacy, 195
  institutional complexity, dealing with, 196
    decoupling, 197
  origin of legitimacy, 196
  SCF-derived propositions, 196, 197,
    198, 200
  theoretically-grounded understanding of
    context, 184
    relevant elements in social space, 198
    systematic analysis of elements, 199
  underestimating importance of
    legitimacy, 195
career timespan
  part of lifetime, 68
  working life to date, 71
career timetable, 120
career trajectory, 120
career transition, 50, 76, 99, 210
  key features of, 77

model of, 209
catalysis, as analogy for applying SCF, 168,
  243, 255
causality, 60, 249
  attribution of, 251
  reverse, 159
CEO succession, 157, 165, 208
  and strategic change, 167
  and top management turnover, 167
  as career transition, 211
  career literature, lack of reference to, 210
  controversies in literature, 209
  insider, 158
  insider/outsider successor, 204, 209
    coevolution, 207
    contenders/followers, 204
    SCF reconstructing, 205
  outsider, 158, 166
    SCF reconstructing, 211
    chaining, 212
    ontic perspective, 211
CEO turnover, 167
chaining, 85, 87, 160, 163, 172, 211, 212, 215,
  216, 219, 225
chronology, 46, 59, 64, 98, 249
client capture. *See* professional service firm
clique formation, 177
coevolution, 172, 205, 207
  and fitness, 173
  coupled dancing, 178
  definition, 173
  degradation to super-competition, 176
  fitness landscape, 174
    and evolution, 174
    and organizations, 174
    of focal actor and collective actors'
      careers, 88
    of focal and other career actors'
      careers, 159
  processes, 167
  theory, 174, 178
  typology, 175
coevolution and mentoring, 172
  applying *NK[C]* tuning, 179
  degrading relationships, 177
  fitness, 173, 174
  fitness landscape, 175
  importing from coevolution theory, 174
  SCF-derived propositions, 180
  suboptimality, 177
cognitive ability and career success, 187
collective career, 88
commonality of interest, nascent, 12, 240
communicative action, 116
community of practice, 28, 48, 49

comparative career studies, 198, 245
    career systems, 246
    views on career success, 246
comparing, 45, 46, 98
    operation of ontic perspective, 55
complementarity theory, 172, 181
    complementary properties, 181
    negative effects, 181
complementarity theory and mentoring, 173
    combinations of properties, effect on
        mentoring, 182
    equivalizing, 180
    formal vs. informal programs, 182
    mixed ethnicity dyads, 182
    relationship constellation, 183
complexity catastrophe. See NK[C] simulation
conceptual combination, 256
conceptual pact, 115, 122, 124, 125, 128
    between OMC and life course
        researchers, 128
condition, 58, 64, 70, 71, 72, 82, 95, 98
    affected by anticipated position, 80
    anticipation of, 79, 83, 87, 156, 223, 228
    change in, 58
    link between two points in time, 78
    of career actor, 54, 55
    rate of change, 77
configurational theory, 181
construct, 45, 64, 92, 98
context, 102, 129, 162
    importance of, 246
    culture, 246
    institutions, 246
    in organizational research, 47
    AMO (abilities, motivation,
        opportunities), 47
    behavioral formula by Lewin, 47
    internal organizational, 164
    of career, 28, 48
    perceived, 162
    social, 153
conversation, 115, 124, 125
    across disciplinary boundaries, 5, 10,
        111, 114
    role of SCF, 128
    and discourse, 116
    as antidote to fragmentation, 115
    as exchange among equals, 117
    between academic discourses relevant for
        career studies
    typology, 202
    between career discourses, 122
        contribution of SCF, 122
        contribution of SCF, limitations to, 123
        lack of, 12, 112

obstacles, 124
    SCF focus on understanding, 130
    between discourses generally, 14
    characteristics
        absence of predefined goals, 116
        equal status of participants, 116
        need for establishing common ground
            (conceptual pact), 115, see also
            conceptual pact
        for understanding, strengthening social ties,
            116, 117
        interpersonal function of, 116
        transactional function, lack of, 116
    coordination: semantic, lexical, syntactic, 115
    core construct, 45
        ontic perspective, 54
        spatial perspective, 49
        temporal perspective, 59
    creating reality, 46
    cumulative research, 147, 157, 243

decoupling, 192
defamiliarization, 255
definition, 63
    definiendum, 63
    definiens, 63
    definientia, 63, 72
    differentia specifica, 63
    genus proximum, 63
    superordinate concept, 63
degrading relationships. See coevolution and
        mentoring: degrading relationships
description, distinguished from theory, 94
developmental stage, 85
difference, for producing information, 42, 44,
        see also guiding difference
discourse, 243
    and conversation, 116
    career focus, little use of OMC, 203
    SCF contribution, 204
dispositional traits
    and career success, 187
distinction, 41, 43, 44
    Ego/Alter, 45, 56, 64, 98, 212
    form of, 44
    in/out, 45, 98
    precedes/follows, 45
    division of labor, 48, 49

efficiency myth, 193
Ego. See distinction: Ego/Alter
emotional arousal, 151
empirical research
    cross-sectional, 154
    longitudinal, 120, 154

practical limitations, 119
retrospective, 154
entity having career, 29
    actor, 31
    human being, 30
    individual, 30
    person, 31
    subject, 30
entrainment, 62, 88
envy, science or physics, 93
epidemiology, use of mapping in, 148
episodes, 50
evenhandedness, 130
existential philosophy, 28, 53, 54
expatriate, 16
extraversion, 164

feed-forward, 87
field, 11. *See* fragmentation
    controversy about implications of
        disorganization, 114
    embryonic. *See* career as embryonic field
        of
        career studies, 22
        management information systems, 114
        management studies
            disarray, 112
        organizational studies, 92
    proto-. *See* career as proto-field
    relational, 58
    scientific. *See* scientific field
    state of paradigm development, 113
    temporal, 58
field, scientific. *See* scientific field
firm performance
    and top management turnover, 168
    as measure of CEO success, 167
    cause of CEO turnover, 167
    effect on CEO succession of deviation from
        expected, 167
    moderation by CEO succession
        type, 167
fitness as evolutionary success, 173
fitness landscape. *See* NK[C] simulation, *see*
    coevolution
five factor model of personality, 125, 163,
    211, 254
    and career success, 119, 187
focal career actor. *See* career actor: focal
fragmentation, 112, 115, 117, 122, 126
    detrimental effect on field, 113
fragmented adhocracy, 9, 112
    career studies as, 9, 12, 240
framework, 96, 98
    SCF as a. *See* SCF: as a framework

free rider, selection of, 176
fundamental attribution error, 250

general mental ability, 129
generalized other, 82
genotype, 174
geographical space. *See* social space
GLOBE study, 186
goals, individual, 116
guiding difference, 41, 42, 44, 45, 98, 116
    of
        ontic perspective, 56
        spatial perspective, 50
        temporal perspective, 59
gulf between vocational career research and
    OMC studies, 10, 131

habitus, 106
heuristic model, 74, 92, 99, 149, 241, 254
    basic building block. *See* basic building
        block
    connection with theory, 75, 78
    elaborated, 89
    extended, 85
    guiding speculation, 75
    proposition, 227, 230, 232
historian, 242
HRM policies and practices, 129
human capital, 129
    and career success, 187

ideal types, 124, *see also* career research ideal
        types
    "ideal" and desirability, 118
    boundaryless career, as not one, 118
    in social sciences, 117
    of
        career taxonomies, 118
        occupations, 117
        organizational international "career
            logics," 118
        organizations, 119
        taxonomies of social constructs, 117
    traditional and boundaryless career, 118
    traditional and new career, 118
imagination, 255
impression management, 196
imprinting, 82, 96, *see* career imprint and
    career trajectory
income, 125
indication, 42, 43
institutional
    change, 223
    complexity. *See* neo-institutional theory
    entrepreneur, 223

institutional (cont.)
  forms, 132
  logic. *See* neo-institutional theory:
    institutional logic
  theory, 184, *see also* neo-institutional theory
interactional expertise, 123
interpretative phenomenological analysis, 250
interpretive scheme, 254

job choice, 119

Kuder Occupational Interest Inventory, 125

labor market
  contest, 80
  internal, 77
  perceived, 160
  tournament, 80
learning experiences, 152
legitimacy. *See* neo-institutional theory
Leitdifferenz. See guiding difference
life course
  definition, 126
  psychological perspective, 126
life course studies
  and OMC, 126
  paradigmatic principles, 127
  similarity to career as defined by SCF, 127
liminal state, 51
locus of control and career success, 187
lone ranger, 232

management information systems, field of, 114
management studies, field of: disarray, 112
Mandela, Nelson, succession to Presidency,
  213–19
  coevolution of career with other political
    actors, 216
  factors influencing transition to presidency
    international support, 215
    Nobel Peace Prize, 213
    release from prison, 213
    transition into office, 213
    understanding by chaining transitions in
      time, 215
mapping, 45, 46, 98
meaning
  constructed from career narrative, 249
  research dealing with, 250
  transformation of data into, 46
mentor, 170, 171, 179
mentoring, 88
  and race, 172
  and religion, 172
  as synergistic relationship, 175

career support, 170
definition, 170
developmental network, 170
dyadic, 170
dysfunctional, 177
ecological perspective, 170
mixed-ethnicity dyads in, 182
ontological system, 170
phases, 170
programs, 182
protégé, 171, 179
psychosocial support, 170
relational, 172
relationship constellation, 170
SCF equivalizing, 172
SCF equivalizing using
  coevolution theory. *See* coevolution and
    mentoring
  complementarity theory. *See* complentarity
    theory and mentoring
configuration theory, 172
SCF importing using coevolution theory. *See*
  coevolution and mentoring
SCF reconstructing, 171
  chaining, 172
  ontic perspective, 171
  temporal perspective, 171
mentorship. *See* mentoring
mobility
  intergenerational, 77
  inter-organizational and career success, 187
  intra-organizational, 120
model, 96, 97, 98
  generic transition, 209
  heuristic. *See* heuristic model
  process, 154
  situation, 115
  situational, 124
  typology, 96

narcissism and career success, 187
narrative, 36, 61, 67
Nash equilibrium. *See* NK[C] simulation
National Longitudinal Survey of Youth, 129
neo-institutional theory
  and rational explanation, 189
  context
    institutional, 190, 191
    differentiated, 190
    organizational, 189
  efficiency vs. legitimacy, 192
  foundations of, 189
  institutional complexity, 192, 196
  institutional logic, 193, 223
    career-relevant, 197

multiple, 193
interpretative scheme, 191
isomorphism, 192
legitimacy, 191, 193
  as feature of career actor and social
    space, 194
meaning of institution, 191
normative, regulative, cognitive pillars,
    190, 198
role system, 191
routines, 191
network
  benefits, 154, 156
  property, 153
  social, 164
  structure, 154, 156
NK[C] simulation, 176
  complexity catastrophe, strategies for
    avoiding, 178
  fitness landscape, 176, 178
  mentorship, parameter meaning, 178
  Nash equilibrium
    failure to reach, 176
    optimal fitness as, 176
  tuning, 178

object, social construction of, 36
objective career. See career: objective
observation, 41
  second order, 44
occupation, 152, 160
occupational choice, 124
Ockam's razor, 121
office, 51
ontic, 16, 53
  definition, 16
  enquiry, 54
ontic perspective, 17, 54, 58, 103, 124, 131,
    151, 211
  core construct, 54
  guiding difference, 56
  operation, 55
ontical, 53, see ontic
ontology, 53
operation, 45, 98
  of the ontic perspective, 55
  of the spatial perspective, 48
  of the temporal perspective, 59
opinion leader, 229
optimal fitness. See NK[C] simulation
optimal matching, 67
organization
  as context factor, 140
  studies, 92, 169
organization and management career (OMC), 8

and life course studies, 126
definition of, 7
discourse, working within, 202
field history, 130
  1960s and 1970s, 132
  1960s/70s
    behavior and organizations, 135
    career studies, 136
    conceptualizing organizations, 133
    dominance of large organizations, 133
    individual and individual
      development, 133
    learning and development, 135
    SCF reconstructing, 137
    social science discourse, 133
  1980s, 138
    OMC changes, 140
    organizational changes –
      deconglomeration, 138
    SCF reconstructing, 140
  1990s to date, 141
    boundaryless career, 142
    organizational boundarylessness, 141
    SCF reconstructing, 143
  Chicago School, 131
    SCF reconstructing, 144
  fragmentation of, 9
  origins, 131
    Cornell, 131
    Massachusetts Institute of Technology
      (MIT), 131
    outside North America, 131
  studies
    as a field, 9
    as focus for this book, 241
    growing consciousness of it as field, 140
  studies, field of, 3
    agentic focus, 244
    increasing focus over time, 145
organizational
  hypocrisy, 192
  socialization, 196
  sponsorship and career success, 187
  structure, 120
  theory, 57
organizations as important element of social
    space, 136

Panama Papers affair, 228
paradigm
  change, 113
  development, 113
  scientific, 102
  wars, 113
paradigmatic consensus, problems with, 113

path
    dependence, 60, 121, 228
    independence, 121
pattern, 66, 70, 71
    contrast with sequence, 66
    emerging from chance, 72
performance accomplishments, 151
personality. *See* career success: and personality
    differences between I/O and vocational
        psychology, 125
person–environment fit, 125
perspective, 15, 16, 92, 98, 119, 120, 124
    as modes of observation, 44, 54
    career as application of spatial, ontic,
        temporal, 29, 241
    constructs emerging from, 241
    core operation of, 241
    interplay between, 62
    on social enquiry, 29
    ontic. *See* ontic perspective
    SCF perspectives, 63, 103
    spatial. *See* spatial perspective
    temporal. *See* temporal perspective
political science, 93
position, 28, 51, 64, 66, 70, 71, 82, 83, 95, 106
    anticipation of, 80, 83, 87, 228
    solidification of, 51
positive organizational scholarship, 172
possible worlds, 49, 59
power, 53, 116
    internal allies, availability of, 164
    internal significance, 164
    sources
        language, 123
        position, 164
        positioning in communication network, 164
precedes/follows, 59, 60, 98
process model, 154
professional service firm, 219
    client capture, 220, 221, 228, 230
    client relations, 229, *see also* professional
        service firm:SCF reconstruction
    economic significance, 219
    environmental pressures, 223
    gender composition of client and PSF, 227
    governance forms of, 223
    interconnected careers of partners and
        firm, 223
    model of PSF and context, 222
    P^2 – professional partnership, 220
    predicting outcomes, 228, 232
    SCF model of strategic change, 222, 229
        acting in interest of one's career, 230
        architecture for examining change, 234
        initial decision, 230

    propaging decision through PSF, 233
    SCF reconstruction, 223
        chaining, 225
        coevolution of professionals' careers, 225
        interactions between actors, 224
        path dependence, 228
        relations with clients, 225
    SCF-derived propositions, 232, 233
    shift from social trustee to commercial,
        220, 228
    and socialization practice change, 220
    change in meaning of
        professionalism, 221
    shift in relations with clients, 221
    and innovation capacity, 222
    social network structure, 229
    strategic change, 225
    strategy, 228
        as emergent process, 228
    up or out, 222
professionalism
    commercial, expert, entrepreneurial, 220
promotion, 119
    internal, 120
    number of, 125, 153, 154, 156
    record
        effect on career sponsorship, 157
        influence on actor's social space, 157
protean career, 184
protégé. *See* mentoring
psychological contract breach and career
        success, 187
psychological success, 184

rationality myth, 192
Red Violin, The, 36
reproductive success, 174
retirement, 128
RIASEC model, 125
rites de passage, 50
role, 52, 66, 76, 82, *see also* transition
    integrated, 66
    models, other, as source of self-efficacy, 151
    segmented, 66

salary, 119, 153, 156
SCF, 16
    and theory, 14
    avoiding the micro-trap, 244
    balanced research, 131, 137, 144
    bivalent research, 140, 144
    coevolutionary angle, 219
    common language, 122
    elements of the, 46
    establishing common ground, 124, 128

focused research, 143, 144
framing individual decision processes,
        234
function of, 255
heuristic model. *See* heuristic model
social space, multifaceted view, 164
stages of application, 98
SCF as a
catalyst. *See* catalysis, as analogy for
        applying SCF
common language, 14–17
framework, 14, 92, 99, 122, 199
heuristic, 147
heuristic framework, 128
shared language, 5
SCF contribution
bridging levels of analysis, 223
catalyst. *See* catalysis, as analogy for
        applying SCF
conversation between career discourses,
        129, *see also* career discourse
developing career theory, 252
facilitating conversation, 243
facilitating role, 123, 168, 169
future research, 249
    career studies – contributing to the future
        of the planet, 247
    causality, 251
    comparative career studies. *See*
        comparative career studies
    experiments, 251
    meaning, 249
    methods and methodology, 250
    special groups, 244
    systematic approach to key career studies
        issues, 243
    taking social seriously, 244
    theory building, 251
new research questions, 196,
        199, 200
providing discipline-independent view of
        career, 241
reframing research topics, 208
supporting
    building bridges, 256, *see also* SCF
        contribution: conversation between
        career discourses
    conceptual combination, 256
    conversation across boundaries, 240
    defamiliarization, 255
    imagination, 255
    OMC insight dissemination, 204
systematic approach to key career studies
        issues, 243
taking chronology seriously, 249

SCF heuristic model. *See* heuristic
        model
SCF, application of
    equivalizing, 105, 169, 172
    importing, 106, 169
    reconstructing, 102, 148, 169
        looking for missing connections, 148,
            151, 153, 156, 158, 206
        mapping existing model, 148, 149
        stepping outside model bounds, 149, 160,
            163, 166
    selecting, 100
    understanding, 105, 169
science, 100
scientific discipline, 93
scientific field, 100, 111
    management studies as a, 112
    meaning of term, 8
    paradigmatic requirements for, 113
scientific method, 93
self-efficacy, 150, 151, 162
    and career success, 187
sense-making, 70
    prospective, 61
    retrospective, 26, 61, 67
sequence, 65
    contrast with pattern, 66
sequencing, 45, 46, 60, 61, 98, 251
    operation of temporal perspective, 59
situation model, 115, 122
situationalism vs. dispositionalism, 120
social
    actor, 241
    capital, 152
    chronology, 16, 241, *see also* chronology
    network, 80, 164
    resources, 154, 156
    space, 16, 28, 81, 82, 87, 207
        anticipation of, 82, 223
        conceptualization of, 188
        effect on position, 83
        enactment of, 81
        moderating transition, 80, 83
        or geographical space, 52
        rules in, 53
    structure, effect on action and its
        outcome, 82
Social Chronology Framework. *See* SCF
social cognitive career theory (SCCT), 150,
        152, 160
social identity theory, 82
social resources theory, 152
socialization
    anticipatory, 79
    sex-role, 150

socialization experiences, 152, 160
affecting self-efficacy, 162
shaping labor market perception, 162
socialization processes, 160
varying across national cultures, 160
varying across societal strata, 160
sociodemographic factors and career
success, 187
sociolect, 10, 123
space
bounded social and geographic, 70,
71, 72
marked, 42
unmarked, 42
spatial perspective, 17, 47, 58, 98, 103, 131
core construct, 49
guiding difference, 50
operation, 48
status, 52
occupational, 125
passage. See transition, status passage
stock ownership, of top management, and CEO
succession, 157
strategic action, 116
strategic management, 11
strategy as
emergent process. See professional
service firm
pattern in stream of decisions, 228, 229, 234,
see also professional service firm
strength of weak ties theory, 152
Strong Interest Inventory, 125
structural holes theory, 152
structuration theory, 254
subjective career. See career: subjective
subjective career success. See career success,
subjective
super-competition, 175
synergy, 175

temporal alignment, 88
temporal personality, 211
temporal perspective, 17, 58, 98, 103, 119, 132,
163, 249, 251
core construct, 59
guiding difference, 59
operation, 59
theorizing, 92, 98
about organizations, 133
theory, 96, 98
"real," "good," 93, 94
difference between social and physical
sciences, 93
evolution of definition, 93

explanatory function, 94
general, 252
grand, 98, 252
in organizational studies, 94
in social sciences, 252
meta-theory, 95
middle range, 98, 253
predictive function, 94
theory of career
building of a, 254
general, 94, 95, 253
middle-range, 253
versions of, 95
theory of everything, 94
theory of practice, 105, 106
capitals, 106
field, 106
time, 28, 57
A series of, 60
anthropology of, 57
axis of intention, 60
axis of succession, 60
B series of, 59
clock time, 57
concepts of, 61
cyclical, 57
dimensions of
discrete vs. continuous vs. epochal
structure, 57
novel vs. cyclical vs. punctuated, 57
real vs. epiphenomenal, 57
referent anchor past, present or
future, 57
subjective or objective, 57
discounting, 119
event time, 57
geography of, 57
in career, 249
life cycle, 57
social psychology of, 57
socially constructed, 57
sociology of, 57
types of, 57
universes of, 61
top management team turnover, 167, see CEO
succession
tournament, 121, 154
transition, 58
career. See career transition
macro work role, 76
micro role, 76
period, 77
role, 76
status passage, 59, 76

taxonomies, 77
work role, 76
work—non-work, 77
translation, 114
trap, "fragmentation," "specialization," 114

understanding, 116
up or out, 222

vacancy chain, 120
verbal persuasion, 151
vocational career studies, 7
vocational psychology, 77, 124

wicked problem, 229
work career. *See* career, work
work-life balance, 128